Class at Bat, Gender on Deck
and Race in the Hole

Class at Bat, Gender on Deck and Race in the Hole

A Line-Up of Essays on Twentieth Century Culture and America's Game

by RON BRILEY

McFarland & Company, Inc., Publishers
Jefferson, North Carolina, and London

Library of Congress Cataloguing-in-Publication Data

Briley, Ron, 1949–
    Class at bat, gender on deck and race in the hole : a line-up of
essays on twentieth century culture and America's game / by
Ron Briley.
        p.   cm.
    Includes bibliographical references and index.

    ISBN 0-7864-1590-8 (softcover : 50# alkaline paper) ∞

    1. Baseball — Social aspects — United States.   2. Baseball — United
States — History — 20th century.   I. Title.
GV867.64.B75   2003
796.357'0973 — dc21   2003007197

British Library cataloguing data are available

Manufactured in the United States of America

Cover image ©2003 Corbis Digital Stock

McFarland & Company, Inc., Publishers
    Box 611, Jefferson, North Carolina 28640
        www.mcfarlandpub.com

 McFarland

Enclosed please find:

Wood. **Reel Baseball**

Publication date: Available Now
Price: $29.95

This book is sent to you:

_____ with the compliments of the author/publisher.

 _XX_ for examination.

_____ as your desk copy, with our compliments.

_____ for review. We ask that you include our website
address (**www.mcfarlandpub.com**) and our order
line (**800-253-2187**) in any review. **Send one copy**
of your published review, preferably via e-mail as
a PDF file (or a link for online reviews), to
bcox@mcfarlandpub.com. Alternately, publications
and tear sheets can be mailed to Beth Cox,
McFarland, Box 611, Jefferson NC 28640.

www.mcfarlandpub.com
orders 800-253-2187

Class at Bat, Gender on Deck and Race in the Hole: A Line-up of Essays on Twentieth Century Culture and America's Game

Ron Briley

335 pages $35 softcover
Notes, index
ISBN 0-7864-1590-8 2003

Reviews: "analysis of the Houston franchise and its inability to deal with its Latino ballplayers is illuminating...deals intelligently with the evolution of the players' union...makes some wise judgments about the conflicts"—*Choice;* "unique...an educational pleasure"—*Crosswinds Weekly*; "every essay is worth reading...enjoyable and informative reading"—*Unholy Troika.*

Nineteen essays by Briley focus on major league baseball as it reflected the changing American culture from about 1945 to about 1980. He examines the era through the lens of race, gender and class—categories which have increasingly become essential analytical tools for scholars.

The accounts of Roman Mejias and Cesar Cedeno offer some disturbing insights regarding the acceptance of Latinos in baseball and American society. In one essay, Briley refers to baseball as the heart of the nation's democratic spirit, noting that the son of a rural farmer could play alongside a governor's son and both would receive only the praise that their playing merited. However, in writing about the Milwaukee Braves' move to Atlanta, the lamentations of fans—that baseball had succumbed to the age of affluence—are compared to the changing patterns of demographics and economic power in American society. Even with the increased participation of women on the field with teams like the Silver Bullets, the final essay comments on organized baseball's perception of them as primarily spectators.

Ron Briley has taught history for 25 years and is Assistant Headmaster at Sandia Preparatory School. His baseball essays have been published in such journals as *Baseball History, Nine* and *Cooperstown Symposium.* He lives in Albuquerque, New Mexico.

McFarland

Enclosed please find:

Briley. **Class at Bat, Gender on Deck and Race in the Hole**

Publication date: Available Now
Price: $35.00

This book is sent to you:

_____ with the compliments of the author/publisher.

 XX for examination.

_____ as your desk copy, with our compliments.

_____ for review. We ask that you include our website address (**www.mcfarlandpub.com**) and our order line (**800-253-2187**) in any review. **Send one copy** of your published review, preferably via e-mail as a PDF file (or a link for online reviews), to bcox@mcfarlandpub.com. Alternately, publications and tear sheets can be mailed to Beth Cox, McFarland, Box 611, Jefferson NC 28640.

www.mcfarlandpub.com
orders 800-253-2187

Reel Baseball: Essays and Interviews on the National Pastime, Hollywood and American Culture

Stephen C. Wood *and* J. David Pincus

326 pages $29.95 softcover
64 photographs & illustrations, notes, index
ISBN 0-7864-1389-1 2003

Reviews: "accessible essays...invites the attention of the fan of both movies and baseball...recommended"—*Choice*; "spectacular study...a sweeping baseball filmography...recommend[ed]"—*Against the Grain;* "[readers] can spend many happy hours with [this book]"—*Burlington County Times;* "a real treat"—*True Review;* "carefully researched"—*University of Arkansas Research Frontiers;* "an arresting work...academic yet accessible essays and interviews...inspects the cultural meshing of film and baseball in a thoughtfully provocative manner...a read as satisfying as a run-scoring double laced into the gap"—*Arkansas Democrat Gazette.* "the volume fills a long-overdue gap in critical discourse"—www.*Reconstruction;* "a fascinating collection...highly recommend"—*The Providence Journal.*

Not only are movies and baseball two of America's favorite pastimes, they are integral parts of our culture. Small wonder that the two frequently merge in Hollywood's use of baseball themes, jargon, and icons.

This work on baseball in the movies is organized into four sections examining different aspects of the cultural intersection between film and baseball. In the first three sections—"Baseball in Baseball Films," "Babe Ruth and the Silver Screen," and "Baseball in Non-Baseball Films"—essays by scholars in various disciplines cover such topics as symbols, the role of family, baseball as a facilitator of violence, and the American mythos.

The fourth section consists of interviews with directors (such as Ron Shelton and Penny Marshall), actors (Kevin Costner, James Belushi), and baseball personnel (broadcaster Vin Scully, coach Rod Dedeaux) who have worked in baseball films.

Stephen C. Wood is chair of the communication studies department at the University of Rhode Island. **J. David Pincus** has held positions in the communications and business departments at California State University, Fullerton, the University of Southern California, and the University of Arkansas. He lives in Fayetteville, Arkansas.

To my family —
Pam, Shane, Meghan, Rosemary, and Kathleen —
who have made it all possible

Acknowledgments

"Ruth and Cobb as Cultural Symbols: The Development of a Mass Consumer Ethic for Baseball in the 1920s," was originally presented at the 1995 Hofstra University conference "Baseball and the 'Sultan of Swat': Commemorating the 100th Birthday of Babe Ruth."

"Don't Let Hitler (or the Depression) Kill Baseball," copyright © 2001 by M.E. Sharpe, Inc. From Nancy Beck Young, William D. Pederson, and Byron W. Daynes, eds., *Franklin D. Roosevelt and the Shaping of American Political Culture* (Armonk, NY: M.E. Sharpe, 2001), pages 119–133. Reprinted with permission.

"Where Have You Gone William Bendix? Baseball as a Symbol of American Values in World War II," originally appeared in *Studies in Popular Culture*, 8:2 (1985), pages 18–29. Reprinted with permission of the editors.

"Amity Is the Key to Success: Baseball and the Cold War," originally appeared in *Baseball History*, 1:3 (Fall, 1986), pages 4–19. Reprinted with permission of Penton Media, Inc.

"'Do Not Go Gently into that Good Night': Race, the Baseball Establishment, and the Retirements of Bob Feller and Jackie Robinson," copyright © 1998 by M.E. Sharpe, Inc. From Joseph Dorinson and Joram Warmund, eds., *Jackie Robinson, Race, Sports, and the American Dream* (Armonk, NY: M.E. Sharpe, 1998), pages 193–204. Reprinted with permission.

"The Limits of Baseball Integration: Louisiana, The Texas League, and Shreveport Sports 1956–1957," was originally published in *North Louisiana Historical Association Journal*, 28 (Fall, 1997), pages 153–162. Reprinted with permission of the editors.

"Ten Years After: The Baseball Establishment, Race, and Jackie Robinson," was originally published in Alvin Hall and Peter Rutkoff, eds., *The Cooperstown Symposium on Baseball and American Culture, 1997 (Jackie*

Robinson) (Jefferson, NC: McFarland, 2001), pages 137–151. Reprinted with permission of the publisher.

"More Legacy of Conquest: Long-Term Ramifications of the Major League Baseball Shift to the West," *Journal of the West*, Vol. 36, No. 2 (April, 1997), pages 68–78. Copyright © 1997 by Journal of the West, Inc. Reprinted with permission of *Journal of the West*, 1531 Yuma, Manhattan, KS 66502 USA.

"The Houston Colt .45s: The Other Expansion Team of 1962," was originally published in *East Texas Historical Journal*, 32 (1994), pages 59–74. Reprinted with permission of the editor.

"Milwaukee and Atlanta, a Tale of Two Cities: Eddie, Hank, and the 'Rover Boys' Head South," was originally published in *Nine: A Journal of Baseball History and Social Policy Perspectives*, 6 (1997), pages 29–47. Reprinted with permission of the editor.

"'The Times Were A-Changin': Baseball as a Symbol of American Values in Transition, 1963–1964," originally appeared in *Baseball Research Journal 17* (1988), pages 54–60. Reprinted with permission of the Society for American Baseball Research.

"It Was 20 Years Ago Today: Baseball Responds to the Unrest of 1968," was originally published in Peter Levine, ed., *Baseball History: An Annual of Original Baseball Research* (Westport, CT: Meckler Publishing, 1989), pages 81–94. Reprinted with permission of Penton Media, Inc.

"Baseball and America in 1969: A Traditional Institution Responds to Changing Times," originally appeared in *Nine: A Journal of Baseball History and Social Policy Perspectives*, 4 (1996), pages 263–281. Reprinted with permission of the editor.

"The Oakland A's of 1972–1975 and the Counterculture in Baseball: Undermining the Hegemony of the Baseball Establishment," was originally published in *Nine: A Journal of Baseball History and Social Policy Perspectives*, 1 (1993), pages 142–162. Reprinted with permission of the editor.

"As American as Cherry Pie: Baseball and Reflections of Violence in the 1960s and 1970s," was originally published in Alvin Hall and Peter M. Rutkoff, eds., *The Cooperstown Symposium on Baseball and American Culture, 1999* (Jefferson, NC: McFarland, 2000), pages 115–132. Presented at the Cooperstown Symposium in 1999, the piece was also honored by the 1999 SABR/Macmillan Award presented at the national Society for American Baseball Research conference. Reprinted with permission of the publisher.

"Roman Mejias: Houston's First Major League Latin Star," was originally published in *Nine: A Journal of Baseball History and Social Policy Perspectives*, 10 (Fall, 2001), pages 73–92. Reprinted with permission of the editor.

"Houston's Latin Star Cesar Cedeno and Death in the Dominican Republic: The Troubled Legacy of Race Relations in the Lone Star State," originally appeared in Alvin Hall and William Simons, eds., *The Cooperstown Symposium on Baseball and American Culture, 2000* (Jefferson, NC: McFarland, 2001), pages 219–236. Reprinted with permission of the publisher.

"The Albuquerque Dukes and the Summer of 1981: The Best Baseball in America," was originally published in *Nine: A Journal of Baseball History and Social Policy Perspectives*, 3 (1994), pages 66–84. Reprinted with permission of the editor.

"Baseball and the Women's Question: Participation, Gender Stereotypes, and the Consumption Ethic," originally appeared in Alvin Hall and Thomas L. Altherr, eds., *The Cooperstown Symposium on Baseball and American Culture, 1998* (Jefferson, NC: McFarland, 2002), pages 182–202. Reprinted with permission of the publisher.

Contents

Preface

Over the last twenty years, I have found baseball a useful vehicle through which to gain a better understanding of twentieth-century America. Accordingly, I have devoted my scholarship to examining the complex relationship between baseball and American culture, a task which has enhanced my teaching of American history. The following nineteen essays were previously published or presented at scholarly conferences, and full bibliographical entries are provided in the endnotes for each one.

The bulk of the essays in this collection deal with the period between 1945 and 1980, and examine major league baseball during this crucial period through the lens of race, gender, and class—categories which increasingly have become essential analytical tools for scholars. The essays primarily focus upon major league baseball as a reflection of changing American values and culture and are arranged chronologically by the time period covered rather than by when they were written. Thus, there is some overlap, but I trust there is also coherence.

The first piece on Ty Cobb and Babe Ruth as manifestations of a transformation in American culture from the ethos of production to consumption was originally presented at the Hofstra University conference commemorating the centennial of Ruth in 1995. The piece is the only one regarding the 1920s, but the essay does introduce the concept of consumption — a key theme of the final essay on major league baseball's approach to women as consumers.

The next essay is from a volume on Franklin Roosevelt and American culture to which I contributed articles on baseball and cinema. This selection focuses on how baseball ownership, along with Roosevelt, dealt with the challenges of the Depression and World War II to the continuity of the game. It is also a bridge to the next piece on baseball as a symbol of American values in World War II, which primarily considers how the sport was portrayed in mass circulation periodicals of the war years. Base-

1

ball as a reflection of American values in the early Cold War years of the late 1940s and early 1950s is discussed in "Amity is the Key to Success," originally published in *Baseball History*.

There are three pieces that cover the year 1956, a crucial year because it marks the retirement of Jackie Robinson amid a great deal of self-congratulatory rhetoric on the part of major league baseball. The essay contrasting the retirements of Jackie Robinson and Bob Feller, both leaving the game after the 1956 season, suggests that the media and baseball establishment responded to these two men in a fashion which might be construed as institutional racism. The limits of baseball integration are apparent in how the Texas League dealt with the Shreveport Sports and a Louisiana state law forbidding blacks and whites from playing integrated baseball in the 1956 and 1957 seasons. The Robinson retirement, Louisiana segregation legislation, and the general state of baseball segregation in 1956 is the subject of "Ten Years After: The Baseball Establishment, Race, and Jackie Robinson." There is some overlap in these three pieces, but they draw attention to the gap between the rhetoric and reality of the 1950s, providing ample fodder for the social activism of the 1960s.

In addition to race issues, baseball expansion and the extent to which a corporation/sports franchise owes allegiance to its fan base or the bottom line of profitability in a capitalist marketplace were major concerns of the late 1950s and early 1960s. "The Long-Term Ramifications of the Major League Baseball Shift to the West" suggests that many of the franchise transfers to the West were not necessarily well thought-out and were representative of efforts to economically exploit the West in the tradition described in Patricia Nelson Limerick's new Western history opus *Legacy of Conquest*. The West has not proven to be an El Dorado for many settlers, prospectors, explorers, or baseball executives. However, some trends in recent years, such as the success of the Arizona Diamondbacks, would point to some revision of the essay's conclusions. As specific examples of the difficulties caused by expansion, essays on the first season of the Houston Colt .45s, who were largely ignored in the media fascination with Casey Stengel and the New York Mets, and the bitterness of the Milwaukee community toward the Braves ownership, who moved the franchise to Atlanta following the 1965 season, are included.

The changing winds blowing through American culture and baseball during the 1960s and 1970s are considered in four pieces. "The Times Were A-Changin': Baseball As a Symbol of American Values in Transition, 1963-1964" was originally published by the Society for American Baseball Research in the *Baseball Research Journal*. To examine in some depth the changes taking place in American culture and baseball during the turbulent late 1960s, essays are included that detail the 1968 and 1969 seasons. Perhaps the most symbolic baseball representation of the upheavals sweeping American society in the early 1970s was the emergence of the Oakland A's dynasty, characterized by long hair, moustaches, and a confrontational style with teammates, opponents, and ownership. Opposing Cincinnati's well-groomed Big Red Machine in the 1972 World Series, the A's were perceived as manifestations of the counterculture in baseball. Americans were also increasingly concerned with the role of violence in a society plagued by the Vietnam War, campus unrest, political assassinations, and racial confrontations. The essay "As American as Cherry Pie: Baseball and Reflections of Violence in the 1960s and 1970s," which was awarded the MacMillan SABR Baseball Research Award in 1999, examines baseball violence within the context of growing unrest in American society.

While much of the literature on baseball and race tends to focus on Jackie Robinson and African Americans, the racial composition of major league baseball in the 1990s and the scholarship of individuals such as Sam Regalado draw our attention to the role of Latinos in baseball and American culture. While the case of Fernando Valenzuela in Los Angeles suggests the promise of social mobility for Latinos in American life, two essays about Roman Mejias with the Houston Colt .45s and Cesar Cedeno with the Houston Astros point out the travails of Latin American ball players in Texas, a state with a troubling legacy of racial conflict between Latinos (most of Mexican ancestry) and Anglos. The accounts of Mejias and Cedeno offer some insights regarding the acceptance of Latinos in baseball and American society.

When the 1981 big league season was disrupted by a prolonged labor stoppage, the attention of baseball fans was drawn to the minor leagues and teams such as the Albuquerque Dukes, who enjoyed a superlative season. The essay on the 1981 season presents the success story of the Albuquerque Dukes on and off the playing field. However, the baseball business is a fickle one, and following the 2000 baseball season the Albuquerque franchise was sold to Portland, and the Dukes were no more. Albuquerque business interests, though, managed to purchase the Calgary Cannons and are pursing a renovated stadium to provide luxury boxes and greater amenities. The role of marketing in baseball is quite apparent in that the new Albuquerque franchise will be called the Isotopes, a name first suggested by the television series *The Simpsons*.

The concluding essay takes us back to the question of consumption in American culture by discussing how the baseball establishment has responded to the changing gender roles in American culture. While women's participation on the field has increased with teams such as the

Silver Bullets, organized baseball has continued to place women in the stereotypical sphere of consumption, suggesting the traditional market-place approach of the game on the major league level.

In conclusion, these nineteen essays on major league baseball in his-torical and cultural perspective offer an avenue through which to exam-ine changing perceptions of race, gender, and class in the United States during the twentieth century. They suggest to readers that baseball may be used to explore important questions about American society, economic power, and culture as we begin the twenty-first century. Interrogating baseball should enhance our understanding of the larger culture.

While most of these pieces have been previously published, it is my hope that bringing these writings together will provide readers and teach-ers who would like to use these essays in the classroom with a model for using baseball as an interpretive and analytical tool for the examination of recent American history. The whole of these essays should carry greater weight than its individual parts.

Preparing these essays over the last twenty years has been a labor of love on my part, but they could not have been completed without the input and assistance of so many individuals. I would like to thank Bill Kirwin, who, as a friend and as an editor of *Nine: A Journal of Baseball History and Social Policy Perspectives*, has always encouraged my work. Anyone who is able to organize an academic conference in conjunction with spring train-ing will always enjoy my respect. My first academic presentation on base-ball was for the North American Society for Sport History, and the boys of summer at NASSH (Steve Gietschier, Sam Regalado, Richard Crepeau, Larry Gerlach, and Jules Tygiel), with whom I have shared many a podium, have been sources of support and inspiration.

For anyone interested in baseball, a pilgrimage to Cooperstown is essential, and in recent years I have been fortunate to make this an annual excursion to participate in the Cooperstown Symposium on Baseball and American Culture. Alvin Hall does a marvelous job organizing these con-ferences, and individuals such as Peter Rutkoff, William Simons, and Thomas Altherr have prepared the proceedings for publications which are available from McFarland & Company. Bill Gates and his staff at the Base-ball Hall of Fame have also contributed to this volume by assisting my navigation through the extensive clipping files available at the Hall's library.

I also owe a great deal of gratitude to my students at Sandia Prepara-tory School and the University of New Mexico-Valencia Campus, whose intellectual curiosity and friendship have made teaching much more than a job for me. I must also thank Sandia Prep Headmaster Dick Heath, whose generous support of professional development has made it possible for me to actively participate in scholarly conferences. For instilling a passion for history during my undergraduate days at West Texas State University, a debt of gratitude is owed to Professor Peter Peterson. My mother deserves acknowledgement for never giving up on me, even when I was flunking some high school courses. I would like to thank my children — Pam, Shane, Meghan, and Rosemary — for making life so wonderful. Last, but never least, I would like to express my appreciation and love for my wife Kathleen, whose assistance with this book was invaluable. She makes every task and day special.

1

Ruth and Cobb as Cultural Symbols: The Development of a Mass Consumer Ethic for Baseball in the 1920s

In the transitional years of 1919–1920, following the First World War, America as well as the institution of baseball went through challenges and changes which altered the nature of American culture. While scholars of political history note disillusionment over the war and defeat of the League of Nations, the Red scare, labor and racial unrest, and a shift from the progressivism of Woodrow Wilson to the normalcy of Warren Harding, social and cultural historians focus upon a transition from the values of production to consumption. In *Culture as History*, Warren Susman argues that in the early 1920s a conflict emerged in America between two cultures, "…an older culture, often loosely labeled Puritan-republican, producer capitalist culture, and a newly emerging culture of abundance."[1]

While this emerging cultural conflict was often contested in the popular arenas of the mass media, darkened movie theaters, and sport, an exchange in the intellectual journal *Dial* indicated that contemporary scholars were only too aware of the cultural messages encoded in a popular pastime such as baseball. In July, 1919, Morris R. Cohen informed readers of the *Dial* that baseball was America's national religion, embodying all the moral value of war. The national "zest for combat and conquest" was exemplified in the rivalry between cities for baseball championships, and Cohen concluded by arguing for the internationalization of baseball as a way to direct national rivalries in a more healthy fashion. Cohen's former student Louis Finkelstein was appalled by the glorification of nineteenth-century values. Instead of extolling competi-

7

tion and conquest, Finkelstein emphasized the cooperative aspects of play, asserting, "The less of rivalry that we have, the less we insist on the self, whether it takes the form of the aggrandizement of one's individuality, one's nation or one's race, the nearer will we approach our ideal. "[2]

This exchange between Cohen and Finkelstein represents a debate regarding the values of production — associated with words such as competition, rivalry, conquest, and individualism — and consumption — reflected by the key words of plenty, play, leisure, gratification, and personality — which raged throughout the decade of the 1920s. In baseball, the ideas put forth by Cohen and Finkelstein are perhaps demonstrated in the careers of two of the sport's greatest stars, Ty Cobb, who still holds the major league record for lifetime batting average at .366 and retired from the game in 1928, and Babe Ruth, who as a slugging sensation revolutionized the game, hitting fifty-nine home runs in 1921 and sixty in 1927. In *A Brief History of American Sports*, Elliot J. Gorn and Warren Goldstein describe Cobb as an "acquisitive, calculating, aggressive" individual who "made the most of his lean build and terrific speed and took instant advantage of every opportunity." Cobb perceived baseball as a Darwinian "survival of the fittest" in which the Georgia native was determined to exploit the weakness of his opponents and subdue them. On the other hand, Gorn and Goldstein perceive Ruth as "a player of power rather than calculation," who "was that rare 'natural' who seemed to have been born with an instinctive knowledge of the game; unlike Cobb, he never appeared to think about strategy, or guard or control his strength."[3] Accordingly, Cobb, with his aggressive tactics, emphasizing singles and base stealing, or scientific baseball as traditionalists liked to call it, appeared to embody the work ethic and Social Darwinist view of nineteenth-century industrial capitalism, while Ruth focused the game's attention on the instant gratification of the home run, spending a great deal of his free time playing hard at drinking, eating, and seeking female companionship.

Much of baseball scholarship tends to support the thesis of Gorn and Goldstein. In Ken Burns's and Geoffrey Ward's *Baseball: An Illustrated History*, the companion volume to the eighteen hour documentary film *Baseball* directed and produced by Burns, much is made of the fact that in an era of conspicuous consumption, Ruth was perhaps the most conspicuous consumer of them all. Having spent most of his youth confined within the walls of St. Mary's Industrial School for Boys, Ruth had little opportunity to sample the offerings of the mass consumption society. However, when he began to earn large sums for his phenomenal slugging abilities, Ruth made up quickly for lost time, "drinking bourbon and ginger ale before breakfast, changing silk shirts six and seven times a day, and becoming a favored customer in whorehouses all across the country."[4] Ruth biographers have well documented the large fellow's appetite as well as his involvement with the emerging advertising industry of Madison Avenue. Ruth endorsed everything from candy bars to Girl Scout cookies, including several different brands of breakfast cereal; in addition to extolling the virtues of various cigarette companies when he only smoked cigars.[5] Despite evidence that Ruth was most compatible with the culture of mass consumption, many scholars have still attempted to place Ruth within the context of the nineteenth-century Horatio Alger rags to riches myth of the self-made man of frontier or small town America. For example, Richard Crepeau, in his study of baseball as a symbol of American values in the 1920s, observes, "Define the rugged individual in a mass ritual role on a stretch of grass in the middle of a concrete-and-asphalt urban center. Personify all of these feelings in a larger-than-life figure, and what begins to appear is the outline of 'The Great Babe Ruth.'"[6]

However, the perception of Ruth as a manifestation of traditional American values espousing rugged individualism and productivity has not been accepted by all scholars. In his multi-volume history of baseball, Horatio Seymour offers some valuable insights on the symbolic value of Babe Ruth. Seymour concedes that Ruth's life fits the model of a Horatio Alger hero in his ascent from boyhood poverty to adult adulation and wealth. But Seymour argues, "Unlike the Alger heroes, Ruth did not struggle upward laboriously by dent of hard work and patient penny-pinching, and his way of life was foreign to their stuffy moralistic code." Indeed, Seymour concludes that much of Ruth's popular appeal was due to his defiance of traditional conventions of hard work and self-denial as he glorified in the conspicuous consumption of everything from alcohol to automobiles. In a similar vein, Warren Susman describes Ruth as "an ideal hero for the world of consumption. Americans enjoyed the Babe's excess; they took comfort in the life of apparently enormous pleasures that Ruth enjoyed."[7]

If scholars have found Ruth's personal habits and his offensive weapon of the home run to have symbolic value for a cultural transformation in America, what of Ruth's contemporaries on the playing field? How did they perceive the shift from the era of Cobb and the stolen base to Ruth and the home run? Sam Crawford, an outstanding outfield teammate of Cobb on the Detroit Tiger teams of the early twentieth century, acknowledged that many observers focused on Cobb's speed. But Crawford asserted that the key to Cobb's success was not natural ability. Rather, it was his speed in thinking and ingenuity. Crawford believed, "He didn't outhit the opposition and he didn't outrun them. He outthought them!" Ruth, with the ability to ensure run production with one swing of his mighty bat, was the polar extreme of Cobb's scientific baseball, and players recognized that he represented an important change in the sport. For example, the college-educated Boston outfielder Harry Hooper realized that with Ruth's coming, the game had changed. Hooper, a teammate of Ruth's until his trade to the Yankees following the 1919 season, recollected, "But sometimes I can't believe what I saw: this nineteen-year-old kid, crude, poorly educated, only lightly brushed by the social veneer we call civilization, gradually transformed into the idol of American youth and the symbol of baseball the world over — a man loved by more people and with an intensity of feeling that perhaps has never been equaled before or since."[8]

And how did the great Cobb himself react to the revolution in baseball values wrought by Babe Ruth and the home run explosion of the 1920s? While Cobb's best biographer Charles C Alexander has downplayed the cultural symbolism of Cobb and attributed his intense drive and determination to an effort to please his father who was accidentally shot and killed by his mother during Cobb's early years in baseball, Cobb made little secret of his contempt for Ruth and the changes in the sport and American life symbolized by the Yankee outfielder in the 1920s. Cobb was unmerciful in his bench jockeying of Ruth, vilifying the Yankee great with profanity and racial slurs that Ruth shared some African-American (certainly a term Cobb would never have used) ancestry. On more than one occasion, Cobb's acid tongue provoked near physical confrontations between the two men. However, in his memoirs, Cobb had kinder things to say about Ruth the man, but not about the values which Ruth and his legacy brought to the game. Cobb ridiculed the passive nature and instant gratification of the home run (values more in tune with the American consumption ethic), while extolling the aggression and sacrifice (production values) of the hit and run play or stolen base. According to Cobb, during his day, "Teams fought for runs like tug-of-war teams fight for an inch of turf. It was thrilling, full of heat, sweat and fury." Indeed, baseball to Cobb was the moral equivalent of war, and he had no use for the civilians of modern day baseball. Cobb preferred players from an earlier production-oriented capitalism who were "less interested in a bonus, a business manager, and a bowling alley than in fighting to win."[9] Thus, Cobb ended his life an embittered, although wealthy (he had invested his early baseball earnings in the fledgling Atlanta-based Coca-Cola company and, in turn, became a millionaire) individual who lamented the decline of traditional American values both off and on the ball field. Accordingly, scholars of American culture as well as players of the period observed that the 1920s were a transitional time in which American values of production symbolized by Cobb and the stolen base were being overshadowed by the consumption ethic of Babe Ruth and the home run. But to what extent was this change evident to millions of Americans who flocked to ball games in the era of what many commentators labeled "the golden age of American sports?" The spectacular rise of spectator sports in the decade was not welcomed by everyone. Progressive reformers, such as the editors of the *Nation*, bemoaned the loss of "athletism" as an ideology of the strenuous life, associated with the growth of republican values, to be replaced by the more passive mass spectator sports in which the people become mere consumers of a game. And historian-journalist Frederick Lewis Allen referred to the decade as the "ballyhoo years" in which hoopla over sporting events and Babe Ruth gained more public attention than the more significant issues of politics and foreign affairs.[10]

A perusal of popular magazines from the decade, such as *Collier's, Literary Digest, Outlook*, and *Saturday Evening Post*, reveals a society which did not forget affairs of state, but, nevertheless, did take its leisure activities such as baseball most seriously. While periodicals gave considerable space to baseball and its sporting challengers of boxing, college football, tennis, and golf, a more important consideration is in what language and symbols did the popular magazines describe the sport and its heroes. Was a cultural shift from production to consumption values evident to the general reading public who avidly followed spectator sports such as baseball and cultural heroes like Ruth? An examination of periodical literature in the popular press between 1920 and 1928 reveals that the embracing of a consumer ethic, with its accompanying values of play, leisure, self-fulfillment, personality, and celebrity, was an essential element of popular culture in the 1920s.

As the American economy and political culture grappled with the transition from war to peace in 1919, the sport of baseball was confronted with accusations that the 1919 World Series between the Chicago White Sox and Cincinnati Reds had been "fixed" by gamblers and eight Chicago players, who in exchange for cash payments made sure that Cincinnati was victorious. Political journals such as the *New Republic* and *Nation* lamented the degree to which gambling and underworld interests had gained influence within the business of baseball. For a solution, these journals of progressive political opinion called for a return to a sense of play with athletes of character and enforcement of a moral code. While the eight indicted players were acquitted by a Chicago jury, the newly appointed Commissioner of Baseball Judge Kenesaw Mountain Landis believed in the moral imperatives called for by the *New Republic* and *Nation*, banishing for life the eight Chicago players from organized baseball.[11]

While Landis in his authoritative manner attempted to instill moral

integrity in the sport, he could not put spectators in the seats of major
league baseball stadiums. That task would fall to George Herman "Babe"
Ruth, who following the 1919 season had been sold by the Boston Red Sox
to the New York Yankees. Ruth, who had joined the Boston franchise in
1915, following a successful 1914 campaign with the Baltimore Orioles of
the International League, was an outstanding pitcher and hitter for the
Red Sox, leading the team to World Series victories in 1916 and 1918, while
establishing a major league record with twenty-nine home runs during the
1919 season. However, Red Sox owner and Broadway producer Harrison
Frazee was in debt and agreed to sell Ruth to Colonel Jacob Ruppert, the
New York brewer who owned the Yankees, for $125,000 cash and the prom-
ise of a $300,000 personal loan for which Fenway Park was offered as secu-
rity. The dollar amounts involved in this sale got the attention of
consumer-oriented Americans. However, an article in the *Literary Digest*
argued that Ruth was a bargain as he was the only player in the American
League in 1919 who had scored over a hundred runs (103) or driven in a
hundred (112). In the spirit of conspicuous consumption, the article went
on to point out that Ruth had slugged four grand slam home runs, observing, "The thrill of cleaning up with 'three on' comes into the career of
many players only once in a lifetime. With Ruth it now is a habit." And
to underscore that indeed the times were changing, the *Literary Digest* concluded the piece by contrasting Ruth's statistics with the 1919 figures
amassed by Cobb, who while hitting for an average of .378, only drove in
seventy runs.[12]

In his first season with the Yankees, Ruth was up to the expectations
raised by his extravagant sale price. The Yankee slugger exceeded his previous marks, hitting for an average of .376, driving in 137 runs, establishing a new record with fifty-four home runs, and well earning his
1920-1921 salary figure of $40,000. The fixation upon the statistical achieve-
ments and price tag of Ruth was a reflection of what cultural historian
Susman calls the "mechanization of life" which "produced particular middle-class delight in what could be measured and counted."[13] And the four
base swats of Ruth were certainly the focus of media speculation. In *Current Opinion*, the Yankee slugger was lauded as "the most talked-of American," while a profile in the *Independent* used the consumption vocabulary
of personality and celebrity to label Ruth an idol worshipped by millions
of Americans. However, Ruth's background at St. Mary's Industrial School
in Baltimore still made it easy to describe Ruth in Horatio Alger terms.
Thus, Stanley Reid in the *Independent* found Ruth's youth at St. Mary's to
be exemplified by "good, plain, hearty food, kindly guidance and teaching and tip top athletic training."[14] But Ruth would make up for his early

material deprivations by establishing records for distance clouts, impatience, and an insatiable appetite, perhaps exemplified by his marriage to Helen Woodford, a sixteen-year-old waitress whom he met on his first day in the major leagues, and an ensuing reputation for chasing women despite his status as a married man.[15]

While interpretations of Ruth's humble origins may differ, it was clear that a new era was dawning in baseball as Cobb's average in 1920 fell to .334, and the *New York Times*, noting the Georgia Peach's fading numbers, asserted, "Ruth has stolen all of Cobb's thunder."[16] If any more evidence was needed for the passing of an era, it was provided in the terms used by the *Providence News* to describe Cleveland shortstop Ray Chapman, who was killed late in the season by a pitch thrown by Yankee hurler Carl Mays. The obituary praised Chapman as the leading sacrifice hitter in the league, asserting, "Down through the years he team-worked for victory, never sulking, always optimistic, praising the other fellow. He was the gentleman of his profession, who sought no adornment, but wished well the way of all."[17] The rhetoric of self-sacrifice and limitations would not suffice for the "ballyhoo years" of Babe Ruth in the 1920s and titles such as the Sultan of Swat or the Caliph of Clout. The modern mass media appeal of Ruth was most evident when he agreed to star in a fictionalized film account of his life entitled *Headin' Home*, which was released in September, 1920, and for which Ruth was to be paid $50,000. Home run leaders and not sacrifice leaders were the stars and subjects of the emerging film industry which espoused the virtues of a mass consumer society.[18]

While Ruth was criticized for missing some games near the end of the 1920 season in order to complete his film appearance, reporter Hugh S. Fullerton, who had played an instrumental role in breaking the 1919 World Series Black Sox scandal, gave the Sultan of Swat full credit for baseball's rapid recovery from questions of impropriety. Fullerton observed that in 1920 baseball had enjoyed its greatest season, playing before more than twelve million spectators, while the Yankees with their "star-attraction" of Ruth entertained nearly two and one-half million fans. Even more paying customers were expected for the 1921 campaign as baseball enthusiasts could not seem to get enough of heavy hitting and home runs. Meeting this challenge, Ruth responded by swatting fifty-nine home runs, shattering his own record for the third year n a row and leading the Yankees to the pennant, although they were defeated in the World Series by the New York Giants. Commentators such as F. C. Lane were quoted as believing Ruth had instituted a new system of baseball with the home run (the number of home runs had risen from 507 in 1911 to 629 in 1920) which supplanted the hit and run tactics of Cobb. Speaking of Ruth, Lane maintained, "He has batted home runs at so dizzy a pace that he has fired the imagination of the entire country. He has not only slugged his way to fame, but he has got everybody else doing it. The home run fever is in the air. It is infectious. There is a disposition on the part of managers not to hold their own men back, but rather to encourage them.... Babe has not only smashed all records, he has smashed the long accepted system of things in the batting world, and on the ruin of that system, he has erected another system, or rather lack of system whose dominant quality is brute force." The adulation of the crowd, the success of the team on the field, and his financial gains encouraged other players and managers to emulate the instantaneous gratification of the home run. Less and less was the Puritan work ethic used to describe Ruth as he was increasingly perceived as a natural. Thus, tests on Ruth performed at Columbia University's Psychological Research Laboratory were reported to prove that the slugger had better eyes and a quicker nervous system than most Americans.[19]

However, not all Americans were comfortable with the enthroning of Ruth as the king of the consumer culture in the sporting world. Spokesmen for the progressive ideology of "athletism," such as the *Louisville Courier-Journal*, continued to argue for the strenuous life of activity rather than the passive quality of a spectator, maintaining, "Two hours of inactivity in the grand stand or bleachers is not productive of muscle or sinew. The same amount of time spent in tennis, golf, swimming or any number of games would be infinitely better for American manhood." And while consumerism appeared to be dominant over "athletism" in the culture, the high priest of baseball consumerism was not above reproach. During the off-season, Ruth disobeyed the instructions of Commissioner Landis regarding barnstorming playing tours. Landis responded by suspending Ruth for the first thirty-nine games of the 1922 season. Getting off to a late start, Ruth never got in the groove, finishing with only thirty-five home runs and batting only .118 in the World Series which once again the Yankees dropped to the Giants. A frustrated Ruth battled all season with umpires and was suspended three times by American League President Ban Johnson.[20]

Realizing that he might be discarded like last year's cereal brand and shamed by New York State Senator James J. Walker, who convinced Ruth that he had let the boys of New York City down, Ruth vowed to redeem himself over the winter. Sports writer F. C. Lane argued that like Napoleon invading Russia, Ruth had simply let fame and money distract him. And no wonder, as not even the "peerless" Ty Cobb "had even won a tithe of Babe's prestige." However, after a winter working on his farm in rural Massachusetts, Ruth was ready to reclaim his preeminent position in the game. With the new structure of Yankee Stadium in place, Ruth would have a suitable domain in which to demonstrate his talents and thrill the masses who descended upon the Stadium to watch Ruth and consume the product of baseball, complete with home runs, hot dogs, and beer. In a rhetorical flourish, Lane concluded, "The date is set for the return of Napoleon from Elba."[21]

And with a flair for the dramatic, Ruth did not disappoint his legion of followers. Before a crowd estimated at over seventy thousand, Ruth hammered on his first at bat in Yankee Stadium. The Yankees won the game four to one, and "the house that Ruth built" had been christened. Baseball fans continued to pour through the turnstiles at Yankee Stadium, and Ruth regained his slugging crown, clouting forty-one homers in 1923, while hitting for an average of .393 and pacing the Yankees to a World Series triumph over the Giants. In 1924, Ruth upped his home run output to forty-six, but the Yankees finished second to the Washington Senators. As home runs increasingly dominated the game and captured fan interest, traditionalists bemoaned the loss of base stealing techniques and pitching fundamentals overwhelmed by power hitting. In addition, more conservative adherents of baseball feared that the sport was losing its rural roots (although many scholars question this Jeffersonian agrarian origin of the game) and its ability to laugh at itself. The difficult initiations confronted by players when Cobb first broke into the league were a thing of the past. Pranks might injure a player who was a valuable commodity. The trickster was disappearing from baseball to be replaced by the business player who "has the money end of the game uppermost in mind." Themes of combat were being replaced by the turnstiles of the market place.[22] The cause for this state of affairs was much debated in baseball circles with a number of theories developed to explain the emergence of the home run. Some observers argued that the culprit was the introduction of a new more resilient baseball, while others maintained that outlawing the spitball and forcing umpires to toss out discolored balls following the Ray Chapman beaning tipped the balance in favor of the hitters. Nevertheless, after careful study, baseball historian Ben Rader insists that while other factors might have some merit, "the success of Babe Ruth was the most important reason for the hitting revolution."[23]

Having regained his slugging crown in 1923 and 1924, Ruth wallowed in his celebrity status and conspicuous consumption. However, Christopher Walsh, in addition to providing Ruth with numerous endorsement opportunities, as business representative and financial adviser provided some security, convincing Ruth in 1924 to begin investing some of his earnings in annuities that would pay off after Ruth retired from the game.[24]

On the playing field Ruth's status was evident in comparison with his greatest National League rival, Rogers Hornsby of the St. Louis Cardinals, who in 1924 had batted .424 with twenty-five home runs. However, while Ruth was earning $52,000 a year in baseball, Hornsby was making $17,500. Hornsby simply did not understand the importance of publicity in a consumer culture, and when asked about his lack of color, commented, "I have been told that I lack color. I do not fight with umpires, and I am not going to. I don't run wild on the bases, spiking other players. If I have to play dirty baseball, I prefer to play none at all. Color in the popular eye seems to consist of just such things. I go along, minding my own business, doing my best work, and if my work won't speak for me, I will have to go without." But baseball in the 1920s was about a great deal more than just the American work ethic. Arthur Robinson in a piece for *Collier's* observed that Ruth deserved his celebrity status in the game, as, "He has drawn more people to baseball than any player in the history of the game. Everywhere larger ball parks have been built simply because of the interest he has attracted to the game. And baseball salaries have gone up because of him."[25] Thus, Ruth enhanced the popularity of baseball as a consumer product in the crowded market place of the 1920s.

However, personal habits of consumption and gratification once again brought discredit upon Ruth. His friend Robinson described him as eating ten times a day and consuming mass quantities of soda and chewing gum. In fact, Ruth reported to spring training in 1925 thirty pounds overweight, collapsing with a mysterious illness, referred to by one pundit as the bellyache heard around the world, which required abdominal surgery and hospital rest. After rejoining the team, Ruth defied training rules, staying out all night and drinking heavily. His conduct resulted in a suspension from Manager Miller Huggins, and the Yankees fell to seventh place with Ruth hitting only twenty-five home runs. In his private life, Ruth and his wife Helen agreed to separate, but not divorce as Helen was Catholic. Meanwhile, Ruth was free to spend more time with his companion; a widow and model by the name of Claire Hodgson.

Many critics of Ruth were quick to applaud his demise in contrast with Cobb who was celebrating his twentieth season with the Tigers in the role of a player-manager. *Literary Digest* referred to Ruth as the "Naughty Boy" of baseball, while Cobb was portrayed as the "Good Boy." Ed Hughes of the *New York Evening Telegram* related Ruth's "colossal collapse" to the lack of a work ethic, while Joe Vila of the *New York Sun* observed that while Ruth's personal indiscretions resulted in disciplinary action, "Cobb's wonderful record as a player never has been tarnished by fines or suspensions for violating the rules against dissipation." Continuing to extol the work ethic of Cobb, the *Evening Telegram* concluded that Cobb was "the story of a determination to succeed, to be first in the chosen endeavor of life."[26] These champions of Cobb's strenuous life overlooked, of course, the many individuals over whom Cobb had scratched and clawed his way to the top.

Other more astute observers of the sporting scene recognized that there was more to the transformation of American culture in the 1920s than the perpetuation of Social Darwinism. Heywood Broun of the *New York World* said that Ruth was a natural creative artist, and the discipline of training schedules or rigid production values simply did not exist for the Sultan of Swat. In *Collier's*, the veteran sports writer Grantland Rice acknowledged that Ruth violated all traditional rules of economy and thrift, proving that money was not as important "as the game and the glory of the game." Here, Rice celebrated the consumption values of play, self-fulfillment, and celebrity status. As for Ruth, he promised to make another comeback in 1926. In an interview for *Collier's*, he made no apologies for his extravagant consumption, such as owning nine cars of the most expensive American make, or during a hot spell in St. Louis, wearing twenty-two silk shirts in three days and leaving them for the hotel chambermaid. Ruth explained, "I was the Home Run King, and I was just living up to the title. What I do regret is my own foolishness, the messes I have gotten into through bad judgment." In conclusion, Ruth admitted that he had flittered away perhaps over a half-million dollars between 1921 and 1925. "I have been the sappiest of saps, but I'm going to make good all over again — if I can cut out being a chump."[27]

On the baseball field, Ruth certainly made good on his pledge, hitting forty-seven home runs and leading the Yankees to the American League pennant in 1926 before losing the World Series to St. Louis.

He was lauded in the *Literary Digest* for his work ethic in staging a comeback, but almost as if expecting another fall, his transgressions were forgiven due to his child-like personality. Ruth was described as "lovable, big-hearted, simple, careless, reckless, easily led, seldom thinking or caring for consequences."[28] These child-like characteristics relate well to the consumption values of play, leisure, and pleasure, and were quite different from the descriptions of Cobb's career when he announced his retirement at the end of the 1926 season, following a dispute with Commissioner Landis and American League President Johnson over allegations that Cobb had wagered on baseball contests during the 1919 season. Following the dismissal of these charges, Cobb returned to baseball as a player-manager for the Philadelphia Athletics during the 1927 and 1928 campaigns.

Following his retirement from the Tigers in 1926, Cobb was described as "literally a self-made man," who looked back upon his playing career as if it were a combat experience. Replying to questions about his aggressive style of play, Cobb asserted, "I would insist that it is just as sportsmanlike to make the other fellow tremble as to let him make me tremble. At any rate it's fighting a fellow with his own weapons." In addition to images of war, Cobb viewed his approach to the game of baseball as similar to that of the manufacturer. Baseball players must be constantly thinking a play or two ahead, just as "a manufacturer doesn't wait until the last minute to order his raw material."[29] The connection to values of nineteenth-century industrial productivity and capitalism seemed as natural for Cobb as the consumption ethic equations of leisure and play were with the career of Babe Ruth. However, the values of consumption appeared to be dominant over those of production during the 1920s and may explain a great deal of Cobb's discomfort during his last days in baseball.

As Cobb's career was winding down in Philadelphia, Ruth enjoyed his greatest season in 1927 with a record-shattering sixty home runs and four game Yankee sweep of the Pittsburgh Pirates in the World Series. Following his successful 1926 campaign, Ruth was rewarded with a three-year contract, calling for $70,000 a year, which brought little criticism from the nation's fickle newspapers who seemed to have forgotten about their denunciation of Ruth's work ethic during the 1925 season. Praising Ruth's contributions clearly within the consumer ethic of the 1920s, the *Ohio State Journal* concluded that Ruth's salary was due to the fact that "a large section of the public is crazy for amusement and able and willing to pay high for it." Likewise, the *Springfield Republican* editorialized, "Entertaining the public is highly legitimate business. Here is a man who can do something better than any other man alive; the public appreciates it and willingly pays for the sight of it." Drawing upon his financial success and downplaying his extravagant spending, Ruth was even depicted giving his young slugging protégé Lou Gehrig investment tips.[30]

Ruth's assaults upon American League pitchers continued through the 1928 season in which he clouted fifty-four home runs before concluding the season with a World Series sweep of the Cardinals to which Ruth contributed three home runs. Following the Series, Ruth was praised, in the *Literary Digest*, as deserving the adulation of the crowd, for, "He is the greatest slugger of all time and one of the most picturesque batters that ever glowered at an enemy pitcher." The article wished Ruth success with his ambition of becoming a manager once his playing days were at an end.[31] The off-season seemed to find Ruth in a reflective mood when he conducted a series of interviews with Bozeman Bulger of the *Saturday Evening Post*. In these interviews, Ruth made it clear how well he embodied the values of the consumption culture. Discussing money, Ruth estimated that with his baseball salary, exhibition games, stage appearances, and syndicate writing, he had earned at least a million dollars, while extravagantly throwing away at least half of that amount. However, he asserted that he "had a lot of fun." Ruth further revealed that he never had any particular aim in life other than just to play ball. "I still like to play, even if it's just for the fun of it." The values of fun and play were alien to the production ethic espoused by Cobb. Ruth also did not attribute his success to hard work. Rather, he simply had a natural talent, and he resented writers saying that he was lucky to hit a baseball or he might be digging ditches. Ruth retorted, "If a lot of those great writers hadn't had the knack of writing, they might have been plow hands or ditch diggers too. They don't work a lot harder to get to the top of their profession than we do…. As a general rule, the baseball player earns all the glory that he gets, just same as anybody in any other walk of life."[32]

Thus, Ruth seemed ready to enter 1929 comfortable in his status as a symbol of the emerging culture of abundance with its values of plenty, play, leisure, recreation, gratification, and publicity. Scholars, players such as Ruth and Cobb, as well as the general public, evident from a survey of popular periodical literature in the period between 1920 and 1928, recognized that baseball and cultural symbols like Ruth exemplified important transformations in American society. Accordingly, the *New York Evening World* commented upon Ruth's five hundredth career home run late in the 1929 season:

> It is to be bracketed with our skyscrapers, our universities, our millions of automobiles, as a symbol of American greatness. Bells should have been rung when this thing came to pass, and fire-crackers set off, and traffic halted for one minute throughout the length and breadth of the land; in addition, Mr. Ruth should have had his picture taken with Thomas Edison, Harvey Firestone, Charles A. Lindbergh, and Henry Ford. Is not he as eminent as they?[33]

However, the years ushered in by the Great Depression of October, 1929 challenged this celebration of the American consumption ethic. Ruth gained some stability in his personal life following the death of his estranged wife Helen, allowing him to marry Claire Hodgson. On the playing field, Ruth hit over forty home runs in each of the seasons between 1929 and 1932, although the Yankees only appeared in the 1932 Series in which Ruth is alleged to have called a home run shot. In 1933, his skills began to deteriorate, and he ended his career with the Boston Braves in 1935. When Miller Huggins died in 1929, Ruth expected to be named Yankee manager. However, the Yankee front office was never to give Ruth this opportunity, and the great athlete who had revolutionized the game in the 1920s with the consumption values of play, gratification, and celebrity status ended up as bitter as his more driven counterpart, Ty Cobb. In the 1919 *Dial* intellectual exchange, Cohen and Finkelstein spoke of baseball and society having to choose between the values of conflict (Cobb and the production ethic) and cooperation (Ruth and consumerism). It appears in retrospect that baseball, like the larger American society, chose the option of a mass consumer culture embodying the concepts of play as well as greed. However, with the death of Babe Ruth in 1948 much of the fun departed from the game, and we are often only left with the legacy of greed exemplified in the strike and cancelled World Series of 1994.

====

Endnotes

A version of this paper was originally presented at the 1995 Hofstra University Conference, "Baseball and The Sultan of Swat: Commemorating the 100th Birthday of Babe Ruth."

1. Warren I. Susman, *Culture as History: The Transformation of American Society in the Twentieth Century* (New York: Pantheon Books, 1973), p. xx. For other studies which emphasize the cultural shift from production to consumption see Mark Dyreson, "The Emergence of Consumer Culture and the Transformation of Physical Culture: American Sport in the 1920s," *Journal of Sport History*, 10 (Winter, 1989), 261–281; Stuart Ewen, *Captains of Consciousness: Advertising and the Social Roots of the Consumer Culture* (New York: McGraw-Hill, 1976); Stuart and Elizabeth Ewen, *Channels of Desire: Mass Image and the Shaping of American Consciousness* (New York: McGraw-Hill, 1982); Leo Lowenthal, "The Triumph of Mass Idols," in *Literature, Popular Culture, and Society* (Palto Alto, California: Pacific Books, 1968); Richard Merchand, *Advertising the American Dream: Making Way for Modernity, 1920-1940* (Berkeley, California: Beacon Press, 1985); Larry May, *Screening Out the Past: The Birth of Mass Culture and the Motion Picture Industry* (New York: Oxford University Press, 1980); and Richard Wrightman Fox and T. J. Jackson Lears, eds., *The Culture of Consumption : Critical Essays in American History, 1880-1980* (New York: Pantheon, 1983).
2. Morris R. Cohen, "Baseball," *Dial*, 67 (July 26, 1919), 57–58; and Louis Finkelstein, "Baseball and Rivalry," *Dial*, 67 (October 4, 1919), 313.
3. Elliot J. Gorn and Warren Goldstein, *A Brief History of American Sports* (New York: Hill and Wang, 1993), 188-197.
4. Geoffrey C. Ward and Ken Burns, *Baseball: An Illustrated History* (New York: Alfred A. Knopf, 1994), 159.
5. For Ruth biographies see Robert W. Creamer, *Babe: The Legend Comes to Life* (New York: Simon and Schuster, 1974); Marshall Smelser, *The Life that Ruth Built* (New York: Quadrangle, 1975); Robert Smith, *Babe Ruth's America* (New York: Holt, Rinehart & Winston, 1961); Ken Sobel, *Babe Ruth and the American Dream* (New York:

Random House, 1974); and Kal Wagenheim, *Babe Ruth: His Life and Legend* (New York: Praeger Publishing, 1975).

6. Richard C. Crepeau, *Baseball: America's Diamond Mind, 1919-1941* (Orlando: University Presses of Florida, 1980), 74. For other interpretations which tend to place Ruth within the context of traditional American production values see Tristram Potter Coffin, *The Old Ball Game: Baseball in Folklore and Fiction* (New York: Herder and Herder, 1974), 76–101; F. R. Doyd, "The Home Run King," 217–228, in Christopher D. Geist and Jack Nachbar, eds., *The Popular Culture Reader* (Bowling Green, Ohio: Bowling Green University Popular Press, 1983); Roderick Nash, *The Nervous Generation: American Thought, 1917-1930* (Chicago: Rand McNally & Company, 1970), 126–137; and David A. Voigt, *America Through Baseball* (Chicago: Nelson-Hall, 1976), 147–161.

7. Harold Seymour, *Baseball: The Golden Age* (New York: Oxford University Press, 1971), 433; and Warren I. Susman, "Culture Heroes: Ford, Barton, Ruth," 122–149, in Susman, ed., *Transformation of American Society in the Twentieth Century*.

8. Lawrence G. Ritter, *The Glory of Their Times: The Story of the Early Days of Baseball Told by the Men Who Played It* (New York: Collier Books, 1966), 60–61, and 136–137.

9. Charles C. Alexander, *Ty Cobb* (New York: Oxford University Press, 1984); and Ty Cobb with Al Stump, *My Life in Baseball: The True Record* (Garden City, New York: Doubleday & Company, 1961), 273–278.

10. For critics of the rise of mass spectator sports in the 1920s see "Sport is Elected," *Nation,* 119 (September 17, 1924), 278; Dyreson, "Emergence of Consumer Culture and the Transformation of Physical Culture," 261–181; and Frederick Lewis Allen, *Only Yesterday: An Informal History of the 1920s* (New York: Harper & Row, 1931), 155–187.

11. "Baseball on Trial," *New Republic,* 24 (October 20, 1920), 183–184; and "Baseball Scandal," *Nation,* 111 (October 13, 1920), 395–396; Eliot Asinoff, *Eight Men Out: The Black Sox and the 1919 World Series* (New York: Holt, Rinehart and Winston, 1963); and J. G. Taylor Spink, *Judge Landis and Twenty-Five Years of Baseball* (St. Louis: Sporting News, 1947).

12. "Something About 'Babe' Ruth, Price $125,000," *Literary Digest,* 64 (January 17, 1920), 128–130; and "Runs Scored by 'Babe' Ruth," *Literary Digest,* 64 (February 14, 1920), 125–127. For the impact of the Ruth trade on Boston see Dan Shaughnessy, *The Curse of the Bambino* (New York: Penguin, 1990).

13. Susman, "Culture Heroes: Ford, Barton, Ruth," 141.

14. "A New Hero of the Great American Game at Close Range," *Current Opinion,* 69 (October, 1920), 477–478; and Stanley Reid, "Meet the American Idol," *Independent,* 103 (August 14, 1920), 170–171.

15. For the sexual exploits of Ruth see Creamer, *Babe,* 315–334.

16. *New York Times,* as quoted in Ward and Burns, *Baseball: An Illustrated History,* 159.

17. "The Death of Chapman Killed by a Pitched Ball," *Literary Digest,* 66 (September 18, 1920), 92; and Mike Sowell, *The Pitch That Killed* (New York, 1987).

18. For *Headin' Home* see Don Trimble, "Babe Ruth: The Media Construction of a 1920s Sport Personality," unpublished manuscript, presented at North American Society for Sport History meeting, University of Saskatchewan, May, 1994; and on the consumer culture and film see May, *Screening Out the Past.*

19. Hugh Fullerton, "Baseball — The Business and the Sport," *American Review of Reviews,* 63 (April, 1921), 417–420; "Home Runs Are in Season," *Literary Digest,* 69

(May 7, 1921), 55; "Babe Ruth Epidemic in Baseball," *Literary Digest,* 69 (June 25, 1921), 51–54; and "Babe Ruth is Supernormal, Hence the 'Homers,' " *Literary Digest,* 71 (October 1, 1921), 40–43.

20. "Is Professional Baseball Sport," *Literary Digest,* 70 (September 17, 1921), 50–53; "When 'Babe' Ruth was Beaten by John J. McGraw," *Literary Digest,* 75 (December 2, 1922), 57–61; and Charles Alexander, *John McGraw* (New York: Oxford University Press, 1988).

21. "Will Babe Ruth Emulate Napoleon and Come Back," *Literary Digest,* 77 (April 7, 1923), 79–82.

22. " 'Jocking' Versus Business in Baseball," *Literary Digest,* 77 (April 28, 1923), 71–76; " 'Hick' Baseball as the Basis of the Game," *Literary Digest,* 77 (May 19, 1923), 64–68; "Batting Bombardment Causes Decline in Art of Baseball," *Literary Digest,* 77 (June 16, 1923), 56–60; "Baseball Shudders at the Home Run Menace," *Literary Digest,* 80 (January 5, 1924), 57–61; "Enter Baseball — But Where Are the Pitchers?," *Literary Digest,* 80 (March 29, 1924), 50–54; and "Sad Decline of Base-Thievery in Baseball," *Literary Digest,* 82 (August 2, 1924), 52–53.

23. Benjamin G. Rader, *Baseball: A History of America's Game* (Urbana: University of Illinois Press, 1994), 112–116.

24. For the role of Walsh see Creamer, *Babe,* 272–275; and Bozeman Bulger, "And Along Came Ruth," *Saturday Evening Post,* 204 (November, 1928), 6–7.

25. " The Man Who Might Rival 'Babe' Ruth," *Literary Digest,* 83 (October 4, 1924), 58–62; and Arthur Robinson, "My Friend Babe Ruth," *Collier's,* 74 (September 20, 1924), 7–8.

26. "Spanking Baseball's Baby and Petting Its Paragon," *Literary Digest,* 86 (September 19, 1925), 58–66.

27. *Ibid.,* 62; Grantland Rice, "What Draws the Crowds?," *Collier's,* 75 (June 20, 1925), 10 and 44; and Babe Ruth to Joe Winkworth, "I Have Been a Babe and a Boob," *Collier's,* 76 (October 31, 1925), 15.

28. "The Babe's Big Effort to Come Back," *Literary Digest,* 90 (July 31, 1926), 46.

29. "Why Ty Cobb is Tired-And Retired," *Literary Digest,* 91 (November 20, 1926), 54–62; Grantland Rice, "The Winner's Way," *Collier's,* 78 (July 10, 1926), 10; "When Ty Cobb and Tris Speaker March Back to the Diamond," *Literary Digest,* 92 (February 12, 1927), 76–80; and Dayton Stoddart, "What Baseball Has Taught Ty Cobb," *Collier's,* 74 (July 19, 1924), 20–25.

30. "Babe Ruth's $210,000 for Three Years of Swat," *Literary Digest,* 92 (March 19, 1927), 61–64; and John B. Kennedy, "Innocents Abroad," *Collier's,* 81 (April 14, 1928), 20 and 43–44.

31. "Babe Ruth's Record Breaking World Series," *Literary Digest,* 99 (October 27, 1928), 56–64.

32. Bulger, "And Along Came Ruth," 6–7 and 36.

33. "Babe Ruth's Five Hundredth," *Literary Digest,* 102 (September 7, 1929), 62.

2

Don't Let Hitler (or the Depression) Kill Baseball: Franklin D. Roosevelt and the National Pastime, 1932–1945

While a leftist critique of American sport suggests that there is social despair in the idea that athletic contests are "one of the bits of glue that hold our society together,"[1] an examination of American baseball during the 1930s and 1940s reveals that when confronted by the challenges of the Great Depression and World War II, President Franklin D. Roosevelt used the national pastime to ward off despair and retain American pride and morale during a period of crisis. Although his sporting interests were more directed to sailing, hunting, and fishing rather than mass urban spectator contests such as major league baseball, Roosevelt and his speech writers cleverly manipulated baseball metaphors to explain the New Deal and gain political support. Likewise, during the Second World War the President provided a "green light" for baseball's survival and use as a morale booster on the home and war fronts.

On the eve of Roosevelt's inaugural in 1933, Arthur Schlesinger, Jr. painted a very grim portrait of American society. Writing in his first volume of *The Age of Roosevelt*, Schlesinger described a nation on the brink of disaster: " The well-groomed men, baffled and impotent in their double-breasted suits before the Senate committee; the confusion and dismay in the business office and the university; the fear in the country club, the angry men marching in the silent street; the scramble for the rotting garbage in the dump; the sweet milk trickling down the dusty road; the noose dangling over the barn door; the raw northwest wind blasting its way across capital plaza."[2] While Schlesinger may be a bit overwrought, there is no doubt that the new President was confronting a crisis to which the American public expected a governmental response. Thus, in his Second Fireside Chat on May 7, 1933, Roosevelt described his New Deal as a partnership among government and farming and industry and transportation. Making an astute use of baseball metaphor, the President asked the American people to be patient with his programs, explaining, "I do not deny that we may make mistakes of procedure as we carry out the policy. I have no expectation of making a hit every time I come to bat. What I seek is the highest possible batting average, not only for myself but for the team."[3]

The President in 1933 sought to make his goals clear to the American people by appealing to their favorite pastime, the game of baseball. However, in the early years of the depression, major league baseball was also a depressed industry. In 1929, regular season attendance in the major leagues topped nine million for a record sixth straight year, and in 1930, a tight pennant race in the National League, in which the top four teams finished within six games of each other, was mostly responsible for a major league net income of $1,462,000. Nevertheless, it proved impossible for baseball to escape the impact of the massive economic slump, and in 1931 net income declined to $217,000, while the profit margin of major league teams dwindled to 2.3 percent. Financial prospects for the sport dimmed further in 1932 and 1933 with losses of $1,201,000, a margin of 15 percent in the election year of 1932. Net losses totaled $1,651,000 in 1933, for a "loss" margin of 23.9 percent.[4] Major league baseball was certainly in need of a new deal.

In response to the ravages of the depression, the *Sporting News*, a self-proclaimed Bible of baseball, warned that "baseball must get in step with the times. Talking about innovations as being 'bad for precedent,' that they hadn't been 'attempted before' and that what 'was good enough yesterday is good enough today,' won't get the game anywhere."[5] Reflecting Heywood Broun's observation in the *Nation* that baseball reigned as the country's number one sport due to "shrewdness, skill, sentimentality, and downright luck,"[6] the baseball establishment maintained a conservative stance, rejecting profit-sharing proposals and refusing to lower ticket prices, while allowing for some limited experimentation with night baseball. While Herbert Hoover was greeted by Philadelphia Athletics fans at the 1931 World Series by booing and chants of "We Want Beer," the magnates of baseball sought to trim expenses by reducing salaries. According to baseball historian Ben Rader, "...total payrolls dropped from $4 million in 1930 to $3 million in 1933; by 1933 the average player salary had plummeted to $4,500."[7]

Disgruntled star players, such as the Yankees Babe Ruth and Giants Bill Terry engaged in celebrated holdouts, but public opinion rarely sided with the players who had little choice but to accept salary reductions, for the sport's reserve clause bound a player to the team for which he was currently contracted. Under the existing interpretations of baseball's Supreme Court exemption from the nation's antitrust laws, free agency was not an option. Popular resentment against baseball salary squabbles was well reflected in an article for the *Outlook and Independent* which stated, "Somehow, in these days of breadlines and jobless heads of families, one cannot sympathize too deeply with the well-fed, bankroll-padded baseball holdout."[8]

While the major leagues were struggling to stay afloat by trimming expenses, minor leagues were imposing salary ceilings, and some organizations such as the Eastern League were forced by depression conditions to suspend operations. James A. Michener, who during the early 1930s was a high school coach and teacher in Pottstown, Pennsylvania, proclaimed that baseball had passed its period of greatest interest for American youth and was being replaced by other entertainment and sports such as golf. To survive in this crisis mode, many minor league operators resorted to such gimmicks as a pajama parade in Dayton, Ohio, where seven hundred women marched and bleacher spectators selected the prize-winning "fannette." In Huntington, West Virginia, fifteen chickens, each with a ticket to the next game tied round its neck, were turned loose on the field.[9] Thus, minor and major league baseball was able to survive the depression, although the nadir was apparently reached during the winter of 1933 when the legendary Connie Mack, principal owner and field manager of the Philadelphia Athletics, broke up his American League champions of 1929, 1930, and 1931 by selling stars Robert Moses "Lefty" Grove, Mickey Cochrane, and George Earnshaw, expecting to realize approximately $300,000 in the transactions.[10]

Having trimmed expenses, baseball, like the nation, seemed posed by 1934 to bounce back from the worse years of the depression. The baseball establishment appeared willing to embrace Franklin Roosevelt and the New Deal. Despite his conservative Republican proclivities and personal dislike for Roosevelt, Baseball Commissioner Kenesaw Mountain Landis, recognizing that baseball's fortunes were tied to the reforms of the Democratic administration, acknowledged, "Steel, factories, railroads, newspapers, agriculture, baseball — we rode down together, and we'll ride back together. The American people love baseball. They will return as paying customers as soon as they have money."[11] Landis could not bring himself to directly endorse the Roosevelt recovery program, but E. G. Brands, editor of the *Sporting News* which advertised itself on letterhead as the "official publication of organized baseball," wrote to Roosevelt expressing support for the President and asserting that baseball deserved a place in the New Deal coalition. On May 22, 1934, Brands informed the President that "...the National Game is keeping step with your recovery program by giving employment to hundreds of young players and thousands of others through the erection of new parks and in creation of many new jobs in connection with the operation of these parks. Furthermore, baseball is not standing pat on this program, but is planning further extensions the next few years that will place it in the fore-front of all enterprises that are assisting in the rehabilitation of the country. Thought that news of this co-operation, small as it might be, would help to hearten you in your fight to make the country a better one in which to live."[12]

The baseball public appeared to echo the confidence expressed by Brands. The *Literary Digest* reported considerable spring training interest in baseball for the 1934 season and predicted, "...nothing will reflect the progress of the Recovery Program and the NRA as much as baseball attendance this year." Opening season gate receipts seemed to herald better days for baseball, the American economy, and the Roosevelt administration. The New York Giants played to over 73,000 more customers in their first nine games than they had in the same number of games during the 1933 season, while the Boston Red Sox surpassed the first six dates of the previous campaign by 145,000 fans. These figures led New York sportswriter Rob Rennie to speculate that the "...National Road to Ruin now is a thriving thoroughfare. It has been redecorated. People have come out of the shell-holes to which they were blown by the explosion of finance and industry. They are working and playing and seem perfectly content to let a busy tribe of professional worriers do their worrying for them."[13]

Rennie was somewhat optimistic as baseball, like the American economy, was certainly not out of the depression. However, in 1934 the baseball owners lost only $290,000 in comparison with losses of $1,650,000 in 1933. By 1935, baseball ownership reported the first net profit in four years, but not until the affluent society of post World War II America did net profits exceed those of 1930.[14] Thus, the New Deal recovery had stopped the decline of baseball revenues without ownership having to alter the basic corporate structure of the game. Cardinal pitcher Dizzy Dean, who led St. Louis to a World Series victory over the Detroit Tigers in 1934, became a symbol of depression-era baseball. Dean's biographer described the pitcher as " a fourth-grade dropout and one-time cotton picker who laughed at hitters when he struck them out, loved to brag, and said of himself, 'There'll never be another like me.'" But the folk hero image of

Dean was never to alter the dominant position attained by the lords of baseball. In a May, 1935 article for the *Review of Reviews,* Jo Chamberlin praised baseball ownership, observing that for big league club owners baseball was not all sport. It was a serious big business in which baseball magnates "pit their men and money against each other in competition which makes yacht-racing, horses, or polo seem much like matching pennies." According to this interpretation, Dean was simply a popular commodity who was the property of the St. Louis Cardinals baseball club. By 1936, baseball ownership was comfortable enough for the irrepressible Connie Mack to author a baseball piece for the *Saturday Evening Post* entitled, "The Bad Old Days."[15]

While the *Sporting News* expressly acknowledged Roosevelt and the New Deal as playing a major role in the stabilization of organized baseball, the question remains as to whether the public perceived the President as a champion of the game for boosting American morale during the dark days of the depression. An examination of correspondence in the Roosevelt Library at Hyde Park indicates that there was considerable public identification of Roosevelt with the game of baseball. And ever the master politician, FDR was not going to ignore what Presidential baseball scholar George C. Rable termed a public platform in which Presidents could "mouth familiar platitudes about sport and patriotism."[16]

The Roosevelt mastery of communication, so well exhibited in the fireside chats, produced a sense of intimacy between the President and the American people. It was not uncommon for Roosevelt to receive personal letters from his constituents on any number of subjects, and the topic of baseball proved to be no exception during the President's first term in office. For example, a high school baseball enthusiast from Pennsylvania wrote the President because he had read in the newspaper that Roosevelt was a "Baseball Fan." Accordingly, the young man suggested, "…if it would not interfere with governmental circumstances I would be thrilled to receive a short letter from you concerning your choice of the Pennant Winners." In a similar vein, an eighteen year-old youth from Norfolk, Virginia wanted to know whether the President would sponsor his baseball team by purchasing sixteen uniforms. In exchange for Roosevelt's support, the writer offered to advertise the team as the NRA Eagles, concluding, "If you can help us President Roosevelt we will be the happiest boys in the world." Realizing that the President received a season pass to National League ballparks but lived in the American League city of Washington, Samuel L. Rubin of Brooklyn asked for the Chief Executive's pass. Rubin wrote, "I am a young man of 29, and have just recovered from a two year's siege of illness. I have been ordered to spend the next few months in the open air, and since I am ardent baseball fan, you would be doing me a great honor and service, if you should let me have your pass."[17]

In addition to the representative requests from enthusiastic young baseball fans around the country, Roosevelt's baseball correspondence included efforts by Henry Misselwitz of the United Press to develop international baseball between the United States and Japan. Lucile Gibbons, President of the Nassau, New York, Amateur Baseball Alliance, inquired whether the President could not push for the construction of baseball diamonds through the PWA. Gibbons argued, "If the nation has funds with which to build prisons, why not use some of the money as a preventive measure in the checking of crime? Keep our young men and boys interested in clean American sports instead of pool halls."[18] The President could not respond in a personal fashion to this plethora of requests, but he did use baseball imagery and symbolic occasions to identify himself with the national pastime.

But did Roosevelt really enjoy baseball? In a study of Roosevelt's sense of humor and personality, M. S. Venkataramani observes that the President was very fond of stories involving fishing or hunting. A favorite was the account that FDR was almost killed when he was struck a glancing blow by a falling goose or duck which he had shot in flight. Venkataramani, however, includes no baseball anecdotes in his volume. Popular biographer John Gunther also places baseball low on Roosevelt's list of leisure activities, behind such pleasures as sailing, stamp collecting, fishing, and card playing. Gunther describes Roosevelt as a casual fan who liked the game "if it was a lively game full of slugging; a pitcher's duel bored him."[19] Gunther's observation is apparently based upon FDR's letter to James P. Dawson of the *New York Times* which was read at the Fourteenth Annual Dinner of the New York Chapter, Baseball Writers Association of America. The President wrote, "When it comes to baseball I am the kind of fan who wants to get plenty of action for his money. I have some appreciation of a game which is featured by a pitcher's duel and results in a score of one to nothing. But I must confess that I get the biggest kick out of the biggest score — a game in which the batters pull the ball into the far corners of the field, the outfielders scramble and men run the bases. In short, my idea of the best game is one that guarantees the fans a combined score of not less than fifteen runs, divided about eight to seven."[20]

Thus, Roosevelt was a casual fan who did not attempt to discuss the intricacies of the morning box score. His most passionate game was politics. Nor is there any indication that Roosevelt enjoyed playing baseball in his youth. Baseball was often perceived in the late nineteenth and early twentieth centuries as a vehicle for the indoctrination of immigrants into the values of American civilization, but Roosevelt, as his biographers suggest, was brought up to be a "Hyde Park gentleman" or at best a "Genteel Reformer."[21] A product of his social class, Roosevelt loved the rigors of sailing. When he contracted polio, however, FDR's range of activities as a sportsman were considerably limited, and perhaps he began to develop an affinity for spectator sports such as baseball. Regardless of whether his health played any role in FDR's growing awareness of the national pastime, as a politician the President was certainly appraised of the game's symbolic importance to the American people. For the first eight years of his Presidency, Roosevelt attended opening day ceremonies at Griffith Stadium in Washington, tossing the ceremonial first pitch in an "unorthodox, overhand" fashion. FDR informed Washington Senators owner Clark Griffith that he would attend more games, "If I didn't have to hobble up those steps in front of all those people." The Senators owner responded to the President's plea by erecting a special ramp at Griffith Stadium so the President could have direct access to his box.[22]

Roosevelt also made use of baseball imagery in what was perceived as a tight 1936 re-election campaign against his Republican opponent Alf Landon. Speaking before a capacity crowd at Forbes Field in Pittsburgh on October 1, 1936, Roosevelt announced, "A Baseball park is a good place to talk about box scores. Tonight I am going to talk to you about the box score of the Government of the United States. I am going to tell you the story of our fight to beat down the depression and win recovery. From where I stand it looks as though the game is pretty well 'in the bag.'" Continuing with his baseball metaphor, the President observed that the national scoreboard looked pretty bleak in 1933, but that a change in management gave the country an opportunity to win the game. And with New Deal investment in agriculture, industry, small business, and the American people, the box score was being revised. The President concluded, "Compare the scoreboard which you have in Pittsburgh now with the scoreboard which you had when I stood here at second base in this field four years ago. At that time, as I drove through these great valleys, I could see mile after mile of this greatest mill and factory area in the world, a dead panorama of silent black structures and smokeless stacks. I saw idleness and hunger instead of the whirl of machinery. Today as I came north from West Virginia, I saw mines operating. I found bustle and life, the hiss of steam, the ring of steel on steel — the soaring song of industry."[23]

The landslide re-election of the President in 1936 indicated that the American people supported the new management in Washington and the improving box score of national recovery, even if the depression game was not yet complete. During his second term FDR continued his association with baseball, attending games and tossing ceremonial pitches, although not without some embarrassing moments. For example, amidst the bitter political debate surrounding FDR's efforts to alter the composition of the Supreme Court, a plane flew over Griffith Stadium on opening day for the 1937 season, bearing a banner which read, "Play the game, don't pack the court." The irrepressible Roosevelt supposedly laughed heartily and continued to munch peanuts. On opening day of the 1940 season, the President responded to *Washington Post* photographer Irving Schlossenberg's request for just one more photograph opportunity by flinging one additional ball, an errant throw which smashed Schlossenberg's lens.[24] The President was usually able to make more successful application of baseball opportunities and symbols.

Throughout the late 1930s as Americans became uneasy regarding international affairs in Europe and Asia, baseball was used in popular culture as a comforting reminder of traditional American values. The St. Louis Cardinals "Gas-House Gang" captured the public imagination with their work ethic and desire to win. As Cardinals Manager Frankie Frish told the *Saturday Evening Post*, "There's no room for sentiment in baseball if you want to win." This doctrine was to prove most applicable to a nation which would soon engage in an era of total war. In addition to the virtues of hard work and success, Americans cherish the mantle of innocence, which in baseball terms is often extolled in the purity of the country boy who makes it to the big leagues. Accordingly, sportswriter J. Roy Stockton championed the virtues of a young Iowa farm boy named Bob Feller who was destined to become one of the greatest pitchers in the history of the game. Feller's message to young boys wishing to climb the ladder of baseball success was "to get plenty of rest and to eat, sleep and think baseball."[25]

Seeking to expound upon baseball as a symbol of traditional values in an age of uncertainty, organized baseball prepared for the 1939 opening of the Baseball Hall of Fame and Museum in Cooperstown, New York. Even though ample evidence existed that Abner Doubleday did not develop baseball in Cooperstown and that 1939 was not the centennial of the game, Roosevelt endorsed the project and associated himself with the nostalgic values of baseball. In approaching the Baseball Hall of Fame and Museum, the President echoed sentiments he had expressed in a 1936 letter to C. F. Drake, editor of *the Chicago Cubs News*, calling baseball the national pastime "because it stands for the fair play, clean living and good sportsmanship which are our national heritage." On the eve of the Cooperstown "centennial," FDR sent a similar message, observing that baseball "has become through the years, not only a great national sport, but also the symbol of America as the melting pot. The players embrace all nations and national origins and the fans equally cosmopolitan, make only one demand of them: Can they play the game?"[26] The concept of America as a melting pot would be essential mythology for the American people during World War II (especially in Hollywood productions of the war years), but the reality of American race relations in the late 1930s was better reflected by racial segregation in baseball and the public statement by Yankee outfielder Jake Powell that while serving as a Dayton, Ohio policeman his favorite winter sport was "cracking niggers on the head."[27]

As Roosevelt sought an unprecedented third term in the White House and as international affairs replaced the New Deal in the President's attention, there was less time for baseball. Yet, FDR did make opening day baseball appearances for the 1940 and 1941 seasons, although after the entrance of America into the Second World War he would not attend another major league game.[28] As Doris Kearns Goodwin observes in her history of the Roosevelts and the home front in World War II, the Chief Executive had other concerns. Kearns Goodwin writes, "Yet his leadership of the home front was the essential condition of military victory. Through four years of war, despite strikes and riots, overcrowding and confusion, profiteering, black markets, prejudice, and racism, he kept the American people united in a single cause."[29]

Nevertheless, it would be impossible for the President to ignore the national pastime. Baseball's presence in the ritual of daily life in America was exhibited in the national fascination with Joe DiMaggio's fifty-six game hitting streak during the summer of 1941 while the country prepared for the war which was engulfing Europe and Asia.[30] And as war clouds gathered, baseball executives were concerned about the game's role in American life and legacy of patriotic service. Thus, National League President Ford Frick, when dispatching his usual season pass to the President, wrote, "At the same time may I not on behalf of my league and myself, volunteer to you such services as we may be able to render in this time of crisis. My own background of experience in the World War plus twenty years of newspaper, advertising and public relations work, together with ten years experience in organizing, regulating, supervising and directing recreational programs is, I think, typical." On the other hand, while Frick was volunteering his services, Clark Griffith was writing Roosevelt adviser General Edwin Watson, suggesting that it was the desire of the government to disturb essential industries, like baseball, as little as possible. Therefore, Griffith proposed that the Army devise a draft plan whereby only one player from each club would be called in a season, except in the event that the government declared a state of national emergency.[31]

After the Japanese attack on Pearl Harbor and declarations of war on the United States by Germany and Italy, baseball's lobbying to be classified as an essential industry for the war effort became more public. During the First World War, the 1918 baseball season was cut short as a result of criticism from such organs of public opinion as the *New York Times* and *Stars and Stripes*, which claimed baseball was a drain upon resources needed for conducting the war.[32] To deter such complaints during the Second World War, the *Sporting News* rushed to the sport's defense, maintaining that baseball "has a responsibility to fans and the nation heightened by war. It must go on fighting, buoyed by the fact that it is the fun, the entertainment, the joy, the sports interest of the common people." The publication, however, insisted that baseball was not asking for any special favors as "in all the history of baseball there never was a conscientious objector, or a slacker in the ranks."[33]

Many politicians supported the baseball establishment. Joseph Martin of Massachusetts, Republican leader in the House of Representatives, said it would be foolish to abolish baseball for the duration of the war because the sport was necessary to preserve national morale. On a similar note, Edward A. Kelly, Democratic Representative from Illinois, argued that baseball was needed to provide morale and recreation for the nation during a time of crisis. The colorful Fiorello H. LaGuardia, Mayor of New York City and Director of National Civil Defense, maintained that baseball was the "fun" of the common people and would be his only source of entertainment for the coming summer. Referring to the rumors of Nazi air attacks on New York City, LaGuardia proclaimed, "If we are to be hit, I'd just as soon get hit in Yankee Stadium, the Polo Grounds or Ebbets Field, as I would in my apartment. It seems to me, under the stands in the Stadium is as safe a place as any in the city. I am for baseball now, more than ever."[34]

President Roosevelt, who had consistently identified himself with baseball and used the sport to boost morale during the depression, had no qualms with applying the same reasoning to the national crisis of the Second World War. In a letter to Baseball Commissioner Kenesaw Mountain Landis, Roosevelt wrote, "There will be fewer people unemployed and everybody will work longer hours and harder than ever before, and that means that they ought to have a chance for recreation and for taking their minds off their work even more than ever." Although Roosevelt did not believe baseball represented an essential occupation for draft deferment purposes, he insisted that the professional game should continue even if the league rosters had to be filled with non-draft age players. The *Sporting News* lauded Roosevelt's decision, calling the President the player of the year for recognizing, "No matter how great its military power in the field, no nation at war is stronger than the morale of the people at home."[35]

Roosevelt's position on the continuation of major league baseball agreed with most Americans, especially those young men in the armed services. The Athletic Round Table of Spokane, Washington, conducted a poll in the spring of 1943 regarding the feasibility of maintaining professional baseball. The results were overwhelmingly in favor of the sport; 95 percent of over 130,000 replies opposed abandoning the national pastime during the war emergency. Of 38,000 sailors polled, 99.5 percent approved conducting baseball business as usual. A Gallup Poll commissioned during the same period, utilizing more systematic techniques than the Spokane analysis, did not produce the same spectacular percentages, but did demonstrate a definite sentiment in favor of continuing the sport; 59 percent preferred that baseball be maintained, while 28 percent opposed its operation, and 13 percent remained undecided. The Gallup organization reported that the most typical reply of respondents to the poll was simply, "America wouldn't be the same without baseball." The Spokane and Gallup quantitative conclusions were further substantiated by a letter-writing contest for servicemen conducted by the *Sporting News*. The winning entry, penned by Wayne L. Ashworth of Fort Benning, Georgia, asserted that the game must be continued. Ashworth wrote, "Baseball may suffer setbacks in attendance and gate receipts. Yet do we soldiers discontinue fighting after a few setbacks and defeats? We'll keep fighting until final and complete victory is won — until we can continue to live as free men and to play our sports as free men."[36]

A perusal of correspondence in the Roosevelt Presidential Library also indicates considerable popular support for the President's decision, which was soon followed by a memorandum to Admiral Ernest King requesting that baseball be encouraged for merchant ship crews in Iceland who were encountering morale problems. A school principal in New Jersey wrote, offering congratulation for the President's stand on major league baseball, as the sport was the "greatest civilian morale booster of them all." Some correspondents thought there was little to discuss regarding the central nature of baseball to American life. One postcard in the Roosevelt Papers simply reads, "Don't let Hitler Kill Baseball. Baseball is essential to our country's victory. The soldiers want it, defense workers need it. Need we say more?" Baseball endorsements to the President were also forthcoming from American servicemen such as Marine Staff-Sergeant William Stein, who informed Roosevelt that baseball "keeps our spirits up, gives us something to talk about and promotes sportsmanship." While serving in China and Guam before American involvement in the Pacific War, Stein indicated that he always eagerly read reports of scores and games, for they "brought the states to me very pleasantly."[37]

But not all Americans agreed with the President's perception of baseball's role in the war. After expressing devotion to the national game, Franlau K. Lutz urged FDR to cancel the sport for the duration of the conflict. In simple direct language, Lutz argued, "I can't see a bunch of Ball Players going around the Country, getting big pay, having a good time, While Millions of other boys are fighting, Dying, Being made Cripples, Being made Sightless for their country. No, Mr. President, I can't get excited over a Ball game as long as we are at war." However, dissenting voices, such as Lutz, were drowned out by numerous letters, exemplified in a note by Richard Berlin to Press Secretary Stephen Early, stating, "The majority of the boys in the army, wherever they are, would say to keep those stars on the diamond where they would do more good."[38]

In addition to a rather voluminous public correspondence regarding baseball's morale role in the war, the White House was besieged by members of the baseball establishment more interested in lobbying for financial gain than in assessing the spiritual and philosophical aspects of the game. While the conservative politics of Landis prohibited much official correspondence between the Commissioner's Office and the White House, unofficial inquiries by individual such as Clark Griffith and J. G. Taylor Spink, general manager of the *Sporting News*, focused upon such issues as the President's support for night baseball, morning games for evening workers, travel restrictions, and, of course, the draft status of major league athletes.[39]

After considerable political maneuvering and lobbying activities, major league baseball did make it through the war years. Although by 1945, it was a rather ragged regiment which included one-armed outfielders and fifteen year old pitchers. Nearly seventy percent of all major league players at the time of Pearl Harbor served in the armed forces during World War II; however, many never saw combat and made their military contributions by playing baseball on service teams. Despite manpower shortages, there is little evidence that the President seriously considered discontinuing the game during the war. In 1944, Lieutenant General Brehan Somervell, Chief of the Service of Supply, informed the New York Chapter of the Baseball Writers Association that baseball served a crucial purpose in the winning of the war. Somervell stated, "It has been said that the successes of the British army can be traced to the cricket fields of Eton, and I can say that the sandlots and big league ball parks of America have contributed their share to our military success." In March, 1945, shortly before his death, Roosevelt indicated that he still had an intuitive grasp for the feeling of the American people regarding the national pastime. In response to a reporter's inquiry as to whether manpower shortages would curtail the current season, the President responded that while the quality of play might deteriorate, he "would go out to see a baseball game played by a sandlot team — and so would most people."[40]

However, the wartime leader was unable to see another baseball game as on April 12, 1945 Roosevelt died from a cerebral hemorrhage. Although he was a casual fan and did not attend any major league games during the war years, FDR demonstrated his ability to understand the values and passions of the American people as he adroitly used the sport of baseball as a metaphor and morale booster to help the American people through the difficult days of depression and war. Franklin Roosevelt refused to let either Hitler or the depression kill baseball and endanger American values of teamwork, determination, innocence, success, and democracy embedded within the mythology of the sport. In many ways the affluent society of post World War II, which exposed many of the gaps between American promise and reality, proved to be more destructive of baseball than the depression and Second World War. Today it is difficult to envision baseball, or many other American institutions for that matter, as a symbol around which an articulate and intuitive leader could rally the American people in times of crisis such as was the case for Franklin Roosevelt during the Great Depression and World War II.

Endnotes

This essay was originally published in Nancy Beck Young, William D. Pederson, and Bryon W. Daynes, eds., *Franklin Roosevelt and Popular Culture* (New York: M. E. Sharpe, 2001), 199-214.

1. John M. Hoberman, *Sport and Political Ideology* (Austin: University of Texas Press, 1984), 21.

2. Arthur M. Schlesinger, Jr., *The Crisis of the Old Order, 1919–1933* (Boston: Houghton Mifflin Co., 1957), 5.

3. "The Second Fireside Chat," May 7, 1933, as cited in Samuel I. Rosenman, ed., *The Public Papers and Addresses of Franklin Roosevelt, vol. 2* (New York: Russell and Russell, 1950), 164–165.

4. For the economic conditions of baseball during the depression era see U. S. Congress, *Organized Baseball: Report of the Subcommittee on Study of Monopoly Powers of the Committee on the Judiciary*, House Report, No. 2002, 82 Cong., 2 Sess. (1952), 1600–1615; Bill Rabinowitz, "Baseball and the Great Depression," in Peter Levine, ed., *Baseball History* (Westport, CT: Meckler Books, 1989), 49–59; and Ben G. Rader, *Base-*

ball: A History of America's Game (Urbana: University of Illinois Press, 1994), 126–140. For additional information on baseball in the 1930s see Richard C. Crepeau, *Baseball: America's Diamond Mind, 1919–1941* (Orlando: University Presses of Florida, 1980); David Voigt, *American Baseball: From the Commissioners to Continental Expansion* (University Park: Pennsylvania State University Press, 1970).

5. *Sporting News*, October 3, 1932.

6. "It Seems to Heywood Broun," *Nation*, 129 (October 23, 1929), 457.

7. .Rader, *Baseball*, 138.

8. "The Spotlight on Sports," *Outlook and Independent*, 160 (January 27, 1932), 116–117. For additional contemporary articles which supported the baseball establishment's timid approach to the depression see John Kiernan, "Big League Business," *Saturday Evening Post*, 202 (May 31, 1930), 10, 17, 149–154; and Billy Evans, "Big League Over-Head," *Saturday Evening Post*, 206 (August 5, 1933), 16–17, 60.

9. "Hard Times Hit the Minors," *Literary Digest*, 114 (July 30, 1932), 37; "Is the American Boy Quitting Baseball," *Literary Digest*, 106 (July 12, 1930), 34–35; and "Minor Leagues Take Heart," *Literary Digest*, 114 (August 20, 1932), 33.

10. "The Break-up of the Athletics," *Literary Digest*, 116 (December 23, 1933), 26.

11. G. H. Fleming, ed., *The Dizziest Season* (New York: William Morrow, 1984), 19. For background information on Landis see J. G. Taylor Spink, *Judge Landis and Twenty-Five Years of Baseball* (New York: Thomas W. Crowell Co., 1947).

12. E. G. Brands to Franklin Roosevelt, May 22, 1934, President's Office File, Box 170, "Baseball," Franklin D. Roosevelt Library, Hyde Park, New York.

13. "America Cries 'Play Ball' in a Recovery Season," *Literary Digest*, 117 (April 14, 1934), 30–31; and Rob Rennie, "A Year Ago Baseball Games Were a Gage of National Melancholy, but Today Fans Flock to Make All Sports Events a Measuring Rod of Recovery," *Literary Digest*, 117 (June 16, 1934), 25.

14. U. S. Congress, *Organized Baseball*, 1600.

15. Robert Gregory, *The Story of Dizzy Dean and Baseball During the Great Depression* (New York: Penguin Books, 1932), 2; Jo Chamberlin, "Safe At Home!," *Review of Reviews*, 91 (May, 1935), 47–49; and Connie Mack, "The Bad Old Days," *Saturday Evening Post*, 208 (April 4, 1936), 16–17, 96–99.

16. George C. Rable, "Patriotism, Platitudes and Politics: Baseball and the American Presidency," *Presidential Studies Quarterly*, 19 (Spring, 1989), 363–372.

17. Allen V. Russell to Franklin Roosevelt, June 1, 1935; Vincent Pezzella to Franklin Roosevelt, n.d.; and Samuel L. Rubin to Franklin Roosevelt, April 15, 1935, President's Office File, Box 170, "Baseball," Franklin D. Roosevelt Library, Hyde Park, New York.

18. Henry F. Misselwitz to Stephen Early, September 21, 1934; and Lucile Gibbons to Stephen Early, February 25, 1935, President's Office File, Box 170, "Baseball," Franklin D. Roosevelt Library, Hyde Park, New York.

19. M. S. Venkataramani, *The Sunny Side of FDR* (Athens, Ohio: Ohio University Press, 1973), 259–260; and John Gunther, *Roosevelt in Retrospect* (London: Hamish Hamilton, 1950), 96–100.

20. Franklin Roosevelt to James P. Dawson, January 23, 1937, in Rosenman, ed., *Public Papers and Addresses of Franklin Roosevelt*, vol. 6, 10.

21. Steven A. Riess, *Touching Base: Professional Baseball in the Progressive Era* (Westport, CT: Greenwood Press, 1980); James MacGregor Burns, *Roosevelt: The Lion and the Fox, 1882–1940* (New York: Harcourt, Brace & World, 1956), 6; and Frank Friedel, *Franklin D. Roosevelt: A Rendezvous with Destiny* (Boston: Little, Brown and Co., 1990), 3–15.

22. William B. Mead and Paul Dickson, *Baseball: The Presidents' Game* (Washington, D.C.: Farragut Publishing Company, 1993), 71–80.

23. Campaign Address at Forbes Field, Pittsburgh, "The Only Way to Keep the Government Out of the Red Is to Keep the People Out of the Red," October 1, 1936, in Rosenman, ed., *The Public Papers and Addresses of Franklin Roosevelt, vol. 5*, 401–408.

24. Rable, "Patriotism, Platitudes and Politics," 368; and Mead and Dickson, *The Presidents' Game*, 76.

25. Frank Frisch, "The Gas-House Gang," *Saturday Evening Post*, 209 (July 4, 1936), 12–13, 55–57; and J. Roy Stockton, "Bob Feller-Storybook Ball Player," *Saturday Evening Post*, 209 (February 20, 1937), 12–13, 66–70.

26. "Are We Celebrating a Fake Centennial?," *Current History*, 50 (June, 1939), 53–54; Franklin Roosevelt to C. F. Drake, August 5, 1936; and Franklin Roosevelt to National Baseball Museum, Cooperstown, New York, April 19, 1939, President's Personal File, Box 227, "Baseball," Franklin D. Roosevelt Library, Hyde Park, New York.

27. "Why the Yankees Win," *Nation*, 147 (September 17, 1938), 258.

28. Mead and Dickson, *The Presidents' Game*, 73. In 1942 and 1944, Vice-President Henry Wallace did the opening day honors for Roosevelt, although his performances were eccentric. In 1942, Wallace stunned the crowd by tossing the ceremonial ball over the players' heads and all the way out to second base, some two hundred feet from his seat. In his last opening day performance, Wallace threw the ball to Senators pitcher Alex Carrasquel. Wallace explained that he singled out Carrasquel, a Venezuelan, to emphasize the administration's "Good Neighbor Policy" toward Latin America. In a more subdued fashion, wartime manpower chief Paul V. McNutt performed the ceremony in 1943, and following FDR's death on April 12, 1945, House Speaker Sam Rayburn, wearing a black armband, substituted for the new President, Harry Truman.

29. Doris Kearns Goodwin, *No Ordinary Time: Franklin and Eleanor Roosevelt, The Home Front in World War II* (New York: Simon & Schuster, 1994), 10.

30. Michael Seidel, *Streak: Joe DiMaggio and the Summer of '41* (New York: Penguin Books, 1988).

31. Ford Frick to Franklin Roosevelt, April 5, 1941, President's Office File, Box 170, "Baseball;" and Clark Griffith to General Watson, April 12, 1941, President's Personal File, Box 7299, "Clark Griffith," Franklin D. Roosevelt Library, Hyde Park, New York.

32. For the impact of World War I on major league baseball see Fred Lieb, "The Great Exhumation," *Collier's*, 109 (May 16, 1942), 22, 60–61; and Harold Seymour, *Baseball: The Golden Age* (New York: Oxford University Press, 1971), 244–255.

33. *Sporting News*, December 11, 1941 and January 18, 1942. For the role of the *Sporting News* in baseball and World War II see "Bible of Baseball: *Sporting News*," *Saturday Evening Post*, 214 (June 20, 1942), 9–10. For more specialized accounts of baseball during the Second World War see William B. Mead, *Even the Browns: The Zany, True Story of Baseball in the Early Forties* (Chicago: Contemporary Books, 1978); Richard Goldstein, *Spartan Seasons: How Baseball Survived the Second World War* (New York: Macmillan Co., 1980); and Bill Gilbert, *They Also Served: Baseball and the Home Front, 1941–1945* (New York: Crown Publishers, Inc., 1992). For general accounts of the American domestic scene during World War II see John Morton Blum, *V Was for Victory: Politics and American Culture During World War II* (New York: Harcourt Brace Jovanovich, 1976); and Richard Polenburg, *War and Society: The United States, 1941–1945* (Philadelphia: Lippincott, 1972).

34. *New York Times*, January 9, 1942; and *Sporting News*, February 12, 1942.

35. Franklin Roosevelt to Kenesaw Mountain Landis, January 16, 1942, in Rosenman, ed., *Public Papers and Addresses of Franklin Roosevelt, vol. 7,* 62; and *Sporting News,* January 22, 1942.

36. *New York Times,* March 25, 1943; "Batter (If Still There) Up," *Newsweek,* 21 (May 3, 1943), 82; and *Sporting News,* April 16, 1942.

37. Franklin Roosevelt to Admiral Ernest King, July 11, 1942; Ronald Decker Glass to Franklin Roosevelt, April 14, 1942; Ted Eckhardt to Franklin Roosevelt, February 23, 1943; Staff-Sergeant William Stein to Franklin Roosevelt, February 9, 1943, President's Office File, Box 170, "Baseball," Franklin Roosevelt Library, Hyde Park, New York.

38. Franlau K. Lutz to Franklin Roosevelt, October 13, 1942; and Richard Berlin to Stephen Early, February 6, 1943, President's Office File, Box 170, "Baseball," Franklin Roosevelt Library, Hyde Park, New York.

39. For examples of baseball establishment correspondence to the White House see Clark Griffith to Stephen Early, March 2, 1943, President's Personal File, Box 7299, "Clark Griffith;" Thomas Kirby to M. H. McIntyre, January 19, 1942, President's Office File, Box 170, "Baseball;" and J. G. Taylor Spink to Franklin Roosevelt, January 28, 1944, President's Personal File, Box 227, "Baseball," Franklin Roosevelt Library, Hyde Park, New York.

40. "Baseball Gets Mandate from Army to Carry On," *Recreation,* 38 (August, 1944), 274; and "995th Press Conference," March 13, 1945, in Rosenman, ed., *Public Papers and Addresses of Franklin Roosevelt, vol. 8,* 592.

3

Where Have You Gone William Bendix? Baseball as a Symbol of American Values in World War II

In recalling his experiences during the Second World War, a former infantryman told interviewer Studs Terkel, "World War Two has affected me in many ways ever since. In a short period of time, I had the most tremendous experience of all of life: of fear, of jubilance, of misery, of hope, of comradeship, and of endless excitement. I honestly feel grateful for having been a witness to an event as monumental as anything in history and, in a very small way, a participant."[1] As this comment suggests, the bombing of Pearl Harbor and the long war resulting from that tragic event was both exhilarating and traumatic for Americans. Forced to make enormous sacrifices for the war effort and confronted with the social upheaval of a crisis environment, many Americans relied upon traditional symbols and institutions to express their system of values. One such institution was professional baseball.

The social and psychological importance of sports has been suggested by several students of American recreation and leisure.[2] And baseball, "the national pastime," has been felt to be the sport most closely identified with the American society. A subcommittee report of a 1952 House Judiciary Committee examining organized baseball noted, "Other sports flourish for a brief season and then sink to the background to await a rebirth of interest in the next season. Baseball, however, remains of public interest both in season and out. Whether it is in June or December, the public is interested in the national game."[3] Statistical evidence supported the subcommittee's conclusion regarding the popularity of baseball. From 1940 to 1945, public expenditures for professional baseball games totaled $112.1 million, while expenditures for all other major sports, including horse racing, only reached a figure of $93.1 million.[4]

Baseball has also been extolled by numerous writers and scholars. Journalist Roger Angell poetically described baseball as an ageless sport in which "time is seamless and invisible, a bubble within which players move at exactly the same space and rhythms as their predecessors."[5] Novelist Marvin Cohen also marveled at the timeless and traditional qualities of baseball. According to Cohen:

> Baseball goes on, essentially unaltered, though the nation itself goes through violent historical upheavals and the times are always changing. Violence is on the land today. But the game of baseball remains its peaceful self. It's constant, enduring, and links the century together in our land — the twentieth century, when so much happened and baseball remained essentially placid in the midst of all. It's dependable and goes on. Fashions come and go, and wars, and social problems, economic crises, political climates. Baseball outlives them all.[6]

In a similar vein, historian Richard C. Crepeau portrayed baseball as a great democratic game of the people, "played by and for them," which "most nearly typifies American institutions and teachings."[7] In an article for the *Massachusetts Review,* George Grella argued, "Anyone who does not understand the game cannot hope to understand the country."[8]

Despite the accolades, the impact of baseball during World War II may best be appreciated by television viewers of the late show. One of the more popular movie scenarios of World War II action in the Pacific theater was the casting of character actor William Bendix as a Marine from Brooklyn with a fanatical interest in the hometown Dodgers. Inevitably, Bendix becomes the target of a Japanese sniper, and in his dying gasp asks for the score of the Dodgers' game, which is then being announced on a nearby short wave radio set. Of course, the Dodgers have won the game, and Bendix dies with a smile on his face as the Marines' Hymn plays in the background.[9]

While such a scene may seem sentimental to contemporary audiences, it evidently was quite successful during the war; Bendix was repeatedly killed by film script writers as he heard of his beloved Dodgers' latest victory. In his study of Jackie Robinson, Jules Tygiel describes the World War II period as the golden age of Dodger baseball. According to Tygiel, "Dodger devotees flocked to Ebbets Field in record numbers and dying Hollywood soldiers asked for Brooklyn scores before passing on to their next feature film."[10] What this scenario apparently indicates is an intensity of feeling for both the patriotic qualities of the soldier dying for his country and the sport which was the national pastime.

Perhaps the first place to examine the intensity of feeling for baseball is in the decision to continue the operation of major league baseball during the war. World War I did not offer such a precedent. The 1918 season had been cut short as a result of criticism from such organs of public opinion as the *New York Times* and *Stars and Stripes,* which claimed baseball was a drain upon resources needed for the war.[11] But when such criticisms were voiced following America's declaration of war against Germany and Japan in 1941, the *Sporting News,* the so-called Bible of baseball, rushed to the sport's defense. The *Sporting News* maintained that the continuation of baseball would encourage morale. Baseball, editorialized the paper, "has a responsibility to fans and the nation heightened by war. It must go on fighting, buoyed by the fact that it is the fun, the entertainment, the joy, the sports interest of the common people."[12] However, the paper was quick to note that baseball was not asking for any special favors or deferments. In fact, the trade publication insisted that "in all the history of baseball there never was a conscientious objector, or a slacker in the ranks."[13] The position of baseball management was exemplified by Warren C. Giles, General Manager of the Cincinnati Reds, who maintained that his team would rather finish last than "win the pennant, World Series, and make a great profit with even one player of military age who could not justify his reasons for being in the service."[14] Player reaction was demonstrated by Detroit slugger Hank Greenberg who had been discharged from military service two days before the attack on Pearl Harbor. "We are in trouble," Greenberg explained, "and there is only one thing for me to do— return to the service."[15]

Many politicians supported the baseball establishment. Joseph Martin of Massachusetts, Republican leader in the House of Representatives, said it would be foolish to abolish baseball for the duration of the war because the sport was necessary to preserve national morale. On a similar note, Edward A. Kelly, Democratic Representative from Illinois, argued that baseball was needed to provide morale and recreation for the nation during a time of crisis.[16] The colorful Fiorello H. LaGuardia, Mayor of New York City and Director of National Civil Defense, maintained in February of 1942 that baseball was the "fun" of the common people and would be his only source of entertainment for the coming summer. Referring to the rumors of Nazi air attacks on New York City, LaGuardia proclaimed, "If we are to be hit, I'd just as soon get hit in Yankee Stadium, the Polo Grounds or Ebbets Field, as I would in my apartment. It seems to me, under the stands in the Stadium is as safe a place as any in the city. I am for baseball now, more than ever."[17]

President Franklin D. Roosevelt agreed. In a letter to Baseball Commissioner Kenesaw Mountain Landis, Roosevelt wrote, "There will be fewer people employed and everybody will work longer hours and harder than ever before, and that means that they ought to have a chance for recreation and for taking their minds off their work even more than ever."[18] Although Roosevelt did not believe baseball represented an essential occupation for draft deferment purposes, he argued that the professional game should continue even if the league rosters had to be filled with non-draft age players. In a 1945 press conference Roosevelt said the quality of play might deteriorate, but he "would go out to see a baseball game played by a sandlot team — and so would most people."[19] The *Sporting News* lauded Roosevelt's decision, calling the President the player of the year for recognizing, "No matter how great its military power in the field, no nation at war is stronger than the morale of the people at home."[20]

Roosevelt's position on the continuation of major league baseball struck a responsive chord with most Americans, especially those young men in the armed services. The Athletic Round Table of Spokane, Washington, conducted a poll in the spring of 1943 regarding the feasibility of maintaining professional baseball. The results were overwhelmingly in favor of the sport; 95 percent of over 130,000 replies opposed abandoning the national pastime during the war emergency. Of 38,000 sailors polled, 99.5 percent approved conducting baseball business as usual.[21] A Gallup Poll commissioned during the same period, utilizing more systematic techniques than the Spokane analysis, did not produce the same spectacular percentages, but did demonstrate a definite sentiment in favor of continuing the sport; 59 percent preferred that baseball be maintained, while 28 percent opposed its operation, and 13 percent remained undecided. The Gallup organization reported that the most typical reply of respondents to the poll was simply, "America wouldn't be the same without baseball."[22] The Spokane and Gallup quantitative conclusions were further substantiated by a letter-writing contest for servicemen conducted by the *Sporting News*. The winning entry, penned by Wayne L. Ashworth of Fort Benning, Georgia, asserted that the game must be continued. Ashworth wrote, "Baseball may suffer setbacks in attendance and gate receipts. Yet do we soldiers discontinue fighting after a few setbacks and defeats? We'll keep fighting until final and complete victory is won — until we can continue to live as free men and to play our 'sports' as free men."[23]

Officials of major league baseball attempted to justify the faith expressed in the sport. At their annual meeting in 1942, major league club owners made plans to aid the war effort and curtail expenses. They agreed to reduce team traveling, to increase night games so that baseball could be viewed by more working people, to set aside receipts from the All-Star game for an armed services bat and ball fund, and to allocate 10 percent of all employees' salary toward the war effort.[24] Organized baseball proved to be successful in its fund-raising endeavors, contributing approximately two million dollars to the United Service Organization, the American Red Cross, and other service organizations. In addition, major league baseball promotions accounted for over a billion dollars of war bond purchases.[25] Thus, baseball evidently fulfilled the morale function Roosevelt had perceived.

A more careful analysis of contemporary statements on baseball, however, reveals that many individuals believed that the national pastime provided something more. Some commentators insisted that baseball symbolized the differences between the American and Japanese civilizations. For example, former college baseball umpire Hap O'Conner, who had been officiating games in Japan before the war, exclaimed that the Japanese had abandoned baseball because "they would never beat us at it anyway" as he had never seen an Oriental capable of hitting a home run.[26] Such opinions were even expressed on the floor of the U.S. Senate when Scott W. Lucas of Illinois told his colleagues "that the treacherous Japs dropped baseball because it is an American game."[27] One of the most extraordinary statements regarding the relationship between baseball and Japan was an editorial in the *Sporting News* following the attack on Pearl Harbor. In an emotional outburst, the Bible of baseball exhibited the racism and fervor of war hysteria by stating that despite seventy years of Japanese baseball the Asiatic land was never converted to the sport:

> American baseball does not breed a punctilious politeness saying "So Sorry" between a grimacing yellow mask, but through our great game runs an inherent decency, fair dealing, love of the game and respect for one's opponents. That is the very soul of baseball. We may cut a few corners on the playing area, but we do not stab an honorable opponent in the back, nor do we crush out his brains with a bat while he is asleep, before even challenging him to a match. So, we repeat, Japan was never converted to baseball. They may have acquired a little skill at the game, but the soul of our national game never touched them. No nation which has had an intimate contact with baseball as the Japanese, could have committed the vicious, infamous deed of the early morning of December 7, 1941, if the spirit of the game ever had penetrated their yellow hides.[28]

Many commentators who stressed that baseball symbolized cultural differences between America and Japan rarely articulated the values that baseball supposedly represented. Other advocates, however, were willing to make direct statements about baseball's positive attributes. John Kiernan, sportswriter for the *New York Times,* said America would defeat the Axis powers because American youth, unlike their German and Japanese counterparts, had grown up on the competition of baseball, and war was simply competition of a greater intensity. Kiernan also praised baseball for its democratic qualities.[29] Baseball as a game characterizing democracy was elaborated upon by Bob Quinn, President of the Boston Braves baseball club. Quinn argued that the national pastime was "the most democratic of games, for the Governor's son may play alongside the son of humble parents, and the only favoritism that either gets is what he earns by merit in playing."[30] While usually dwelling on the morale functions of baseball, the *Sporting News* was not adverse to utilizing the democracy theme. Thus, in a piece praising Hank Greenberg's decision to return to military service, the paper observed that Greenberg's parents had immigrated to the United States from Romania "because the way of living there did not correspond to their ideas of going through life." In America, the Greenbergs prospered. "Their son had an equal opportunity with the sons of all other people in this country, and achieved a notable position in a notable profession."[31] Accordingly, to Kiernan, Quinn, and the *Sporting News,* baseball was American society in microcosm.

Most advocates of the sport simply emphasized its importance as a morale booster. But the views expressed by Kiernan, Quinn, and the *Sporting News* were shared by many Americans who accepted baseball as a symbol of national values. This could account for the popularity of the William Bendix image. A way to test such an hypothesis is to read popular literature of baseball during the war period.[32]

Two of the most widely circulated magazines of the day were the *Saturday Evening Post* and *Collier's.* An analysis of articles on baseball in these two publications from 1942 to 1945 should give one some idea of what values and attitudes were associated with baseball.[33]

Certainly, the most important concept expressed in the literature, and similar to ideas developed by Kiernan, Quinn, and the *Sporting News,* was a portrayal of baseball as a democratic game in which the poor boy was able to make good through hard work in the American Horatio Alger tradition.[34] While scholars such as Steven Riess have questioned the degree of social mobility in professional baseball, the Alger concept was especially emphasized during World War II in regard to major league players.[35] For example, Roger Bistwell, in an essay lauding the achievements of Boston Red Sox rookie pitcher Dave Ferriss, observed that Ferriss's father was a Mississippi farmer of moderate means whose dream in life had been for his son to become a major league baseball player. Although his father had died two years earlier, in 1945 the poor lad from Mississippi had established himself as one of the top pitchers in baseball.[36] Unlike the Horatio Alger stories of American fiction, however, the saga of Dave Ferriss did not necessarily conclude upon an optimistic note. After successful seasons in 1945 and 1946, the Boston pitcher became ineffective and won his last major league game in 1948 when he was still only twenty-seven years of age.[37]

Perhaps the most famous World War II baseball story regarding an individual overcoming enormous obstacles to reach the pinnacle of the big leagues was the odyssey of one-armed St. Louis Brown outfielder Pete Gray. Gray, a natural right-hander, lost his right arm in a childhood accident. However, according to a portrayal in *Collier's*, this son of a Lithuanian-American coal miner refused to make excuses and told his father, "He guessed coal mining would be too tough a goal, and that maybe he'd better be a big league ballplayer." To demonstrate Gray's drive for success in baseball, authors William A. Jones and Harman W. Nichols recount an incident that happened to the ballplayer when he was thirteen years old. Gray scored the winning run in a sandlot game by running over the catcher and dislodging him from the ball. The irritated catcher informed Gray, "If it wasn't for your handicap, smart guy, I'd bust your face in." Gray immediately struck the catcher and proclaimed, "What handicap."[38] Despite some impressive minor league statistics, though, the one-armed outfielder played only one season for the Browns, batting a mere .218 in 77 games. Most observers believed Gray only made it to the majors because of the severe manpower shortage in filling rosters in 1945, and his personality was considered abrasive by many of his St. Louis teammates.[39] While Gray's achievements were limited, he, nevertheless, did succeed at playing in the majors and served as an excellent symbol of what drive and determination could accomplish.

Most performers alluded to as the Horatio Alger type did not suffer the fate of Dave Ferriss and Pete Gray. In a *Saturday Evening Post* article, Stanley Frank pointed out that New York Yankee outfielder Charley "King Kong" Keller, who compiled a .286 batting average in thirteen major league seasons, had been born on a Maryland farm where he "was making muscles at the age of seven, getting up at four o'clock in the morning to help with the chores on his father's farm."[40] Evidently, Keller's indoctrination into the work ethic on his father's farm produced beneficial results as Frank reported that the outfielder had completed college and saved enough money for a farm of his own while performing for the Yankees. In another article, Boston Red Sox outfielder Ted Williams was praised for his driving ambition and effort to become a major league baseball player,

Williams, observed author Cleveland Amory, had since his early child-hood desired to become an "immortal" of the baseball world.[41] With his selection to the Baseball Hall of Fame in 1966, Williams certainly realized his ambition. The ambitious Williams, who lost playing time to both World War II and the Korean War, was the subject of some criticism in 1942 when his draft board reclassified him from I-A to 3-A as he was the sole means of support for his ill mother. The *Sporting News* defended Williams as a self-made man of character and talent, while urging him to pay no attention to malicious gossip. The paper concluded, "The same sort of spirit that helped him hit .406 last year ought to help him knock out that kind of pitching."[42]

The image of the aggressive, ambitious, hard-working young man making his way to the pinnacle of the baseball world was not reserved simply for Ted Williams and other players. This stereotype applied equally to various officials of the game. Such a fact is not surprising as Steven M. Gelber has pointed out that baseball is an integral part of such modern American capitalist values as a scientific world view, appreciation for ratio-nality, competition between groups with cooperation within the group, and an understanding that failure can occur.[43] Representative of this approach is Malcolm W. Bingay's portrayal of Detroit Tiger owner Walter K. Briggs who, as a devoted young Tiger fan, had difficulty obtaining tickets for the 1907 World Series between Detroit and the Chicago Cubs. Agitated by this problem, Briggs vowed to make his fortune and then purchased the team so he would always be guaranteed a seat. In 1936, related Bingay, Briggs's success in the business realm culminated when he became sole owner of the Detroit franchise.[44]

The Horatio Alger element was even more evident in the career of Branch Rickey who served as President of the St. Louis Cardinals and the Brooklyn Dodgers during the war years. Rickey, born into rural poverty in Stockdale, Ohio, was an extremely intelligent young man determined to obtain an education. From a small salary he earned teaching in coun-try schools, Rickey saved enough money to attend Ohio Wesleyan Col-lege. Following his graduation, Rickey obtained a law degree from the University of Michigan. He paid for his schooling by playing professional baseball during summer vacations. After a mediocre playing career, he used his legal training to move into the business end of the sport where he was destined to become one of the highest paid officials in major league baseball. According to J. Roy Stockton of the *Saturday Evening Post*, Rickey's climb to fame and financial security was a result of hard work and uncompromising determination.[45]

Other images of American life are reflected in the baseball literature of the *Saturday Evening Post* and *Collier's*. Teamwork, certainly an important quality in a nation at war, was a favorite element in baseball reporting. Phil Rizzuto, New York Yankee shortstop, described to baseball fans how his teammates had nurtured him through his first season in the major leagues. The crucial aspect of Rizzuto's story was the role of Frank Crosette, the Yankee's regular shortstop, whom the young rookie was being groomed to replace. Crosette did everything possible to help Rizzuto perform more efficiently because he realized that the younger player would be a greater asset to the entire team.[46] In addition to appealing to readers involved in a coordinated national effort to defeat the Axis powers, Rizzuto's example favorably reflects the tendency of most Americans to view their history from a consensus perspective which has emphasized teamwork and cooperation rather than conflict.

Indeed, baseball analogies may have convinced Americans that teamwork and concentrated group effort were capable of overcoming almost any obstacle, for such a belief correlates well with the attributes of discipline and work contained in the Horatio Alger model. For example, one of the major surprises of the baseball world occurred in 1944, when the St. Louis Browns, a perennial loser, won the American League pennant. This abrupt change, according to Kyle Crichton in *Collier's*, was due to great team spirit.[47] A more likely explanation, however, was offered by another Browns fan who, observing that military manpower needs had drained most quality players from the opposition, said, "It took a world war to win the St. Louis Browns a pennant, and to me it seemed a small enough price to pay."[48] Nevertheless, the Browns, despite their great spirit, were not destined to win the World Series, They were defeated by their inner-city rivals, the St. Louis Cardinals.

The Cardinals were the best club in baseball during the war years, winning the National League pennant in 1942, 1943, and 1944, in addition to capturing the World Series in 1942 and 1944. The success of the Cardinals was popularly attributed to their outstanding team effort.[49] Billy Southworth, manager of the St. Louis franchise, believed his team's triumph over the New York Yankees for the 1942 world championship represented the passing of individualism in baseball. While once Cardinal players had damaged teammates' bats because of rivalry for the league batting title, in 1942 all worked for a team victory. Southworth concluded, "Cohesive thinking and coordinated movement of an intelligent team will always beat a team of individual stars." The successful manager, and theorist of team cooperation, evidently believed that his ideas were not limited to the realm of sport. After obtaining the championship in 1942, Southworth congratulated his players and then ordered them to spend the winter furthering the nation's war effort.[50] The Southworth family practiced what the manager preached. Billy Southworth, Jr. was the first ballplayer to enlist in the military, serving with distinction in the Army Air Corps until his death in a crash at New York's LaGuardia Field only a few months before the end of the war.[51] Southworth's stress upon group accomplishments does not completely contradict the values of individualism expressed in the Horatio Alger stories. Individual success was not achieved at the expense of friends and associates, which might be translated as teammates. Cooperation within the group and competition without were the values stressed. Achievements of any worth were gained through discipline and work; the very qualities for which the Cardinals were often praised.

In addition to symbolizing the values of cooperation, work, and discipline, the Cardinals also exemplified the importance of youth and ideas. The American fighting forces in World War II were certainly dependent upon young males to fulfill their manpower needs, while youth striving for success was a crucial element of the Horatio Alger image. Charles Dexter, writing in *Collier's,* pointed out that Southworth was named manager of the St. Louis club because of his reputation for understanding young men who dominated the Cardinal roster with the average age on the team being just under twenty-five. After the conclusion of the 1943 season, Dexter noted that many Cardinal players were being drafted into the armed services, and he predicted that the youthful athletes from St. Louis would bring their fellow soldiers "speed, savvy, and never-say-die spirit."[52]

The youth cult in baseball during the war years was popular in many quarters. The young baseball hero was viewed as the all-American boy who was honest, good in athletics but not too interested in intellectual pursuits, maintained high moral standards, worked and played hard, and always expressed concern for his mother. Thus, Dave Ferriss, after pitching his first victory in the major leagues, was described as celebrating his success by eating some ice cream and telephoning his mother in Mississippi to give her the good news.[53] Ted Williams was portrayed as an example for other young Americans to follow since he did not smoke or drink alcoholic beverages.[54] The following characterization of Brooklyn Dodger outfielder Pete Reiser exemplifies the image of the all-American boy. Pete grew up in the St. Louis tradition, fighting the usual battles with gangs from other neighborhoods, like the Sherman Street Creeps or the Marcus Street Rats, playing ball after school, catching the latest installment of the Western thriller on a Saturday afternoon, wearing a special suit on Sundays, and rooting for the Cardinals and the Browns.[55]

The *Sporting News* also praised the young Reiser for not becoming "big-headed" after the 1941 season in which the Dodger outfielder was the first rookie ever to win the batting title. Reiser celebrated his good fortune and demonstrated his all-American qualities by purchasing a new home for his parents. His mother pronounced Pete, "The greatest boy that ever lived."[56]

On a more professional level, the qualities sought in a young player by a major league scout were vividly described by Harold Parrott in an article for the *Saturday Evening Post*. Parrott maintained that two types of athletes were blacklisted by professional talent scouts; the bolsheviks who always criticized management and the pussycats who cringed from violent physical contact.[57] Therefore, major league baseball was interested in aggressive youth, but only those who would vent their hostilities upon the opposition and not on established baseball interests. Thus, the *Sporting News* advised players not to become holdouts for higher contracts during the war: "The fans are in no frame of mind for reading about extended scrapes relating to sums which these fans could not earn in five years—some of them in a decade."[58] Following the suggestions of Parrott and the *Sporting News,* hard working and loyal Cleveland Indian short-stop Lou Boudreau became a big league manager in 1942 at the tender age of twenty-four.[59] This stress upon youthful aggressiveness conjoins the World War II and Horatio Alger beliefs in which, in the final analysis, there is no substitute for victory and success. The baseball articles in the *Saturday Evening Post* and *Collier's* rarely referred to such concepts as sportsmanship; instead they concentrated upon winning at almost any cost as long as one's competitiveness and aggression were focused upon opponents or the enemy rather than teammates or established interests. Thus, in a nostalgic piece about former player Bill Lange, Talbert Josselyn contended that Lange was one of the most successful base stealers in baseball history because he utilized his tremendous size to knock down opponents who attempted to tag him.[60] Larry Gilbert, perhaps the most famous of minor league managers, reduced this concept to a simple maxim. "Make winning so pleasant," stated Gilbert, "and losing so unpleasant that hustle is automatic."[61] One of the greatest practitioners of this philosophy was outfielder Pete Reiser of the Dodgers who was praised for his hustle and aggressiveness in constantly running into walls in pursuit of long fly balls.[62] While such activities sometimes resulted in spectacular catches, Reiser more often suffered a concussion for his endeavors. Nevertheless, Reiser exemplified the courage of those who sought victory in war and financial enterprise regardless of the tremendous odds against them.

All the images presented by baseball, however, were not favorable. Most noticeable was the exclusion of blacks. They were segregated into Negro leagues just as the armed services divided units on a racial basis. The incompatibility of this racism in baseball with American war aims was pointed out by many sources. The *New York Times* commented:

> Baseball has come to be, through the years, something of a symbol of the
> United States. It is a democratic game, where the boy from a back lot can
> rise from rags to comparative riches through skill and stamina. If we are
> willing to let Negroes as soldiers fight wars on our team; we should not
> ask questions about color in the great American game.[63]

The recruitment of Jackie Robinson by the Dodgers and Branch
Rickey in the winter of 1945 began a change, but racism and the rising aspirations of blacks were to remain problems in baseball and American society during the post-war era.

Also, post-war changes in the structure of organized baseball would
render it less likely to serve as the breeding ground for simple American
success stories as that of Branch Rickey who rose from a reserve catcher
to the Presidency of a major league baseball club. Sportswriter Dan Parker
said in the fall of 1945 that organized baseball was just about to undergo
a fundamental change, as new club owners and the newly inducted Commissioner of Baseball, former Kentucky Senator Happy Chandler, were
emphasizing the image of the sport more than its competitive aspects.[64]
Parker's speculations match those of author John Brooks. In *The Great
Leap,* Brooks argues that such a transformation from competition to image
consciousness has characterized large American business concerns since
World War II.[65] Indeed, the big business quality of baseball was evident
in 1952 when a subcommittee of the Judiciary Committee investigated the
monopolistic structure of the sport.[66]

Confronted in the post-war period with problems of race, monopoly, drugs, and even union organization among players, major league baseball — in common with American society which was concerned with
similar questions — no longer seemed to exemplify the simple virtues contained in the Horatio Alger model.[67] These perplexities of the post-war
era, however, do not obliterate the images reflected in the pages of the *Saturday Evening Post* and *Collier's* from 1942 to 1945. Baseball served the
nation during the war. It was a symbol of the American success epic and
when William Bendix, near cinema death, inquired as to the state of the
Dodgers, he was, in fact, asking if the American dream remained intact.
For most Americans during the war years, regardless of objective realities,
the answer to Bendix's question remained "yes" the Dodgers have won,
and "yes" the American dream of success is alive and well.

===

Endnotes

This essay was originally published in *Studies in Popular Culture*, volume 8, number 2 (1985), 18-32.

1. Studs Terkel, *The Good War: An Oral History of World War II* (New York: Pantheon Books, 1984), 16.

2. For the role of sport in shaping American society see Robert Boyle, *Sport — Mirror of American Life* (Boston: Little, Brown and Co., 1963); Foster Rhea Dulles, *America Learns to Play* (New York: Appleton Century Co., 1940); Roland Garrett, "The Metaphysics of Baseball," *Philosophy Today*, 20 (Fall, 1976), 209–226; James Michener, *Sport in America* (New York: Random House 1976); Frederic Logan Paxson, "The Rise of Sport," as cited in Frederic Logan Paxson, *The Great Demobilization and Other Essays* (Madison: University of Wisconsin Press, 1941); Benjamin G. Rader, *American Sports: From the Age of Folk Games to the Age of Spectators* (Englewood Cliffs, New Jersey: Prentice Hall, 1983); and Leverett T. Smith, Jr., *The American Dream and the National Game* (Bowling Green, Ohio: Bowling Green University Popular Press, 1975).

3. U.S. Congress, *Organized Baseball: Report of the Subcommittee on Study of Monopoly Power of the Committee on the Judiciary, House Report*, No. 2002, 82 Cong., 2 Sess. (1952), 7.

4. *Ibid.*, p. 12.

5. Roger Angell, *The Summer Game* (New York: Viking Press, 1972), 30.

6. Marvin Cohen, *Baseball the Beautiful: Decoding the Diamond* (New York: Links Books, 1974), 120. It is interesting to note that baseball has received more serious literary treatment than other American sports. For surveys of baseball and literature see C. Candelaria, "Literary Fungos; Allusions to Baseball in Significant American Fiction," *Midwest Quarterly*, 23 (Summer, 1982), 411–425; Michael V. Oriard, *Dreaming of Heroes: American Sports Fiction, 1868–1980* (Chicago: Nelson-Hall, 1982); Anton Grobani, ed., *Guide to Baseball Literature* (Detroit: Gale Research Co., 1975); and Robert J. Higgs, *Laurel and Thorn: The Athlete in American Literature* (Lexington: The University of Kentucky Press, 1981).

7. Richard C. Crepeau, *Baseball: America's Diamond Mind, 1919-1941* (Orlando: University Presses of Florida, 1980), 25.

8. George Grella, "Baseball and the American Dream," *Massachusetts Review,* 16 (Summer 1975), 550.

9. The relationship of Brooklyn, William Bendix, baseball, and World War II is discussed in Roger Kahn, *The Boys of Summer* (New York: Random House, 1971), xiv. Representative Bendix films of the World War II era include *Wake Island* (1942), *Guadalcanal Diary* (1943), and *Lifeboat* (1944). For the role of Hollywood in World War II see Joe Morella, Edward Z. Epstein, and John Griggs, *The Films of World War II* (Secaucus, New Jersey: The Citadel Press, 1973); Colin Shindler, *Hollywood Goes to War* (Boston: Routledge and Kegan Paul, 1979); and Lewis Jacobs, "World War II and the American Film," *Cinema Journal* (Winter, 1967-1968), 1–21.

10. Jules Tygiel, *Baseball's Great Experiment: Jackie Robinson and His Legacy* (New York: Oxford University Press, 1983), 181.

11. For the impact of World War I on major league baseball see Fred Lieb, "The Great Exhumation," *Collier's*, 109 (May 16, 1942), 22, 60–61; and Harold Seymour, *Baseball: The Golden Age* (New York Oxford University Press, 1971), 244–255.

12. *Sporting News*, January 15, 1942. For the role of the *Sporting News* in baseball and World War II see "Bible of Baseball: *Sporting News*," *Saturday Evening Post*, 214 (June 20, 1942), 9–10. For general accounts of baseball during the Second World War see William B. Mead, *Even the Browns: The Zany, True Story of Baseball in the Early Forties* (Chicago: Contemporary Books, 1978); Richard Goldstein, *Spartan Seasons: How Baseball Survived the Second World War* (New York: Macmillan Co., 1980); David Voigt, *American Baseball: From the Commissioners to Continental Expansion* (University Park: Pennsylvania State University Press, 1970); and J.G. Taylor Spink, *Judge Landis and Twenty Five Years of Baseball* (New York: Thomas W. Crowell Co., 1947). For general accounts of the American domestic scene during World War II see John Morton Blum, *V Was For Victory: Politics and American Culture During World War II* (New York: Harcourt Brace Jovanovich, 1976); and Richard Polenburg, *War and Society: The United States, 1941-1945* (Philadelphia: Lippincott, 1972).

13. *Sporting News*, December 11, 1941.

14. *Ibid.*, January 29, 1942.

15. *Ibid.*, December 18, 1941.

16. *New York Times*, January 9, 1942.

17. *Sporting News*, February 12, 1942.

18. Franklin D, Roosevelt to Kenesaw Mountain Landis, January 16, 1942, as cited in Samuel 1. Rosenman, ed., *The Public Papers and Addresses of Franklin Roosevelt, vol. 7* (New York: Russell and Russell, 1950), 62.

19. Franklin D. Roosevelt, 995 Press Conference, March 13, 1945, as cited in Rosenman, ed., *The Public Papers and Addresses of Franklin Roosevelt, vol, 8*, 592,

20. *Sporting News*, January 22, 1942.

21. *New York Times*, March 25, 1943.

22. "Batter (if still there) up," *Newsweek*, 21 (May 3, 1943), 82.

23. *Sporting News*, April 16, 1942.

24. *New York Times*, February 3, 1942.

25. U.S. Congress, *Organized Baseball: Report of the Subcommittee on Study of Monopoly Power of the Committee on the Judiciary, House Report*, No. 2002, 82 Cong., 2 Sess. (1952) 9. For a more complete account of baseball fund raising activities during the war see Goldstein, *Spartan Seasons*, 63–96.

26. *New York Times*, March 26, 1943. For background studies on the role of baseball in Japan see Richard C. Crepeau, "Pearl Harbor: A Failure of Baseball?," *Journal of Popular Culture*, 15 (Spring, 1982), 67–74; Donald Roden, "Baseball and the Quest for National Dignity in Meiji Japan," *American Historical Review*, 85 (June, 1980), 511–534; Robert Whitney, *The Chrysanthemum and the Bat: Baseball Samurai Style* (New York: Dodd, 1977); and Robert Objski, "Baseball is the National Game of Japan," *Baseball Research Journal*, 5 (1976), 21–27.

27. U. S. Congress, *Congressional Record*, 78 Cong., 2 Sess., 91 (1943), 9 and 514.

28. *Sporting News*, December 18, 1941.

29. *New York Times*, December 10, 1941.

30. *Ibid.*, December 20, 1942.

31. *Sporting News*, December 18, 1941.

32. This technique for analyzing social and cultural values has been skillfully applied in a number of historical studies. Two of the more important works utilizing such an approach are Henry Nash Smith, *Virgin Land: The American West as Symbol and Myth* (Cambridge, Massachusetts: Harvard University Press, 1950); and William K. Taylor, *Cavalier and Yankee* (New York: Harper and Row, 1957).

33. In 1942, *Collier's* enjoyed a circulation figure of 2,909,794, while the *Satur-*

day Evening Post listed circulation at 3,348,875. For 1942 periodical figures see Percy H. Johnson, ed., *N. W. Ayer and Son's Directory of Newspapers and Periodicals* (Philadelphia: N. W. Ayer and Sons, Inc., 1942).

34. For the Horatio Alger symbol in American society see John Tebbel, *From Rags to Riches: Horatio Alger, Jr., and the American Dream* (New York: MacMillan Co., 1963); Gregory G. Sojka, "Going from 'Rags to Riches' with Baseball Joe: Or a Pitcher's Progress," *Journal of American Culture*, 2 (Spring, 1979), 113–121; and Richard Bowerrnan, "Horatio Alger, Jr.; or, Adrift in the Myth of Rags to Riches," *Journal of American Culture*, 2 (Spring, 1979), 83–112.

35. Steven A. Riess, "Professional Baseball and Social Mobility," *Journal of Interdisciplinary History*, 11 (Autumn, 1980), 235–250.

36. Roger Bistwell, "Fantastic Ferriss," *Collier's*, 116 (July 21, 1945), 21 and 35.

37. All baseball statistics utilized in this paper may be found in Hy Turkin and S. C. Thompson, *The Official Encyclopedia of Baseball* (New York: A. S. Barnes and Co., 1970).

38. William A. Jones and Harman W. Nichols, "One Wing and a Player," *Collier's*, 112 (September 4, 1943), 26 and 43.

39. For additional information on Gray's career see Mead, *Even the Browns*, 203–218; Goldstein, *Spartan Seasons*, 208–210; and Bill Borst, *Last in the American League: An Informal History of the St. Louis Browns* (St. Louis: Krank Press, 1978).

40. Stanley Frank, "The Yankee's Second Gehrig," *Saturday Evening Post*, 216 (July 3, 1943), 72.

41. Cleveland Amory, "I Wanna Be An Immortal," *Saturday Evening Post*, 214 (January 19, 1942), 30, 73–74.

42. *Sporting News*, March 12, 1942. For an interesting account of Williams's career see Lawrence Bardassaro, "Ted Williams: The Reluctant Hero," *Journal of American Culture*, 4 (Fall, 1981), 66–74.

43. Steven M. Gelbes, "Working at Playing: The Culture of the Workplace and the Rise of Baseball," *Journal of Social History*, 17 (Summer, 1983), 3–22.

44. Malcolm W. Bingay, "The Fan Who Bought the Ball Park," *Saturday Evening Post*, 215 (March 6, 1943), 18, 83–84.

45. J. Roy Stockton, "A Brain Comes to Brooklyn," *Saturday Evening Post*, 215 (February 13, 1943), 24–25, 54–60. For additional information on Rickey see Harvey Frommer, *Rickey and Robinson: The Men Who Broke Baseball's Color Barrier* (New York: MacMillan Co., 1982); David Lipman, *Mr. Baseball: The Story of Branch Rickey* (New York: G. P. Putnam's Sons, 1966); Arthur Mann, *Branch Rickey: American in Action* (Boston: Houghton Mifflin, 1957); Kahn, *The Boys of Summer*; and Tygiel, *Baseball's Great Experiment*.

46. Phil Rizzuto, "They Made Me a Big-Leaguer," *Saturday Evening Post*, 214 (April 11, 1942), 11, 38–41.

47. Kyle Crichton, "The Unbelievable Browns," *Collier's* 114 (September 2, 1944), 14.

48. Mead, *Even the Browns*, ix.

49. The Cardinal emphasis upon teamwork is discussed in "The Kids," *Time*, 40 (October 12, 1942), 77–79; and "Birds of Fine Feather," *Newsweek*, 22 (September 20, 1943), 94.

50. Billy Southworth, "The Greatest Ball Club on Earth," *Saturday Evening Post*, 215 (June 5, 1943), 87–89.

51. Goldstein, *Spartan Seasons*, 6.

52. Charles Dexter, "Baseball's Billy the Kid," *Collier's*, 112 (October 9, 1943), 71.

53. Bistwell, "Fantastic Ferriss," *Collier's,* 116 (July 21, 1945), 35.

54. Amory, "I Wanna Be An Immortal," *Saturday Evening Post,* 214 (January 19, 1942), 74.

55. Tom Meany, "Pistol Pete — National Leaguer No. 1," *Saturday Evening Post,* 215 (September 26, 1942), 39.

56. *Sporting News,* December 25, 1941.

57. Harold Parrott, "Baseball's Baby Snatchers," *Saturday Evening Post,* 217 (April 21, 1945), 20 and 92.

58. *Sporting News,* February 26, 1942.

59. Franklin Lewis, "The Old College Try," *Collier's,* 109 (June, 1942), 42, 59–60.

60. Talbert Josselyn, "Better than the Best," *Collier's,* 116 (July 7, 1945), 69–71.

61. Fred Russell, "They're Simply Wild about Larry," *Saturday Evening Post,* 214 (May 30, 1942), 38.

62. Meany, "Pistol Pete — National Leaguer No, 1." *Saturday Evening Post,* 215 (September 26, 1942), 37. Reiser's style of play greatly shortened his career as he was able to only participate in five full seasons, in which he compiled an outstanding batting average of over .300.

63. *New York Times,* November 20, 1945.

64. Dan Parker, "Comes the Baseball Revolution," *Saturday Evening Post,* 218 (October 6, 1945), 18–19, 106–107.

65. John Brooks, *The Great Leap* (New York: Harper and Row, 1958), 38–72.

66. U.S. Congress, *Organized Baseball: Hearings Before a Subcommittee on Study of Monopoly Power of the Committee on the Judiciary, House Report,* No. 2002, 82 Cong., 2 Sess. (1952).

67. For the complex issues confronting post-war America and baseball see Douglass C. North and Roger Leroy Miller, *Abortion, Baseball, and Weed: Economic Issues of Our Times* (New York: Harper and Row, 1971).

4

Amity Is the Key to Success: Baseball and the Cold War

Numerous explanations have been offered to describe the insecurities that befell American society in the late 1940s and early 1950s. Following the sacrifices for a war effort, which Studs Terkel termed *The Good War*, Americans were ready to bask in the sunshine of peace and prosperity, but, instead, the American century was frustrated by the emergence of the Cold War and the witch hunts of the McCarthy period. Post war anxieties have been analyzed in such concepts as the affluent society, the organization man, the "inner" directed versus the "outer" directed, and the search for a liberal consensus.[1] Of these explanations, perhaps the concept of the ideology of a liberal consensus best describes the early years of the post war period.

The liberal consensus was based upon two cornerstone assumptions: that the structure of American society was sound and that the spread of communism was a clear and present danger to the United States. Americans desired security symbolized by the white picket fences of suburbia and by the gray flannel suit of the corporate ladder climber. Increasing prosperity would solve all of America's problems. There was no need for dissent. The American government was as understanding and reasonable as Jim Anderson in *Father Knows Best* and Ward Cleaver in *Leave It to Beaver*.

However, the corporate state, increased productivity, and technology failed to usher in a safe and secure world. As Michael Harrington documented in *The Other America*, pockets of poverty remained unseen in the tranquil suburbs of the Andersons and Cleavers. Spy scandals, the explosion of an atomic bomb by the Soviet Union, and a shooting war in Korea would remind Americans that the world was a very unpredictable place. Frustrated by the failure of the liberal consensus to provide the promise land, many Americans sought scapegoats in the anti-communist crusades of the post war era. For many, it seemed an alien ideology was frustrating America's just goals of democracy and an open door economic policy. The cancer of communism was making America and the world ill, and numerous would-be doctors volunteered to exorcise the malignancy; only to discover the patient was suffering from numerous diseases and complications.

The story of the Cold War and the Second Red Scare has been well documented in regard to political, military, and diplomatic affairs.[2] In more recent years, scholars have investigated the conjunction between popular culture and the anti-communist crusade, often focusing upon the red scare in Hollywood.[3] A fertile but largely unexplored field is sporting activities which have been recognized by many scholars as fulfilling various psychological and social needs by providing traditional symbols and values in a rapidly changing and frightening world.[4] While Americans enjoy a wide spectrum of athletic endeavors, baseball provides an ideal laboratory for examining the immediate post World War II period. From 1940 to 1945 alone, public expenditures for professional baseball games totaled $112.1 million, while expenditures for all other major sports, including horse racing, only reached a figure of $93.1 million.[5]

More importantly, aside from its dominant economic position, baseball traditionally has served as a unique symbol of American values, in part by the outstanding quality of literature produced regarding the sport. For example, Roger Angell described baseball as an ageless sport in which "time is seamless and invisible, a bubble within which players move at exactly the same pace and rhythms as their predecessor;" while in an article for the *Massachusetts Review,* George Grella, paraphrasing Jacques Barzun, succinctly made the case for baseball, stating, "Anyone who does not understand the game cannot hope to understand the country."[6]

In recent years, American historians have followed the suggestions made by Barzun and Grella, recognizing that baseball represents a unique cultural influence through which American values may be examined. For example, in his study of baseball in the progressive era, Steven A. Riess emphasized the role of writers in making the sport appear relevant to the needs of middle-class Americans. According to Riess, "The national pastime was portrayed in such a way that it supplied some of the symbols, myths, and legends society needed to bind its members together." A similar role for the sport in the 1920s and 1930s was suggested in the work of Richard Crepeau, who argued that for the inner war years baseball was the game that "most nearly typified American institutions and teachings." Historians have also discovered a fertile field in baseball biography. Jules Tygiel utilized the story of Jackie Robinson to comment on racial relations in post World War II America, while Peter Levine examined the efforts of A. G. Spalding to use baseball as a vehicle to impose some order upon the chaos of post Civil War industrialization. Levine concluded that the popularity of baseball in late nineteenth-century America "was surely related to its ability to offer a visual tie with a rural past to new urban audiences, to assure them that order prevailed even in 'the turmoil of the modern city,' and to demonstrate that traditional values could be incorporated into the new demands of a complex society."[7]

But while baseball as a symbol of American values has gained attention, little has been written directly on the Cold War.[8] Yankee domination of the playing field and the challenge of the Brooklyn Dodgers have captivated baseball fans and writers, but baseball as a reflection of American values under the stress of the Cold War and McCarthyism still requires analysis. This study proposes to examine the sport as it responded to the demands of the post war liberal consensus.

During the Second World War spokesmen for organized baseball maintained that the sport symbolized the democratic virtues of American society. Baseball had fought the war against fascism, now it would be enlisted in the struggle against communism. The other cornerstone of the liberal consensus, that American society was basically sound and most problems could be solved by an expanding economy, also concerned the sport. In the period between 1946 and 1954, baseball would directly confront the problems of racism, union organization, monopoly, and challenges to the reserve clause, baseball's own version of the loyalty oath. In coping with these difficulties, organized baseball would emphasize the values of consensus, in which the loyalty of the organization man would be rewarded. There was no reason to rock the boat. Baseball executives, like businessmen and government bureaucrats, were looking out for the welfare of the individual. In the age of McCarthy and Eisenhower, conformity appeared to be the norm.[9]

Along with most Americans, baseball entered the post war era with confidence. The end of the war in 1945 witnessed a new high of nearly eleven million fans attending major league games. This mark was shattered in 1946 as over eighteen million fans jammed major league parks, perhaps representing a "pent up" demand for the sport following the turbulent war years. Attendance continued to climb in 1947 and 1948, reaching a figure of over twenty million in the latter year.[10]

Why was baseball so successful following the war? Spokesmen for the sport emphasized the importance of consensus. In a January 19, 1948 speech before the first Minor League Executives Conference, Branch Rickey of the Brooklyn Dodgers, the man who had brought Jackie Robinson to the major

leagues in 1947, listed his attributes for success in the sport: honesty, loyalty, accuracy, dependability, industry, aptitude, friends, and opportunity.
Rickey concluded, "One must believe the sport is making a worthwhile
contribution to the welfare of the community and country and give an
unconquerable devotion to it. Equip yourselves with the habiliments of
success—dress, look and act like it."[11]

In pursuit of the goals outlined by Rickey, the Presidents of the American and National Leagues emphasized dress codes for players and sought
to crack down on profane language emerging from the field. In a similar
vein, a March 3, 1948 editorial in the *Sporting News*, the Bible of baseball,
praised the practice of owners polling the players before making major
changes. Recognizing that polling could be overdone and that players
remember their place, the publication, nevertheless, asserted, "Amity is the
prime essential for success."[12] Amity was extolled and dissent was deplored,
as there was room in the baseball consensus for the players. In symbolic
fashion, as the values of consensus and the organization man become
increasingly voiced by officials of the game, Babe Ruth, the individualist
who defied tradition and training rules, passed away on August 16, 1948.

However, as the Cold War intensified in 1949 and scapegoats were
sought by HUAC, baseball, along with the nation, seemed to lose some of
its confidence in success and the American century, while continuing to
pledge its allegiance to the other cornerstone of the consensus—anti-communism. The *Sporting News* prayed for peace and "that these young men
who are being taken in our first peacetime draft will not be forced to
fight."[13] On January 21, 1949, in Columbus, Ohio, the staunch anti-communist Senator from Ohio John W. Bricker addressed the second Annual
Conference of Minor League Executives. Bricker sought to enlist baseball
in the Cold War, maintaining that the sport was essential to the American way of life. In a rhetorical excess, Bricker asserted, "While the marching hordes in China are spreading the doctrine of communism, officials
of the national pastime are helping to make democracy work in this country by giving every youth a chance to carve out his own career."[14] Thus,
Senator Bricker envisioned baseball as serving an important role in the
indoctrination of American youth and combating what the Senator perceived as the alien influence of communist ideology into the United States.
In accordance with this role for baseball, Jackie Robinson was called before
HUAC to refute the testimony of Paul Robeson that black Americans would
not fight in a war against the Soviet Union. The star second baseman of
the Dodgers confessed that he was no expert on communism, and blacks
in the United States still needed to struggle for equality, but blacks would
fight for their country. Robinson testified, "They'd do their best to help

their country stay out of war; if unsuccessful, they'd do their best to help their country win the war — against Russia or any other enemy that threatened us."[15]

Baseball was also viewed as a means by which American values might be extended into the third world and gain new friends in the ideological struggle with communism. For example, U. S. Ambassador to Venezuela, Walter J. Donnelly won praise for championing the game in that country. Expressing his admiration for Donnelly, a belligerent Dan Parker of the *New York Mirror* insisted, "If more ambassadors used sports instead of double talk as their medium of expression, I'm sure the world would be much better off, and to test the theory, I'd like to see the new envoy to Moscow introduce himself in the Kremlin by fetching Uncle Joe Stalin a resounding whack on the noggin with one of Joe DiMaggio's castoff bats."[16] On a more practical level, the San Francisco Seals of the Pacific Coast League toured Japan in the fall of 1950 on a good will visit promoted as an effort to prevent the spread of communism in that Asian nation. According to Seals' coach Del Young, "When we got there the Communists were on the soap boxes on almost every street corner. But we hadn't been there long before they disappeared in the crowds. I don't think they'll get far now." The San Francisco club played before 500,000 Japanese fans and lunched with General Douglas MacArthur, who assured them there was "no substitute for victory."[17]

While baseball had signed on in the Cold War, the game itself was not free from the type of subversion which worried Joseph McCarthy and HUAC. Baseball's subversion concerned the case of players jumping to the Mexican League in violation of the sport's reserve clause, which bound the player to the exclusive service of one club. Baseball Commissioner A. B. "Happy" Chandler had banned the jumping players from returning to organized baseball. In response to Chandler's decision, former New York Giants outfielder Danny Gardella challenged the reserve clause in the courts as a violation of anti-trust law. Chandler defended his action with the rhetoric of loyalty and subversion which was becoming prevalent in American life, labeling the jumpers as "disloyal" and urging all supporters "to stand by the flag of Organized Baseball."[18] Faced with Chandler's patriotic appeal, some jumpers disassociated themselves from the Gardella case and threw themselves upon the mercy of the commissioner in a situation not unlike those "naming names" of former communist associations before Congressional committees. Former Dodger catcher Mickey Owen petitioned Chandler for reinstatement, pleading, "I think Danny is wrong. I would never sue baseball. Baseball didn't make us go to Mexico. I want to play baseball, not destroy it. Baseball must have the reserve clause."[19]

Perhaps because of Owen's appeal or, more likely, due to the threat of Gardella's law suit, and despite his insistence that the jumpers were a challenge to the integrity of the game, Chandler reinstated the delinquent players in June, 1950. The *Sporting News* praised Chandler for reinstating the players and declared them ideologically sound. The paper observed that Chandler had "removed the bitterness from their hearts and put them on the way of winning back all the emoluments and privileges that were theirs before they departed."[20] The editorial did not mention that allegedly Gardella had dropped his law suit in favor of a generous cash settlement from the club owners.

With its internal affairs apparently in order, baseball next had to confront the challenge of the Korean War and whether the sport would continue during this military engagement as it had been allowed to do during World Wars I and II. The conflict in Korea, and the fear that fighting on that distant peninsula might result in a third world war, frightened many Americans. Moreover, Commissioner Chandler reportedly speculated that the draft might call up as much as 75 percent of current major league rosters. Such gloomy assessments led to questions regarding whether baseball would receive the same type of green light bestowed by President Roosevelt during World War II. Many baseball representatives, however, refused to accept a reduced position for the game. Frank Lane, general manager of the Chicago White Sox, used the World War II experience and patriotic slogans as arguments for continuing the game. Lane insisted, "Next to religion, no other agency played such a large part in maintaining our morale both at home and at actual battlefronts in World War II, and I repeat that unless actual enemy attacks on the shore of the United States prescribe otherwise, professional baseball should be encouraged to continue its operations as long as it possibly can do so."[21] Thus, baseball would do its duty in the shooting war as well as in the ideological Cold War, asking for no favors, but maintaining its role of indoctrination and morale.

Although many minor leaguers and some well known established stars were taken by the draft, the feared global conflict did not occur, and baseball did, indeed, continue its struggle against communism. Branch Rickey took time from his beloved Dodgers to assail the American educational system. Baseball's elder statesman argued, "If the schools would teach American history and basic Christianity, they would mark an end to subversion, secret cells, and false isms."[22] The Yankee Clipper, Joe DiMaggio, also contributed by visiting the troops in Korea. DiMaggio got close enough to the front to ascertain that Korea was not a mere police action, but instead represented a full scale shooting war. The Yankee star marveled, "Troops can't even brush their teeth in the contaminated water without first boiling it. And they bathe out of their helmets." Meanwhile, in Venezuela Ambassador Donnelly was organizing a Chico Carrusquel day to combat communism, while press attaché Frederick Kuhn chased away communist protestors from the embassy with a baseball bat, proclaiming, "I did catch one of the little Reds. Fortunately, however, I dropped the bat and just gave him a beating with my hands. It's the leaders we're after, not the kids." And in Philadelphia, Phillies pitcher Curt Simmons, the first major league player to be drafted in the Korean conflict, bemoaned his defeat by the Cincinnati Reds before he departed for the army. Simmons quipped, "I hope I have better luck against those Reds in Korea."[23]

Despite baseball's service to ideological soundness, troop morale, and manpower, major league attendance took a dive in 1950, dropping over 13 percent from 1949.

While the *Sporting News* blamed declining crowds on the weather and the emergence of television, baseball owners evidently had another scapegoat in mind, when, at the St. Petersburg winter meeting, they announced the contract of Commissioner Chandler would not be renewed. The decision by the owners led some observers to question whether baseball magnates were really committed to the Cold War. Reports that Chandler was dismissed because he suggested that baseball might have to be placed in mothballs in the event of total mobilization led Harold Russell, National Commander of Amvets who had lost both of his hands in the Pacific before earning an Oscar for *The Best Years of Our Lives,* to suggest that owners were placing profits over patriotism. Russell observed, "We remember the strange crop of deferments during World War II that were necessary to keep baseball going and, incidentally, to keep profits rolling in at the ticket windows."[24]

Faced with dissension in the ranks, the *Sporting News,* in a house divided editorial, called for a return to consensus and warned of character assassinations and unfounded rumors; a most appropriate comment for the McCarthy period. Club owners failed to heed the warnings of the *Sporting News* and, instead, launched a boomlet for the deposed General Douglas MacArthur as Baseball Commissioner. While President Truman was soundly booed throwing out the first pitch at the Senators home opener, thirteen year old Arthur MacArthur, son of the General, was being treated as royalty at the Giants home opener in the Polo Grounds. Escorted by thirty-six patrolmen, young MacArthur was personally greeted by Managers Leo Durocher of the Giants and Chuck Dressen of the Dodgers. In addition to these public displays, Warren Giles, President of the Cincinnati Reds, insisted, "General MacArthur could run anything for me," while owner Lou Perini of the Boston Braves exclaimed, "General MacArthur has my vote if he is available and wants the job." Even Chandler got into the national act of bestowing accolades on the General, asserting that he would resign immediately if MacArthur would accept the position. Certainly, owners who were ready to submit to the leadership of General MacArthur viewed themselves absolved from critics who doubted their commitment to the Cold War. But, alas, the Old Soldier stated that although he might have loved the job fifteen years earlier, he was now too old for the position.[25]

MacArthur was not the only military figure considered for the position of Commissioner. Erle Crocke, Jr., head of the American Legion, openly indicated his interest in the office, but his partisan political statements antagonized some supporters. After a citation to editor J. Taylor Spink for wartime editions of the *Sporting News*, Crocke could not resist criticizing Democratic foreign policy in Korea. The Legionnaire asserted, "More than 11,000 American lives sacrificed in a fight-but-don't win war in Korea have demonstrated with tragic impact the complete bankruptcy of American foreign policy in the hands of a State Department staffed by lukewarm and apologetic Americans."[26]

If Crocke was a bit strident for some owners, there was still a consensus that the sport required discipline and identification with the war effort which a general could provide. Thus, on August 21, 1951, the owners named Major General Emmett "Rosey" O'Donnell to the post. Truman, however, maintained that he could not release the General from active service. Leaderless and confronting new challenges to the reserve clause, baseball selected an in-house candidate, Ford Frick, President of the National League. The *Sporting News* announced its approval of the selection, lauding Frick as an organization man who would well represent baseball in a corporate age, utilizing business techniques to enhance baseball's position within the post war affluent consensus:

> Taking over now is a practical baseball man, fashioned in the mold of a schooled executive. The problems he must meet are different than those forced by Landis and Chandler. Like the president of a big corporation — for baseball has become big business in every sense of the term — he must concern himself with selling the product he represents, with meeting competition, with instituting more economical operation and with shaping policies to satisfy both the legislative and judicial dictates of the nation.[27]

Frick would need his organizational and business skills to combat the charges raised by Congressman Emmanuel Celler whose subcommittee on monopoly was investigating allegations of antitrust violations against the sport. Congressman Celler questioned numerous aspects of organized baseball; including the "blacklisting" of the players who had jumped to the Mexican League, the reserve clause, the "mere pittance" of a $5,000 annual salary for major league players, the failure to expand in the last fifty years despite the considerable geographical shifts in U. S. population, and, finally, the domination of the sport by reactionaries "who have the financial interest." While baseball executives rushed to the defense of the sport, it was essential to present players before the Committee who would follow the party line and deny that the reserve clause represented any form of involuntary slavery. Thus, Granny Hamner, the Philadelphia Phillies Player Representative, testified, "But as far as the reserve clause is concerned and our ability to deal with the owners on salary, everything is great. Players are making more money, living under better conditions and leading a better life than ever before in the history of baseball. Let the game alone."[28] Knowing the fate of those who had challenged the owners and reserve clause, players lined up behind Hamner to demonstrate their allegiance in baseball's own version of the loyalty oath. Salary figures from the 1970s and 1980s would later illustrate what the reserve clause really meant to players.

Baseball owners had selected a "true believer" and patriot in Ford Frick who raised the banner of the sport against Celler's accusations in Congressional testimony and a series of speeches around the country. An attack upon baseball was an assault upon America itself, as Frick asserted that the sport was at the heart of the nation's democratic spirit and well entitled to its position within the postwar consensus. The banker and the mechanic could sit together in the stands voicing their democratic right of free speech in criticizing the umpire, while on the field, race, creed, and color made no difference, only a player's individual talent counted. Thus, speaking before the Rotary Club of Columbus, Ohio, on December 3, 1951, Frick insisted that American civilization could be defined through baseball. In somewhat of an oversimplification, he observed, "If Germany had had baseball, World War II would have been prevented, and if Russia had a sports program like the Americans, with a chance to let off steam, there would be no danger of communism." Frick continued that America was safe as long as boys went to bed with catcher's mitts under their pillows. Even in an age of "uncertainty and questioning" baseball was doing its job of indoctrinating youth in the virtues of democracy, and the game would "remain a proud part of our ideal way of life."[29]

Accordingly, baseball, like America itself, which had entered the post war world with such confidence, found itself in the early 1950s in an age of uncertainty. Already confronted with a manpower shortage due to selective service, and declining attendance figures, baseball would lose one of its star gate attractions when Ted Williams of the Boston Red Sox was drafted in January, 1952. Despite the lamentable loss of Williams, and with the sword of the forthcoming Celler's Committee report hanging over baseball's head, the *Sporting News* reiterated the sport's commitment to the war effort. The baseball publication proclaimed:

> In the diplomatic language of the United Nations, the fighting in Korea is a police action, but it kills many and wounds still more. These men must be replaced, and strength of the armed forces generally must be built to the point at which the peace will be guaranteed — or that any more inclusive war will be won certainly and quickly. Baseball, as always in its history, is proud to send its players to their appropriate places in their effort.[31]

Baseball officials breathed a sigh of relief and felt rewarded for their patriotic effort when the Celler's Committee report was released in May, 1952. The report paid homage to baseball as America's national pastime and extolled the democratic values of the game. And, of most importance to baseball executives, no legislation regarding baseball's business structure was recommended until the courts had a chance to rule on the controversial reserve clause. Congressman Celler, however, strongly suggested that organized baseball should take the opportunity given by the Committee to get its internal house in order.[32] Accordingly, the *Sporting News*, Commissioner Frick, and other officials of the game began to wage a campaign for correcting any inequities in the reserve clause, clarifying the territorial rights of major and minor league franchises, and the first major league franchise expansion in over fifty years.

Despite the new lease on life given the sport by the Celler's Committee, 1952 remained a troubling year for baseball. Attendance again declined as paid admissions were down over 8 percent from 1951, itself hardly a banner season. A multitude of factors were blamed for baseball's difficulty: huge bonuses for signing young players, selective service, the domination of the sport by the New York Yankees, lack of good business promotion skills by some owners, players who were more interested in salaries and golf rather than competition and the game itself like old-timers such as Ty Cobb, competition from television, and the fact that children were watching Westerns rather than playing baseball. The sport also experienced new external and internal challenges. Baseball, which prided itself as the most democratic of games, found itself attacked for the reserve clause in the Soviet youth magazine *Smena*. The Soviets alleged, "Players are bought and sold like sheep and then, when they are worn out and usually crippled as a result of injuries, they are thrown out on the street to die of starvation."[33]

While surprised that baseball's structure could be utilized for anti-American propaganda, major league representatives did not react to such criticism by relinquishing control over players; instead, events in late 1953 witnessed even greater efforts to insure conformity on the part of players. For example, many in baseball were incensed when Chicago White Sox outfielder Jim Rivera, who had served time in prison for a previous sexual offense, was accused of rape. The charges were eventually dropped as the courts determined sexual relations between Rivera and the woman were voluntary, but guardians of public morality were outraged. Commissioner Frick placed Rivera on indefinite probation and warned the Chicago club that they would be responsible for Rivera's conduct "on and off the field." The *Sporting News* used the Rivera case to call for a morals clause in all major league contracts, emphasizing "the necessity for careful screening of the game's prospects in the future, the adoption of safeguards that will prevent similar situations and, above all, the tremendous obligation of all in Organized Ball to conduct themselves in such a manner that no discredit can be brought upon America's no. 1 sport by their actions."[34] Although the morals clause did not become a standard part of the players' contract, the comments of Frick and the *Sporting News* clearly emphasized the importance of the players being organization men.

That there was little room for the individual in baseball was further demonstrated in December, 1952, when Jackie Robinson, in a television interview, chided the Yankees for failing to place any black players on their major league roster. Many in baseball were outraged by Robinson's allegations of racism against baseball's dominant organization. Baseball was playing an important role in enlarging America's liberal consensus by bringing blacks into the mainstream of American society. To allege otherwise would undermine the consensus and give aid and comfort to America's enemies. Robinson's statements, just as Rivera's actions, were viewed as disloyal. The *Sporting News*, for example, once again reminded Robinson of his important role as a symbol for black Americans:

> Organized Baseball is playing a fine and influential role in the practical application of the founding fathers insistence that all men are created equal. All sorts of social barriers which formally were raised against the Negroes have been broken down — simply because so many of them are in the majors. Almost without exception, the trail blazers of this new deal for their race have seen the wisdom of remaining in the game as skilled performers, not as social crusaders. It is to be hoped that Robinson will return to the ranks of the majority.[35]

While never making a formal apology, Robinson downplayed the incident and returned to the consensus. Martin Luther King, Jr., would later explain to the *Sporting News* and other representatives of the liberal consensus why black Americans could not wait.

Having worked to insure conformity within its own playing ranks, baseball's position within America's liberal consensus would be ratified by events in 1953. Only weeks before the opening of the season, baseball's first franchise shift in over fifty years occurred as the owners gave permission for Lou Perini to move his Braves from Boston to the greener pastures of Milwaukee. However, American League magnates blocked the transfer of flamboyant Bill Veeck's St. Louis Browns to Baltimore. The transfer would eventually be approved following the 1953 season with Veeck selling his share of the club. Some viewed these maneuverings as baseball's equivalent of McCarthyism, as more conservative owners schemed to remove Veeck from the game.[36] In addition to the geographical expansion of the sport, proponents of baseball were convinced that the signing of a Korean armistice in July, 1953 would improve the quality of play with the return to the diamond of such stars as Williams. And, indeed, attendance did tend to level off in 1953, as the season witnessed a decline of only 1.8 percent, although a great deal of this leveling was due to the enthusiastic reception Milwaukee gave to the Braves.

However, to the executives of organized baseball the best news of the year came in November when the Supreme Court, in a seven to two decision, announced that baseball was a sport and not a business and therefore not subject to federal anti-trust legislation. Although the decision of the court did not necessarily agree with economic realities and the increasing emphasis within the sport on business techniques and organization, baseball officials applauded the court's reasoning. Ford Frick, just returning from a good will barnstorming tour of Japan, lauded the decision as a vote of confidence for baseball. But aware of baseball critics such as Congressman Celler, Frick asserted, "Baseball must re-survey itself and make territorial changes to keep pace with the economic and population shifts in this country in the last fifty years." Such a policy would silence some critics, as well as line baseball's coffers. The *Sporting News* termed the deliberations of the court a Thanksgiving present for the game, concluding, "That historic decision, for all practical purposes, gave the game back to the men who finance and operate it and took its problems out of the hands of constitutional lawyers. Some of the problems remain, but it's strictly up to baseball to deal with them effectively."[37] Thus, baseball executives were firmly in the saddle and outside forces, such as government, would not attempt to grab the reins. Baseball's position within the liberal consensus appeared assured.

Opening day of 1954 brought new optimism to the sport as 448,935 fans watched home openers; the best turnout since 1948. The Korean War was over, and some of the worst excesses of McCarthyism would be exposed in the Army-McCarthy hearings. Perhaps the age of uncertainty was over, and Americans would be able to enjoy some of the prosperity promised by The Good War. As another sign of stability in baseball, a new pension plan agreement was produced between the owners and the Players Association. J. Norman Lewis, lawyer for the players, praised the agreement, stating, "This is a new trend, a more business-like arrangement. We are bringing order out of chaos." The *Sporting News* applauded the return of amity to the game, expressing the view that while there would continue to be disagreements between the players and management, everyone could agree on "the continuation of baseball at a level profitable for all." For those who feared that the formation of a Players Association would lead to unionization, American League Player Representative and Yankee pitcher Allie Reynolds asserted, "We have neither the time nor the equipment, nor the urge, to do anything but let the magnates operate the game. The operation belongs to them."[38] Thus, on the major league level, organizational values were replacing the values of rugged individualism as baseball sought its place within the emerging post war consensus. Like America itself in the late 1940s and early 1950s, internal and external challenges had undermined the confidence of the national pastime, and frustrations often led to rhetorical outbursts and imposed conformity. But by 1954, a sense of renewed optimism returned to the sport as the corporate consensus values of amity appeared at last to prevail.

But, what of traditional values? Old loyalties seemed submerged in a search for profits exemplified by franchise shifts. Had, indeed, baseball succumbed to the age of affluence? Was the Cold War rhetoric of baseball only meaningless platitudes utilized to obscure corporate demands for profit? The Cold War, McCarthyism, and affluent society did place considerable strain on the institution of baseball, and, certainly, organized baseball found a niche in the emerging postwar liberal consensus. Yet, while baseball was utilized by individuals like Senator Bricker and Ambassador Donnelly in the ideological struggle against communism, to many other Americans it simply remained a symbol of traditional values in a confusing world.

Thus, in a prayer celebrating the return of organized baseball to Peoria, Illinois in 1953, Reverend William E. Cousins viewed baseball analogies as essential to explaining the qualities of the American fighting man. Reverend Cousins asserted, "We are not a military nation, but the spirit of those serving our country's cause has had all the value of a secret weapon.

You can't beat men who won't give up, who believe that the game isn't over till the last out. You can't discourage men who keep swinging for the fence even after two strikes have been called. You can't frighten men who will never quit until God Himself pulls them out of the lineup." But, perhaps one of the most direct and honest statements about the sport was made by former P.O.W. Sergeant Jim W. Richardson, who commented on attending an August 26, 1953 contest between the Phillies and Braves, "I sat behind the catcher, and when I ate my first hot dog with mustard I knew I was really back in the States."[39] While baseball was undergoing fundamental structural changes in a more organized society, the basic rules and traditions of the game remained an oasis for many Americans in a turbulent world.

<hr>

Endnotes

This essay was originally published in *Baseball History*, vol. I: 3 (Fall, 1986), 4-19. *Baseball History* was published by Meckler Publishing.

1. For historical interpretations and sociological insights into the Cold War period of the late 1940s and early 1950s see John K. Galbraith, *The Affluent Society* (Boston: Houghton-Mifflin, 1970); William H. Whyte, Jr., *The Organization Man* (New York: Simon and Schuster, 1957); David Riesman, Nathan Glazer, and Reuel Denny, *The Lonely Crowd* (New York: Doubleday, 1955); and Geoffrey Hodgson, *America in Our Time* (New York: Doubleday, 1976).

2. For example, on the origins of McCarthyism and the emergence of an anti-communist ideology see David Caute, *The Great Fear: The Anti-Communist Purge Under Truman and Eisenhower* (New York: Simon and Schuster, 1978); Richard M. Freeland, *The Truman Doctrine and the Origins of McCarthyism: Foreign Policy, Domestic Politics, and Internal Security. 1946-1948* (New York: Knopf, 1972); Robert Griffith, *The Politics of Fear: Joseph McCarthy and the Senate* (Lexington: University Press of Kentucky, 1970); Thomas C. Reeves, *The Life and Times of Joe McCarthy* (New York: Stein and Day, 1982); and Athan G. Theoharis, *Seeds of Repression: Harry S. Truman and the Origins of McCarthyism* (Chicago: Quadrangle, 1971).

3. On Hollywood and the Red Scare see Eric Bentley, ed., *Thirty Years of Treason* (New York: Viking, 1971); Peter Biskind, *Seeing is Believing; How Hollywood Taught Us to Stop Worrying and Love the Fifties* (New York: Pantheon Books, 1983); Larry Ceplair and Steven Englund, *The Inquisition in Hollywood: Politics in the Film Community, 1930-1960* (Berkeley: University of California Press, 1979); and Nora Sayre, *Running Time: Films of the Cold War* (New York: Dial Press, 1978).

4. For the role of sport in shaping American society see Robert Boyle, *Sport — Mirror of American Life* (Boston: Little, Brown and Co., 1963); Foster Rhea Dulles, *America Learns to Play* (New York: Appleton Century Co., 1940); Roland Garrett, "The Metaphysics of Baseball," *Philosophy Today,* 20 (Fall, 1976), 209–226; James Michener, *Sport in America* (New York: Random House, 1976); Frederic Logan Paxson, "The Rise

of Sport," as cited in Frederic Logan Paxson, *The Great Demobilization and Other Essays* (Madison: University of Wisconsin Press, 1941); Benjamin G. Rader, *American Sports: From the Age of Folk Games to the Age of Spectators* (Englewood Cliffs, New Jersey: Prentice Hall, 1983); and Leverett T. Smith, Jr., *The American Dream and the National Game* (Bowling Green, Ohio: Bowling Green University Popular Press, 1975).

5. U.S. Congress, *Organized Baseball; Report of the Subcommittee on Study of Monopoly Power of the Committee on the Judiciary, House Report*, No. 2002, 82 Cong., 2 Sess. (1952), 12.

6. Roger Angell, *The Summer Game* (New York: Viking Press, 1972), 30. For other works which evoke the spirit of baseball see Donald Hall, *Fathers Playing Catch with Sons: Essays on Sport (Mostly Baseball)* (San Francisco: North Point Press, 1985); and Thomas Boswell, *Why Time Begins on Opening Day* (New York: Doubleday and Co., 1984).

7. George Grella, "Baseball and the American Dream," *Massachusetts Review,* 16 (Summer, 1975), 550; Jacques Barzun, "America at Play," *Atlantic,* 193 (February, 1954), 40–41; Steven A. Riess, *Touching Base: Professional Baseball and American Culture in the Progressive Era* (Westport, Connecticut: Greenwood Press, 1980), 5; Richard C. Crepeau, *Baseball: America's Diamond Mind, 1919-1941* (Orlando: University Presses of Florida, 1980), 25; Jules Tygiel, *Baseball's Great Experiment; Jackie Robinson and his Legacy* (New York: Oxford University Press, 1983); and Peter Levine, *A. G. Spalding and the Rise of Baseball: The Promise of American Sport* (New York: Oxford University Press, 1985), 146.

8. On baseball and the Cold War see Philip Roth, *The Great American Novel* (New York: Holt, Rinehart, and Winston, 1972); Richard C. Crepeau, "Not the Cincinnati Reds: Anti-Communism in Recent Baseball Literature," *Arete: The Journal of Sport Literature,* I (Fall, 1983), 87–97; and Howard Senzel, *Baseball and the Cold War: Being a Soliloquy on the Necessity of Baseball* (New York: Harcourt Brace Jovanovich, 1977).

9. For baseball in the late 1940s and early 1950s see Peter Golenbock, *Dynasty* (New York: Prentice-Hall, 1975); Peter Golenbock, *Bums: An Oral History of the Brooklyn Dodgers* (New York: Signet, 1973); and David Quentin Voigt, *American Baseball, Vol. III: From Postwar Expansion to the Electronic Age* (University Park: The Pennsylvania State University Press, 1983).

10. For an interesting discussion of major league attendance figures in the post war period see Bill James, *The Bill James Historical Baseball Abstract* (New York: Villard Books, 1986), 193, 209.

11. *Sporting News,* February 4, 1948. For background on Rickey see Arthur Mann, *Branch Rickey: American in Action* (Boston: Houghton-Mifflin Company, 1957); and David Lipman, *Mr. Baseball: The Story of Branch Rickey* (New York: G. P. Putnam's Sons, 1966).

12. *Sporting News,* March 3, 1948. On the role of the *Sporting News* in baseball see *First Hundred Years, 1886-1986* (St. Louis: Sporting News, 1986).

13. *Sporting News,* November 24, 1948.

14. *Ibid.,* February 2, 1949.

15. Ibid., July 27, 1949. For background information on Robinson see Jules Tygiel, *Baseball's Great Experiment: Jackie Robinson and his Legacy;* and Jackie Robinson, *I Never Had It Made: An Autobiography* (New York: G. P. Putnam's Sons, 1972).

16. *Sporting News,* April 20, 1949. On the history of baseball diplomacy see Richard Crepeau, "Pearl Harbor: A Failure of Baseball?," *Journal of Popular Culture,* 15 (Spring, 1982), 67–74; and Donald Roden, "Baseball and the Quest for National Dignity in Meiji Japan," *American Historical Review,* 85 (June, 1980), 511–534.

17. *Sporting News*, November 16, 1949.

18. *Ibid.*, March 30, 1949.

19. *Ibid.*, February 23, 1949. On the importance of naming names before Congressional committees see Victor Navasky, *Naming Names* (New York: Viking Press, 1980).

20. *Sporting News*, November 2, 1949.

21. *Ibid.*, September 6, 1950. On baseball during World War II see Richard Goldstein, *Spartan Seasons: How Baseball Survived the Second World War* (New York: Macmillan Co., 1980); William B. Mead, *Even the Browns: The Zany, True Story of Baseball in the Early Forties* (Chicago: Contemporary Books, 1978); and Ron Briley, "Where Have You Gone William Bendix? Baseball as a Symbol of American Values in World War II," *Studies in Popular Culture*, 8 (1985), 18–32.

22. *Sporting News*, September 3, 1950.

23. *Ibid.*, December 4, July 26, August 9, 1950. On the Korean War see Joseph C. Goulden, *Korea: The Untold Story of the War* (New York: Times Books, 1982); and Donald Knox, *The Korean War — Pusan to Chosin: An Oral History* (New York: Harcourt Brace Jovanovich, 1985). For additional background on DiMaggio see Maury Allen, *Where Have You Gone, Joe DiMaggio?: The Story of America's Last Hero* (New York: Signet Books, 1975).

24. *Sporting News*, December 27, 1950.

25. On the MacArthur boomlet for Commissioner see *Sporting News*, April 25, May 2, May 9, May 23, July 25, and August 22, 1951. On Chandler's difficulties see Arthur Mann, *Baseball Confidential: Secret History of the War Among Chandler, Durocher, MacPhail and Rickey* (New York: McKay, 1951). For MacArthur's interest in sport see William Manchester, *American Caesar: Douglas MacArthur, 1880-1964* (Boston: Little Brown and Co., 1978).

26. *Sporting News*, May 23, 1951.

27. *Ibid.*, September 26, 1951. For the development of post war America's organizational society see John Brooks, *The Great Leap: The Past Twenty-five Years in America* (New York: Harper and Row, 1968).

28. *Sporting News*, August 8, 1951. For more critical accounts of the reserve clause see Curt Flood, *The Way It Is* (New York: Trident Press, 1970); Douglass C. North and Roger Leroy Miller, *Abortion, Baseball, and Weed: Economic Issues of Our Times* (New York: Harper and Row, 1971); and Lee Lowenfish and Tony Lupien, *The Imperfect Diamond: The Story of Baseball's Reserve System and the Men Who Fought to Change It* (New York: Stein and Day, 1980).

29. *Sporting News*, December 12, 1951. For more information on Frick see Ford C. Frick, *Games, Asterisks, and People: Memoirs of a Lucky Fan* (New York: Crown, 1973).

30. Williams had already served in World War II, and his career statistics would be diminished by his two service hitches. For additional information on Williams see Lawrence Bardassaro, "Ted Williams: The Reluctant Hero," *Journal of American Culture*, 4 (Fall, 1981), 66–74; and Ted Williams and John Underwood, *My Turn at Bat: The Story of My Life* (New York: Simon and Schuster, 1968).

31. *Sporting News*, January 9, 1952.

32. U. S. Congress, *Organized Baseball; Report of the Subcommittee on Study of Monopoly Power of the Committee on the Judiciary, House Report*, No. 2002, 82 Cong., 2 Sess. (1952).

33. *Sporting News*, September 24, 1952.

34. *Ibid.*, November 19, 1952.

35. *Ibid.*, December 10, 1952. For a more detailed discussion of Robinson's allegations see Tygiel, *Baseball's Great Experiment,* 295–298.

36. Voigt, *Baseball in America, Vol. Ill: From Postwar Expansion to the Electronic Age,* 17. For additional information on Veeck see William Veeck, Jr., *Veeck-as in Wreck* (New York: Bantam, 1963).

37. *Sporting News,* November 18 and November 25, 1953.

38. *Ibid.*, April 21, April 28, and September 1, 1954.

39. *Ibid.*, May 6 and September 30, 1953.

5

Do Not Go Gently into That Good Night: Race, the Baseball Establishment, and the Retirements of Bob Feller and Jackie Robinson

On July 22, 1969, Organized Baseball officially celebrated its centennial with the All-Star Game in Washington D.C. and a White House reception hosted by President Richard Nixon. However, the controversial Nixon was not the focal point of political fireworks that day, as prior to the White House reception, Hall of Fame players Bob Feller and Jackie Robinson squared off at a press conference in the Sheraton Park Hotel.

Irritated by African-American charges of racism in baseball and American society, the conservative Feller lashed out at Robinson for his criticism of baseball hiring practices. The former Cleveland pitcher asserted, "Robinson has always been bush. He's always been a professional agitator more than anything else. He's just ticked off because baseball never rolled out the red carpet when he quit playing and offered him a soft front office job." Feller argued that there had been no discrimination in the sport since Robinson integrated the game, and, furthermore, baseball contributed more to minority groups than almost any other institution in the country. Feller ended his diatribe by concluding, "Ability alone is what should count in the front office, too. I think there will be a Negro with that ability." Obviously, Feller did not believe that African-Americans in 1969 were yet ready for the responsibilities of management.

An angry Robinson retorted that Feller had grown little since 1947, Robinson's rookie season, continuing to bury "his head in the sand." Perhaps expressing some resentment that he was employed as a fast food chain executive rather than in baseball management following his playing days, Robinson proclaimed, "My big thing is I don't believe that the black players are getting an equal opportunity with the whites after their playing days are through."[1]

This 1969 exchange was not the first time that the two stars had crossed swords. In 1946, Feller, who was considered somewhat of an expert on the Negro Leagues due to his postseason barnstorming tours against black competition, told reporters that he could see no future for Jackie Robinson in the major leagues. The Cleveland pitching star maintained that Robinson had "football shoulders and couldn't hit an inside pitch to save his neck. If he were a white man, I doubt they would consider him big league material."[2] While Robinson took exception to these remarks and interpreted them as being racially biased, Feller insisted that he bore no racial animosity toward the former UCLA football player. He was simply basing his opinion on professional observations. According to his memoirs, Feller easily retired Robinson the six times he faced him during a 1946 West Coast barnstorming tour, striking him out three times on ten pitches in San Diego. Feller stood by his assertion that Robinson could not hit the high fast ball.[3] Whether Feller's comments were professionally based or tinged with racial superiority, there was certainly hard feelings between the two players, and, according to Robinson biographer David Falkner, Feller had initially asked not to share the same platform during their 1962 inauguration into the Baseball Hall of Fame.[4]

Although their Cooperstown plaques are placed side by side, suggesting that personal antagonism did not interfere with baseball integration, the reactions of the baseball establishment and press to the retirements of Robinson and Feller provide evidence that considerable racism remained in the sport and American society, probably continuing to fuel Robinson's resentment toward Feller.

As far as baseball's self-proclaimed Bible, the *Sporting News,* was concerned, the sport, a decade after the breaking of baseball's color barrier, was a model for racial integration and toleration. In an editorial commentary, the paper reminded readers, "The Negro in Organized Ball is so completely taken-for-granted these days that it must be difficult for younger fans to recall the time little more than a decade ago, when both majors and minors raised an invisible but effective barrier on the color line."[5] Yet, the story of the Robinson and Feller retirements casts a very different light on the baseball establishment's racial enlightenment. Following his announcement that he was leaving the playing field, Feller was awarded a job as a spokesman for the Motorola Corporation and toured the country as a good will ambassador for baseball. On the other hand, Robinson's retirement was controversial with allegations that he had betrayed his baseball employers by first breaking his decision in a *Look* magazine exclusive. Robinson accepted a position as personnel director for the Chock Full o'Nuts Company, and reporters questioned whether Robinson possessed the proper qualifications for personnel supervision, although no one seemed to question Feller's capabilities to speak for Motorola. In addition, Robinson commenced on a speaking tour for the NAACP which was not covered by the baseball press with the reverential tones reserved for Feller's engagements. The differing treatment given Feller's and Robinson's departures from the game indicates the amount of institutional racism remaining within the baseball establishment and exposes as a sham the *Sporting News* editorial that baseball had solved its racial problems. After ten years baseball still did not understand Robinson, as the former Dodger star challenged racism in the nation and its self-proclaimed pastime.

The Feller retirement story broke first, but was not unexpected. During the 1956 baseball campaign, the former ace of the Cleveland staff appeared in only nineteen games, winning none and losing four, striking out only eighteen, and compiling an earned run average of almost five runs per game.[6] Feller reportedly wanted to come back for one more season and conclude his career on a more positive note. Cleveland management made it clear that they would be willing to give him his release so that he could hook up with another club, but the right-hander was not in the Indians' plans for 1957.[7]

Accordingly, at a December 28, 1956 luncheon at Municipal Stadium in Cleveland, Feller announced his departure from the game he loved. The proud athlete maintained that he could still pitch, but he did not wish to leave his Cleveland home. Feller turned down the offer of an administrative position with the Indians, stating, "I expect to devote all my energies to the insurance business, to civic activities, and to my job as president of the Baseball Players Association."[8] Although he was sometimes a thorn in the side of management, Feller was given permission by the owners to continue his service as president of the Players Association through the completion of a new pension plan, which Feller the insurance executive may have understood better than many baseball owners.

Reaction to the retirement announcement poured in from across the country, praising the Cleveland star's accomplishments on and off the playing field. Arthur Daley of the *New York Times* wrote a piece on Feller's career, while storm clouds were beginning to break over the end of Robinson's playing days. The key to Feller's success, according to Daley, was that the Cleveland hurler never became "swell-headed." During the peak of his career, Feller lost three years to the Navy and World War II, denying him an opportunity to garner 300 wins in his twenty-year major league tenure. Yet, Daley observed that Rapid Robert Feller "never uttered a complaint nor let himself grow wistful at the might-have-been."[9]

The *Sporting News* treated the Feller retirement story in a similar fashion. After noting his three no-hitters and twelve one-hitters, the Bible of Baseball extolled Feller's achievements off the field of play, calling him "one of the outstanding individuals of our time." The paper concluded, "As the years passed, it became evident that here was no run-of-the-mill citizen of baseball, content to win as many games as possible and earn as much as he could. Feller became a smart businessman, but he also interested himself in the welfare of others— including his colleagues on the diamond."[10]

In fact, *Newsweek* carried this theme so far as to argue, "In a business-minded age, he was probably the best businessman that baseball's player ranks ever produced." The *Newsweek* profile described Feller as the quintessential corporate organizational man of the 1950s. With outside business investments in General Mills, Gillette, Wilson, and others, he was incorporated into Ro-Fel, Inc. According to *Newsweek,* "If you wanted a ball game pitched, some insurance sold, a newspaper column written, a radio or banquet speech made, or even a new luxury gimmick thought up for a car, Feller was your man."[11] And like the great philanthropists of the late nineteenth century, he was perceived as a man who worked for the benefit of his community, giving speeches for civic clubs, churches, and schools. His climb from the corn fields of Iowa to the pinnacle of athletic and financial success epitomized the American dream of social mobility contained in the stories of Horatio Alger. Thus, Feller seemed well suited to assume the mantle of an ambassador for baseball and corporate spokesman for the radio and television firm, Motorola.

Following negotiation of a new pension plan, which Feller lauded as making baseball more attractive to the youngsters of America, he was off on a baseball promotional tour sponsored by Motorola. Feller's speaking engagements enjoyed detailed coverage by the *Sporting News,* who saw no conflict of interest between corporate sponsorship and the free publicity provided by the paper's features on Feller, Motorola, and baseball. In fact, the paper made its editorial position quite clear, writing, "His sponsorship is commercial, but far from considering this a reason to withhold publicity, the *Sporting News* salutes the Motorola people for their recognition of Feller as an ideal ambassador and for their confidence in baseball as a medium of appeal to their prospective customers."[12]

As Motorola's Youth Baseball Counselor, Feller visited fifty-four cities during the summer of 1957. A typical Feller schedule, such as an August visit to Bangor, Maine, called for a morning arrival and meeting with city officials. After changing into his uniform, Feller was taken via motorcade to the local ballpark, where enthusiastic youngsters were treated to a baseball clinic and Feller lecture. Feller's talks usually consisted of baseball adaptations of Ben Franklin's *Poor Richard's Almanack* emphasizing the value of hard work. A favorite Feller saying was, "It takes a lot of practice to be a good bunter."[13]

Also included on Feller's itinerary was a visit to Texas League Park in Shreveport, Louisiana. In 1956, the Louisiana state legislature passed a law barring inter-racial athletic contests in the state. Texas League clubs complied with the law by withholding black players in Shreveport. Evidently, Feller and Motorola had no problems with legitimizing segregation by scheduling Shreveport on the tour. Feller told approximately a thousand youngsters in Shreveport that the keys to baseball success were: listening to your coaches, finding the right playing position, practicing, and displaying enthusiasm. Feller failed to acknowledge that these qualities still did not allow a black youngster in Louisiana to compete with white players. [14]

While Organized Baseball did not protest Feller's Shreveport appearance, his testimony before the House Subcommittee on Monopolies, investigating baseball's financial and legal structure, did evoke controversy. After suggesting that the owners were arrogant and that the players should have a role in selecting the Commissioner, Feller's promotional appearance at the Brooklyn Dodgers-owned Los Angeles Wrigley Field was canceled. Nonetheless, these disputes with management did little to change Feller's image as an ambassador for the game. The *Sporting News* concluded that with his promotional work and service as player representative, Feller placed baseball "in a position to compete with industry for the service of young people."[15] The paper encouraged other players to follow in the path of Feller and become involved in the work of promoting baseball. His spectacular pitching career, business acumen, and enthusiasm for the game continued to make Bob Feller a promotional fixture in minor and major league baseball parks for the next forty years. However, Jackie Robinson's retirement would not go so smoothly, raising questions about racial attitudes within the baseball establishment.

By the conclusion of the 1956 season, in which the New York Yankees edged Brooklyn for the World Series championship, it was apparent that the illustrious career of Jackie Robinson was winding down. Battling injuries and health problems, Robinson's playing time in 1956 was limited to 117 games. However, his games played, batting average, home runs, and runs batted in were all improvement over his 1955 marks.[16] Thus, many in baseball were shocked to learn on the morning of December 13, 1956 that Brooklyn had traded Robinson to their fierce National League rivals, the New York Giants, for cash and journeyman pitcher, Dick Littlefield. In an official statement, Robinson stated that he was disappointed and having to comfort his crying son, Jackie, Jr. However, trades were part of baseball, and he spoke of his relationship with the Brooklyn club in diplomatic terms, stating, "There are no hard feelings. The Brooklyn club had to protect its own best interests. I thought I helped Brooklyn last year and didn't figure to be traded." Robinson concluded that he would wait until January 10, 1957 to inform Giants owner Horace Stoneham whether he would retire or play for the Giants.[17]

Dodger fans were outraged. The *New York Times* quoted one Brooklyn partisan as proclaiming, "I'm shocked to the core. This is like selling the Brooklyn-Battery Tunnel. Jackie Robinson is a synonym for the Dodgers. They can't do this to us." (Of course, this fan did not realize the Robinson trade was only the beginning of Dodger management's betrayal of Brooklyn.) Despite outrage among the Dodger faithful and Robinson's hint that he might retire, the baseball establishment's assumption was that business would go on as usual. Giants owner Stoneham did not believe Robinson would retire. Instead, Robinson, whom Stoneham labeled the "greatest competitor I've ever seen in baseball," would play first base for the Giants in 1957. Referring to Jackie Robinson Jr.'s tearful reaction to the trade, the *Sporting News* insisted, "Jackie, Sr., being an adult, recognizes the expediency that exists in this world with which he must cope and has displayed no tear-stained-face to the public. He is now a Giant and will play ball for the Giants with the same fiercely competitive spirit he displayed for so long as a Dodger. That is the only way Robinson knows how to play."[18] However, when Robinson engaged in a bit of his own expediency regarding the announcement of his retirement, the *Sporting News* and baseball establishment yelled foul.

While Brooklyn fans were dismayed with the trade, Robinson was less surprised and was already making plans for his departure from the game. Robinson did not get along well with Dodgers manager Walter Alston, and his relationship with the Dodgers front office deteriorated when Walter O'Malley maneuvered to force Branch Rickey out of Brooklyn. From a peak figure of $39,000, Robinson's salary suffered slight reductions for each of his last three seasons in Brooklyn. In his memoirs, Robinson commented unfavorably on the racial views of O'Malley, alleging that the Dodger President perceived him as an "uppity Nigger."[19]

Accordingly, on December 10, 1956, Robinson met with William Black, President of Chock Full o'Nuts, a fast-food restaurant chain in the New York City area. Black, whose employees were predominantly African-American, offered Robinson a position as Vice-President in charge of personnel at an annual salary of fifty-thousand dollars. That evening Robinson attempted to reach Dodger General Manager "Buzzy" Bavasi and inform him of his intentions. However, Bavasi, who was negotiating with the Giants, was unavailable. The next day, Robinson signed a contract with Black. That same evening, Robinson was told that he had been traded to the Giants. He did not advise Dodger officials that he had decided to retire from baseball and accept a position with Chock Full o'Nuts. The reason for Robinson's apparent duplicity was an exclusive contract for fifty thousand dollars which he had signed with *Look* magazine.[20] The contract stipulated that Robinson's retirement would first be announced in a magazine exclusive.

Yet, the story broke early before the magazine hit the newsstands. A few *Look* subscribers received advance copies, and *Look* executives scrambled to call a press conference for Robinson. When asked why he had chosen to work through a magazine deal and not keep his employer informed of his intentions, Robinson replied, "I had given my best to Brooklyn for eleven years and my debt to baseball has been paid." Buzzy Bavasi did not agree, insisting that Robinson owed an obligation to the Dodgers as well as the sportswriters of New York. Bavasi told reporters, "And this is the way he repays the newspapermen for what they've done for him. He tells you one thing and then writes another for money. You fellows will find out that you've been blowing the horn for the wrong guy." An angry Robinson retorted, "After what Bavasi said, I wouldn't play ball again for a million dollars."[21]

The New York press immediately weighed into the Robinson-Bavasi debate. Red Smith of the *New York Herald Tribune* rebuked Robinson for his lack of loyalty to the Dodgers, asserting, "But for the Dodgers, the Jackie Robinson of this last decade would not have existed. The fact that he gave them full value on the field and the fact that after eleven years they sold his contract without consulting him, these do not alter the fact that everything he has he owes to the club. His debt to the Dodgers had precedence over any agreement to sell a story to *Look,* and with his mind already made up at the time of the trade he was honor bound to speak up." Dick Young of the *New York News,* who often chastised Robinson, maintained that the Brooklyn great did not owe anything to reporters or the Dodgers. Young was more upset that Robinson, in his *Look* press conference of January 6, had criticized baseball for lacking sentiment. Rallying to the defense of the national pastime, Young argued, "So Robinson should have quit, which certainly is his privilege, without smearing the game that has earned him $500,000 in ten years. Baseball has as much sentiment as any business he can name, much more than the cream cheese sandwich business, for one." On the other hand, Joe Williams of the *New York World Telegram* insisted that Robinson would be a "dope" to not take *Look's* lucrative offer. Seeking to take a more neutral position, the *Sporting News* editorialized that while Robinson had every right to sell his story, the Bible of Baseball preferred the "outstanding example" of dignified retirement established by Bob Feller.[22]

In the much maligned *Look* article, Robinson simply maintained that his decision to leave the game was based on financial security for his family. He concluded the article by noting, "I know I'll miss the excitement of baseball, but I 'm looking forward to new kinds of satisfaction. I'll be able to spend more time with my family, My kids and I will get to know each other better.... They won't have to look for me on TV."[23] However, shortly after his retirement, Robinson agreed to postpone assuming his duties with Chock Full o'Nuts, while he commenced on a speaking and fund-raising tour on behalf of the NAACP. Perhaps as biographer David Falkner suggests, Robinson's retirement was also related to the athlete's decision to make a larger commitment and contribution to the burgeoning civil rights movement.

On December 8, 1956, two days before he met with William Black, Robinson received the prestigious Spingarn Medal, awarded annually "for the highest achievement of an American Negro." Ed Sullivan, columnist and television celebrity, presented the gold medal at a New York dinner sponsored by the NAACP. Among the previous recipients present were Ralph Bunche, W. E. B. DuBois, and Thurgood Marshall. The award citation placed Robinson's contributions in historical perspective, proclaiming, "The entire nation is indebted to him for his pioneer role in breaking the color line in Organized Baseball. Through sheer ability and exceptional competitive zeal, he won popular acclaim of sports lovers of all races and demonstrated that there were no fore-ordained racial restrictions upon the ability to play the National Game. He opened the doors of the major leagues for Negro stars whose skill, zest, and stamina have entered the national sport."[24]

Perceived as a symbol of opportunity and struggle for African-Americans, Robinson could hardly refuse when NAACP Executive Secretary Roy Wilkins asked Robinson to chair the organization's 1957 Freedom Fund drive. While a novice as a public speaker, under the tutelage of veteran NAACP organizer Franklin Williams, Robinson became a successful orator and fund raiser, proudly pointing out that the 1957 tour was able to garner a million dollars for the NAACP coffers. Echoing the sentiments of Martin Luther King, Jr., Robinson argued that African-Americans were out of patience and could no longer wait for equal rights. He told a Chicago audience, "We have waited almost one hundred years for these rights. In my view, now is the time for Negroes to ask for all of the rights which are theirs."[25]

It is worth noting the courage which Robinson displayed in embracing the cause of the NAACP. In the late 1950s, opponents of racial integration attempted to brand the civil rights organization as a subversive tool of the Communist Party and Soviet Union. For example, appearing before the Louisiana Joint Legislative Committee on Segregation, African-American Manning Johnson, who had been a minor Communist Party official in New York, attacked Martin Luther King, Jr., and the NAACP. The vitriolic Johnson described King as a "dastardly misleader who is taking his race down the road of violence, bloodshed, revolution, and possible communism in the South." In concluding his testimony, Johnson denounced the NAACP as a "communist vehicle designed to initiate the overthrow of the government."[26]

However, sport coverage of the Robinson speaking tour failed to acknowledge his courage and determination. Instead, publications such as the *Sporting News* focused upon baseball questions Robinson fielded during press conferences. The Robinson image projected by the *Sporting News* was not the crusader for racial equality, but rather a hot-headed commentator who antagonized fellow players and baseball executives. For example, at a speaking engagement in Wauhegan, Illinois, Robinson stated that too much night life cost the Milwaukee Braves the 1956 National League pennant. Braves players replied to the criticism by labeling Robinson a "rumor monger." Braves shortstop Johnny Logan maintained that Robinson was "just popping off to keep his name in the headlines."[27] As if a man whose mission to raise a million dollars for an institution under attack needed the publicity of alleged night life in Milwaukee.

On a more serious note, Robinson was quoted as describing former teammate Roy Campanella as "washed up." An angry Campanella retorted that he was tired of Robinson "popping off." The burly catcher criticized Robinson for demonstrating a negative attitude toward baseball, asserting, "Instead of being grateful to baseball, he's criticizing it. Everything he has he owes to baseball. That beautiful house of his, and this new job of his, too. Does he think those people would have had anything to do with him if he had never played baseball."[28] The two men initially quarreled over Campanella's failure to join Robinson in challenging segregated housing for the black Brooklyn ball players. The antagonism between Campanella and Robinson reflected a debate within the African-American community about the necessity of pushing for racial integration going back to the days of Booker T. Washington and W. E. B. DuBois.

But Campanella's complaints failed to silence Robinson who observed that it was "strange" that no African-American players could make the major league rosters of Detroit, Philadelphia, and Boston. While speaking in Detroit, the former Brooklyn star further acknowledged that he was puzzled by the fact that "for some reason there are no Negro players on the fields of Detroit. Detroit is a great sports town. But you can't help but wonder about the absence of Negro players in both football and baseball."[29]

While Robinson insisted that he was speaking honestly, seeking a better nation for all Americans, former playing field opponents of Robinson continued to label the Dodger great a trouble-maker. Giants pitcher Sal Maglie, no stranger to baseball rhubarbs, was quoted as saying Robinson was unpopular with the players due to self-promotion. Maglie believed Robinson, who had expressed interest in managing, would never be given the reins of a major league club. Maglie concluded, "I don't think any ball club would take a chance on Jackie, because you just couldn't get anybody to play for him after the way he's been rapping other players."[30]

Despite business success, political involvement, and a respected role in the civil rights movement, one of Robinson's greatest disappointments was that he was never allowed to try his hand at piloting a major league franchise. Writing in 1972, Robinson observed, "I felt that any chance I might have had of moving up to an administrative job with the Dodgers or any other team was mighty slim. Had I been easy going, willing to be meek and humble, I might have had a chance. But this fact has not changed much even today. There are many capable black athletes in the game who could contribute greatly as managers or in other positions of responsibility, but it just isn't happening."[31] In fact, Robinson never lived to see his dream of an African-American manager, for Frank Robinson was not named to manage the Cleveland Indians until 1975, three years after the death of the pioneering Dodger great.

Baseball's reluctance to provide opportunities for black managerial experience on the playing field and executive suite demonstrated that the sport had serious problems with institutional racism long after the playing career of Jackie Robinson had supposedly erased racial barriers in the sport. In addition, an examination of the retirement stories of Bob Feller and Jackie Robinson suggests a lack of racial understanding if not overt racism. Despite some criticism of management, Bob Feller was welcomed into the baseball establishment and corporate America. Feller was extolled as the embodiment the American success epic: a farm boy who rose from the cornfields of Iowa to athletic and corporate success. Robinson was also a good fit for the Horatio Alger imagery so dear to the American mythology of success and social mobility. Through hard work and a fierce competitive spirit Robinson surmounted racial barriers to become one of the nation's outstanding athletes and role models. And although Chock Full o'Nuts lacked the executive pedigree of the Motorola Corporation, Robinson also found success within the economic and business spheres. Yet, he was never embraced by the baseball establishment. Feller became an ambassador for baseball, citing clichés about the value of hard work, while failing to challenge racial segregation in a city such as Shreveport. Robinson, on the other hand, left the playing field to champion the standard of racial equality. Nevertheless, the baseball press viewed him as a troublemaker when he drew attention to continuing racial segregation in cities such as Philadelphia, Boston, and Detroit. Although only two weeks separated the officially-announced retirements of Robinson and Feller, the reaction of the baseball world to their departures reveals much about the great racial divide within American society.

Endnotes

This essay originally appeared in Joseph Dorinson and Joram Warmund, eds., *Jackie Robinson: Race, Sports, and the American Dream* (New York: M. E. Sharpe, 1998), 193-204.

1. For the Feller and Robinson confrontation during the centennial ceremonies, see *Sporting News,* August 9, 1969.
2. For Feller's 1946 comments on Robinson, see Jules Tygiel, *Baseball's Great Experiment: Jackie Robinson and His Legacy* (New York: Random House, 1983), 76; and Jackie Robinson, *I Never Had It Made* (New York: G. P. Putnam's Sons, 1972), 48.
3. Bob Feller with Bill Gilbert, *Now Pitching: Bob Feller* (New York: Harper-Perennial, 1990), 140–141.
4. David Falkner, *Great Time Coming: The Life of Jackie Robinson from Baseball to Birmingham* (New York: Simon & Schuster, 1995), 294.
5. *Sporting News,* May 22, 1957.
6. For statistics see John Thorn and Pete Palmer, eds., *Total Baseball: The Ultimate Encyclopedia of Baseball* (New York: HarperPerennial, 1993) 1,491.
7. For a management perspective on the Feller retirement see Ira Berkow, ed., *Hank Greenberg: The Story of My Life* (New York: Times Books, 1989), 221–222. For Feller's thoughts on retirement see Bob Feller, "I'll Never Quit Baseball," *Look,* 20(March 20, 1956), 53–54.

8. *Sporting News,* January 2, 1957; and *New York Times,* December 29, 1956.

9. *New York Times,* January 7, 1957.

10. *Sporting News,* January 9, 1957.

11. "Ro-Fel, inc.," *Newsweek,* 49 (January 7, 1957), 44.

12. *Sporting News,* February 13 and May 15, 1957.

13. *Ibid.,* August 14, 1957.

14. *Ibid.,* May 1, 1957.

15. *Ibid.* July 3 and 17, 1957; November 6, 1957.

16. Thorn and Palmer, eds., *Total Baseball,* 1, 182.

17. *Sporting News,* December 19, 1956; *New York Times,* December 14, 1956; and "If You Can't Beat Him," *Time,* 68 (December 24, 1956), 42.

18. *New York Times,* December 14, 1956; *Sporting News,* December 19 and 26, 1956; and "After Ten Years," *Newsweek,* 48 (December 24, 1956), p. 49.

19. For Robinson's perspective of O'Malley see Robinson, *I Never Had it Made,* 100–115.

20. For Robinson's negotiations with William Black see Falkner, *Great Time Coming,* 249–251; and Robinson, *I Never Had It Made,* 130–134.

21. *Sporting News,* January 16, 1957; and *New York Times,* January 7, 1957.

22. *Sporting News,* January 16, 1957.

23. Jackie Robinson, "Why I'm Quitting Baseball," *Look,* 21 (January 22, 1957), 99–102.

24. *New York Times.,* December 9, 1956; and *Sporting News,* December 19, 1956.

25. For Robinson's Freedom Foundation tour see Robinson, *I Never Had It Made,* 137–146; and Falkner, *A Great Time Coming,* 253–262.

26. For the public hearings of the Louisiana Joint Legislative Committee on Segregation see *Shreveport Times,* March 7, 8, 9, and 10, 1957. For background information of Manning Johnson see Harvey Klehr, *The Heyday of American Communism* (New York: Basic Books, 1984), 400–401 and 471–472.

27. *Sporting News,* January 23, 1957.

28. *Ibid.,* February 6, 1957. For the Robinson-Campanella relationship see Robinson, *I Never Had It Made,* 110–111. For additional background information on Campanella see "Big Man From Nicetown: Roy Campanella," *Time,* 66 (August 8, 1955), 50–55; and Roy Campanella, *It's Good To Be Alive* (Boston: Little, Brown, 1959).

29. *Sporting News,* February 27 and 6, 1957.

30. *Ibid.,* February 6, 1957. For the temperamental Maglie see Robert W. Creamer, "An Angel of Darkness Named Sal the Barber," *Sports Illustrated,* 2 (June 6, 1955), 43–44; and Millan J. Shapiro, *The Sal Maglie Story* (New York: Julian Messner, 1957).

31. Robinson, *I Never Had It Made,* 130.

6

The Limits of Baseball Integration: Louisiana, the Texas League, and Shreveport Sports, 1956–1957

In September, 1956, the *Sporting News,* speaking on behalf of Organized Baseball, printed a self-congratulatory editorial lauding the sport's tenth year of racial integration. The paper observed that with over forty "Negro" players on major league rosters, "their place in the game is secure." On a rather smug note, the *Sporting News* stated that while challenges to racial segregation in the schools were rocking the nation, baseball offered a model for peaceful reconciliation of racial strife. The editorial concluded, "The National Game does not presume to advise other segments of the population, or other sports, on how to handle this complicated and emotional problem. It merely points with satisfaction to its own record of gradual, voluntary, and peaceful advance toward the complete fulfillment of the code that a player should not be judged on the basis of creed, connections or color, but on the basis of ability alone."[1] Organized Baseball's commitment to this philosophy of democratic opportunity and racial toleration would be tested, and found wanting, by events taking place in the state of Louisiana.

In July, 1956, the Louisiana state legislature approved House Bill 1412, which, among other measures to ensure continued racial segregation in the state, prohibited blacks and whites from participating in interracial sporting events anywhere in the state. Despite protests from the NAACP and some concerns expressed by the business community regarding the economic consequences of this legislation, Governor Earl Long, explaining that he was "just a poor little old man going along with the majority," signed the legislation, which was to go into effect on October 15, 1956. Clarence Lewis, field secretary of the NAACP, pointed out that while Hitler was censured for his racial prejudice against black athletes, such as Jesse Owens in the 1936 Olympics, if the 1956 Olympics were to be held in Louisiana, "colored athletes could not even compete." *Newsweek* predicted that national condemnation of the athletic segregation legislation would result in the shuffling of college football and basketball schedules, while in baseball the Shreveport Sports would be expelled from the Texas League due to the number of black players in the league.[2]

While the forecast of *Newsweek* proved accurate in regard to intercollegiate basketball and football, professional baseball was not as adamant in its opposition to segregation. Major league exhibition games scheduled for Louisiana in the spring of 1957 were canceled, but the segregationist Shreveport Sports baseball club retained its good standing in the integrated Texas League. The segregation issue was placed in the hands of Texas League President Dick Butler, who said he would seek a compromise solution, assuring all concerned that there would be no legal challenge by Organized Baseball to the Louisiana interracial sports ban. Finding a middle ground would not be easy. Art Routzong, general manager of the Houston Buffaloes, announced that his team would play the best players possible, regardless of race. However, he did put forth the idea that Houston might be willing to withdraw black players, if Shreveport would reciprocate by benching equivalent starting players. Crusty Bonneau Peters, long time President of the Shreveport franchise (an independent club with no major league working agreement), sounding a bit like Arkansas Governor Orville Faubus, shunned compromise, asserting, "If these clubs want to play at Shreveport, they'll just have to play under the laws of Louisiana. I'm not going to do anything about it."[3]

Engaging in delicate diplomacy, League President Butler orchestrated an agreement which essentially catered to the stubborn Peters. Clubs with black players on the roster would be allowed an extra man above the league-imposed player limit of eighteen. Franchises such as Houston and Dallas, who each had five black roster players, were to be placed at a considerable competitive disadvantage when they journeyed to Shreveport. This agreement allowed *Sporting News* correspondent Jack Gallagher to portray the January 20, 1957 midwinter meeting of Texas League management as conciliatory. According to Gallagher's report, "Only minor business occupied the directors, thus portraying the Texas League as one circuit without problems—a rarity in these times."[4]

This report may suggest why neither Baseball Commissioner Ford Frick nor the *Sporting News* elected to speak publicly on the Shreveport issue. In the mid 1950s, minor league baseball was in serious financial difficulty. In 1949, minor league attendance peaked at nearly 42,000,000 fans, with 464 teams represented in 59 leagues. But turnstile counts dipped by more than 7,000,000 in 1950, followed by another 7,000,000 the next season. Blamed upon television, air conditioning, increased leisure choices in the suburbs, and the growing availability of major league broadcasts, attendance problems plagued minor league baseball throughout the 1950s. By the end of the decade minor league fan support tumbled to just a little over 12,000,000 in only 21 leagues.[5] It was an inopportune time to antagonize traditional supporters of baseball in the state of Louisiana. Accordingly, Organized Baseball searched for innovative ways that the major league game might support and preserve its life line of the minor leagues. At its annual meeting in 1956 the National Association, Organized Baseball's governing body for the minor leagues, voted to commend the major leagues for the establishment of a one-half million dollar stabilization fund. The *Sporting News* editorialized that the sport must close ranks and "operate as one big family, each member sensitive to the needs of all the others." [6] Issues of racial integration in Louisiana would have to take a seat in the back of baseball's bus, while the sport concentrated upon securing its financial foundation,

The Texas League and baseball establishment were also reluctant to take on the hostile political environment in Louisiana. Vehement opposition to racial integration was evident on the eve of the 1957 baseball season with the public hearings of the Louisiana Joint Legislative Committee on Segregation. Committee Chair Willie Rainach announced that the hearings would focus upon a "planned conspiracy" to foster racial unrest in Louisiana and throughout the South. Among the witnesses called by the committee were Assistant New Orleans Police Superintendent Guy Bannister, a twenty-year veteran of the FBI (in Oliver Stone's film *JFK.,* actor Ed Asner portrayed Bannister as a conspiratorial intelligence agent involved in the murder of President John Kennedy), and former Communist Party officials Joseph Kornfedder and Manning Johnson. The hearings highlighted the testimony of the African-American Johnson, who had been a minor party operative in New York, for his vitriolic attack upon Martin Luther King and the NAACP. Johnson described King as a "dastardly misleader who is taking his race down the road of violence, bloodshed, revolution, and possible communism in the South." In concluding his testimony, Johnson denounced the NAACP as a "Communist vehicle designed to initiate the overthrow of the government."[7]

In response to the accusations of the Committee on Segregation, Reverend T. J. Jemison, pastor of the Baton Rouge Mount Zion Baptist Church and leader of a state voter registration drive, acknowledged that communism constituted a threat to the United States, but reminded Louisiana residents of the "grave threat which fascism presents to our nation and the world through the techniques of smear, guilt by association and accusation which was the method employed in the recent hearings of the Joint Legislative Committee on Segregation."[8]

It was in this racially-charged atmosphere that the Shreveport Sports prepared to open the 1957 Texas League season. League President Butler recognized that a number of clubs were dissatisfied with the arrangement whereby one or more of its regulars might be forced from the playing field during road trips to Shreveport. A defensive Butler complained to reporters, lamenting, "If you can come up with a better solution, I'd be happy to have it."[9] Clearly, pulling the club from Shreveport as a statement in favor of integration was unacceptable to Butler and baseball officials. With minor league baseball apparently on its deathbed, the baseball establishment tried to keep the patient alive in Shreveport despite the moral ambiguities and compromises involved in working around the Louisiana segregation statutes.

But was the Shreveport franchise worth this effort? The Sports recorded a first place finish in 1954, before losing in the first round of the Texas League playoffs. In 1955, Shreveport improved its record by capturing its first Texas League championship. The 1956 campaign witnessed the home run exploits of Ken Guettler who slammed sixty-two balls over the walls of Texas League parks, yet paid admissions to Texas League Park in Shreveport continued to decline, falling from 204,231 in 1952 to 40,919 in 1956.[10]

Accordingly, the focus of Shreveport ownership was not on challenging racial apartheid, but rather on getting fans (and the assumption here seems to be white fans) out to the ballpark and away from the television set. To retain a league franchise, Shreveport management established a preseason goal of selling 125,000 tickets. The *Shreveport Times* supported the ticket drive by extolling the virtues of seventy-eight year old Spanish-American War veteran Walter Swedley, who, although blind and bed-ridden, purchased five tickets. Despite the example set by Swedley and the efforts of Sports President Bonneau Peters to fill the team with "local color" (eleven of the twenty white players on the Sports spring training roster were from the Arkansas, Louisiana, and Texas region), the ticket campaign fell short of its goal. Nevertheless, Peters announced that he was pleased with the total of eighty-five hundred tickets sold. In an open letter to Shreveport baseball supporters, Mr. Pete, as he was affectionately known, stated, "For my part, the drive has given me new confidence that the people of this city and area do want baseball, and will not give it up without

a battle. I can promise them here and now that if the preseason enthusiasm is any indication of what we can expect during the season, Texas
League ball is safe not only for 1957, but for years to come."[11] Peters did
not prove to be a very good prognosticator, for the 1957 campaign would
be the last one for Shreveport in the Texas League until 1968 when it reen-
tered the league as an integrated team which included a working agreement with the Atlanta Braves.

But with eighty-five hundred ticket sales in the bank, the Shreveport
club, led on the field by player-manager Mel McGaha, entered the 1957
baseball season with enthusiasm. The Sports opened on the road, defeating Houston, who was picked to win the Texas League flag, 3 to 1 behind
the three-hit pitching of Dave Newkirk. The opening-day win was destined to be the highlight of the 1957 campaign for the Sports. The second
game in Houston was rained out, and the teams resumed their series at
Texas League Park in Shreveport. Houston complied with the Louisiana
segregation statutes, defeating the Sports 9-2 before 2,972 supporters.[12]

Meanwhile, the baseball establishment continued to ignore the issue
of racial segregation in Louisiana sport. Former Cleveland Indian star
pitcher Bob Feller, who retired from the game in December, 1956, appeared
at a Texas League Park youth rally sponsored by the Motorola Corporation, who had signed Feller to conduct a promotional tour for the company and baseball. Feller told approximately a thousand youngsters in
Shreveport that the keys to baseball success were: listening to your coaches,
finding the right playing position, practicing, and displaying enthusiasm.
Feller apparently failed to acknowledge that these qualities would not allow
a black youngster in Louisiana to compete with white players. And the
Sporting News maintained its editorial position that baseball had already
solved its racial issues. In a May 22, 1957 editorial, the paper reminded
readers, "The Negro in Organized Ball is so completely taken-for-granted
these days that it must be difficult for younger fans to recall the time little more than a decade ago, when both majors and minors raised an invisible but effective barrier on the color line."[13]

While Feller and the Sporting News could pretend that racial segregation did not exist in Louisiana baseball, visiting clubs in Shreveport
enjoyed no such illusions. Houston, Austin, Fort Worth, Dallas, and San
Antonio were forced to bench black players in compliance with Louisiana
law. The biggest problem was with the Dallas club which had to sit three
starting black players, yet they swept a four game series at Shreveport in
mid-May. By the end of May, the Sports record was a dismal sixteen wins
against twenty-two losses. The team was already twelve and one-half games
behind front-running Dallas, and fan support at Texas League Park was

dwindling. The home field racial advantage made no difference to the lackluster Shreveport players.[14]

By July, the Shreveport club was mired in last place and only a few hundred fans were frequenting contests at Texas League Park. At the Texas League all-star game meeting in Dallas, Peters announced that the Shreveport franchise was for sale. Although Peters hoped that Shreveport investors would step forward to purchase the team, he made it clear that "the present organization is not going to operate it next year." Complaining that he was "tired of seeing only 500 people come out to the ball park," Peters cited poor attendance and the lack of a major league working agreement as forcing him to sell after twenty years with the club. However, Peters insisted that a black boycott of the team had no effect on attendance or his decision to put the team up for sale. On the other hand, a well organized NAACP boycott of the New Orleans Pelicans of the Southern Association, dating back to a 1955 decision of the club to not accept five black players assigned to the franchise by the parent Pittsburgh Pirates team, indicated that black economic power might have a role to play in Louisiana sport.[15]

Nevertheless, baseball's self-proclaimed Bible, the *Sporting News,* continued to ignore the racial implications of the Shreveport situation. In an editorial regarding the sale of the Shreveport franchise, the paper saluted Peters and his fellow investors for their efforts to maintain an independent club free from the dictates of a working agreement with a major league team. But the editorial concluded that the days of the independents were over, commenting, "Now they have come to the end of the road, but they deserve a salute from all in the game for their long and courageous fight. Their withdrawal should serve to focus attention on the handicaps faced by independents and, it is hoped, will help to speed the day when a greater measure of autonomy and well-being can be restored to the minors."[16] Not once in this benediction to the entrepreneurial spirit of Peters was there any mention of the fact that Shreveport investors operated a segregated minor league baseball franchise in violation of the platitudes of racial harmony and equality espoused by the *Sporting News* and the baseball establishment.

On the field, the Sports continued with their hapless ways. By season's end, Shreveport was in last place with a record of fifty-nine victories and ninety-five defeats, a winning percentage of under .400 percent. The Sports were forty-three games behind first place Dallas and seven games behind next-to-last (seventh place) Oklahoma City. Shreveport attendance in 1957 dwindled to a meager 40,919.[17] With the entire Texas League gate off approximately 27 percent from 1956, league officials made little effort to save the floundering Shreveport and Oklahoma franchises.

Despite the optimistic guarantees of Peters, Shreveport was out of organized baseball in 1958, although the city obtained a Southern Association
franchise for the 1959 season. The failure of baseball leadership to confront the issue of racial apartheid embodied in House Bill 1412 exposed a
great deal of hypocrisy in the national pastime. It did not have to be that
way.

In the fall of 1957, West Point was scheduled to play the Tulane football team in New Orleans. In a telegram to President Eisenhower, Pennsylvania Congressman James G. Fulton protested the military academy's
participation in a segregated athletic contest. Fulton urged the President
to use his powers as commander-in-chief to "institute a general order
establishing as a policy the equality of sports competition and integrated
seating at all athletic contests in which our service teams participate."
Responding to the exhortations of Fulton and other exponents of racial
integration, Secretary of the Army Wilber M. Brucker announced that the
Tulane-Army football game was to be transferred from New Orleans to
West Point because of the Louisiana sports segregation statute. Representative Fulton proclaimed the army's decision as "an important step in the
segregation issue," while some Southerners, such as Tulane Athletic Director Dick Baumback, were angered by the army's action. Baumback insisted
that initially the service academy had no problem with the Louisiana
statute, but then "there was trouble in Little Rock. Northern politicians
had placed pressure on West Point due to the actions taken by Arkansas
Governor Faubus to block school integration.[18] However, what Baumback
failed to acknowledge was that in responding to such lobbying efforts, West
Point was making a point of support for the principles of integration and
equality of opportunity. These were principles for which the baseball establishment was not willing to make a stand in Louisiana.

While less forceful in formulating a response to apartheid than West
Point, the National Boxing Association, at its annual meeting in September, 1957, discussed Louisiana athletic segregation laws, but a boycott of
the state was not approved. Nevertheless, the case of lightweight boxing
contender Ralph Dupas cast the segregation legislation of Louisiana in a
negative light. Following the passage of House Bill 1412, witnesses appeared
before the Louisiana State Athletic Commission, testifying that Dupas was
a Negro named Duplessis and insisting that he should not be sanctioned
as a white fighter. With his livelihood at stake, Dupas did not directly challenge the Louisiana ban on interracial athletic competition. Instead, it was
incumbent upon Dupas to prove that he was white. Since Dupas was delivered at birth by a midwife and did not have an official birth certificate stating that he was white, the Athletic Commission ruled that it could not

certify him to box white fighters. Dupas then filed a suit in civil court demanding that the New Orleans Health Department issue him a white birth certificate. In November, Judge Rene A. Viosca allowed Dupas to resume his boxing career by ordering the New Orleans Health Department to issue a birth certificate listing his parents as white. Dupas did not challenge the segregationist policies of Louisiana. He accepted the ground rules of the segregationist system, persevering in having himself declared as white.[19] The publicity generated by the Dupas case and its almost Nazi-like emphasis upon proving the purity of one's blood line gave Louisiana athletic apartheid a black eye.

While some in the boxing community questioned the ban on interracial athletic competition, and many Northern college football programs, such as that of West Point, confronted the athletic ban by canceling or moving games, the sport of baseball, which extolled itself as the model for racial integration in the sports world with Jackie Robinson, was found wanting in its willingness to compromise the principles of racial integration. An examination of baseball's response to sport apartheid in Louisiana with the case study of the Shreveport Sports of 1957 indicates that racial prejudice was still powerful within American society and the baseball establishment. The willingness to compromise with segregation in Louisiana did not bode well for the pace of integration in major league baseball, which in 1957 contained approximately only forty players of African-American descent and no blacks on the rosters of the Detroit Tigers, Philadelphia Phillies, and Boston Red Sox. In 1957, baseball could take pride in the accomplishments of Jackie Robinson, but it was no time to be self-congratulatory as the national pastime was found wanting on the moral principles raised by the civil rights movement's challenge to racial segregation. Baseball's conspiracy of silence in Shreveport could be interpreted as giving legitimacy to the Manning Johnson's of the world who denounced the civil rights struggle as communist subversion. The Shreveport Sports and the Texas League in 1957 were not baseball's finest hour.

Endnotes

This essay was originally published in the *North Louisiana Historical Association Journal*, 28 (Fall, 1997), 153-162.

1. *Sporting News,* September 9, 1956.
2. "Segregation Snafu," *Newsweek.* 48 (July 30, 1956), 79–80. For additional back-

ground information on Louisiana history and the state's practices of segregation see Joe Gray Taylor, *Louisiana: A Bicentennial History* (New York: Norton, 1976); Edwin Adams Davis, *Louisiana: A Narrative History* (Baton Rouge: Claitor's Publishing Division, 1971); Dewey W. Grantham, *The South in Modern America: A Region at Odds* (New York: HarperCollins, 1994); and T. N. Davis, "Spanish Moss and Segregation," *America,* 99 (May 24, 1958), 249–250.

3. *Sporting News,* October 24, 1956. The Louisiana law which went into effect on October 15, 1956 prohibited racially-mixed athletic contests in the state, providing penalties for participants ranging from sixty days to one year in jail and fines from $100 to $1,000.

4. *Sporting News,* January 30, 1957. Preseason Texas League rosters included five black players at Houston and Dallas, while San Antonio and Austin each counted two players, with one each at Fort Worth and Tulsa. The Shreveport and Oklahoma City franchises listed no black players.

5. For minor league attendance woes see Bill O'Neal, *The Texas League. 1888-1987: A Century of Baseball* (Austin: Eakin Press, 1987), 108; and Neil J. Sullivan, *The Minors: The Struggles and the Triumph of Baseball's Poor Relation from 1876 to the Present* (New York: St. Martin's Press, 1990).

6. *Sporting News,* December 26, 1956.

7. For the public hearings of the Louisiana Joint Legislative Committee on Segregation see *Shreveport Times.* March 7, 8, 9, and 10, 1957. For background information on Johnson see Harvey Klehr, *The Heyday of American Communism* (New York: Basic Books, 1984), 400–401 and 471–472. It is also interesting to note that following his retirement from baseball in January, 1957, Jackie Robinson commenced on a fundraising speaking tour for the NAACP.

8. *Shreveport Times,* March 16, 1957.

9. *Sporting News,* April 10, 1957.

10. For an overview of Shreveport's history in the Texas League see O'Neal, *Texas League,* 302–309.

11. *Shreveport Times,* March 7 and 12, and April 14, 1957.

12. *Ibid.,* April 15 and 17, 1957.

13. *Sporting News,* May 1 and 22, 1957. For additional information on Bob Feller see Bob Feller with Bill Gilbert, *Now Pitching, Bob Feller* (New York: HarperPerennial, 1990).

14. *Sporting News,* May 22, 1957; and *Shreveport Times*, May 31, 1957.

15. *Sporting News,* July 24 and 27, 1957.

16. *Ibid.,* August 7, 1957.

17. *Shreveport Times,* September 9, 1957; and *Sporting News,* September 18, 1957.

18. *Shreveport Times,* September 5, 17, and 22, 1957.

19. *Ibid..* August 27, September 9, and November 1, 1957.

20. For the slow pace of baseball integration see Larry Moffi and Jonathan Kronstadt, *Crossing the Line: Black Major Leaguers, 1947-1959* (Jefferson, N.C.: McFarland, 1994).

7

Ten Years After: The Baseball Establishment, Race, and Jackie Robinson

In September, 1956, the *Sporting News,* speaking on behalf of Organized Baseball, printed a self-congratulatory editorial lauding the sport's tenth year of racial integration. The paper observed that with over forty "Negro" players on major league rosters, "their place in the game is secure." On a rather smug note, the *Sporting News* reported that while challenges to racial segregation in the schools often resulted in violent confrontations, baseball offered a model for peaceful reconciliation of racial strife. The editorial concluded, "The National Game does not presume to advise other segments of the population or other sports, on how to handle this complicated and emotional problem. It merely points with satisfaction to its own record of gradual, voluntary, and peaceful advance toward the complete fulfillment of its code that a player should not be judged on the basis of creed, connections or color, but on the basis of ability alone."[1]

The baseball establishment in 1956 was especially proud of African-American players such as Harry Simpson of the Kansas City A's, who, after leading his team in runs batted-in, had no problems reaching terms for a new contract with Kansas City management. In an interview with reporters, Simpson expressed his gratitude to baseball for giving him an opportunity, insisting that all African-American ball players should be appreciative of baseball's racial policies. Simpson stated, "Here I am making more than a great percentage of the men of my race. Here I am on a ball club where I've been given every chance in the world to make good. What more could I possibly want? That's everything there is." The *Sporting News* was appreciative of the sentiments espoused by Simpson, editorializing, "Naturally, the good things of the game seem especially gratifying to a big leaguer who, as a boy, probably assumed his color would make it impossible for him even to enjoy them. But Simpson's words would have been every bit as valid had he made no mention of his race. They apply with just as much force to all big leaguers, regardless of nationality, background, or pigmentation."[2]

However, these noble sentiments were less than apparent on the playing field as the roster of major league teams contained approximately only forty players of African-American descent. In 1956, only thirteen African-American players were added to major league rosters, and clubs such as the Philadelphia Phillies, Detroit Tigers, and Boston Red Sox had no black players. Like Southern reaction to the Supreme Court's 1954 Brown decision on school desegregation, the baseball establishment did not exactly move with all deliberate speed to integrate the sport. Baseball officials explained their actions by citing such concerns as the reaction of Southern white players to black teammates, the many minor league clubs in the South, spring training facilities in the South, potential race conflict among spectators, and the quality of black athletes.

These excuses constituted a rather feeble effort to conceal the continued racism within the baseball establishment. Accordingly, historian Ben Rader maintained that by the mid-1950s, "...many if not all clubs had unwritten understandings to restrict the total number of blacks. Driven in part by the profit motive, the owners tried to calculate whether increasing the number of black players would result in more wins and thereby increase attendance or whether it would adversely effect the identification of white fans with their teams and thereby reduce attendance and revenues." In a similar vein, Robinson biographer Jules Tygiel argued, "Baseball's failure to integrate more rapidly reflected not only a persistent hostility to blacks, but prevailing racial attitudes and assumptions, and widely shared player development strategies. Many teams stalwartly resisted desegregation. Others moved haltingly, bypassing established Negro League stars in favor of young prospects and demanding higher standards of performance and behavior from black players than white." Black athletes such as Curt Flood, who starred for the St. Louis Cardinals and later gained notoriety by challenging baseball's reserve clause, insisted that white ownership was most concerned with sexual politics and interracial dating between African-American ballplayers and white women.[3]

Thus, there was an assumption within the baseball community that unacknowledged racial quotas existed for some teams. Indeed, many teams had only one black athlete, as was the case of the New York Yankees and Elston Howard. In an article on Howard, reporter Dan Daniel made it clear that more than playing ability was evaluated as a factor in the advancement of African-American athletes in the major leagues. Reflecting wide spread racial stereotyping within the baseball establishment, Daniel's reporting raised no protest when he observed that Howard stayed with the Yankees not only because he was a fine player, but also because the African-American athlete was "quiet, well-behaved, and a fine asset to the off-the-field tone of the club." Daniel praised Howard for raising no objection when he could not stay with the team at the Emerson Hotel in Baltimore due to city segregation ordinances. Concluding on what could certainly be interpreted as a racist tone, Daniel wrote, "The Yankees would like to find another Negro player. But they insist that he be of the Howard stamp, and that is not going to be easy. In fact, at the moment, it's impossible."[4] In addition to indulging in racial stereotypes regarding character, the Yankee management seemed to accept a double standard based on race. While Howard was expected to always demonstrate exemplary behavior, and the Yankees refused to call up African-American Vie Power from the minor leagues, the "party" antics of white stars such as Mickey Mantle, Billy Martin, and Whitey Ford were tolerated.

While management continued to display condescending attitudes regarding race, racial taunts had not disappeared from the playing field. In a late August contest between the Brooklyn Dodgers and Milwaukee Braves, Jackie Robinson fired a ball into the Braves dugout, narrowly missing the head of pitcher Lew Burdette, who turned down a challenge by Robinson to fight. Burdette had called the African-American athlete a "watermelon head." However, the *Sporting News* reporter covering the incident failed to describe the taunting as racially motivated. Instead, he wrote, "It was assumed that the pitcher referred to Robinson's girth, which had been given prominent display in a photograph which appeared recently in a national sports publication."[5] Even if commentators refused to acknowledge racist language, Robinson would no longer tolerate it.

While black players continued to struggle with segregated housing and racism on the playing field, the baseball establishment made clear its lack of understanding and commitment to racial segregation with the manner in which it handled the end of Jackie Robinson's illustrious career and the challenge of segregation with the Shreveport Sports of the Texas League.

By the conclusion of the 1956 season, in which the New York Yankees edged Brooklyn for the World Series championship, it was apparent that the illustrious career of Jackie Robinson was winding down. Battling injuries and health problems, Robinson's playing time in 1956 was limited to 117 games. However, his games played, batting average, home runs, and runs batted in were all an improvement over his 1955 marks.[6] Thus, many in baseball were shocked to learn on the morning of December 13, 1956 that Brooklyn had traded Robinson to their fierce National League rivals, the New York Giants, for cash and journeyman pitcher Dick Littlefield. In an official statement, Robinson stated that he was disappointed and having to comfort his crying son, Jackie, Jr. However, trades were part of baseball, and he spoke of his relationship with the Brooklyn club in diplomatic terms, stating, "There are no hard feelings. The Brooklyn club had to protect it's own best interests. I thought I helped Brooklyn last year and didn't figure to be traded." Robinson concluded that he would wait until January 10, 1957 to inform Giants owner Horace Stoneham whether he would retire or play for the Giants.[7]

Dodger fans were outraged. The *New York Times* quoted one Brooklyn partisan as proclaiming, "I'm shocked to the core . This is like selling the Brooklyn-Battery Tunnel. Jackie Robinson is a synonym for the Dodgers. They can't do this to us." (Of course, this fan did not realize the Robinson trade was only the beginning of Dodger management's betrayal of Brooklyn.) Despite outrage among the Dodger faithful and Robinson's hint that he might retire, the baseball establishment's assumption was that business would go on as usual. Giants owner Stoneham did not believe Robinson would retire. Instead, Robinson, whom Stoneham labeled the "greatest competitor I've ever seen in baseball," would play first base for the Giants in 1957. Referring to Jackie Robinson Jr.'s tearful reaction to the trade, the *Sporting News* insisted, "Jackie, Sr., being an adult, recognizes the expediency that exists in this world with which he must cope and has displayed no tear-stained-face to the public. He is now a Giant and will play ball for the Giants with the same fiercely competitive spirit he displayed for so long as a Dodger. That is the only way Robinson knows how to play."[8] However, when Robinson engaged in a bit of his own expediency regarding the announcement of his retirement, the *Sporting News* and baseball establishment yelled foul.

While Brooklyn fans were dismayed with the trade, Robinson was less surprised and was already making plans for his departure from the game. Robinson did not get along well with Dodgers manager Walter Alston, and his relationship with the Dodger front office deteriorated when Walter O'Malley maneuvered to force Branch Rickey out of Brooklyn. From a peak figure of $39,000, Robinson's salary suffered slight reductions for each of his last three seasons in Brooklyn. In his memoirs, Robinson commented unfavorably on the racial views of O'Malley, alleging that the Dodger President perceived him as an "uppity Nigger."[9]

Accordingly, on December 10, 1956, Robinson met with William Black, President of Chock Full o' Nuts, a fast-food restaurant chain in the New York City area. Black, whose employees were predominantly African-

American, offered Robinson a position as vice-president in charge of personnel at an annual salary of fifty-thousand dollars. That evening Robinson attempted to reach Dodger General Manager "Buzzy" Bavasi and inform him of his intentions. However, Bavasi, who was negotiating with the Giants, was unavailable. The next day, Robinson signed a contract with Black. That same evening, Robinson was told that he had been traded to the Giants. He did not advise Dodger officials that he had decided to retire from baseball and accept a position with Chock Full o'Nuts. The reason for Robinson's apparent duplicity was an exclusive contract for fifty thousand dollars which he had signed with *Look* magazine. The contract stipulated that Robinson's retirement would first be announced in a magazine exclusive.[10]

Yet, the story broke early before the magazine hit the newsstands. A few *Look* subscribers received advance copies, and *Look* executives scrambled to call a press conference for Robinson. When asked why he had chosen to work through a magazine deal and not keep his employer informed of his intentions, Robinson replied, "I had given my best to Brooklyn for eleven years and my debt to baseball has been paid." Buzzy Bavasi did not agree, insisting that Robinson owed an obligation to the Dodgers as well as the sportswriters of New York. Bavasi told reporters, "And this is the way he repays the newspapermen for what they've done for him. He tells you one thing and then writes another for money. You fellows will find out that you've been blowing the horn for the wrong guy." An angry Robinson retorted, "After what Bavasi said, I wouldn't play ball again for a million dollars."[11]

The New York press immediately weighed into the Robinson-Bavasi debate. Red Smith of the *New York Herald Tribune* rebuked Robinson for his lack of loyalty to the Dodgers, asserting, "But for the Dodgers, the Jackie Robinson of this last decade would not have existed. The fact that he gave them full value on the field and the fact that after eleven years they sold his contract without consulting him, these do not alter the fact that everything he has he owes to the club. His debt to the Dodgers had precedence over any agreement to sell a story to *Look,* and with his mind already made up at the time of the trade he was honor bound to speak up." Dick Young of the *New York News,* who often chastised Robinson, maintained that the Brooklyn great did not owe anything to reporters or the Dodgers. Young was more upset that Robinson, in his *Look* press conference of January 6, had criticized baseball for lacking sentiment. Rallying to the defense of the national pastime, Young argued, "So Robinson should have quit, which certainly is his privilege, without smearing the game that has earned him $500,000 in ten years Baseball has as much sentiment as any business he can name, much more than the cream cheese sandwich business, for one." On the other hand, Joe Williams of the *New York World Telegram* insisted that Robinson would be a "dope" to not take *Look's* lucrative offer. Seeking to take a more neutral position, the *Sporting News* editorialized that while Robinson had every right to sell his story, the Bible of Baseball preferred the "outstanding example" of dignified retirement established by Bob Feller, who announced his retirement several weeks before Robinson and had accepted a position as corporate spokesperson for the Motorola Corporation.[12]

In the much maligned *Look* article, Robinson simply maintained that his decision to leave the game was based on financial security for his family. He concluded the article by noting," I know I'll miss the excitement of baseball, but I 'm looking forward to new kinds of satisfaction. I'll be able to spend more time with my family. My kids and I will get to know each other better.... They won't have to look for me on TV."[13] However, shortly after his retirement, Robinson agreed to postpone assuming his duties with Chock Full o'Nuts, while he commenced on a speaking and fund-raising tour on behalf of the NAACP. Accordingly, Robinson's retirement was also related to the athlete's decision to make a larger commitment and contribution to the burgeoning civil rights movement. Commenting upon the athlete's statement that he was ready to accept responsibility to his race and country, Robinson biographer Arnold Rampersad wrote, "Most immediately, he was making this sacrifice in order to aid black people living under Jim Crow down south."[14]

On December 8, 1956, two days before he met with William Black, Robinson received the prestigious Spingarn Medal, awarded annually "for the highest achievement of an American Negro." Ed Sullivan, columnist and television celebrity, presented the gold medal at a New York dinner sponsored by the NAACP. Among the previous recipients present were Ralph Bunche, W. E. B. DuBois, and Thurgood Marshall. The award citation placed Robinson's contributions in historical perspective, proclaiming, "The entire nation is indebted to him for his pioneer role in breaking the color line in Organized Baseball. Through sheer ability and exceptional competitive zeal, he won popular acclaim of sports lovers of all races and demonstrated that there were no fore-ordained racial restrictions upon the ability to play the National Game. He opened the doors of the major leagues for Negro stars whose skill, zest, and stamina have entered the national sport."[15]

Perceived as a symbol of opportunity and struggle for African-Americans, Robinson could hardly refuse when NAACP Executive Secretary Roy Wilkins asked the athlete to chair the organization's 1957 Freedom

Fund drive. While a novice as a public speaker, under the tutelage of veteran NAACP organizer Franklin Williams, Robinson became a successful orator and fund raiser, proudly pointing out that the 1957 tour was able to garner a million dollars for the NAACP coffers. Echoing the sentiments of Martin Luther King, Jr., Robinson argued that African-Americans were out of patience and could no longer wait for equal rights. He told a Chicago audience, "We have waited almost one hundred years for these rights. In my view, now is the time for Negroes to ask for all of the rights which are theirs."[16]

It is worth noting the courage which Robinson displayed in embracing the cause of the NAACP. In the late 1950s, opponents of racial integration attempted to brand the civil rights organization as a subversive tool of the Communist Party and Soviet Union. For example, appearing before the Louisiana Joint Legislative Committee on Segregation, African-American Manning Johnson, who had been a minor Communist Party official in New York, attacked Martin Luther King, Jr., and the NAACP. The vitriolic Johnson described King as a "dastardly misleader who is taking his race down the road of violence, bloodshed, revolution, and possible communism in the South." In concluding his testimony, Johnson denounced the NAACP as a "communist vehicle designed to initiate the overthrow of the government."[17]

However, sport coverage of the Robinson speaking tour failed to acknowledge his courage and determination. Instead, publications such as the *Sporting News* focused upon baseball questions Robinson fielded during press conferences. The Robinson image projected by the *Sporting News* was not the crusader for racial equality, but rather a hot-headed commentator who antagonized fellow players and baseball executives. For example, at a speaking engagement in Wauhegan, Illinois, Robinson stated that too much night life cost the Milwaukee Braves the 1956 National League pennant. Braves players replied to the criticism by labeling Robinson a "rumor monger." Braves shortstop Johnny Logan maintained that Robinson was "just popping off to keep his name in the headlines." As if a man whose mission to raise a million dollars for an institution under attack needed the publicity of alleged night life in Milwaukee.[18]

On a more serious note, Robinson was quoted as describing former teammate Roy Campanella as "washed up." An angry Campanella retorted that he was tired of Robinson "popping off." The burly catcher criticized Robinson for demonstrating a negative attitude toward baseball, asserting, "Instead of being grateful to baseball, he's criticizing it. Everything he has he owes to baseball. That beautiful house of his, and this new job of his, too. Does he think those people would have had anything to do with him if he had never played baseball." The two men initially quarreled over Campanella's failure to join Robinson in challenging segregated housing for the black Brooklyn ball players.[19] The antagonism between Campanella and Robinson reflected a debate within the African-American community about the necessity of pushing for racial integration going back to the days of Booker T. Washington and W. E. B. DuBois.

But Campanella's complaints failed to silence Robinson who observed that it was "strange" that no African-American players could make the major league rosters of Detroit, Philadelphia, and Boston, While speaking in Detroit, the former Brooklyn star further acknowledged that he was puzzled by the fact that "for some reason there are no Negro players on the fields of Detroit. Detroit is a great sports town. But you can't help but wonder about the absence of Negro players in both football and baseball."[20]

While Robinson insisted that he was speaking honestly, seeking a better nation for all Americans, former playing field opponents of Robinson continued to label the Dodger great a trouble-maker. Giants pitcher Sal Maglie, no stranger to baseball rhubarbs, was quoted as saying Robinson was unpopular with the players due to self-promotion. Maglie believed Robinson, who had expressed interest in managing, would never be given the reins of a major league club. Maglie concluded, "I don't think any ball club would take a chance on Jackie, because you just couldn't get anybody to play for him after the way he's been rapping other players."[21]

Despite business success, political involvement, and a respected role in the civil rights movement, one of Robinson's greatest disappointments was that he was never allowed to try his hand at piloting a major league franchise. Writing in 1972, Robinson observed, "I felt that any chance I might have had of moving up to an administrative job with the Dodgers or any other team was mighty slim. Had I been easy going, willing to be meek and humble, I might have had a chance. But this fact has not changed much even today. There are many capable black athletes in the game who could contribute greatly as managers or in other positions of responsibility, but it just isn't happening."[22] In fact, Robinson never lived to see his dream of an African-American manager, for Frank Robinson was not named to manage the Cleveland Indians until 1975, three years after the death of the pioneering Dodger great.

While Robinson was displaying his courage on the civil rights front, the baseball establishment was demonstrating its timidity in fighting segregation. In July, 1956, the Louisiana state legislature approved House Bill 1412, which, among other measures to ensure continued racial segregation in the state, prohibited blacks and whites from participating in interracial sporting events anywhere in the state. Despite protests from the NAACP and some concerns by the business community regarding the economic consequences of this legislation, Governor Earl Long, explaining that he was "just a poor little old man going along with the majority," signed the legislation, which was to go into effect on October 15, 1956. *Newsweek* predicted that national condemnation of the athletic segregation statute would result in the shuffling of football and basketball schedules, while in baseball the Shreveport Sports would be expelled from the Texas League due to the number of black players on league rosters.[23]

While the forecast of *Newsweek* proved somewhat accurate in regard to intercollegiate basketball and football, professional baseball was not as adamant in its opposition to segregation. While major league exhibition games scheduled for Louisiana in the spring of 1957 were canceled, the segregationist Shreveport Sports baseball club retained its good standing in the integrated Texas League. While Commissioner Ford Frick was silent on the issue, the segregation problem was placed in the hands of Texas League President Dick Butler, who said he would seek a compromise solution, assuring that there would by no legal challenge by organized baseball to the Louisiana interracial sports ban. Finding a middle ground would not be easy. Art Routzong, general manager of the Houston Buffaloes, announced that his team would play the best players possible, regardless of race. However, he did put forth the idea that Houston might be willing to withdraw black players, if Shreveport would reciprocate by benching equivalent starting players. Crusty Bonneau Peters, long time President of the Shreveport franchise (an independent club with no major league working agreement) sounded a bit like Arkansas Governor Orville Faubus when he shunned compromise, asserting, "If these clubs want to play at Shreveport, they'll just have to play under the laws of Louisiana. I'm not going to do anything about it."[24]

Engaging in delicate diplomacy, League President Butler orchestrated an agreement which essentially catered to the obstinate Peters. Clubs with black players on the roster would be allowed an extra man above the league-imposed player limit of eighteen. Franchises such as Houston and Dallas, who each had five black roster players, were to be placed at a considerable competitive disadvantage when they journeyed to Shreveport. This agreement, or sellout, allowed *Sporting News* correspondent Jack Gallagher to portray the January 20, 1957 annual midwinter meeting of Texas League management as conciliatory. According to Gallagher's report, "Only minor business occupied the directors, thus portraying the Texas League as one circuit without problems—a rarity in these times."[25]

Despite the baseball establishment's lack of understanding and sensitivity in responding to the retirement of Robinson, along with a lack of courage in confronting racial segregation in Shreveport, the *Sporting News* continued to extol the sport's race record. In a May 22, 1957, editorial, the paper reminded readers, "The Negro in Organized Ball is so completely taken-for-granted these days that it must be difficult for younger fans to recall the time little more than a decade ago, when both majors and minors raised an invisible but effective barrier on the color line."[26]

Those who maintained that baseball was color blind pointed to a June 13, 1957 confrontation between Larry Doby, the first African-American player to integrate the American League, and New York Yankee pitcher Art Ditmar. In the first inning of the game at Comiskey Park, Ditmar brushed Doby back with a high and tight fast ball. After sprawling in the dust, Doby charged the mound and landed a left hook to the jaw of Ditmar. The Chicago and Yankee dugouts emptied, and a full scale brawl ensued. Following the game, Doby and teammate Walt Dropo, along with the Yankees Billy Martin and Enos Slaughter, were fined by League President Will Harridge. Shirley Povich of the *Washington Post* described the fight as historic for the sport of baseball. Povich wrote, "The Doby-Ditmar episode had special significance because for the first time a Negro player was daring to get as assertive as the white man whose special province Organized Ball had been for nearly a hundred years.... There is no intent here to condone what Doby did; merely to point out the consequences fell far short of Civil War or succession or a violent sense of outrage except among Ditmar's Yankee teammates who dashed to his assistance, but in no more anger than if his attacker had been a white player." While the fisticuffs between Doby and Ditmar did prove that black and white players could have altercations on the field without setting off race riots in the stands, Povich went too far in the conclusions he drew from the fight. Povich asserted, "There's no call now to brief the Negro player who is breaking into the big leagues. The chances are that any discrimination in his mind are more fancied than real. Anyway, the novelty of the Negro player in the majors long since wore off. They are no longer a gate attraction because of the color of their skin. It's the glint of their batting averages and other skills that count."[27]

Tell that to Larry Doby, who continued to endure segregation and Jim Crow during the White Sox's spring training in Tampa, Florida. Doby had to find housing with black families as he could not stay at the team hotel, and black players were given meal money to eat on their own. Accordingly, Doby told biographer Joseph Thomas Moore, "Not many people realize this, but I was segregated in spring training for 10 out of 13 years, right through the spring of 1959. Now do you see what I mean when I say that there were constant reminders that I was black? Was I imagining things when I was segregated? Does anyone think that the prejudice which caused segregation in the South didn't exist in the North?"[28]

A similar gap between myth and reality was evident in descriptions of Hank Aaron's 1957 pennant-winning home run for the Milwaukee Braves. On September 23, Aaron clubbed an eleventh inning home run giving the Braves a four to two victory over the St. Louis Cardinals. The first National League pennant for the Milwaukee club set off impromptu street parades in the brewing capital, while Aaron's teammates carried him off the field on their shoulders. According to the *Sporting News,* this moment represented the democratic spirit of baseball. Aaron was depicted as exemplifying the Horatio Alger success epic of America in which any individual, regardless of race or social class origin, may obtain success through hard work, drive, and determination The *Sporting News* wrote, "A few years ago, Henry Aaron, one of a large family of children, was just another Negro boy playing softball on the sandlots of Mobile, Alabama. Now he is a national figure, a star on a pennant-winning team, the hero of the flag-clinching game, a World's Series participant, his name familiar to every follower of baseball. More than that, he is a popular member of the Braves, acclaimed and respected by his fellow players and by fans with no thought of his color. For, as the pennant-clinching scene proved again, outstanding achievement depends only on ability, and not on race, creed or background, in the real fellowship of sports."[29]

Notwithstanding the democratic credo endorsed in the *Sporting News* editorial, Aaron's baseball career demonstrated that discrimination and racial bigotry were still major factors in American society and the sport of baseball. The perception of being treated as an interchangeable commodity to be transferred from Milwaukee to Atlanta for the 1966 season weighed heavily upon Aaron. Even though Milwaukee had a relatively small African-American population, and its own history of racial discrimination,[30] Aaron, who grew up in Alabama, was not eager to return to his native region. In his memoirs Aaron, who finished his playing career with the Milwaukee Brewers, insisted that he never got over the trauma of the Braves departure from the Wisconsin city.

Aaron needed reserves of character and talent as he dealt with the challenges of life in Atlanta. He and his wife were able to purchase a beautiful home, although, of course, it was located in a segregated neighborhood. As a prominent African-American player, Aaron received several hate letters a week, in addition to hearing the racial insults hurled in his direction at the ballpark. Aaron's wife Barbara was even arrested when she tried to drive into the stadium, as a white guard, who did not recognize her, stopped the car, pulled his gun, and verbally abused her. The charges were dropped after intervention from the mayor's office. Aaron responded the only way he knew, with his bat. In his memoirs, Aaron asserted, "I knew that, as a black player, I would be on trial in Atlanta, and I needed a decisive way to win over the white people before they thought of a reason to hate me. And I believed that the way to do all of this was with home runs."[31] Aaron's decision to let his bat do the talking culminated in the surpassing of Babe Ruth's career home run mark, which, ironically, seemed to increase the racial abuse to which the Braves outfielder was subjected.

The reality of the discrimination encountered by players such as Hank Aaron, Larry Doby, and Elston Howard; the failure of Organized Baseball to challenge segregation in Shreveport; the criticism of Jackie Robinson as a rabble rouser following his baseball career and commitment to the civil rights struggle; and the slow progress of racial integration in the major leagues (franchises in Boston, Detroit, and Philadelphia had no black players on their major league rosters), all indicate that baseball ten years after Jackie Robinson was hardly a model of racial integration and toleration. Baseball spokespersons, such as the *Sporting News,* who assumed that baseball had put racial issues behind it by the 1956 and 1957 seasons, were as much out of step with the changes occurring in America as those in Congress who assumed the rather innocuous Civil Rights Bill of 1957 would satisfy those courageous individuals mounting assaults upon Jim Crow and racism in America. For in 1956-1957 the civil rights movement was just beginning to gather steam, and much sacrifice would be needed to topple the structure of Jim Crow. While Organized Baseball congratulated itself for integrating some black players, the sport remained silent about Shreveport and much of the discrimination in spring training sites. On the other hand, black players such as Robinson, Doby, and Aaron knew the movement for equality was only gathering momentum ten years after Robinson began his career with the Dodger organization.

And where are we today fifty years after Jackie Robinson? There is much about baseball and American society of which Robinson would probably be proud. The kind of overt racism to which Robinson was subjected is no longer tolerated in American society, and it is most appropriate that Organized Baseball is honoring Robinson's memory. Robinson was also a businessman, and he would welcome a growing black middle class; however, the overall economic gap between rich and poor, where black Americans are over represented, continues in grow in America. And it is easy to assume that Robinson would be most concerned with the discrepancy between the number of young African-American males, ages eighteen to twenty-four, in penal institutions as opposed to educational institutions.

The number of African-American managers in baseball has increased in recent years, but after expressions of concern following the racist comments of Dodgers' executive Al Campanis on the fortieth anniversary of Robinson's Dodger career, baseball management has not been forthcoming with opportunities for African-Americans in the executive suite. Currently, Bob Watson, of the New York Yankees, is the only black general manager. And the percentage of African-American players in baseball is down to 17 percent, as black athletes increasingly turn to careers in football and basketball. As we honor Jackie Robinson's fiftieth anniversary, it is no time to be overly self-congratulatory. Just as baseball and America in 1956 and 1957 had a long way to travel in regard to an egalitarian society, we still have a distance to go. But as we proceed in our endeavors to achieve a just society let us not grow complacent and always keep in mind the courageous legacy of Jackie Robinson.

Endnotes

This essay was originally published in Peter M. Rutkoff, ed., *The Cooperstown Symposium on Baseball and American Culture, 1997 (Jackie Robinson)* (Jefferson, North Carolina: McFarland & Company, 2001), 137-151.

1. *Sporting News,* September 9, 1956.
2. *Ibid.,* November 21 and 28, 1956. For additional information on Harry "Suitcase" Simpson see Larry Moffi and Jonathan Kronstadt, *Crossing the Line: Black Major Leaguers. 1947-1959* (Jefferson, North Carolina: McFarland, 1994), 65–67.
3. On the progress, or lack thereof, of major league baseball integration see Moffi and Kronstadt, *Crossing the Line;* and Jules Tygiel, *Baseball's Great Experiment: Jackie Robinson and His Legacy* (New York: Random House, 1983), 285–286; and Curt Flood with Richard Carter, *The Way It Is* (New York: Trident Press, 1970), 100–102.
4. On Elston Howard see *Sporting New,.* February 1, 1956; Elston Howard, "It's Great to Be a Yankee," *Ebony,* 10 (September, 1955), 50–54; Barry Stainback, "Have the Yankees Held Back Howard?," *Sport,* 32 (December, 1961), 46–47; and Moffi and Kronstadt, *Crossing the Line,* 133–136.
5. *Sporting News,* September 5, 1956. On Lew Burdette see Bob Wolff, "Burdette, the Dodger Baiter," *Sport,* 16 (April, 1984), 24–31.
6. John Thorn and Pete Palmer, eds., *Total Baseball: The Ultimate Encyclopedia of Baseball* (New York: HarperPerennial, 1993), 1, 182.
7. *Sporting News,* December 19, 1956; *New York Times,* December 14, 1956; and "If You Can't Beat Him," *Time,* 68 (December 24, 1956), 42.
8. *New York Times,* December 14, 1956; *Sporting News,* December 19 and 26, 1956; and "After Ten Years," Newsweek, 48 (December 24, 1956), 49.
9. For Robinson's perspective of O'Malley see Jackie Robinson, *I Never Had it Made* (New York: G. P. Putnam's Sons, 1972), 100–115.

10. For Robinson's negotiations with William Black see David Falkner, *Great Time Coming: The Life of Jackie Robinson from Baseball to Birmingham* (New York: Simon & Schuster, 1995), 249–251; Arnold Rampersad, *Jackie Robinson: A Biography* (New York: Alfred A. Knopf, 1997), 303–309; and Robinson, *I Never Had It Made*, 130–134.

11. *Sporting News*, January 16, 1957; and *New York Times*, January 7, 1957.

12. *Sporting News*, January 16, 1957.

13. Jackie Robinson, "Why I'm Quitting Baseball," *Look*, 21 (January 22, 1957), 99–102.

14. Rampersad, *Jackie Robinson*, 316–317.

15. *New York Times*, December 9, 1956; and *Sporting News*, December 19, 1956.

16. For Robinson's Freedom Foundation tour see Robinson, *I Never Had It Made*, 137–146; Falkner, *Great Time Coming*, 253–262; and Rampersad, *Jackie Robinson*, 314–330.

17. For the public hearings of the Louisiana Joint Legislative Committee on Segregation see *Shreveport Times*, March 7, 8, 9, and 10, 1957. For background information on Manning Johnson see Harvey Klehr, *The Heyday of American Communism* (New York: Basic Books, 1984), 400–401 and 471–472.

18. *Sporting News*, January 23, 1957.

19. *Ibid.*, February 6, 1957. For the Robinson-Campanella relationship see Robinson, *I Never Had It Made*, p. 110–111; and Rampersad, *Robinson*, 291–292. For additional background information on Campanella, see "Big Man From Nicetown: Roy Campanella," *Time*, 66 (August 8, 1955), 50–55; and Roy Campanella, *It's Good To Be Alive* (Boston: Little, Brown, 1959).

20. *Sporting News*, February 27 and 6, 1957.

21. *Ibid.*, February 6, 1957. For the temperamental Maglie see Robert W. Creamer, "An Angel of Darkness Named Sal the Barber," *Sports Illustrated*, 2 (June 6, 1955), 43–44; and Millan J. Shapiro, *The Sal Maglie Story* (New York: Julian Messner, 1957).

22. Robinson, *I Never Had It Made*, 130.

23. "Segregation Snafu," *Newsweek*, 48 (July 30, 1956), 79–80.

24. *Sporting News*, October 24, 1956. The Louisiana law which went into effect on October 15, 1956 prohibited racially-mixed athletic contests in the state, providing penalties for participants which would range from sixty days to one year in jail and fines from $100 to $1,000.

25. *Sporting News*, January 30, 1957. Preseason Texas League rosters included five black players at Houston and Dallas, while San Antonio and Austin each counted two African-American players, and one each at Fort Worth and Tulsa. The Shreveport and Oklahoma City franchises listed no black players.

26. *Sporting News*, May 22, 1957.

27. *Ibid.*, June 26, 1957.

28. Joseph Thomas Moore, *Pride Against Prejudice: The Biography of Larry Doby* (New York: Praeger, 1988), 112.

29. *Sporting News*, October 2, 1957.

30. Joe William Trotter, *Black Milwaukee: The Making of an Industrial Proletariat, 1915-45* (Urbana: University of Illinois Press, 1988).

31. Henry Aaron with Lonnie Wheeler, *I Had a Hammer: The Hank Aaron Story* (New York: HarperCollins, 1991), 179–184.

8

More Legacy of Conquest: Long Term Ramifications of the Major League Baseball Shift to the West

In an April 2, 1995 piece for the *New York Times Magazine*, veteran sportswriter Robert Lipsyte bemoaned the loss of traditional American values in baseball. Lipsyte argued that the ideas championed in a sport such as baseball — "honoring boundaries, playing by the rules, working together for a common goal, submitting to authority" — were the characteristics which allowed Americans to conquer the Western frontier. Obviously irritated by the 1994-95 major league baseball players strike, Lipsyte concluded that the changes in baseball, such as the shifting of franchises and free agency, "have made it impossible to count on a player, a team, an entire league still being around for next year's comeback. The connection between player and fan has been irrevocably destabilized, for love and loyalty demand a future. Along the way, those manly virtues of self-discipline, responsibility, altruism, and dedication seem to have been deleted from the athletic contract with America."[1]

It is worthy of note that in his jeremiad, Lipsyte uses the imagery of the American frontier. Like Frederick Jackson Turner in his frontier thesis, Lipsyte perceives the Western experience as the embodiment of traditional American values of progress and improvement. An older generation of American scholars would certainly agree with Lipsyte's perspective. For example, in *The American West in the Twentieth Century*, Gerald D. Nash maintains that for much of the twentieth century the American West "has been ahead of the rest of the nation by about one generation." In support of his conclusion, Nash points to the emergence of a consumer-oriented

economy hospitable to social dissent, the application of science and technology to modify the environment, the growth of service industries, a
political cooperation between government and private business, and cultural experimentation.[2] Seeking to tap the economic and cultural possibilities described by Nash, major league baseball executives turned to the
West, establishing franchises in Los Angeles and San Francisco in 1958, followed by expansion and realignment to include Houston, Anaheim, San
Diego, Seattle, Oakland, Dallas, Denver, and Phoenix by 1998.

While this expansion has reaped tremendous profits, especially with
the Los Angeles Dodgers and Colorado Rockies, and brought major league
baseball to millions who were long denied this opportunity by the Eastern Establishment of the sport, the blessings of the westward movement
in baseball have proven to be mixed. The origins of the lack of community and civic-mindedness among professional athletes, of which Lipsyte
complains, may be found in the franchise relocations set off by the Dodgers
move from Brooklyn to Los Angeles.

A younger generation of Western historians might well have warned
the lords of baseball that the Western experience is one of complexity
rather than unimpeded progress. In her pioneering work *The Legacy of
Conquest: The Unbroken Past of the American West*, Patricia Nelson Limerick emphasizes the American West as an epic of conquest with consequences for the conqueror and conquered. Thus, from the perspective of
the New Western History, the American West is a place where sexism,
racism, exploitation of the environment, and capitalistic cycles of prosperity and recession characterize the region. Limerick asserts, "A belief in
progress has been a driving force in the modern world as a depository of
enormous hopes for progress, the American West may well be the best
place in which to observe the complex and contradictory outcome of that
faith."[3] Limerick's conclusions on the broader implications of Western history may also be applicable when considering the long term ramifications
of the major league baseball shift to the West.

Seeking an El Dorado in the West, baseball ownership found lucrative financial veins to exploit. However, this expansion brought with it
troubling questions which have yet to be resolved: the impact of franchise
shifts on minor league operations such as the Pacific Coast League, civic
loyalties to abandoned cities such as Brooklyn and Washington, the economic future of small markets such as Seattle, and a general loss of place,
community, and time as the major league baseball map stretches across
four time zones, reflecting the mobile nature of American society which
in the search for new opportunities is always in danger of losing its identity.

During the 1957 season, the western outpost of major league baseball was Kansas City, demonstrating the Eastern domination of baseball. Indeed, stability reigned between 1903 and 1953, until the owners approved the shift of the Boston Braves to Milwaukee, followed by the move of the St. Louis Browns to Baltimore in 1954, and the realignment of the Philadelphia Athletics to Kansas City in 1955. However, the great quest for new markets and opportunities in the West was set off by the departure of the Brooklyn Dodgers and New York Giants for the greener pastures of Los Angeles and San Francisco. These franchise shifts and major league expansion were the products of demographic changes in American society as well as political pressures.

In 1951, New York Congressman Emmanuel Celler's subcommittee on monopoly investigated allegations of antitrust violations against baseball, which traditionally enjoyed antitrust exemption dating back to a 1922 Supreme Court ruling written by Oliver Wendell Holmes. Congressman Celler questioned numerous aspects of organized baseball, including the reserve clause, the "mere pittance" of a $5,000 minimum annual salary for major league players, and the failure to expand in the last fifty years despite the considerable geographical shifts in American population.[4] However, the final report of the subcommittee paid homage to baseball as America's national pastime and extolled the democratic values of the game. And, of major significance to baseball executives, no legislative remedies for the plight of organized baseball were suggested, allowing the court's antitrust exemption to stand. However, Congressman Celler strongly urged organized baseball to take the opportunity given by the subcommittee to get its house in order.[5] In response to critics of the sport, Baseball Commissioner Ford Frick, asserted, "Baseball must resurvey itself and make territorial changes to keep pace with the economic and population shifts in this country in the last fifty years."[6] Accordingly, the path was paved for the first franchise transfer in over fifty years, the move of the Boston Braves to the untapped Midwestern market of Milwaukee.

In 1957, with rumors circulating in the nation's press that the Dodgers and Giants might be moving west, Commissioner Frick was once again confronting the investigative powers of Congress, where bills were again introduced calling for baseball to be stripped of its antitrust exemption. Seeking neither to antagonize representatives who sought the expansion of major league baseball nor those who feared the loss of valuable franchises, Frick played the role of the careful bureaucrat, pointing out that in meetings between minor and major league executives expansion as well as reclassification of many minor league cities were under consideration. However, a wary Frick told Congress that tampering with baseball's legal status might endanger this orderly process of change. Predicting chaos if Congress interfered with baseball, Frick argued that without clear territorial rules established by organized baseball, "Clubs presumably could relocate at will and without notice or compensation to other clubs and leagues. Under these conditions, I question whether responsible persons would be willing to invest in unprotected clubs in either major league or national association cities. I am also apprehensive that, under those conditions, baseball would not be sufficiently well organized to finance and operate the players pension plan."[7] Prick's obfuscation and threats to renege on negotiated agreements with the players, along with the testimony of other executives and players, convinced Congress to forestall legislative action. But it was clear that the sport would have to expand to head off further legislative inquiry.

Demographics also reinforced Congressional demands for realignment. In the affluent post World War II society the West experienced unprecedented growth rates. For example, in the thirty year period between 1945 and 1975 the population of Houston climbed from 385,000 to 1,400,000; Phoenix from 65,000 to 755,000; and San Jose from 68,000 to 446,000. And Texas surpassed New York in population, trailing only California whose gross domestic production would make it one of the ten leading economic powers in the world. In *Power Shift: The Rise of the Southern Rim and Its Challenge to the Eastern Establishment,* Kirkpatrick Sale identified six pillars to the economic emergence of the West; agribusiness, defense spending, technology, oil, real estate, and leisure, of which sports such as baseball constituted a vital component.[8]

Confronted with aging ballparks and urban population shifts which reduced suburban attendance, the Giants and Dodgers decided to gamble on the growing economic prosperity of the West. As David Voigt noted, their westward movement "rocked the foundations of the major leagues."[9] Efforts by Branch Rickey and William Shea to launch a third major league with the Continental League in 1959 resulted in a compromise whereby the threat of a rival league was crushed by absorbing the more promising Continental sites into the existing major league structure. Thus, in 1961, the American League added the Los Angeles Angels and Washington Senators (the original Senators departed for Minnesota after the 1960 season), while in 1962 National League expansion brought the New York Mets and Houston Colt .45s into the major league fold.

While certainly welcomed in the virgin territories of the West, in his history of baseball Ben Rader demonstrated that Westward expansion was the type of mixed blessing which Patricia Limerick attributed to the Western experience. Rader observed, "By the 1950s and 1960s, baseball could no longer ignore the shifting character of leisure in American cities, the rapid growth of new metropolises, or the new technological marvel of television. In response, the big leagues moved to exploit the new population centers, embarked on a new stadium-building boom, and sought to control the dangers and capitalize on the opportunities presented by television." But an orgy of expansionism, from sixteen teams playing a 154 game schedule in 1950 to 1990 with twenty-six teams in twenty-four cities playing a 162 game schedule, failed to solve the problems of major league baseball. A 70 percent increase in the number of regular season games enhanced gross attendance, but per game attendance continued "to lag proportionately to the population areas served by big league clubs," and the game has never recovered the popularity that it lost in the 1950s.[10]

The chief architect of baseball's paradigm shift was the owner of the Brooklyn Dodgers Walter O'Malley, who has been described as a heartless greedy despot for abandoning Brooklyn. The devil perception of O'Malley is well developed in Peter Golenbock's *Bums* in which the author dismisses O'Malley's complaints of declining attendance as a "red herring," pointing out that the Dodgers were the most profitable team in baseball.[11] However, Neil J. Sullivan, in his study of the Dodger franchise relocation, paints a very different portrait of the Dodger owner. According to Sullivan, O'Malley was forced to abandon a deteriorating Ebbets Field, but he would have been willing to stay in Brooklyn if the New York City government had been more accommodating in acquiring title to land for the construction of a new stadium. Municipal and county government in Los Angeles was forthcoming, assisting O'Malley in the acquisition of Chavez Ravine where the owner built Dodger Stadium. Rather than greedy exploiter, Sullivan perceives O'Malley as an opportunistic businessman who was willing to take a chance on the unproven Los Angeles market, despite court challenges and a voter initiative questioning the Chavez Ravine agreement between Los Angeles and Dodger ownership.[12] While tears were shed in Brooklyn over what Doris Keams Goodwin described as an "invidious act of betrayal,"[13] citizens of Southern California thronged to the vacuous Los Angeles Coliseum, exceeding two million fans in the Dodgers pennant-winning season of 1959. In the spirit of civic boosterism, the *Los Angeles Times* celebrated the Dodger World Series triumph by editorializing, "Their triumph is that they have created one of those centers of attachment that the Metropolitan area of Los Angeles needed so desperately. The team has made the people for a couple of hundred miles around aware that they have a common interest. A major league baseball club does not a city make, but in our agglomeration of Southern California communities any joint enterprise which excites a wide interest serves as a sort of civic glue."[14] The Los Angeles love affair with the Dodgers continued to grow after the opening of Dodger Stadium in 1962, with season attendance figures of over three million fans annually the norm by the mid-1980s. However, the Dodgers were not able to create a sense of community which would prevent Los Angeles from exploding in racial tension during the 1960s and 1990s.

While the Dodger exodus from Brooklyn and love affair with Los Angeles has attracted the attention of numerous academics and journalists, the history of the Giants move from New York to San Francisco has received far less scrutiny, perhaps because the Giants never developed the geographical attachment to a New York City borough such as Brooklyn. In addition, Giants owner Horace Stoneham was often perceived as having been duped by the crafty Water O'Malley into abandoning New York. In reality, Stoneham had considerable incentive in his own right for seeking gold in California. The Polo Grounds were deteriorating, attendance had slumped to only slightly over 600,000, and the citizens of San Francisco pledged the construction of a new ballpark for the Giants.

Even though the Giants opened the 1958 season in Seals Stadium which seated fewer that 23,000 spectators, Stoneham was able to double his home attendance. The Giants also enjoyed instant gratification on the playing field, finishing third in 1958 and remaining in contention for the 1959 National League pennant until the last week of the season. Fortunately, they did not win and have to play in October as Seals Stadium had already been booked for a convention of the American Medical Association.[15] With the opening of Candlestick Park in 1960 attendance soared to 1.8 million, a new club record. However, Candlestick Park proved to be a somewhat cold, windy, and inhospitable site from which to witness a baseball game, and attendance soon declined. Club owners did little to relieve the plight of the Giants when in 1968 they allowed Charles Finley to move the Kansas City Athletics across the bay to Oakland. Fluctuating attendance figures and the failure of Bay Area voters to approve public construction of a replacement stadium for Candlestick have led to repeated discussions of another franchise shift for the Giants. (In 1992, National League owners blocked a transfer to St. Petersburg, Florida.)

Why did the Giants fail to find El Dorado in the West as had the Dodgers? The ambiguous legacy of the Western conquest was again apparent. Perhaps the instant success of the Giants spoiled Bay Area fans who had a rich legacy of successful minor league baseball with the San Francisco Seals and superstars such as Joe DiMaggio. While the imperialistic perpetrators of baseball's manifest destiny seemed somewhat impervious to this tradition, the players were not. Thus, Giant outfielder Hank Saur lamented that San Francisco fans never embraced Willie Mays the way New York City loved the centerfielder. Saur complained, "They never treated him like the superstar that he was. Supposedly, they were still partial to San Francisco-native Joe DiMaggio as baseball's great centerfielder." A sensitive Mays was only too aware of the situation and blamed Manager Bill Rigney for establishing unrealistic expectations in an effort to stir up fan interest. A disgruntled Mays also encountered racism in finding housing in San Francisco which he had not encountered in New York. San Francisco crowds adopted the Latino Orlando Cepeda, who never played in New York, as their favorite.[16]

Perhaps the Giants could never quite replace the indigenous Seals, DiMaggio, and Pacific Coast League, along with the many other cultural options available in San Francisco. In his survey of minor league baseball, Neil Sullivan argues that if the Pacific Coast League had been allowed to evolve into a major league status, "...with its character, traditions, and rivalries intact, it would have made a special contribution to major league baseball. Instead, the majors engulfed the West Coast by transferring three of its historic franchises and creating three new ones. Baseball in the West is a hodgepodge of clubs from the eminent Dodgers to the marginal Mariners with little to suggest the deep traditions of the game in that part of the country."[17]

Indeed, the search for gold in the West by the Dodgers and Giants, along with Congressional pressures and the threat of antitrust legislation, set off a new wave of expansionism akin to the European imperialist scramble for African colonies following the Berlin Conference in the late nineteenth century. In 1961, the American League moved into Southern California with the Los Angeles Angels under the ownership of cowboy actor and singer Gene Autrey, a most appropriate symbol for Western baseball. In 1962, playing in Dodger Stadium, the Angels challenged the dominant New York Yankees for the pennant, before fading in the final weeks and settling for a most respectable third place finish in the standings. The success of the Angels caught the attention of the Hollywood crowd, and the young Angel players developed a considerable reputation for the party scene. Following his no-hitter in May, 1962, Angel left-hander Bo Berlinsky became involved with Hollywood starlet Mamie Van Doren. Veteran pitcher Art Fowler, taking note of the Hollywood publicity, described Van Doren as a sweet person, but he recalled, "You never knew about Belinsky. He was supposed to be a pool hustler. He couldn't play pool worth a shit. But he wasn't a bad person."[18] However, in 1963 the Angels came back to earth, and most of the Hollywood crowd deserted them for the more consistently successful Dodgers. In 1965, the Los Angeles Angels became the California Angels, and in 1966 they moved to their current home in Anaheim. While Autrey opened his saddlebags and spent lavishly in the free agent market, the team never captured the hearts of Southern California like the Dodgers, nor an American League pennant, although coming close in 1982 and 1986. The Angels have struggled to establish a tradition and identity of their own in Anaheim where they are overshadowed by Walt Disney's version of the California dream.

Another Western city which has struggled to find its major league baseball identity is Houston, which as a proposed site for a team in the defunct Continental League was awarded a National League franchise in 1962. Appealing to the frontier image still associated with Texas and its largest city, the initial logo for the Houston team was the Colt .45s, often shortened to Colts, a symbol of the gun considered to have played a leading role in the taming of the West. According to historians of Houston this was perhaps a fitting image for the city. Francisco A. Resales and Barry J. Kaplan maintain nineteenth-century values have retained a stronghold in Houston, remarking, "Individualism, opportunity, capitalism, limited government, virtual dogma in American government before the 1929 crash, have remained sacred in Houston."[19]

Overwhelmed by the publicity generated by their hapless expansion cohorts the New York Mets and the irrepressible Casey Stengel, the Colts played in the virtual obscurity of a temporary structure, Colt Stadium, with a seating capacity of 32,000 and located on the same lot as the projected domed stadium. Relief pitcher Hal Woodeschick described the problems of playing in hot and muggy Houston, observing, "It was so hot in Houston. And we had no dome, so we started playing our home games at night. The problem was that the mosquitoes were worse at night. We'd get to the ballpark and watch it rain every day between 4 and 5 in the afternoon. Then the groundskeepers would go through the stands with an insecticide fogger to kill the mosquitoes. The ballplayers would have to be sprayed before every game. If we didn't have the stuff on our bodies, they would eat us up in the bullpen."[20]

In addition to combating mosquitoes, Houston players were expected to wear Western suits on the road. On a road swing from Cincinnati to Chicago, ten players refused to wear the suits, complaining that the outfits had caused negative comments and contributed to a "circus-like" atmosphere. In Chicago, airline passengers reportedly asked Colts players such questions as "Where is the rodeo?" and "Where's your horse?" But Manager Harry Craft made clear that wearing the cultural symbols was not a negotiable issue. He reminded the players they had voted for the Western suits before the season, and they would wear them. The early 1960s represented a time period in which management dominated, and player options were limited through strict enforcement of the reserve clause. Conformity and compliance were still the watchwords of ballplayers, and player representative catcher Hal Smith announced that the Colts would adhere to the wishes of management.[21]

However, in 1965 Houston management attempted to shed the frontier image with the opening of the Harris County Domed Stadium, now called the Astrodome. The Colt .45 logo was abandoned in favor of the rainbow-colored Astros, a futuristic look for a city which played a key role in the nation's space program. Despite changes in symbolic imagery, baseball attendance in Houston has been inconsistent and the team has yet to win a National League pennant.

Still seeking gold in the West and the growing California market, American League owners approved the transfer of the Kansas City A's to Oakland for the 1968 season. Following the 1955 move of the A's from Philadelphia to Kansas City, the team's attendance and on the field play improved, but in 1967 the team finished last for the third time in four years and fan interest lagged. However, with their bright kelly-green uniforms, mustaches, and long hair, the youthful Oakland A's seemed to embody the values of the counterculture which found a home in the Bay Area during the late 1960s and early 1970s. In reality, these modern fashions were encouraged by A's owner Charles Finley, a businessman whose journey from the steel mills in Birmingham, Alabama and Peoria, Illinois to a multi-million dollar Chicago insurance executive personified the Horatio Alger saga of rags to riches and nineteenth-century production values. Finley, seeking to boost sagging ticket sales, paid Oakland players $300 each to adorn themselves with facial hair. The A's owner sought to co-opt the fashion of the counterculture, but did not count on having to deal with the questioning of authority inherent in the movement.

Thus, led by such outstanding players as Joe Rudi, Vida Blue, Catfish Hunter, Reggie Jackson, Rollie Fingers, and Sal Bando, the A's won world championships in 1972 (when the A's defeated the well disciplined and groomed Big Red Machine from Cincinnati), 1973, and 1974, before Finley, in response to increasing player demands, disassembled his dynasty.[22] Despite tremendous success on the playing field, Oakland attendance lagged behind performance, and many in major league baseball still question whether the Bay Area is able to support two major league franchises.

Following the Oakland franchise transfer, baseball expansion in 1969 placed new Western franchises in San Diego and Seattle. The National League San Diego Padres wanted to tap the Southern California market which had proven to be so lucrative for the Dodgers and to a lesser extent for the Angels. Baseball was not an instant success in San Diego with only one winning season during the first fifteen years, and home attendance for the inaugural 1969 campaign barely topped half a million. By 1974, team owner Arnholt Smith was prepared to sell the franchise to a buyer who would move the team to Washington, D.C. However, a white knight emerged in Ray Kroc, head of the McDonald's fast food empire, who purchased the team and kept it in Southern California. With aggressive marketing techniques , as well as the acquisition of fine athletes such as Tony Gwyn and Kevin McReynolds, the Padres attendance improved, and the team appeared in the 1984 World Series. However, following the death of Kroc, the team was sold to new ownership in 1990, and the Padres have been unable to find a niche in the hearts of Southern Californians. Attracting neither the fans nor the radio-television contracts available to the neighboring Dodgers, the Padres have sold or traded outstanding young players such as Fred McGriff and Gary Sheffield. Operating on a shoestring budget for the major leagues, the Padres in 1994 fielded a team which many detractors thought was more befitting the Pacific Coast League franchise which the National League had displaced in 1969.[23]

The 1969 American League expansion team in Seattle fared even worse than the Padres. The Seattle Pilots played their home games in the refurbished minor league Sick's Stadium, finishing last and drawing fewer than 700,000 spectators. Following this disastrous inaugural campaign, whose underside has been well chronicled by Jim Bouton's infamous *Ball Four*, the Pilots moved to Milwaukee and became the Brewers.[24] After an eight year absence and threats of legal action, the American League returned to the Pacific Northwest with the Mariners in 1977. Despite a domed stadium to prevent costly rain-outs and the emergence of a superstar in Ken Griffey, Jr., the Mariners have struggled on and off the field. With a troubled financial picture, the future of major league baseball in the Pacific Northwest remains dubious.[25]

The failure of the Western San Diego and Seattle markets to materialize did not discourage Bob Short from moving his Washington Senators (a 1961 expansion team to replace the original Senators who transferred to Minnesota) to Arlington, Texas (midway between Fort Worth and Dallas). A bitter Senators broadcaster Shelby Whitfield blasted Short for the transfer, stating that Arlington Stadium was inadequate, parking poor, the press unreceptive, and football was king. Whitfield acidly remarked, "All the seats were out in the open, directly under the sun or exposed to showers, and the stadium was notorious in the area for its toilet facilities. In Texas they like their baseball with plenty of beer, and beer and baseball don't quite go well together if you a don't have a handy 'john.'"[26] Perhaps there was something to the sour grapes of Whitfield as the Rangers, despite a traditional Western frontier image and logo, failed to provide much excitement either on the field or at the box office. Nevertheless, a group of investors headed by George W. Bush purchased the team in 1989, and their signing of free agent Nolan Ryan brought considerable interest to the franchise. The 1994 opening of a new ballpark in Arlington with plenty of facilities has also rekindled fan appreciation, but the Rangers have yet to produce a divisional winner and remain second cousins to the Dallas Cowboys.

The El Dorado sought in the West by baseball owners after the initial successful strike in Los Angeles was finally found in 1991 with the awarding of a National League franchise to Denver. Expecting to draw approximately two million paying customers, the Colorado Rockies, in a Denver metropolitan area of two million, drew over four and one-half million fans to their inaugural campaign in 1993. The unexpected bonanza was attributed to geography, demographics, pent-up demand, and a solid Denver history of supporting big league sports franchises, as well as minor league baseball. Bob Howsam, former major league general manager with Cincinnati, played a key role in bringing major league baseball to Denver after many years with the minor league Denver Bears. Howsam knew Denver would be successful, but he believed the phenomenal attendance figures owed something to luck and timing. Howsam observed, "It just happened to come along at the right time, and the stadium was large enough, and this region is prospering economically right now. People in the mountain region have some dollars in their pockets to spend on entertainment." Frank Haraway, a retired *Denver Post* sportswriter who served as the Rockies official scorer in 1993, simply believed the Eastern Establishment of baseball had underestimated the potential of the region. Haraway quipped, "I always felt that major league sports people back east pretty much looked down the groove of their nose at us, and imagined that all we did out here was dodge behind trees and shoot Indians."[27] While the staggering attendance figures at Mile High Stadium (also home of the Denver Broncos football team) were a most pleasant surprise for the Eastern Establishment, they also surpassed the estimation of Denver baseball officials who were scrambling to add additional seating capacity to Coors Field for the Rockies 1995 season.

Having found a Western gold mine in Denver, baseball owners, even in the midst of their long winter of discontent during the 1994-95 strike in which the 1994 World Series was lost, voted to add the Arizona Diamondbacks to the ranks of major league baseball for the 1998 campaign. Boston Red Sox executive John Harrington, chairman of the expansion committee, admitted that during the prolonged labor negotiations of 1994–95 was probably not the ideal time to announce expansion plans. However, in defense of the committee's decision to expand to Arizona and Tampa, Harrington explained, "But if you understand the pressure brought on us by Congress to expand — especially by the Florida and Arizona delegations — you would know why. They wanted teams and we would have lost Phoenix as a viable candidate if we had waited past April 1." The Phoenix group of investors had until that date to benefit from a tax approved by Maricopa County (Phoenix) voters that would raise $253 million of the $280 million price tag for a retractable-roof stadium.[28] Thus, baseball attempted to expand to avoid Congressional threats of antitrust legislation and fill coffers with an estimated three million annual ticket sales in Arizona. These were similar to the reasons given for baseball's initial Westward movement in 1958

Even supposing that Phoenix proves to be a rich vein to tap like the Dodgers and Rockies, what conclusions are we to draw about the long term ramifications of the major league baseball shift to the West? First, this brief survey of baseball in the West suggests, as Larry Gerlach eloquently argued in a recent article on baseball historiography, that much research remains to be done on baseball in the region.[29] Nevertheless, perhaps some tentative conclusions are worthy of consideration. To place baseball within the historiographical debate between the traditionalists and New Western historians, it is obvious that the major league baseball shift has not brought unqualified growth and progress. To use the phrase coined by Patricia Limerick, the legacy of conquest has been ambiguous. The expansion of the major league baseball frontier to the West did democratize the game by bringing the major leagues into a better balance with the demographic alignment of America in the late twentieth century. But this expansion brought with it the destruction of distinguished minor league traditions such as that of the old Pacific Coast League as well as the extinction of baseball loyalties in Eastern cities such as Brooklyn and Washington. In addition, expansion in baseball in the search for lucrative new markets and to avoid Congressional antitrust actions has encouraged baseball management to seek a safety valve of frontier expansion rather than deal with its problems. Accordingly, expansionism has only accelerated the greed factor in professional baseball deplored by Robert Lipsyte in his piece for the *New York Times Magazine.*

In *Lords of the Realm: The Real History of Baseball*, John Helyar argues that to baseball executives expansion was "always a response to a problem," spreading the talent pool thinner, increasing upward pressures on salaries, while removing the scarcity that had undergirded the value of franchises. Helyar writes that all of this changed in 1993 when attendance surged past seventy million, smashing the old attendance mark by 24 percent. The new franchises in Colorado and Florida counted for over seven and one-half million of this increase. However, these figures have just increased the greed in baseball which Helyar deplores. Helyar concludes, "The Lords and the agents, the lawyers and the czars, had done their best to kill baseball. There was something about the national pastime that made the people in it behave badly. They were, perhaps, blinded by the light of what it represented — a growing distillate of America. Men fought to control it as though they could own it. They wallowed in dubious battle, locked in ugly trench warfare for dominion over the green fields. The money poured into the game and men gorged and gouged over it — made damned fools of themselves over it."[30]

Major league baseball's paradigm shift to the West is part of the portrait of greed painted by Helyar. Rich baseball veins have been found in Los Angeles and Colorado, and possibly Arizona, but the picture and future of baseball in Anaheim, Seattle, San Diego, Oakland, San Francisco, Arlington, and Houston remain unclear. For baseball to reach its promise as the American game more than Westward expansion, albeit with its democratic elements, is needed. The game and its officials must be willing to reach negotiated settlements with politicians, agents, players, and umpires which will establish a solid affordable foundation for the game and which will still place baseball within the financial grasp of the American family. Until these issues are resolved expansion will only be a panacea and the ambiguous legacy of conquest will persist.

Endnotes

This essay was originally published in *Journal of the West*, 36 (April, 1997), 68–78. Copyright 1997 by Journal of the West, Inc. Reprinted with permission of *Journal of the West*, 1531 Yuma, Manhattan, KS 66502 USA. World Series victories by the Arizona Diamondbacks in 2001 and Anaheim Angels in 2002, along with the construction of new parks in Arlington, Seattle, San Francisco, and Houston have certainly improved the prospects of baseball in the West since this piece was written. However, baseball still struggles with economic problems as the 2002 labor agreement and flap over contraction well document. The history of baseball in the West continues to fit well within the boom and bust cycles described by Limerick in *Legacy of Conquest*.

1. Robert Lipsyte, "Why Sports Don't Matter Anymore," *New York Times Magazine* (April 2, 1995), 51–52.

2. Gerald D. Nash, *The American West in the Twentieth Century: A Short History of an Urban Oasis* (Englewood Cliffs, New Jersey: Prentice-Hall, 1973), 296–305. For a journalistic account which lends support to Nash's thesis see Neil Morgan, *Westward Tilt: The American West Today* (New York: Random House, 1961).

3. Patricia Nelson Limerick, *The Legacy of Conquest: The Unbroken Past of the American West* (New York: W. W. Norton & Company, 1987), 18–32. For the intensity of the contemporary historical debate on Western history see Gene M. Gressley, ed., *Old West/New West: Quo Vadis?* (Worland, Wyoming: High Plains Publishing Company, 1994).

4. *Sporting News*, August 8, 1951.

5. U.S. Congress, *Organized Baseball: Report of the Subcommittee on Study of Monopoly Power of the Committee on the Judiciary, House Report*, No. 2002, 82 Cong., 2 Sess. (1952).

6. *Sporting News*, November 18, 1953.

7. U. S. Congress, *Organized Professional Team Sports, Hearings Before the Antitrust Subcommittee of the Committee on the Judiciary*, 85 Cong., 1 Sess. (1957), 128–129.

8. Kirkpatrick Sale, *Power Shift: The Rise of the Southern Rim and its Challenge to the Eastern Establishment* (New York: Vintage Books, 1976), 17–53.

9. David Voigt, *American Baseball. Volume III: From Postwar Expansion to the Electronic Age* (University Park: The Pennsylvania State University Press, 1983), xxvi.

10. Ben G. Rader, *Baseball: A History of America's Game* (Urbana: University of Illinois Press, 1994), 172–185.

11. Peter Golenbock, *Bums: An Oral History of the Brooklyn Dodgers* (New York: G.P. Putnam's Sons, 1984), 432. For other sources critical of O'Malley see Roger Kahn, *The Boys of Summer* (New York: Harper and Row, 1971); and Harold Parrott, *The Lords of Baseball* (New York: Praeger, 1976).

12. Neil J. Sullivan, *The Dodgers Move West* (New York: Oxford University Press, 1987).

13. Doris Kearns Goodwin, as quoted in Geoffrey Ward and Ken Burns, *Baseball: An Illustrated History* (New York: Alfred A. Knopf, 1994), 307.

14. *Los Angeles Times*, October 9, 1959.

15. For the early years of the San Francisco Giants see Charles Einstein, *A Flag for San Francisco* (New York: Simon and Schuster, 1962), 7–25

16. Danny Peary, *We Played the Game: 65 Players Remember Baseball's Greatest Era, 1947-1964* (New York: Hyperion, 1994), 398; Willie Mays with Lou Sahadi, *Say Hey: The Autobiography of Willie Mays* (New York: Simon and Schuster, 1988), 146–147; and in Peary, *We Played the Game*, 395–396, Giants pitching star Johnny Antonelli discusses relations between African-American and Latino players.

17. Neil J. Sullivan, *The Minors* (New York: St. Martin's Press, 1990), 228. Also on the Pacific Coast League see Paul J. Zingg and Mark D. Medeisos, *Runs, Hits, and an Era: The Pacific Coast League, 1903-58* (Champaign: University of Illinois Press, 1993); and Bill O'Neal, *The Pacific Coast League, 1903-1988* (Austin, Texas: Eakin Press, 1990).

18. Peary, *We Played the Game*, 548–549; William Leggett, "Halos, Hopes, and Belinsky, Too," *Sports Illustrated*, 17 (July 3, 1962), 16–17; Maury Allen, *Bo: Pitching and Wooing* (New York: Dial Press, 1973); and Ross Newham, *The California Angels* (Garden City, N. Y.: Doubleday, 1982).

19. Francisco A. Rosales and Barry J. Kaplan, eds., *Houston: A Twentieth Century Urban Frontier* (Port Washington, N. Y.: Associated Faculty Press, 1983), 3; Ron Briley, "The Houston Colt .45s: The Other Expansion Team of 1962," *East Texas Historical Journal*, 32 (1994), 59–74; and Clark Nealon, Robert Nottebart, Stanley Siegel, and James Tinsley, "The Campaign for Major League Baseball in Houston," *The Houston Review*, 7 (1985), 3–46.

20. Peary, *We Played the Game*, 533.

21. *Houston Chronicle*, May 29 and 31, 1962.

22. For the Oakland A's and Finley see Ron Briley, "The Oakland A's of 1972-1975 and the Counterculture in Baseball: Undermining the Hegemony of the Baseball Establishment," *Nine: A Journal of Baseball History and Social Policy Perspectives*, 1 (Spring, 1993), 142–167; Herbert Michelson, *Charlie O.: Charles Oscar Finiey vs. the Baseball Establishment* (New York: Bobbs-Merrili, 1975); Bill Libby, *Charlie O. and the Angry A's* (New York: Doubleday, 1975); Tom Clark, *Champagne and Baiony: The Rise and Fall of Finley's A's* (New York: Harper and Row, 1976); and Wells Twombly, "Charlie O. and the Missouri Mule," *New York Times Magazine* (July 15, 1973), 12–13.

23. For the Padres see John Curtis, "How We Did It," *San Diego Magazine*, 34 (September, 1982), 123–135; Ron Fimrite, "San Diego Love Story: Two Big Macs with Lots of Trimmings," *Sport*, 58 (September, 1974), 79–88; Joe Gergen, "San Diego Padres Survived a Most Humble Beginning," *Baseball Digest*, 44 (February, 1985), 55–58; and Steve Wulf, "You've Got to Hand It to the Padres," *Sports Illustrated*, 41 (October 15, 1984), 28–34.

24. For the Seattle Pilots see Jim Bouton, *Ball Four* (New York: Dell Publishing, 1970); and Carson Van Lindst, *The Seattle Pilots Story* (New York: Marabou Publishing, 1993).

25. For the Seattle Mariners see Jim Kaplan, "Ringing in the New: Toronto and Seattle Expansion Teams," *Sports Illustrated*, 46 (January 10, 1977), 88–89; and Tray Ringolsby, "Shipwrecked in Seattle," *Sport*, 75 (March, 1984), 61–72.

26. Shelby Whitfield, *Kiss It Goodbye* (New York: Abelard-Schuman, 1973), 248–249. For other interesting pieces on the Rangers see Ron Fimrite, "Texas is Not a Lone Star Team," *Sports Illustrated*, 44 (May 17, 1976), 18–21; Norm Hitges, "How Bad Will the Texas Rangers Be?," *D, The Magazine of Dallas*, 3 (May, 1976), 52–54; and Harold Peterson, "New Home on the Ranger: Washington Senators Now Texas Rangers," *Sports Illustrated*, 36 (May 1, 1972), p. 59.

27. Alan Gottlieb, *In the Shadow of the Rockies: An Outsiders Look Inside a New Major League Baseball Team* (Niwot, Colorado: Roberts, Rinehart, Publishers, 1994), 11–18. For baseball in Denver also see Mark Foster, *The Denver Bears: From Sandlots to Sellouts* (Boulder, Colorado: Pruett Publishing Company, 1983), and "Coors Field Is a Hit," *Baseball Weekly*, 28–30.

28. "Phoenix Gets a Team," *Baseball Weekly*, 8–11.

29. Larry Gerlach, "Not Quite Ready for Prime Time: Baseball History, 1983-1993," *Journal of Sport History*, 21 (Summer, 1994), 103–137.

30. John Helyar, *Lords of the Realm: The Real History of Baseball* (New York: Villard Books, 1994), 460–463 and 553–554.

9

The Houston Colt .45s: The Other Expansion Team of 1962

The date is October 15, 1986, and the scene is the Astrodome in Houston, Texas. Astros outfielder Kevin Bass steps to the plate with two out and tying run Denny Walling waiting at second base. Bass, facing veteran New York Mets relief pitcher Jesse Orosco, works the count full. Orosco delivers a wicked slider, and Bass is unable to make contact. The Mets win seven to six, clinching the National League pennant. The Orosco-Bass confrontation put the finishing touch on a sixteen inning, four hour and forty-two minute spectacular which sportswriter Jerry Izenberg termed "the greatest game ever played."[1] The New York franchise would go on to appear in its third World Series, defeating Boston in seven games. Houston would once again remain at home and play second fiddle to the Mets, just as they had when the two franchises entered the National League twenty-five years earlier.

The 1962 season was viewed as a very important one by officials of Organized Baseball. Despite the 1961 drama surrounding the assaults of Mickey Mantle and Roger Maris on the sixty home run mark of Babe Ruth, baseball attendance declined slightly. Attendance was down 5.6 percent from 1960, and only the Tigers, Yankees, and Reds demonstrated any significant increases. Meanwhile, the National Football League set an attendance record in 1961. The Associated Press followed up these box office receipts with a poll of sportswriters and broadcasters as to whether professional football would replace baseball as the nation's number one sport in the next ten to twenty years. In a narrow decision of over two hundred individuals polled, football won by three votes. In response, Baseball Commissioner Ford Frick observed that baseball, unlike other sports, was not seasonal and maintained year around interest, playing only a lesser role than God and school in American families. Faced with the threat of the Continental League attempting to form a third major league and Congress looking into depriving baseball of its anti-trust exemption, Frick also placed considerable faith in franchise expansion, observing, "Getting New York and Houston into the National League was a good move and its going to help increase attendance throughout the country in 1962."[2] But the two new franchises failed to receive equal attention from the nation's media. While in 1986, Houston was defeated on the playing field by an eventual world champion; in 1962, Houston, fielding a competent expansion entry, was overlooked by sportswriters and fans in favor of a New York Mets team which established modern day records for futility.

Of course, there were many reasons for the national attention focused on the 1962 Mets. They resided in the nation's media center and were able to attract such skilled chroniclers as Jimmy Breslin. The Mets were also well represented by General Manager George Weiss and Manager Casey Stengel who recalled the glory days of the New York Yankees in the 1950s. Having to compete with the popular Yankees for the New York market, Weiss decided that the Mets would draft well-established veterans to fill the expansion roster. Players such as Gil Hodges, Don Zimmer, Charley Neal, Gus Bell, and Richie Ashburn adorned the roster, providing the Mets with older hands who were household names to baseball fans in New York and throughout the country. While the team was old and very short of pitching, Stengel remained quotable, and the nation became infatuated with such lovable losers as former Yankee "Marvelous" Marvin Throne-berry.[3] Indeed, the Mets proved to be so bad that they did restore some of the interest in baseball which many in the game feared was being lost to professional football.

Meanwhile, ignored in the national hoopla over Stengel and the Mets, a solid first year expansion franchise had been established in Houston. While not as frustrating for Houston fans as Bass's swing and miss in 1986, the overshadowing of Houston by the Mets in 1962 remains disconcerting. The story of Houston's workmanlike, professional approach to fielding an expansion team deserves an audience.

Appealing to the frontier images still associated with Texas and its largest city, the initial logo for the Houston team was the Colt .45s, often shortened to Colts, a symbol of the gun which was considered to have played a leading role in the winning of the West. According to historians of Houston this may be a fitting image for the city. Francisco A. Resales and Barry J. Kaplan maintain nineteenth-century values have retained a stronghold in Houston, remarking, "Individualism, opportunity, capitalism, and limited government, virtual dogma in American government before the 1929 crash, have remained sacred in Houston." The Houstonian sense of individualism has also been apparent in the desire to conquer a harsh environment. In his history of the city, David G. McComb described Houston as the most air-conditioned city in the world, stating, "There is nothing closer to hell in modern America than to be caught after a rain in a Houston traffic jam at midday in an unair-conditioned car. It is possible, at that moment, to appreciate the plight of a steamed clam, and the situation does nothing to improve human temperament."[4] The Houston way of coping with this environment has been to build huge structures of steel and concrete, while paying little attention to zoning and creation of open spaces.

This approach was evident in Houston's initial efforts to capture a National League franchise. In 1958, Harris County voters approved a twenty million dollar revenue bond issue for a combined football-baseball stadium, but when interest developed in an indoor air-conditioned facility, it was necessary in 1961 to go back to the electorate and get approval for twenty-two million dollars in general obligation bonds. With the bond issues indicating popular support, the Houston Sports Association, led by George Kirksey, Craig Cullinan, and William Kirkland, applied for a major league franchise and agreed to lease the proposed facility at a rent sufficient to pay off the bonds. However, the Harris County Domed Stadium, or the Astrodome as it would eventually be called, was not ready for the inaugural 1962 campaign. The Colt .45s would have to compete against the Mets without the publicity of the world's first indoor park for baseball.[5]

Instead, the Colt .45s would play in a temporary structure, Colt Stadium, with a seating capacity of 32,000 and located on the same lot as the projected domed stadium. The playing dimensions of Colt Stadium were 360 feet down the foul lines, 420 feet in center, and 395 feet in left and right power alleys. In jest, the *Sporting News* reported, "Our scouts tell us that Colt Stadium extends from the Pecos on the west to the Sabine on the east, and from the Red River on the north to the Gulf of Mexico on the south. The Gulf side is the comparatively short fence because even Texas peters out in this southerly direction."[6] This playing surface dictated a decision to invest in young players who could run, catch, and throw.

Unlike the Mets who emphasized name players in the draft, Houston selected younger athletes, many of them out of the talented Los Angeles Dodger system. Among the players assembled by Houston were Dodger products Norm Larker, Bob Lillis, and Bob Aspromonte; former Giants bonus baby Joe Amalfitano; Boston Red Sox shortstop Don Buddin; and outfielder Al Spangler from the Milwaukee Braves. For pitching help the

Colts selected such players as veteran Dick Farrell from the Dodgers, Bob Bruce from the Tigers, and knuckleballer Ken Johnson who had won six while losing two for the National League champion Cincinnati Reds.[7]

To guide this group of young players, Houston management pegged former Baltimore Orioles manager Paul Richards as general manager and former journeyman outfielder and skipper of the Kansas City Athletics Harry Craft as manager. Craft had a fine reputation for handling young players, earned while managing in the Yankee farm system. In fact, Craft had guided Mickey Mantle in his first two professional seasons, and the Yankee outfielder continued to sing the praises of Craft, asserting, "Craft was more like a father to me than a manager. I guess I was lucky to have him my first two years. He started me out right." Houston management believed Craft could exercise patience with their young talent and start them out right. Philosophically, Craft emphasized treating young players with courtesy and respect. Players making mistakes would be dealt with firmly by the manager, but there would be no public criticism. Craft concluded, "Have confidence in your players and win their respect and you've taken a giant stride in the direction of building a winning club."[8]

Taking fifty-four players to training facilities in Apache Junction, Arizona, Craft and his team got off to a rough start in the Cactus League exhibition season, dropping their first two contests. However, working hard under the direction of Richards and Craft, the Colts completed their Arizona Cactus League schedule in first place with a mark of fourteen wins and seven losses. Manager Craft, not wanting expectations in Houston to run too high, played down the Cactus League success, observing, "We've done a lot of experimenting and so have the other teams. We've played against a lot of people we won't be seeing after April 10 (opening day). The important thing was that our players really got to work, and their morale was terrific. But I'll tell you we'll take any championship we can get."[9]

While Craft sought to lower expectations, the Colts created additional excitement by starting the season in Houston with a three game sweep of the Chicago Cubs. The opening day crowd of 25,271 was somewhat of a disappointment, but numbers were held back by some threatening weather and unresolved parking problems. Thirty-year-old, five foot-seven inch Bobby Shantz went the distance for the Colts, holding the Cubs to just five hits in an 11 to 2 victory. Offensive punch was provided by former Pirate Roman Mejias who blasted a pair of three-run home runs.[10] Houston continued its mastery of the Cubs on April 11 and 12 by tossing consecutive shutouts at the overwhelmed Cubs. Hal Woodeschick and Dick Farrell combined for a 2-0 victory, followed by veteran left-hander Dean Stone's three hitter. Judge Roy Hofheinz, emerging as a principal player within the Houston Sports Association, was excited about the Colts sweep, but offered a somewhat backhanded compliment to the players, commenting, "Who'd have thought we could do it? Why Woodeschick and Stone are rejects, retreads, and they pitch shutouts for us." The only negative note for the Colts was a threat of rain, including a delay in the second game, which kept total attendance for the Cubs series down to 53,445.[11]

The Colts were brought back to earth when they arrived in Philadelphia on April 13 to face the Phillies who would develop into their greatest nemesis. Craft decided to try Farrell in a starting role, and the flame-thrower responded with nine strikeouts while allowing two hits through six innings, but the Colts could muster little offense and went down by a score of 3 to 2. In the final game of the series, Ken Johnson yielded only six hits in seven innings of toil, but was bested by Phillies right-hander Art Mahaffey who blanked the Colts.

From Philadelphia, the Colts traveled to New York to do battle with their rival new franchise which had started the season with four consecutive losses. Due to rain, the Colts were able to play only one game in New York, but while waiting out the weather, Houston sportswriters had ample opportunity to hear and record the comments of Mets manager Casey Stengel. Responding to his team's 0 and 4 start, as well as inclement Eastern weather, Stengel observed, "We can't play in rain or snow. My men are high-class ball players, beautifully built. They're all from California. They can't stand this kind of weather. Why this rain and snow has frozen my brain. And my players had no ski outfits." Then, without missing a beat, the Ole' Professor, mused, "You know once you get that dome up, we won't be able to recognize you guys. Now you look good and healthy and tanned. I won't be able to recognize you after you get light-complected." No wonder that the incompetent Mets were receiving more press than the successful Colts. Poor Harry Craft was no match for his quotable opposite in the Mets dugout. But on the field, Houston asserted its superiority over the Mets with a 5 to 2 win in eleven innings, climaxed by a three-run home run by shortstop Don Buddin.[12]

The Colts finished their first road trip of the season by splitting two games with the Cubs. Of their first eight games Houston had won five. The pitching staff was the talk of the National League, having yielded only thirteen runs. Although not in a league with Stengel, Manager Craft quipped, "If we keep getting this kind of pitching, this is going to be a very interesting summer." Hitting, however, continued to worry the Colts, especially the poor start of outfielder Jim Pendleton, who went only two for fourteen. Pendleton, with a lifetime major league batting average of .260, refused to use race as an excuse for his poor start, although the outfielder was the only African-American on the squad, besides the seldom-used Johnny Weekly who would shortly be optioned to the minors. Pendleton minimized the racial abuses and taunts he received in baseball, insisting, "I turn a deaf ear, that's the best way."[13]

Regardless of the cause, Pendleton broke out of his slump with a three for four performance when the Colts returned home, but the Phillies continued their domination, defeating the Colts 3-1. The Phillies completed a sweep of their two game series with a narrow 4 to 3 triumph on April 22, and for the first time some reporters suggested that the Philadelphia team had a hex of some type over the Colts. The homestand concluded with the Colts dropping three out of five contests with the Cardinals and Braves. After the first eleven home games of the season, the Colts had drawn 202,400 fans for an average of 18,363 per game, a pace approaching a million and a half for the year. Noting the early season success of the Colts, the *Sporting News* editorialized that there would be a day of reckoning for the new franchise and the Texans should watch their bragging, but meanwhile, "The Colts and their friends are having fun. They're enjoying baseball, winning games and being boisterous. Their attitude is refreshing and admirable."[14]

And there was a bit of reckoning on the next road trip as the Cards swept a three game series from the Colts in St. Louis, while the Colts were able to earn a split of a four game set in Milwaukee. During this road trip the Colts also made their first trade of the young season, sending opening day pitcher Bobby Shantz to the Cardinals in exchange for young prospects Carl Warwick and John Anderson. The transaction made it clear that the Colts were continuing to build for the future and that there was not much room for sentiment in the business of baseball. Shantz had trouble regaining strength in his arm following an injury in New York during his second start. A disappointed Shantz remarked, "I hate to go, but I guess this is the way it is when you get old." The veteran understood the business of baseball and left Houston in a classy fashion, insisting, "I have no complaints. I certainly have been treated well by this team."[15]

The Colts returned home on May 8 to face an important set of games with National League power houses Los Angeles and San Francisco. The Colts did not fare well with the coast teams, dropping five of seven contests. Despite being dominated in these games, the Colts drew well, raising their season attendance figure to 350,314, helped by a total of 65,143 for a weekend series with the Giants. After an outstanding start Houston's record had fallen by mid-May to 11 wins against 18 losses. They were in eighth place, eleven and one-half games out of first and only two games ahead of the last place Mets.[16]

The Colts had a tough West Coast road trip awaiting them, but they were attired in new traveling uniforms befitting their logo and the Texas frontier heritage. The Western style suits featured wide-brimmed cowboy hats, bright blue suits, orange ties, and boots. While these outfits may have turned heads in California, Houston continued to have its difficulties with the Giants and Dodgers, dropping five out of seven contests.[17]

On May 21, the Colts returned to the friendly confines of Colt Stadium for the Mets first visit to town. As usual, media attention focused on the irrepressible Casey Stengel. Like his appearances throughout the National League, Stengel was greeted with a standing ovation by the Houston fans. Speaking before an eager Houston press corps, he developed his theory of pitching. Stengel explained, "Pitching is like everything else in baseball. Ought to have it. You can't stand out there and catch those balls in the bleachers. Somebody will break a leg. These ballplayers aren't going to break any legs. I will tell you that." But after Houston swept the two game series with the Mets, Stengel was more gruff. He complained that home plate umpire Al Forman "wasn't too familiar with his calls." A frustrated Stengel concluded, "Maybe it is best we get out of town and try our luck against the Dodgers. We probably have a better chance of beating them than this bunch."[18]

The Colts completed the homestand, splitting two games with the Cincinnati Reds and dropping two out of three to the Pittsburgh Pirates. Crowds declined during the homestand, with only a little over 8,000 fans attending the second game with the Reds, although for twenty-five games the Colts had drawn 406,516, placing them only behind the Dodgers and Giants in total attendance. Fans applauded the exploits of Dick Farrell, the first four-game winner on the staff; Jim Golden who had a gaudy 1.80 earned run average for fifty innings; and Roman Mejias, the Cuban outfielder who had clubbed ten home runs, three more than his previous major league high.[19]

On May 28, the Colts departed Houston for a road trip to Cincinnati, Chicago, and Pittsburgh. After dropping a game to the Reds, the Colts continued to dominate the Cubs, sweeping a two game series. June 1 found the Colts at 19 and 27 in seventh place, fourteen games out of first and five games ahead of the last place Mets. When the team reached Pittsburgh, Craft had to deal with a small player revolt involving the wearing of Western suits on the road. Ten players had not worn the suits from Cincinnati to Chicago, complaining the outfits had caused negative comments and contributed to a "circus-like" atmosphere. In Chicago, airline passengers reportedly asked Colts players such questions as "Where is the Rodeo?" and "Where's your horse?" But Craft made clear this was not a negotiable issue. He reminded the players they had voted for the Western suits before the season, and they would wear them. The early 1960s represented a time period in which management dominated and player options were limited through strict enforcement of the reserve clause. Conformity and compliance were still the watchwords of ballplayers, and player representative catcher Hal Smith announced the Colts would adhere to the wishes of management. With the great Western suit controversy quashed, the Colts moved on to Pittsburgh where they dropped the first two games of the series, but swept their first doubleheader, scoring ten runs in each of the victories.[20]

Enthused with their power showing against Pittsburgh, the Colts returned home for a ten game stretch. They got off to a fine start, taking two out of three contests from the Braves. The Houston team was feeling feisty, and Craft commented on the strong morale of the team, observing, "Our personnel has excellent morale and a measure of confidence. At times talent alone will not get the job done. A team needs morale and we've got it." Morale also remained high among Houston fans, despite the complaints of New York columnist Dick Young that Houston urgently needed the domed stadium due to the "recent mass attack upon players and fans by voracious mosquitoes at the Colt park." After splitting two games with the Dodgers, a doubleheader with Los Angeles on June 10 drew Houston's first sell-out crowd of the year, 33,145, but the fans left disappointed as the Colts were swept. Fortunately, the New York Mets furnished the opposition for the remainder of the homestand, with Houston taking two out of three games. In the final contest of the series, Houston right-hander Bob Bruce recorded his fifth victory of the year in a 10 to 2 triumph. A disgruntled Stengel was once again glad to get his Mets out of Houston, complaining, "We made four errors and it could have been eight. But the big thing is that we are chasing bad balls or taking good pitches. It really was a bad game to watch."[21]

After a break-even homestand, the Colts departed on June 15 for what proved to be a successful road swing to the West Coast. The Colts took four out of five games from the Dodgers and Giants. Harry Craft insisted the Colts had a solid nucleus with Norm Larker at first, Joey Amalfitano at second, Bob Aspromonte at third, Bob Lillis at shortstop, Al Spangler in left field, Carl Warwick in center, and the bedrock of Roman Mejias with sixteen home runs and a .300 batting average in right field. The starting staff of Jim Golden, Ken Johnson, Dick Farrell, and Bob Bruce led the National League in shutouts with seven. And with the work of youngsters like Rusty Staub in the Colt farm system, Craft insisted the Colts were right on target. A euphoric *Houston Chronicle* stated, "The odds are that back home the ex-politico named Roy Hofheinz who turned to baseball is wondering what it costs for the printing of World Series tickets."[22]

However, the West Coast swing proved to be the highlight of the season for the Colts. The next few months were no picnic for the Houston franchise as reality caught up with the expansion team. After losing two out of three to the Mets, the Colts moved into Philadelphia, where the Phillies swept the three games, extending their winning streak to seven over the Colts. The road trip which started out so promising ended with the Colts having dropped six of eleven, and the Phillies replacing the Colts in seventh place. The Colts lead over ninth place Chicago was only five games.[23]

The losing ways continued after the team's return to Houston. After blowing a June 28 exhibition contest to a Texas League all-star team, the Colts made several roster changes, adding veteran pinch hitter Bob Cerv, bonus baby Ernie Fazio from Santa Clara University, and former Cub pitcher Dick Drott, who had completed his military service. But roster moves provided little relief for the current slump, and the accounts of Colt games began to sound more like those of the floundering Mets. After dropping the first game of the homestand on June 30 to the Reds, the Colts broke a five game losing streak when Bob Bruce beat the Cincinnati club, 6-1, in a game shortened to seven innings by a thick fog. The key hit for the Colts was a double by Carl Warwick, which Reds outfielder Marty Keough claimed he never saw. But there were not many other acts of God to bail out the slipping Colts. On July 2, Reds pitcher Joey Jay beat Houston 6 to 1 in a game which featured lumbering Bob Cerv failing to score from second base on an Al Spangler triple. It seems that Cerv believed the Spangler hit was foul and had not been running at a full clip. The disastrous homestand was finished with a three game sweep of the Colts by the Pirates. The Colts had now lost eight of their last ten, and crowds were beginning to dwindle at Colt Stadium. Only a little over six thousand fans, the smallest crowd of the year, had witnessed Bob Cerv's unsuccessful dash toward home plate.[24]

As the Colts prepared for a road trip before the much needed All-Star game break, *Houston Chronicle* sports editor Dick Peebles attempted to place the recent losing ways of the Colts in perspective. Peebles pointed out that the Colts had been predicted to finish tenth, but as the halfway point of the season approached, they were in eighth place, only one game out of seventh. All the Colts had to do to finish in seventh was beat the Phillies, and certainly before the season started, Houston fans would have been well satisfied with any position above tenth place. Early success had simply spoiled Colt fans a bit. However, the road remained unkind to the Colts, who dropped three out of four games in Cincinnati before the All-Star game.[25]

On July 9, Dick Farrell, the only Colts player selected to the All-Star classic, lost both ends of a doubleheader. Tired from his work in Cincinnati, Farrell was not called upon by Reds manager Fred Hutchinson to perform in the interleague contest. Farrell's selection surprised many in the Colt camp. Outfielder Roman Mejias, with nineteen home runs, forty-eight runs batted-in, and a .311 average through games of July 2, was visibly upset that he was not included on the National League roster. Farrell remarked, "With my record, I've got to be surprised." But Farrell, who had hurled in a number of tough luck games, had a deceiving record. Both starting and relieving, he had appeared in twenty-three games, winning five and losing eight, saving five, and posting a fine earned run average of 2.48.[26]

A two day vacation did little to change the fortunes of the Colts. They started the second half by losing a single game in Philadelphia and suffered a three game sweep at the hands of the Pirates. Houston pitching which had once been the mainstay of the team was collapsing, giving up an average of almost seven runs per game in July. Returning to Houston on July 15, the Colts broke their losing streak, splitting a doubleheader with the Cubs. The crowd was small, 6,907, and the temperature a muggy ninety-five degrees, as the Colts played sloppily, committing nine errors in the two games. A frustrated Craft acknowledged the Colts had played so poorly they did not even deserve a split. An angry Paul Richards threatened a major shakeup of the Houston roster, but after cooling off for a day, recanted, counseling, "I don't see how anybody can be disappointed in this team as long as we're ahead of anybody."[27]

Meanwhile, the losses continued to mount for the Colts. The Phillies arrived in Houston on July 17 and proceeded to sweep four contests from the helpless Colts, running their winning streak over the Colts to twelve. Houston had a five game losing streak with twenty-two losses in the last twenty-five games. But Dick Farrell demonstrated a little spunk for the Colts, defeating the Cardinals on July 20 and attempting to keep the team loose with his jokes and bench jockeying. Farrell predicted that the Colts might win fifty of their next seventy games and insisted, "Just wait till we play the big teams. We'll show 'em. We knock off the big ones. Just call us the Houston spoilers." Farrell proved to be a better pitcher than forecaster, as following a four game split with the first division Cardinals, the Giants moved into town and swept three from the Colts. The last game of the series witnessed some dramatics as popular Houston third baseman Bob Aspromonte fulfilled the request of a nine year old blind boy from Arkansas to hit a home run. Aspromonte connected in the eighth inning off Giants reliever Stu Miller, but the story lacked a true story book ending as the Colts fell a run short of winning the game. Joining Aspromonte in the spotlight was Farrell, who, following a public confession that he had tried to get out Stan Musial with a spitball, hit Willie Mays with a pitch on July 24 after the Giants centerfielder had homered the first two times at bat. Mays insisted that Farrell was a good pitcher but a "bush leaguer" for the beaning. The fireworks of the Giants series had pushed season attendance over the 700,000 mark. While the losing ways of the Colts and Houston heat had caused attendance to slow down, the 700,000 figure surpassed the 1961 totals of American League expansion teams in Los Angeles and Washington.[28]

After dropping two out of three in Chicago, the Colts left the Windy City in ninth place as the team prepared for a short break during the second All-Star game of the season. Again Farrell was Houston's only representative on the National League squad, but this time he did pitch, surrendering a three-run home run to Rocky Calavito. While he was pleased to be an All-Star, the Houston hurler made it clear that, like many other players, he did not particularly care for playing a second All-Star tilt.[29]

The Colts moved into the month of August with a record of 37 wins and 65 losses, in ninth place, and 32 games behind first place Los Angeles. However, following a six game split with the Braves and Cardinals on the road, the season reached a new low when the Colts returned to Houston for a fourteen game homestand with the Reds, Braves, Cardinals, and Cubs. The Reds swept a four game series in which the Colts were held scoreless for thirty-eight innings, until they were able to push across an unearned run. The first game of the Reds series was most frustrating and seemed to foreshadow the entire homestead. Dick Farrell pitched twelve scoreless innings, but the Colts lost the game in the thirteenth when Reds journeyman relief pitcher Johnny Klippstein homered. The last game of the homestand, in which the Colts had played poorly and posted only five wins, was the smallest crowd of the year, a total of 4,543 fans. While most of the city was disappointed with the team's August home showing, relief pitcher Russ Kemmerer, an ordained minister, saved two games and was rewarded with an appointment to the staff of Bethany Methodist Church in Houston.[30]

The Colts could certainly use divine intervention as they headed for a visit to their nemesis in Philadelphia. But even Reverend Kemmerer was unable to pull any strings as the Phillies swept a three game series from the Colts, extending their winning streak over Houston to fifteen, with an opportunity to sweep the season series the first week in September in Colt Stadium. The Colts woes continued as the Pirates took two from the hapless Houston club. The longest losing streak of the year hit nine games as the Colts dropped two more games in Cincinnati, but Houston did rebound to take a doubleheader from the Reds on August 27. The Colts followed up this success by winning both games of a two game set in St. Louis. By prevailing in the last four games, the Colts were able to post a mark of four wins and seven losses on the road swing before moving into Chicago for two games. Four victories in a row had allowed Houston to recapture eighth place by a half game over the Cubs, and a split allowed Houston to retain this lofty position before moving home to face a showdown with Philadelphia.

Despite regaining eighth place, the August road trip was a difficult one for many Houston players and morale was low. A discouraged Craft confessed, "We've tried all possible infield and outfield combinations. You'll see a lot of new faces when the player limit is off after August 30." Craft also levied fines against infielders Aspromonte and Larker for throwing their helmets and bats, and many players realized their status for the 1963 season was very questionable. Joe Amalfitano, who had started the season as the Colts second baseman, was only hitting .235 and had been benched in favor of Bob Lillis. The former Giant was reconciled to being traded, while first baseman Norm Larker, who had also suffered through a disappointing season, acknowledged, "We're like soldiers, we're all expendable." Harry Craft agreed, insisting, "We'd trade Dick Farrell if we could benefit." This sense of insecurity led to a scuffle between Hal Woodeschick and rookie catcher Jim Campbell before the August 26 contest in Cincinnati.[31]

Thus, the disgruntled Colts flew home to face the Phillies and considerable hoopla orchestrated by management to attract fans and end the Phillie hex over Houston. Scheduled to pitch the first game of a September 3 doubleheader with the Phillies, Dick Farrell agreed to swap his regular uniform number 43 for number 13. Meanwhile, ladders were erected in front of the Phillies clubhouse. Colts fans bringing Arabian prayer rugs, rabbits' feet, four leaf clovers, or horseshoes were given half-price admission. The finishing touch for Houston management was the hiring of ex-prize fighter Kid Dugan, known for his devastating stare, to put a spell on the Phillies. Kid Dugan confidently told Colts Vice-President George Kirksey that the Philadelphia team "hasn't got a chance."

The circus-like atmosphere was successful in attracting over nineteen thousand curious fans, but the Phillies prevailed, sweeping the doubleheader. Kid Dugan expressed shock, explaining, "May my tongue cleave to the roof of my mouth. I'd rather lost my right arm than see what happened tonight." The Phillies streak over the Colts had reached seventeen, and one more victory would allow the Philadelphia franchise to become the first major league team to ever sweep a season series. However, on September 5, in a contest lacking the exhibitionism of the previous evening and attended by the smallest crowd of the season, the Colts and pitcher Bob Bruce denied the Phillies an opportunity to establish a major league record, defeating Philadelphia 4 to 1. The taciturn Craft summed up the situation succinctly, "You can't lose 'em all." After getting the Philadelphia monkey off their back, the Colts took two games from the Pirates and three from the Mets, establishing a six game winning streak and solidifying their hold on eighth place. While only a little over 8,000 spectators showed up for the last three games with the Mets, the Dodgers last visit to Colt Stadium on September 12 drew almost 29,000 fans. But the Colt winning streak was halted as the Dodgers won 1-0, with hard luck Ken Johnson taking his fifteenth loss of the season.[32]

Before finishing the season with nine games against pennant contenders San Francisco and Los Angeles, the Colts departed for a road trip to Milwaukee and New York. After dropping two one-run decisions to the Braves, the Colts were not excited about playing the Mets who were hopelessly mired in tenth place. They were ready to play the role of spoiler with the coast clubs. Hal Woodeschick summed up Colt attitudes about the New York trip when he quipped, "Wouldn't it be nice if it rained for the next three days." But four games were played with the Mets. The Colts took two twin bills from New York, spoiling Casey Stengel appreciation night. Houston third baseman Bob Aspromonte established a National League record for third sackers of fifty-seven games without an error until he booted a grounder hit by Elia Chacon in the first game of the September 20 doubleheader. The four game set gave final proof to what had been obvious since April. Despite all the media attention focused on Stengel and the aging stars acquired by the Mets, it was clear the Colts had fielded the better expansion team, finishing twenty games ahead of New York in the standings.[33]

The Colts returned home on September 21 to face the Giants for three games. San Francisco won the first game 11 to 5, but Harry Craft was angry as he believed Giants manager Alvin Dark had attempted to run up the score by hit and run plays when the Giants held a large lead. Craft predicted, "It'll come back to haunt them." And it did the next evening as a bases-loaded single by Roman Mejias in the ninth propelled the Colts to a 6-5 victory. However, the Giants dominated the Colts in the final home-game of the season by a margin of 10 to 3. The Colts had completed their home season with a record of 32 wins and 48 losses. The Colts drew 924,456 fans, falling just short of their goal of one million, which had been negated by a team tailspin in July and August and the humid Houston climate. The Colts had also defeated the Mets in the attendance battle, outdrawing the New York club by 1,926 spectators.[34]

The stage was set for an exciting finish as the Colts moved west to face the Dodgers and Giants for the final six games of the 1962 season. The Giants trailed the Dodgers by three games, and the Colts would have an important say in determining the National League pennant. On September 25, the final road swing of the season opened with Dick Farrell facing his former Dodger teammates. Revenge was sweet as Farrell went ten innings, defeating the Dodgers 3 to 2 and notching his tenth victory of the season. The Dodgers bounced back the next day behind left-hander Johnny Podres, who tamed the Colts by a 13 to 1 count. However, the Colts won the series by taking the final game 8-6 behind some excellent relief pitching by Jim Umbright. The Dodger lead was cut to two games, and a disgruntled crowd showered the field with seat cushions after the final out. After rain on Friday, the Colts faced the Giants in a doubleheader on September 29. The Colts managed to salvage a split with the Giants when Bob Bruce tossed a six hitter in the second game. Meanwhile, the Dodgers had dropped two contests to the Cardinals, and Los Angeles entered the final game of the season with a one game lead over San Francisco. The Colts did their best to play the role of spoiler. They sent staff ace Farrell out to face Giant lefty Billy O'Dell before over 40,000 fans. Farrell, as usual, pitched will, but as had been the story all season, the Houston bats fell silent. The Giants triumphed 2-1, and Farrell lost his twentieth contest of the season. The San Francisco victory placed pressure on the Dodgers who dropped a 1-0 contest to the Cardinals, forcing a play-off between the Dodgers and Giants. The Giants eventually prevailed in the best two out of three series, and the Colts had played a pivotal role in deciding the outcome of the National League pennant. A fitting conclusion to what was really a rather successful inaugural campaign.[35]

The Colts compiled a record of fifteen wins and twelve losses for the month of September, their best month of the season. A strong finish and the excitement of being involved in the pennant race tended to erase memories of the Colt swoon in July and August. Optimism was the watchword for Houston management following the 1962 season. Predicted to finish tenth, the Colts achieved eighth place, completing the year with a record of 64 wins and 96 defeats. While finishing thirty-six games out of first and sixteen out of seventh (Philadelphia with their domination of Houston was able to gain seventh place), the Colts completed the season six games ahead of ninth place Chicago and twenty-four ahead of the Mets, who compiled a record of just forty wins against one hundred and twenty losses, The Colts surprising finish was primarily due to a fine pitching staff which achieved an earned run average of 3.80, while compiling a strikeout total of 1,039 and issuing only 467 walks. The hitting star of the franchise was outfielder Roman Mejias with a .286 batting average, 24 home runs, and 76 runs batted in (although 1962 was Mejias's only year in a Houston uniform. In the off-season, he was traded to Boston for American League batting champion Pete Runnels). The team also did well at the box office, ending up sixth in National League attendance. Vice-President George Kirksey summed up the year by observing, "Most of our objectives were realized. We did not lose 100 games or finish last. We licked our expansion twin, the Mets, and outdrew them at the box office. We have a foundation to build on, and by blending our upcoming players in with the 1962 team, should begin the long, hard climb up the National League ladder." Similar sentiments were expressed by Roy Hofheinz, who concluded, "We made great progress in a year, and we look forward to continued hard work and progress. No one in the Houston organization will be satisfied until Houston has a world's champion."[36]

But the championship predicted by Hofheinz has eluded the Houston franchise and no pennants fly under the Astrodome. The competent expansion team of 1962 was no publicity match for Casey Stengel's "Can't Anybody Here Play This Game" Mets. And the futile swing of Kevin Bass in 1986 allowed the Mets to defeat Houston on the playing field and go on to another world championship. In 1980, Houston fans also suffered the agony of defeat in an excellent National League Championship Series with their 1962 rivals, the Philadelphia Phillies. The last thirty-one years have been difficult ones for Houston fans, but the glitter of the Astrodome and frustrations of recent seasons should not be allowed to obscure the memory of the Colt .45s who brought major league baseball to Houston and the state of Texas in 1962. The ballpark was hot and muggy with numerous mosquitoes, but the achievements of Dick Farrell, Ken Johnson, Bob Bruce, Jim Golden, Hal Woodeschick, Russ Kemmerer, Norm Larker, Bob Lillis, Joe Amalfitano, Bob Aspromonte, Roman Mejias, Carl Warwick, Al Spangler, Hal Smith, and Jim Pendleton are worth remembering.

Endnotes

This piece was originally published in the *East Texas Historical Journal*, 32 (1994), 59-74. And for a Houston fan, the frustration has not eased since this article's publication in 1994.

    1. Jerry Izenberg, *The Greatest Game Ever Played* (New York: Henry Holt and Company, 1987).
    2. For the problems confronting baseball in 1962 see *Sporting News*, January 24 and 31, 1962.
    3. On the inaugural season of the New York Mets see *Sporting News*, January 10 and February 14, 1962; Jimmy Breslin, *Can't Anybody Here Play This Game?* (New York: Viking Press, 1963); Leonard Schecter, *Once Upon a Time: The Early Years of the New York Mets* (Garden City, N.Y.: Doubleday, 1983); and Robert W. Creamer, *Stengel: The Life and Times* (New York: Simon and Schuster, 1984), 293–303.
    4. Francisco A. Roasales and Barry J. Kaplan, eds., *Houston: A Twentieth Century Urban Frontier* (Port Washington, N.Y.: Associated Faculty Press, 1983), 3; and David G. McComb, *Houston: A History* (Austin: University of Texas Press, 1981). Other good background sources on Houston include George Fuermann, *Houston: The Once and Future City* (Garden City, N.Y.: Doubleday, 1971); and Don E. Carlton, *Red Scare!: Right-wing Hysteria, Fifties Fanaticism, and Their Legacy in Texas* (Austin: Texas Monthly Press, 1983).
    5. For an in-depth discussion of the efforts to bring major league baseball to Houston see Clark Nealon, Robert Nottebart, Stanley Siegel, and James Tinsley, "The Campaign for Major League Baseball in Houston," *The Houston Review*, 7 (1985), 3–46; and for details on the construction of the Astrodome see McComb, *Houston*, 186–190; "Houston's Big New Bubble," *Sports Illustrated*, 21 (August 10, 1964), 26–27; Hy Peskin, "Baseball Under the Dome," *Sport*, 40 (July, 1968), 22–25; F. X. Talbert, "The Incredible Houston Dome," *Look*, 29 (April 20, 1965), 96–98; and "What a Wonder, What a Blunder: Houston's New Enclosed Baseball Stadium," *Life*, 58 (April 23, 1965), 76–78.
    6. For Colt Stadium see *Sporting News*, January 10 and February 21, 1962; and *Houston Chronicle*, January 11 and 25, 1962.
    7. For early Houston draft selections see Sid Sussman, "Gusher in Houston," *Baseball Monthly*, 1 (March, 1962), 14–18; *Houston Chronicle*, January 7, 1962; and *Sporting News*, February 21, 1962.
    8. For background information on Harry Craft see *Houston Chronicle*, January 21, 22, 23, 24, 25, and 26, 1962.
    9. For the early exhibition schedule see *Houston Chronicle*, March 11, 12, 13, and 14, 1962. For an excellent summary of the Colts exhibition season see *Sporting News*, April 11, 1962.
    10. For the Colts home opener see *Sporting News*, April 18, 1962; and *Houston Chronicle*, April 11, 1962. For background information on opening day hero Shantz see Lester J. Biederman, "Wee Shantz Pitched Big," *Baseball Digest*, 24 (March, 1965), 91–93; and June Benefield, "The Bobby Shantz Story," *Zest Magazine: The Houston Chronicle's Magazine of People, Places and Pleasures* (April 8, 1962), 1 and 6.
    11. *Houston Chronicle*, April 12 and 13, 1962. For background information on Roy Hofheinz see Ray Edgar, *Grand Huckster: Houston's Judge Roy Hofheinz, Genius of the*

Astrodome (Memphis, Tenn.: Memphis State University Press, 1980); and Tay Terrell, "Fast Man with a .45," *Sports Illustrated*, 46 (March 26, 1962), 32–41.

12. *Houston Chronicle*, April 14, 15, 17, and 18, 1962. For more quotes from Casey Stengel on the 1962 season see Robert Creamer, "The Return of Casey Stengel," *Baseball Monthly*, 1 (March, 1962), 20–21; Gilbert Millstein, "Musings of a Dugout Socrates," *New York Times Magazine* (August 26, 1962), 17; and Harry T. Paxton, "Casey the Indestructible," *Saturday Evening Post*, 235 (April 7, 1962), 46.

13. *Sporting News*, April 25, 1962; and *Houston Chronicle*, April 15, 19, and 20, 1962. For African-Americans in baseball during the 1962 season see William B. Furlong, "A Negro Ballplayer's Life Today," *Sport*, 33 (May, 1962), 38–39.

14. *Sporting News*, May 2 and 9, 1962; and *Houston Chronicle*, April 22, 23, 25, 26, 27, 28, 29, and 30, 1962.

15. For the Shantz trade see *Sporting News*, May 16, 1962; and *Houston Chronicle*, May 7, 1962.

16. *Houston Chronicle*, May 8, 9, 10, 11, 12, 13, and 14, 1962; and *Sporting News*, May 23, 1962.

17. *Sporting News*, May 23, 1962; and *Houston Chronicle*, May 16, 17, 18, 19, 20, and 21, 1962.

18. *Houston Chronicle*, May 22 and 23, 1962.

19. *Houston Chronicle*, May 24, 25, 26, 27, and 28, 1962. For profiles of Roman Mejias and Jim Golden see *Sporting News*, June 2 and 9, 1962.

20. *Houston Chronicle*, May 29 and 31, June 1 ,2 ,3, and 4, 1962.

21. *Houston Chronicle*, June 6, 7, 8, 9, 10, 11, 12, 13, and 15; and *Sporting News*, June 23, 1962.

22. *Houston Chronicle*, June 16, 17, 18, 19, 20, and 21, 1962; and *Sporting News*, June 23, 1962.

23. *Houston Chronicle*, June 23, 24, 25, 26, and 27, 1962; and *Sporting News*, July 7, 1962.

24. *Houston Chronicle*, June 30, July 1, 2, 3, and 5, 1962; and *Sporting News*, July 14, 1962. For background information on Bob Cerv see Charles Dexter, "Cerv-is with a Smile," *Baseball Digest*, 17 (July, 1958), 51–57; and Joe McGuff, "Cerv begins at 32," *Sport,* 37 (February, 1959), 35–37.

25. *Houston Chronicle*, July 6, 7, 8, and 9, 1962.

26. *Sporting News*, July 14 and 21, 1962. For additional background information on Dick Farrell see Mickey Herskowitz, "Dick Farrell: A Guy Has to Grow Up," *Sport*, 38 (October, 1964), 34–35; and Larry Merchant, "Losing 20 Games Isn't Easy," *Saturday Evening Post*, 236 (June 18, 1962), 58–60,

27. *Houston Chronicle*, July 12, 13, 14, 15, 16, and 18, 1962; and *Sporting News*, July 28, 1962. For profiles of the flashy Bob Aspromonte see Mickey Herskowitz, "No Candy Problem for Aspromonte Now," *Baseball Digest*, 23 (June, 1964), 71–74; and Wilt Browning, "Bob Aspromonte: A Legend in El Dorado," *Baseball Digest*, 28 (July, 1969), 49–51.

28. *Houston Chronicle*, July 18, 19, 20, 21, 22, 23, 24, 25, and 26, 1962; and *Sporting News*, August 4, 1962.

29. *Houston Chronicle*, July 28, 29, 30, and 31, 1962; and *Sporting News*, August 11, 1962. For negative commentary on the second All- Star game see Jim Brosnan, "Two All-Star Games: The Players' View," *Baseball Monthly*, 1 (July, 1962), 1; and Melvin Durslag, "All-Star Baseball Time-Again?," *TV Guide*, 9 (July 28, 1962), 4–5.

30. *Houston Chronicle*, August 1, 2, 3, 4, 5, 6, 7, 8, 9, 10, 11, 12, 13, 14, 15, 16, 17, 18, 19, and 20, 1962; and *Sporting News*, August 11, 18, and 25, 1962.

31. *Houston Chronicle*, August 21, 22, 23, 24, 25, 26, 27, 28, 29, and 30, and Sep-

tember 1 and 2, 1962; and *Sporting News*, September 1 and 8, 1962. For background information on Norm Larker see Arnold Hana, "Larker Never Lets Up," *Sport*, 31 (January, 1961), 50–52.

32. *Houston Chronicle*, September 3, 4, 5, 6, 7, 8, 9, and 13, 1962; and *Sporting News*, September 15 and 22, 1962. On hard luck Ken Johnson see Mickey Herskowitz, "Ken Johnson-A No-Hitter Worth but $1,350," *Baseball Digest*, 24 (June, 1965), 13–15.

33. *Houston Chronicle*, September 16, 17, 18, 19, and 21, 1962; and *Sporting News*, September 22 and 29, 1962.

34. *Houston Chronicle*, September 22 ,23, and 24, 1962; and *Sporting News*, October 6, 1962.

35. *Houston Chronicle*, September 26, 27, 28, 30, and October 1, 1962; and *Sporting News*, October 6 and 13, 1962. On the Giants-Dodgers rivalry with which Houston was caught up at the end of the season see Lee Allen, *The Giants and the Dodgers: The Fabulous Story of Baseball's Fiercest Feud* (New York: G. P. Putnam, 1964); Walter Bingham, "The Race is in the West: San Francisco's Giants and Los Angeles' Dodgers," *Sports Illustrated*, 16 (June 4, 1962), 36–39; and Eric Walker, "The Giants-Dodgers Rivalry," in Laurence J. Hyman, ed., *San Francisco Giants, 1958-1982: Silver Anniversary Yearbook* (San Francisco: Woodford Associates, 1982).

36. *Houston Chronicle*, October 1 and 4, 1962; and *Sporting News*, October 13, 1962.

10

Milwaukee and Atlanta, a Tale of Two Cities: Eddie, Hank, and the "Rover Boys" Head South

On the evening of September 22, 1965, over twelve thousand fans at Milwaukee County Stadium were treated to an exciting baseball game between the Los Angeles Dodgers and Milwaukee Braves. The home town faithful witnessed the removal of Dodger ace Sandy Koufax from the game in the third inning following a grand slam home run by second baseman Frank Bolling and an inside the park four base blow by lumbering catcher/first baseman Gene Oliver. However, after trailing by a margin of 6 to 1, the Dodgers rallied to take a 7 to 6 victory. The Dodger win was their sixth in a row, while the Braves defeat marked their fifth straight and ninth loss in the last eleven games, knocking the Milwaukee franchise from contention for the National League pennant.

While the game that evening was entertaining, the real story was off the field as the Braves, playing the 1965 season in Milwaukee under a court injunction, were hosting their last contest at County Stadium, before departing for the greener pastures of Atlanta and the 1966 baseball campaign. For a while the game seemed to evoke the memory of Milwaukee's enthusiastic embrace of the Braves, as stars Hank Aaron, Eddie Mathews, and Joe Torre were greeted with standing ovations. Yet, when the game ended and the players departed, the fans appeared somewhat lost and reluctant to leave. While the organist played "Auld Lang Syne" and "Till We Meet Again," some members of the crowd broke onto the field, taking turf and bases for souvenirs. Eventually, the Milwaukee faithful filtered out of the park, leaving Robert Wells of the *Milwaukee Journal* to comment, "It was all over. There was nothing left to do but just put aside the pleasant illusion that baseball matters, and go home."[1]

A much different mood was apparent on April 12, 1966 in Atlanta Stadium (later called Atlanta Fulton County Stadium) when 50,671 fans turned out to see the Braves host the Pittsburgh Pirates. Even with enthusiastic support, the Braves could not muster a win as the Pirates prevailed over Braves pitching star Tony Cloninger 3 to 2 in thirteen innings (critics claimed that Braves Manager Bobby Bragan's decision to let Cloninger pitch thirteen frames so early in the season hurt the pitcher's arm and shortened his career). Atlanta sportswriter Furman Bisher praised the city of Atlanta and Mayor Ivan Allen, Jr., for the vision to build an eighteen million dollar stadium to attract the Braves, ushering in "a grand and glorious explosion in sports in the whole South, an explosion that had studiously disassociated itself from such medieval south-of-the Mason Dixon clichés as 'cotton-picking,' 'pickaninny,' 'you-all,' 'hoecake,' and 'salate greens.'"[2]

While Atlanta celebrated the Braves with banquets, fireworks, parades, and the dismissal of public schools for opening day, the commencement of the 1966 baseball season found Milwaukee in a state of depression, well exemplified by a University of Wisconsin student who told the *Milwaukee Journal*, "I loved those Braves, and I grew up with them. I even learned to read with baseball cards. I saw many a wonderful game with my dad, and opening day was a ritual with us. Today, I don't know. I can't even bear the thought of having to listen to the Atlanta Braves on the radio."[3] Meanwhile, Milwaukee County Stadium was renovated, swept, and garnished, just in case some last minute miracle in the courts returned the Braves to the jilted lovers in Wisconsin. In the fantasy world of a "Field of Dreams," it may hold that "if you build it, they will come." However, in the real world of American business (of which professional baseball has always been part), it may depend on one's market share. Thus, the real story of the mid–1960s in Atlanta and Milwaukee was the changing patterns of demographics and economic power in American society, along with the explosive issue of race relations, which many in baseball sought to ignore, assuming the story was over following the ordeal of Jackie Robinson. The transfer of the Braves from Milwaukee to Atlanta was reflective of what journalist Kirkpatrick Sale described as an economic, political, and cultural power shift from the Midwest and East to the Sun Belt following the Second World War. According to Sale, the rise of the Sun Belt in the South and West was based upon a foundation of agribusiness, defense spending, technological development, energy sources such as oil, booming real estate values, leisure opportunities, and a population growth of from about forty million people to nearly eighty million inhabitants between 1940 and 1975.[4] This was a potentially lucrative market for baseball to tap, although a sense of vision and an orderly plan of expansion were missing among baseball moguls. Like the abandonment of areas such as Flint, Michigan by General Motors, the decision of the Braves to desert Milwaukee raises questions regarding the moral and financial responsibilities of a business to the community as well as to its employees. For example, how would African-American players react to leaving a Northern city, such as Milwaukee, for the tumultuous South of the 1960s in which the forces of segregation continued to wage a war of attrition against the civil rights movement? The story of the Braves in Milwaukee and Atlanta in the mid-1960s provides an opportunity to examine in microcosm some of the economic, cultural, and social issues defining modern America.

However, this tale of two cities must first consider a third urban center, Boston, the original home of the Braves. The 1952 season was to mark the end of the Braves eighty-two year history in Boston. Just four years after a franchise record in excess of 1.45 million ticket buyers, the 1952 Braves drew only 281,278 supporters, finishing in seventh place, a dismal thirty-two games out of first place.[5] In March, 1953, only a month before the start of the season, Braves owner Lou Perini asked his National League colleagues to approve moving the club to Milwaukee. While baseball owners blocked the efforts of maverick Bill Veeck to relocate his St. Louis Browns in Milwaukee, approval for Perini, who owned the minor league territorial rights in Milwaukee, was unanimous. The Braves move was the first franchise shift for major league baseball in over fifty years and was closely monitored by baseball magnates. However, baseball historian G. Edward White argues that movement of the Braves franchise (as well as the 1954 transfers of the Athletics from Philadelphia to Kansas City and the Browns from St. Louis to Baltimore) did not alter the fundamental structure of major league baseball, as it neither invaded minor league prerogatives nor radically changed transportation circuits. According to White, "It involved an economically depressed club in a two-team city whose population base was comparatively small...."[6] Thus, White perceives the Braves as the paradigmatic "problem franchise" identified at the 1952 *Hearing Before the Subcommittee on Study of Monopoly Power*, chaired by New York Democrat Emmanuel Celler. White, along with other baseball scholars such as Ben Rader, concludes that the significant change in baseball history occurred when more successful franchises such as the Dodgers and Giants sought greater profits in the El Dorado of California.[7]

While the Dodgers and Giants do appear to represent more of a paradigm shift, it is, nevertheless, difficult to argue with the common sense conclusion reached by David Voigt, who suggests that Perini's fellow owners "waxed green-eyed with envy," as the Braves settled into a new 6.6 million dollar county-financed stadium, drawing 1.8 million fans in 1953.[8] A full blown romance between Milwaukee and its new major league franchise was evident when a crowd of twelve thousand people showed up to welcome the team at the train station, followed by a parade witnessed by approximately 60,00 fans. Braves players were showered with attention, including free services and merchandise, ranging from dry cleaning to automobiles. Johnny Logan, the Braves shortstop during their glory days of the 1950s, continued to live in Milwaukee following his retirement and recalled, "Everywhere you went, people wanted to talk baseball. They gave us free cars, milk, bread, dry cleaning, gas. Cops stopped us to talk baseball, not to give us tickets. Some of the teachers taught the alphabet by using our names."[9]

After this whirlwind courtship, the relationship between the Braves and the city of Milwaukee cooled by the early 1960s. But for the 1950s, Milwaukee was the toast of the baseball world. Following the 1953 campaign which drew 1.8 million fans through the turnstiles, the Braves topped two million fans annually for the next four years, culminating in the figure of 2,215,404 in the World Series championship season of 1957. The Braves lost the 1958 Series to the Yankees, as well as dropping a play-off series to the Dodgers in 1959, and by the early 1960s attendance was beginning to wane. In 1961, the Milwaukee Braves attracted only 1.1 million faithful to County Stadium (the last time the team would draw a million in Milwaukee). Following the 1962 season in which attendance plummeted to 766,921, Perini sold the team to a syndicate of seven Chicago businessmen. During the latter stages of the 1963 season, press speculation arose that the Braves might be headed to Atlanta, and despite a 1964 campaign in which the Braves finished only five games out of first, the rejuvenated team still fell short of a million, bringing in 910,911 fans.[10]

There was considerable speculation as to the roots of Milwaukee's deteriorating relationship with the Braves. Following the 1958 season, popular general manager John Quinn was lured to the Philadelphia Phillies with a lucrative salary and the title of vice-president, to go along with his general manager duties. Field boss Fred Haney left Milwaukee after the 1959 season to return home and assume the position of general manager for the expansion Los Angeles Angels. The new management of the Braves proceeded to trade some of the aging Brave stars such as Joe Adcock and Lou Burdette, in addition to controversial transactions such as the dispatching of young pitching prospect Joey Jay to the Cincinnati Reds for the good field, no-hit shortstop Roy McMillan. Another management issue was the decision of Braves President Joseph F. Caines to discontinue, following the 1958 season, the practice of allowing fans to bring beer into Milwaukee County Stadium. For the Braves clientele, who were working class and could obtain beer at cost in the breweries where many of them were employed, the high price of Stadium beer was a major issue. Although the beer ban was dropped midway through the 1962 season, the damage was already done. Perhaps the disenchantment of Braves fans was best summed up in a column by Red Smith in which the journalist quoted a Milwaukee cab driver as complaining, "Where's Joe Adcock? Where's Johnny Logan? Where's Lou Burdette? They got rid of all the players the fans knew and then expected people to come out to see a lot of bushers they never even heard of. If Fred Haney and John Quinn were still here, they'd never even have gone below two million."[11]

Although the Chicago group, led by Board Chair Bill Bartholomay, maintained that their intention was to keep the Braves in Milwaukee, by July, 1963, they were engaging in exploratory discussions with Atlanta officials, culminating in a February, 1964 Chicago meeting between Atlanta Mayor Ivan Allen and Bartholomay in which the Braves agreed to move to Atlanta for the 1965 season. In exchange, Atlanta committed to the construction of a municipally financed stadium.[12] And, indeed, Atlanta, with a metropolitan population exceeding a million, and the South offered a lucrative market for Northern business investment. In his study of the modern South, Numan Bartley writes that per capita income in the South increased more rapidly than on the national level during the post World War II period, so that by 1960 per capita income in the South was 76 percent of that in the nation. This type of statistical evidence led historian Dewey Grantham to conclude, "The convergence of North and South in the half-century following World War II was nowhere more apparent than in the economic development and diversification, industrialization, dynamic new middle class, and rising income and consumer-oriented lifestyle of Southerners in this period."[13]

One of the chief beneficiaries of this Southern economic growth was Atlanta, the city which billed itself as "too busy to hate." The self-proclaimed capital of the new South hailed itself as a center of transportation, wholesale and retail transactions, business-services income, bank clearings, corporate branch offices, and light industry based around aircraft and automobile assembly plants. According to the candid memoirs of Atlanta Mayor Ivan Allen, the economic and political elite of Atlanta were "white, Anglo-Saxon, Protestant, Atlantan, business-oriented, nonpolitical, moderate, well-bred, well educated, pragmatic, and dedicated to the betterment of Atlanta."[14] While Atlanta was modernized and governed by a relatively progressive business elite, who supported the economic benefits and political prestige involved with the acquisition of a major league sport franchise, women as well as African-Americans, who comprised approximately 40 percent of the city's population, were missing from Mayor Allen's coalition. However, Allen's description of the Atlanta leadership well paralleled that of the Chicago businessmen with whom he was negotiating the fate of major league baseball in Milwaukee.

The secret shuttle diplomacy between Chicago and Atlanta was made public in July, 1964 by a *Sporting News* article (apparently derived from sources within the St. Louis Cardinals organization). According to the *Sporting News*, the Braves were ready to make the shift to Atlanta following the 1964 season. When confronted with the newspaper accounts of an eminent move to Atlanta, Board Chairman Bartholomay and Braves President John McHale hedged in their comments, pointing out that the Braves encountered a forty thousand dollar deficit in 1963, and with reduced television revenues in Milwaukee the club would require an attendance mark of over one million to break even in 1964 (they would draw over 900,000). McHale concluded, "It is only right that from an economic standpoint we be permitted to assess our position at the end of the season."

The citing of the corporate bottom line by club officials enraged Milwaukee County Executive John Doyne, who threatened legal action against the Braves if the team failed to honor the remaining year on its contract with Milwaukee County Stadium. Doyne blasted the power structure of professional baseball, asserting, "If the Braves pull up stakes for Atlanta, it could be the worst mark against baseball since the Black Sox scandal.... How a ball club is permitted to come into a city like this, milk it for a dozen years and then jump elsewhere, I can't understand." Meanwhile, Wisconsin Congressman Henry W. Reuss threatened the baseball establishment with Congressional action removing the sport's antitrust exemption. While National League President Warren Giles gave no encouragement to Milwaukee, Baseball Commissioner Ford Frick sought to downplay passions by observing that if the Braves did move to Atlanta, Milwaukee would be considered for major league expansion.[15]

While the pennant race heated up, the issue of the Braves franchise transfer was placed on the back burner. However, at an October 21, 1964 Braves Board of Directors meeting held in Chicago, a vote was taken to ask National League owners to approve the move of the Braves to Atlanta for the 1965 season. The next day National League owners meeting in New York appeared ready to support the action of Braves management, until served with a restraining order that would force the Braves to adhere with the provisions of their 1965 contract with Milwaukee County Stadium.

Furman Bisher of the *Atlanta Journal and Constitution* described the legal actions of the Milwaukee officials, especially Milwaukee County Executive Eugene Grobschmidt, as spiteful, observing, "We had a stadium eagerly waiting for a team, really lusting for it. Milwaukee had a team that didn't want Milwaukee. Milwaukee, in truth, by this time viewed the team with scorn, but would hold it to its legal truth just for pure damned spite, if nothing else."[16]

At a November 7, 1964, meeting of National League owners in Phoenix, the lords of baseball decided to obey the restraining order and dictated that the Braves fulfill their lease with Milwaukee, but approved the transfer of the club to Atlanta for the 1966 season. This ruling by the baseball establishment called for a lame duck season for the Braves in 1965 and created an acrimonious season for team officials, players, and the citizens of both Atlanta and Milwaukee.

The *Sporting News*, the self-proclaimed Bible of baseball, took a strong position against the Braves transfer, citing the hypocrisy of team management. For example, the paper chastised Bartholomay for his April 11, 1964 comment, "We are positively not moving. We're playing in Milwaukee, whether you're talking of 1964, 1965, or 1975. I hope this is the last time anyone tries to link us with Atlanta or any other city." The report went on to observe that the Braves Chairman uttered these comments one month after making a verbal commitment to Mayor Allen and Atlanta. Clearly, the *Sporting News* was concerned that the situation in Milwaukee might endanger the sport's antitrust exemption.[17]

Such fears seemed justified when Congressman Emmanuel Celler, Chairman of the House Judiciary Committee, agreed to appear on the weekly radio show of Wisconsin Congressman Reuss. Calling baseball a business rather than a sport, Celler suggested that organized baseball "no longer be immunized under the antitrust laws."[18] Celler's remarks and the Milwaukee situation were only one of many threats to the baseball establishment during the pivotal 1965 season. The acquisition of the New York Yankees by the Columbia Broadcasting Corporation also raised serious questions with antitrust implications. Senator Phil Hart of Michigan was holding Senate hearings regarding whether all major sports should be placed under Congressional regulation, and the players, who had never been consulted regarding franchise shifts, were growing more assertive, selecting as their spokesman Marvin Miller of the Steelworkers' Union. And last, but not least, Commissioner Frick was completing a lame duck term. The response of baseball management to these issues was timid and shortsighted. They refused to appropriate pension funds so that Miller and the players' organization could have a New York office, balked at formulating expansion plans, and selected a weak Commissioner, General William Eckert, who had little knowledge of the game and would be subservient to baseball ownership.[19]

On the other hand, the *Sporting News* was quite critical of baseball ownership and legal maneuvers which marred the 1965 baseball season in Milwaukee. The editorial position of the paper was that Milwaukee should support the Braves in 1965 and that their good faith efforts should be rewarded with an expansion franchise in 1966 or as soon as possible. Following the 1965 baseball campaign, the *Sporting News* editorialized that under the circumstances the Braves season attendance mark of 555,584 fans was decent, and that baseball should make expansion its number one agenda item, and Milwaukee should be the number one city on the expansion list. The paper asserted, "Milwaukee wants major league baseball. It wants a major league club under Milwaukee ownership. If it gets this, there will be no question whatsoever about support for the club. It will be there."[20]

Accordingly, Teams, Inc. of Milwaukee, along with representatives from Oakland and San Diego, made an expansion presentation at baseball's annual winter meeting. These efforts were rebuffed by the major league establishment, who maintained that the talent pool was insufficient to support expansion. Editorial reaction by the *Sporting News* was spirited, arguing, "This is the greatest nation on the face of the globe. There is no dearth of baseball talent here. There is only a dearth of desire to encourage and nurture it. Baseball is not suffering from a shortage of anything. Its burdened by a surplus—of can't do men in a can do age." The paper continued to push the expansion issue throughout the early months of 1966, even going so far as to suggest the Braves stay in Milwaukee if a new franchise was unavailable for the beer city. The consistent editorial support for the Milwaukee position led one Atlanta partisan, Lester Wallace of Social Circle, Georgia, to complain that the *Sporting News* was a "snotty" Yankee magazine. Wallace wrote, "Well, in the eyes of God-fearing Southerners, we compare your magazine with LBJ — Nuff said."[21]

Meanwhile, the Braves and the cities of Milwaukee and Atlanta spent the months following the 1965 season wrangling in court. A perusal of the legal depositions by the leading participants, and a sampling of editorial opinion in the *Milwaukee Journal* and *Atlanta Constitution and Journal*, indicates a degree of bitterness which made any type of compromise next to impossible. In December, 1965, Judge Sam McKenzie of Fulton County (Atlanta) Superior Court granted an injunction at the request of the Atlanta Stadium Authority, mandating the Braves to honor their twenty-five year contract to use Atlanta Stadium. In support of Judge McKenzie's ruling, the National League ordered the Braves to fulfill their obligations to Atlanta, and in February, 1966, the city of Atlanta went into federal court in Houston (National League city) and was granted a decision requiring that the Braves observe their contractual agreement with the Atlanta Stadium Authority. All that was left for Milwaukee was for the state of Wisconsin to pursue its allegation that the Braves had violated state antitrust law. During the fall and winter of 1965-1966, the Wisconsin Circuit Court of Judge Elmer Roller processed numerous depositions from officials representing Milwaukee and the Braves baseball club.[22]

Milwaukee City Attorney John T. Fleming agreed to petition, along with the county, pointing out that the taxpayers of Milwaukee had contributed millions toward the construction of a ballpark and related expenses so the National League could conduct professional baseball games. Fleming concluded that the Braves afforded the city entertainment, relaxation, and education. Accordingly, the attorney argued, "The denial of major league baseball and with it a denial of a major league baseball franchise to persons who are genuinely interested in providing baseball for Milwaukee, constitutes a denial of a substantial and significant right to the city." The law suit mirrored the popular indignation displayed by the *Milwaukee Journal*, whose editorial and sports pages satirized the Chicago ownership of the Braves as the "Rover Boys," while characterizing them as practicing "greed, ingratitude, deception, and betrayal."[23]

There was, indeed, considerable animosity in Milwaukee as many citizens participated in a boycott of Coca-Cola products as the corporate headquarters of the soft drink conglomerate were housed in Atlanta. It was also the contention of Milwaukee officials that the Braves had done little to promote the team in 1965, seeking to induce artificially low attendance figures in support of the club's abandonment of the city. In fact, County Board Chairman Grobschmidt, who had quarreled with Braves Manager Bragan during the course of the 1965 baseball campaign, continued to assert that the Braves had not played "the baseball they were capable of." According to Grobschmidt, Bragan told him that there was nothing dumber than a dumb politician, to which the County Executive retorted, "There is nothing dumber than a dumb baseball manager."[24]

Milwaukee's suit questioning baseball's antitrust exemption also enjoyed support from other victims of the baseball establishment. Bill Veeck, whose efforts to move his St. Louis Browns franchise to Milwaukee or Baltimore was blocked by his fellow owners, retained bitter feelings toward baseball ownership. After issuing a public statement deploring the duplicity and greed of Braves ownership, the baseball maverick was asked whether he was considering getting back in baseball. To this inquiry, Veeck quipped, "When I go back to work, I'll probably go into something more legitimate than baseball — like running dope or something."[25] Potentially even more damaging to the baseball power structure was the breaking of a sixteen year silence by former Giants outfielder Danny Gardella, who revealed that baseball owners had paid him sixty thousand dollars to drop his legal challenge to baseball's antitrust exemption. Gardella, who had jumped from the Giants to the Mexican League in the late 1940s, found his return to major league baseball barred by a blacklist. Evidently embittered by the fact that he lost his baseball career and failed in his efforts to even the score with organized baseball, Gardella announced his support for Milwaukee's legal action against the Braves and National League. Sounding almost Marxist in his branding of baseball owners as parasites, Gardella proclaimed, "The same kind of men ran baseball when I was playing. These men are vampires who have been sucking the blood of the American people until nothing is left but the phantom they call baseball. These guys are like spores or mushrooms that suck up nourishment and then move on. If they do this to the American people, we're all lost."[26]

Despite the testimonials of Veeck and Gardella, and the fact that baseball enjoyed a privileged legal position, Braves management and their supporters continued to cloak their rhetoric in the fabric of free enterprise and laissez-faire capitalism. Thus, in the *Atlanta Journal and Constitution*, sports editor Jesse Outlar wrote, "So what's wrong with an owner seeking a profit? The U. S. is supposed to be the land of free enterprise. It has always been the opinion here that a baseball owner has as much right to move as a football or basketball owner, or a brewery or soft drink owner." Outlar maintained that the Milwaukee law suit was spiteful and sought to interfere with the economic development of the South. The Atlanta paper was also generous in its support of Bartholomay, who, according to Outlar, was branded by Wisconsin residents as the "vilest villain since Genghis Khan." Instead, the Braves Board Chair was simply a good businessman like the progressive interests championed by Mayor Allen in Atlanta. There was simply too much competition in the Midwest with the two Chicago clubs and the 1961 addition of the Minnesota Twins, while there was no major league competition in the virgin baseball market of the booming Southeast. Bartholomay insisted that Milwaukee citizen promises to promote the club with season ticket sales and public purchase of stock were not forthcoming, indicating a lack of interest in the club. The Board Chair concluded his deposition by observing that he reluctantly voted to move the club due to the "terrible disappointment and disbelief that the commitment had not been carried out." No such reluctance was expressed by the volatile Braves Manager Bragan, who was the focal point of fan resentment in Milwaukee. The irrepressible skipper asserted that he would not return as manager for three times his forty-five thousand dollar salary if it meant going to work in Milwaukee again. He labeled the Wisconsin city as a "bad baseball town," although Milwaukee would get the last laugh when the Atlanta Braves let Bragan go during the course of the 1966 season.[27]

National League President Warren Giles was given the final word, once again placing the issue within the parameter of free enterprise rhetoric. Giles insisted, "Frankly, it would appear that under the American system of free enterprise only one reason is needed. In the last three years, the Braves suffered some three million dollars in losses. That seems sufficient reason to transfer any business." The case for the National League was presented by its attorney Bowie Kuhn (later to serve as Commissioner of Baseball), who in his memoirs maintained that his heart and responsibilities were not in the same place, for he opposed franchise transfers. Nevertheless, Kuhn and the National League successfully pursued the case through the courts.[28]

On April 13, 1966, Judge Roller rendered his decision on the Milwaukee antitrust case, ruling against major league baseball and ordering the National League to file a 1967 expansion plan, including Milwaukee, by May 16. If the League failed to provide such a plan, the Braves would be dispatched back to Milwaukee. In addition, Roller levied fines and court costs against Braves management, the National League, and each club within the League. National League attorney Kuhn announced that the decision would be appealed. In August, the Wisconsin State Supreme Court overturned Roller's decision, agreeing with him in principle, but concluding that interstate commerce regulation of major league baseball franchise transfers was national policy and a job for the Congress. The Supreme Court refused to review the Milwaukee case, letting the judgment of the Wisconsin State Supreme Court stand, reaffirming that if baseball was to be brought under the umbrella of antimonopoly legislation it would have to be through Congressional action.[29] However, the inactivity of both the Courts and Congress allowed baseball owners to continue their unbridled quest for profits with no countervailing power of community responsibility. The irony of this situation is that in 1970 Milwaukee welcomed the transfer of the Seattle Pilots, renaming them the Brewers, leading Seattle to pursue antitrust litigation until it was granted an expansion franchise, the Seattle Mariners. For most of their history, the Brewers and Mariners have struggled as small market franchises, while after a difficult time in Atlanta, the Braves have emerged as the team of the 90s with a sound scouting system, Ted Turner's money, and the visibility of a super station.

But the structure of the game did change in 1965 with the tapping of Marvin Miller to head the Major League Players Association, which eventually did provide a countervailing force to corporate greed, albeit one with a player "class consciousness" of sorts with just as little community commitment as the big boys. When the decision was made to move the Braves to Atlanta there was no consultation with the players, and there is little evidence that baseball management even considered the ramifications of the civil rights movement, which contributed to the formation of a culture in which players were more assertive, and racial segregation upon African-American players who would be required to play in a region where legal racial separation was still a major factor.

Of course, management in the early 1960s paid scant attention to the opinion of players, whether white or black. Thus, Eddie Mathews, who made the transition from Boston and was the last of the original Milwaukee Braves, expressed anxiety to reporters on September 22, 1965, when he made his last appearance at County Stadium as a member of the Milwaukee Braves. Mathews explained, "I was nervous before the game — after all, this may be the end of the 13 best years of my life. I'm ordinarily not a sentimental guy, but this really shakes me up. I haven't felt this way since we came back from winning the 1957 World Series and the crowd greeted us at the airport. But I'm unhappy too. I'm sorry that the Braves are leaving, if that's the way its got to be. But there's nothing we can do about it."[30] This apprehension of being treated as an interchangeable commodity to be transferred from Milwaukee to Atlanta weighed even more heavily upon Aaron. Even though Milwaukee had a relatively small African-American population and its own history of racial discrimination,[31] Aaron, who grew up in Alabama, was not eager to return to his native region. In his memoirs, Aaron, who finished his playing career with the Brewers, insisted that he never got over the trauma of the Braves departure from Milwaukee.[32]

Yet, the power structure of major league baseball, while it had much to say about the intricacies of antimonopoly legislation, had little comment about the racial implications of a franchise transfer to Atlanta. Perhaps this was because of a certain smugness within the baseball establishment that after Jackie Robinson and the signing of other African-American players, racism in baseball was over, and the sport could serve as a model for racial integration within the United States. This sense of complacency regarding race relations was often reflected in the pages of the *Sporting News.* For example, in May, 1964, the paper editorialized that baseball was exempt from civil rights demonstrations as the sport was "completely integrated." The editorial concluded, "Long ago, baseball proved that Negroes and whites could work together in perfect harmony and understanding. It takes a little time. Almost two decades ago baseball camps were the targets of early civil rights groups. Baseball met the challenge and worked things out."[33]

Ball players of African-American descent understood the fallacy of this argument for both baseball and American society.[34] And certainly Aaron's experience in Atlanta exposed the resiliency of racism in the region and city despite the efforts of an influential black middle class leadership which included Martin Luther King, Sr. Along with the Braves in 1966 came efforts by the Student Nonviolent Coordinating Committee (SNCC) to polarize Atlanta politics along racial lines. SNCC's endeavors failed, and the moderate African-American bourgeoisie of Atlanta remained ascendant.[35] But the black establishment was certainly not part of the progressive elite led by Mayor Allen. And champions of Mayor Allen and his progressive business alliance, such as Furman Bisher of the *Atlanta Constitution and Journal,* could be quite condescending. Bisher asserted that Atlanta was "no Negro paradise by any means, but compared to those in the rest of the Deep South, the city's problems on the racial level have been negligible." However, Bisher was very disconcerted that Northern newspapers, especially those in Milwaukee, had printed stories that Aaron and Lee Maye, another African-American outfielder for the Braves, were reluctant to live in Atlanta and feared for their safety. Braves management dealt with the problem by trading Maye to Houston two weeks into the 1965 season. Bisher described Maye as born in Alabama, but raised in California, where he pursued an off-season career as a "hip" singer. According to Bisher, Maye was "a moody kind, and often sensitive enough to feel that the guy next to him is trying to put something over on him even when he is passing the time of day."[36] In other words, Maye was an African-American who did not know and accept his place. And for that matter, neither did Henry Aaron, but he had a great deal more talent than Lee Maye.

Aaron needed reserves of character and talent as he dealt with the challenges of life in Atlanta. He and his wife were able to purchase a beautiful home, although, of course, it was located in a segregated neighborhood. As a prominent African-American player, Aaron received several hate letters a week in addition to hearing the racial insults hurled in his direction at the ballpark. Aaron's wife Barbara was even arrested when she tried to drive into the stadium, and a white guard, who did not recognize her, stopped the car, pulled his gun, and verbally abused her. The charges were dropped after the intervention of Mayor Allen. Aaron responded the only way he knew, with his bat. In his memoirs, Aaron asserted, "I knew that, as a black player, I would be on trial in Atlanta, and I needed a decisive way to win over the white people before they thought of a reason to hate me. And I believed that the way to do all of this was with home runs." Aaron's decision to let his bat do the talking culminated in the surpassing of Babe Ruth's career home run mark, which, ironically, seemed to increase the racial abuse to which the Braves outfielder was subjected. However, Aaron concluded that, while he was no Jackie Robinson, he made a contribution to the civil rights movement in the South and Atlanta. Thus, Aaron quoted Mayor Allen as proclaiming, "There was a lot of subtle apprehension about how the South's first major-league sports franchise and its black players would go over. Hank played a major role in making the transition and confirming the end of segregation in the South through his thoughtful consideration and exemplary conduct. He taught us how to do it. "[37]

So by the summer of 1966, Hank, Eddie, and the Rover Boys had departed Milwaukee and were entrenched in Atlanta. The economic maneuvers and goals of the Chicago ownership group, headed by Bartholomay, received considerable scrutiny from the factions in the new South advocating modernization and from the industrial centers of the East and Midwest who feared losing jobs and businesses to the Southern rim. However, scant attention was give to the predilections of Mathews and, especially, Aaron. Baseball erroneously assumed that it had solved the racial question. The game of baseball is too much of a reflection of the nation in which it was conceived for that to be the case. The continuing underrepresentation of African-Americans in baseball's management structure, along with the racial commentary of baseball officials such as Al Campanis and Marge Schott, indicate that much remains to be done. And as was the case with Atlanta, where the population in 1966 was approximately 40 percent African-American, little has been done to attract African-American fans to the ballpark.[38]

What conclusions are we to draw from the odyssey of the Rover Boys, Eddie, and Hank to the South? It is a tale of hypocrisy and greed as Milwaukee retakes the Braves from Boston, only to have them stolen by Atlanta. While baseball expansion offers some democratization as new regions and urban centers acquire the opportunity to host major league baseball, franchise transfers, in the constant search for new markets and sources of profit, undermine values of community loyalty. A life-long fan of the Houston Astros can open his/her morning paper, only to discover that the team may move to Washington, D.C.— a two-time victim of franchise relocation. Thus, it may be argued that the transferring of franchises to Milwaukee and Atlanta played a pivotal role in turning baseball fan allegiance from the community to the corporate sector. In the late nineteenth century one rooted for the Brooklyns or the Bostons; now one is a Red Sox or a Dodger fan. Nevertheless, cities continue to engage in unbridled competition for the favors of the baseball corporate sector, offering tax credits, municipal stadiums, and tracts of land, in the hope that a baseball franchise will somehow restore a deteriorating sense of community in urban America. Nor has the emergence of the Major League Players Association done anything to restrain the greed of baseball management. No longer simply chattel to be moved from one city to the next, veteran players now have the option to sell their services to the highest bidder, just like the big boys in the three-piece suits. In recent years, the sport of baseball has suffered through prolonged labor negotiations resulting in strikes and a cancelled World Series. The sport is leaderless and speculation regarding franchise transfers are rampant, as a framework for assuring a competitive balance for small market cities remains elusive. The values of community, loyalty, and the greater good of the game and country continue to lack representation, just as in 1964-1966 when Atlanta and Milwaukee struggled over the Rover Boys and the rights to the services of Eddie Mathews and Hank Aaron.

Endnotes

This piece was originally published in *Nine: A Journal of Baseball History and Social Policy Perspectives*, 6:1 (1997), 29-47.

1. For accounts of the Braves last game in Milwaukee see *Milwaukee Journal*, September 23, 1965: and *Sporting News*, October 9, 1965.
2. For opening day in Atlanta see *Atlanta Journal and Constitution*, April 13, 1966; *Sporting News*, April 30, 1966; and Furman Bisher, *Miracle in Atlanta: The Atlanta Braves Story* (Cleveland: World Publishing Company, 1965), 2.
3. *Milwaukee Journal*, April 13, 1965.
4. Kirkpatrick Sale, *Power Shift: The Rise of the Southern Rim and Its Challenge to the Eastern Establishment* (New York: Vintage Books, 1976), 18–53.
5. For an overview of the Braves in Boston see Gary Caruso, *The Braves Encyclopedia* (Philadelphia: Temple University Press, 1995).
6. G. Edward White, *Creating the National Pastime: Baseball Transforms Itself, 1903-1953* (Princeton, N J: Princeton University Press, 1996), 312–315.
7. Ben Rader, *Baseball: A History of America's Game* (Urbana: University of Illinois Press, 1994), 179–185.
8. David Q. Voigt, *American Baseball, Volume III: From Postwar Expansion to the Electronic Age* (University Park: Pennsylvania State University Press, 1983), xxiv–xxv.
9. For the initial reaction of Milwaukee to the Braves see W. C. Heinz, "Baseball Players' Dream Town: Milwaukee and Her Braves," *Cosmopolitan,* 136 (May, 1954),

88–93; Gilbert Millstein, "More Brooklyn Than Brooklyn: Milwaukee and Its New Ball Team," *New York Times Magazine*, July 5, 1953, 10–11; and "Sausages, Sauerbraten, and Sympathy for the Milwaukee Braves," *Life*, 35 (July 6, 1953), 39–42. Johnny Logan is quoted in the *Milwaukee Journal*, September 22, 1965. For a profile of Logan see Red Gleason, "Johnny Logan's a Fighter," *Sport*, 21 (June, 1956), 42–45.

10. For a discussion of attendance figures in Milwaukee see Caruso, *Braves Encyclopedia*, 345–348.

11. For explanations regarding the loss of enthusiasm in Milwaukee for the Braves see Charles Dexter, "Milwaukee's Fight for Baseball," *Baseball Digest*, 25 (December, 1964), 6–7; William Furlong, "Milwaukee's Troubles: Too Many Stars Are Hard to Handle," *Sport*, 29 (February, 1960), 12–15; Frank Graham, Jr., "The Inside Story of the Braves Dissension," *Sport*, 33 (February, 1962), 36–37; Caruso, *Braves Encyclopedia*, 324–325; and *Milwaukee Journal*, September 22, 1965.

12. For the negotiations between Atlanta and the Braves ownership see Bisher, *Miracle in Atlanta*; and Ivan Allen, Jr., *Mayor: Notes on the Sixties* (New York, 1971).

13. For the post World War II economic development of the South see Numan V. Brantley, *The New South,!945-1980* (Baton Rouge: Louisiana State University Press, 1995), 146; Dewey W. Grantham, *The South in Modem America: A Region at Odds* (New York: HarperCollins, 1994), 339; Richard M. Bernard and Bradley R. Rice, eds., *Sunbelt Cities: Politics and Growth Since World War II* (Austin: University of Texas Press, 1983); Carl Abbott, *The New Urban America: Growth and Politics in Sunbelt Cities* (Chapel Hill: University of North Carolina Press, 1987); and David R. Goldfield, *Cotton Fields and Skyscrapers: Southern City and Region* (Baton Rouge: Louisiana State University Press, 1982).

14. For the development of Atlanta see Tojman A. Hartshorn, *Metropolis in Georgia: Atlanta's Price as a Major Transaction Center* (Cambridge: Harvard University Press, 1976); Bradley R. Rice, "If Dixie Were Atlanta," in Bernard and Rice, eds., *Sunbelt Cities*, 31–57; and Allen, *Mayor*, 30–31.

15. *Sporting News*, July 11 and 18, 1964; and August 1, 1964.

16. Bisher, *Miracle in Atlanta*, p. 107.

17. For the *Sporting News* reaction to the Braves transfer see November 7, 1964; and January 23, 1965.

18. For Celler's remarks see *Milwaukee Journal*, February 6, 1965; and *Sporting News*, February 20, 1965.

19. For baseball ownership's limited response to the challenges facing the sport in 1965 see John Helyar, *Lords of the Realm: The Real History of Baseball* (New York: Villard Books, 1994), 16–38.

20. *Sporting News*, October 9, 1965.

21. *Sporting News*, January 29, 1965; April 2, 23, and 30, 1965; and May 21, 1965. It is interesting to note that economist Andrew Zimbalist is in agreement with the *Sporting News*, arguing the myth of a talent shortage for Major League baseball. In fact, Zimbalist asserts that expansion is one of the major solutions to contemporary difficulties plaguing the sport. For the views of Zimbalist see *Baseball and Billions: A Probing Look Inside the Big Business of Our National Pastime* (New York: Basic Books, 1992).

22. For a summary of legal actions regarding Milwaukee, Atlanta, and the Braves, see Bisher, *Miracle in Atlanta*, 178–179.

23. *Milwakee Journal*, September 16 and 22, 1965.

24. For the Coca-Cola boycott see Hank Aaron with Lonnie Wheeler, *I Had a Hammer: The Hank Aaron Story* (New York: HarperCollins, 1991), 174–175; and Bisher, *Miracle in Atlanta*, 69–71. For Grobschmidt's testimony, see *Milwaukee Journal*, September 28, 1965.

25. For the views of Bill Veeck on the Braves franchise shift from Milwaukee to Atlanta and the baseball establishment see Bill Veeck, *The Hustler's Handbook* (New York: G. P. Putnam, 1963); and *Sporting News,* March 5, 1966.

26. On Danny Gardella see *Sporting News,* March 12, 1966.

27. *Atlanta Journal and Constitution,* February 3, 1966; January 14, 1966; and January 28, 1966. For additional background information on Bragan see Milton Gross, "Bobby Bragan Comes of Age," *Baseball Digest,* 27 (June, 1963), 59–61; and Donald Honig, *The Man in the Dugout* (Chicago: Follett Publishing Co., 1977), 7–30.

28. *Atlanta Journal and Constitution,* February 26, 1966; and Bowie Kuhn, *Hardball: The Education of a Baseball Commissioner* (New York: Times Books, 1987), 20–22.

29. For Judge Roller's decision see *Milwaukee Journal,* April 14, 1966. For the appeal process see *Sporting News,* April 23, 1966; August 13, 1966; and December 24, 1966.

30. *Milwaukee Journal,* September 23, 1965. For additional information on Mathews, who joined with Aaron to eclipse the teammate home run mark of Babe Ruth and Lou Gehrig, see Robert Creamer, "Matinee Idol Into Mature Hero," *Sports Illustrated,* 8 (June 2, 1958), 36–42; Eddie Mathews, "My Fifteen Years with the Braves," *Sport,* 42 (August, 1966), 28–31; and Al Hirshberg, *The Eddie Mathews Story* (New York: Julian Messner, 1960).

31. Joe William Trotter, *Black Milwaukee: The Making of an Industrial Proletariat, 1915-45* (Urbana: University of Illinois Press, 1988).

32. Aaron, *I Had a Hammer,* 178.

33. *Sporting News,* May 7, 1964.

34. For the experience of African-American players after Jackie Robinson see Jules Tygiel, *Baseball's Great Experiment: Jackie Robinson and His Legacy* (New York: Vintage Books, 1969), 211–344; Larry Moffi and Jonathan Kronstadt, *Crossing the Line: Black Major Leaguers, 1947-1959* (Jefferson, North Carolina: McFarland & Company, 1994); Curt Flood with Richard Carter, *The Way It Is* (New York: Tndent Press, 1970); and Dick Allen with Tim Whitaker, *Crash: The Life and Times of Dick Allen* (New York: Ticknor & Fields, 1989).

35. Clayborne Carson, *Struggle: SNCC and the Black Awakening of the 1960s* (Cambridge: Harvard University Press, 1981), 224–226.

36. Bisher, *Miracle in Atlanta,* 167–171.

37. Aaron, *I Had a Hammer,* 179–184.

38. Rader, *Baseball,* 214.

11

The Times Were A-Changin': Baseball as a Symbol of American Values in Transition, 1963–1964

Folk-rock artist Bob Dylan's "The Times They Are A-Changin'," written shortly before President Kennedy's assassination in 1963 and released in album form in 1964, well reflects the winds of change which would assault the established structure of organized baseball during the turbulent 1960s.[1] Just as the Vietnam War, the civil rights movement, college demonstrations, the counterculture, and violence in the streets would challenge the traditional values of many Americans, so did the issues of free speech, racial unrest, player organization, economic grievance, and the reserve clause force baseball traditionalists to reexamine the "national pastime." By the end of the decade many traditionalists, who supported so-called old fashioned values and the sport of baseball, would bemoan the changes made in American society and join with Simon and Garfunkel in recalling the glory days of the past and wonder, "Where Have You Gone Joe DiMaggio?"[2] However, these "nattering nabobs of negativism" may have overestimated the extent of change, as the 1980s would witness the election of a conservative President and the reemergence of baseball as America's favorite spectator sport. In fact, there may be some correlation between these two events as one must remember Ronald Reagan's career in show business began with his re-creation of White Sox and Cubs games over Iowa radio.[3]

But certainly the 1960s were a divisive time and brought change to both baseball and American society. Although some historians remain skeptical of contemporary history, the 1960s have received serious atten-

157

tion by scholars. Also alterations in the relationship between players and baseball management have provoked study,[4] but what of baseball as a symbol of values during this turbulent time? Advocates of baseball praise the stability of the sport. An individual who died in 1900 could be resurrected today and still easily follow the flow of a major league baseball game. It might not be so easy to make such a statement for the spectator sports of football and basketball. Nevertheless, this stable traditional game was rocked by change in the 1960s, as was the rest of the nation, and survived with many of its fundamental values intact. Perhaps through focusing on the institution of baseball we may learn something about America and how the times were a-changin' in the 1960s.

While the social and psychological importance of sports has been suggested by many students of American recreation and leisure, baseball, the "national pastime," has often been viewed as the sport most closely identified with American cultural and social values.[5] For example, a subcommittee report of the House Judiciary Committee in 1952 examining organized baseball asserted, "Other sports flourish for a brief season and then sink to the background to await a rebirth of interest both in season and out. Whether it is in June or December, the public is interested in the national game."[6] Baseball has also been extolled by numerous writers and scholars, producing some outstanding literature which has led some to dub baseball as the "intellectual's game."[7] Thus, writing in the *Massachusetts Review*, George Grella, paraphrasing Jacques Barzun, succinctly made the case for baseball, stating, "Anyone who does not understand the game cannot hope to understand the country."[8]

In recent years, American historians have followed the suggestions made by Barzun and Grella, recognizing that baseball represents a unique cultural perspective through which American values may be examined. Peter Levine's biography of A. G. Spalding focused upon the efforts of Spalding and other baseball pioneers to utilize the sport as a means by which to impose some order upon the chaos of post Civil War industrialization; while Steven Riess, in his study of baseball in the progressive era, emphasized the role of sportswriters in making the sport appear relevant to the needs of middle class Americans. According to Riess, "The national pastime was portrayed in such a way that it supplied some of the symbols, myths, and legends society needed to bind its members together." A similar role for the sport in the 1920s and 1930s was suggested in the work of Richard Crepeau, who has written that for the inner war years baseball was the game that "most typified American institutions and teachings." And Jules Tygiel utilized the story of Jackie Robinson to produce considerable insights into race relations in post World War II America.[9]

Thus scholars have found baseball a fertile field in which to investigate established American values. This would appear to be especially true for World War II and the Cold War of the late 1940s and early 1950s as baseball was identified with patriotic and traditional values threatened by the external enemies of fascism and communism. In fact, viewers of the late show may still be treated to scenes of character actor William Bendix dying in action in the Pacific theater, while asking for the score of a Dodgers' game with his last gasp of air.[10] Baseball in the Cold War era lacked the sentimentality of a William Bendix, but the sport easily fit into the post World War II era liberal consensus. The ideology of the liberal consensus was based upon two cornerstone assumptions: the spread of communism was a clear and present danger to the United States, while the structure of American society was fundamentally sound and postwar difficulties would be solved by an expanding economy. Thus in coping with such postwar issues as racism, union organization, monopoly, and challenges to the reserve clause, organized baseball would emphasize the values of consensus in which the loyalty of the organization man was rewarded. Conformity was the norm, and there was no reason to rock the boat. Baseball executives, like businessmen and government bureaucrats, were looking out for the welfare of the individual.[11] However, the consensus came apart in the 1960s as minorities, women, and young people, both off and on the playing field, challenged the assumptions commonly held in the liberal consensus.

Perhaps the best time to begin an investigation into the breakdown of the liberal consensus in the institution of baseball would be the year 1963, when Bob Dylan was composing his anthem of national unrest and visions of Camelot were destroyed by an assassin's bullet. It would be increasingly difficult for complacent Americans to ignore the violence and winds of change shaking their windows and rattling their walls.

Facing increased competition from football and other sources of entertainment in an affluent society, baseball entered 1963 with some foreboding, but the *Sporting News*, the major trade paper of the game and referred to as the Bible of baseball, insisted that there was nothing fundamentally unsound with the game. Publisher C. C. Johnson Spink labeled as "rubbish" the claims of professional football to be the sport of the 1960s. Of course, baseball needed some cosmetic surgery to keep up with the times, but the sport did not require a major operation. Spink advocated better marketing, speeding up the game, better coordination between organized baseball and the college game, orderly expansion from the current two ten team leagues, and a free agent draft to help provide additional talent for second division clubs.[12] This program hardly represented a radical overhaul of the game and fit well within the concept of the liberal consensus in which baseball was a successful business that could solve any difficulties through the liberal values of orderly expansion, efficiency, and reason.

These values were also apparent in Organized Baseball's emphasis upon conformity and the organization man. While baseball might occasionally censure such corporate figures as maverick Bill Veeck, who had owned the Cleveland Indians and St. Louis Browns, most rhetoric regarding institutional values was reserved for the players whom owners most feared being infected with the virus of change. But players were quick to assert their loyalty and praise the magnanimous nature of the owners. Player representative Gene Woodling of the New York Mets insisted that players "have it so good that we just don't know what to ask for any more." Bob Friend of the Pittsburgh Pirates described player-management relations as "Utopian" and gave the credit for this state of affairs to Judge Robert Cannon, legal counsel for the Major League Baseball Players Association.

Cannon, who had held the position of counsel since 1959, gave the owners and Baseball Commissioner Ford Frick full credit for this harmonious consensus. Rather than conflict, Cannon preached cooperation and insisted that the players had an obligation to the owners "to get out and preach the baseball gospel, spread good will, and improve public relations toward the game." To paraphrase Charles Wilson of General Motors, what was good for the owners was good for baseball. The players' legal counsel also took a somewhat paternalistic view of his position as he informed players, while visiting 1963 spring training camps, that he would not present any player request which he considered unreasonable as "the best interests of the game should forever be paramount." Cannon also believed, "No player has a right to criticize publicly the club for which he is playing." Any complaints were to be submitted to the players' office which would process them through proper channels. In other words, Cannon as the players' representative preached the virtues of the organization man, or as Congressman Sam Rayburn often said, "To get along you have to go along."[13]

However, it was difficult for many players to function within the narrow confines and norms established by Judge Cannon. Baseball has a long history of individualism, and the winds of change encouraged this tendency, while management was determined to deal severely with dissenters. Thus, in March, 1963, the Sporting News lauded the Mets for releasing forty year old outfielder Gene Woodling following his public criticism of management's handling of Marv Throneberry's contract dispute.[14] This was the same Woodling who had praised player-management relations in January. But perhaps it did not take all that much courage to release an aging outfielder. Baseball had a more difficult time dealing with California pitcher Bo Belinsky, who authored a no-hitter during his rookie campaign of 1962. Belinsky increasingly made headlines for his nocturnal activities and relationship with Hollywood sex symbol Mamie Van Doren. Angel officials, embarrassed by Belinsky's antics, insisted that the young pitcher should keep his mind on baseball and returned him to the minors during the 1963 season. Writing in the *Sporting News*, sportswriter Dan Daniel wondered what all the excitement was about. After all, in comparison with such figures of the 1920s and 1930s as Rabbit Maranville, Belinsky's activities paled. But Daniel concluded that baseball had changed in the postwar era from a game to a business, and "the old tomfoolery finds itself precluded."[15]

Of course, the sport did attempt to accommodate some young eccentric players who could still be placed within the consensus. Thus, Yankee management was willing to accept rookie Joe Pepitone with his long hair, but emphasized his Italian ancestry and the fact that he was married with two children.[16] While the Yankees tried to portray Pepitone as unthreatening and simply a happy-go-lucky kid who did not mean any disrespect, the literary activities of Cincinnati Reds relief pitcher Jim Brosnan were viewed with alarm by some in baseball management circles.

Brosnan, an effective pitcher with the Reds, made himself *persona non grata* with Cincinnati President Bill DeWitt for his 1962 publication of *Pennant Race*, which chronicled the 1961 Reds climb to the National League pennant. DeWitt found Brosnan's account to be irreverent and earthy, while placing a muzzle on future publications by referring to the players' contract which forbids players from making statements which may be considered detrimental to baseball. Needless to say, DeWitt's censure did not sit well with a disgruntled Brosnan who failed to fit the mold of the organization man. An effort was made to resolve this situation in May, 1963 when the Reds shipped Brosnan to the Chicago White Sox of the American League. Chicago General Manager Ed Short stated that Brosnan would not be permitted to publish during the season, as such writing might undermine the morale and spirit of the White Sox, but management could not control a player's off season endeavors. Although he was not given complete freedom of expression, Brosnan announced he was glad to be with the White Sox and could live with the compromise.[17] Thus, as college campuses began to hear the refrains of free speech movements, organized baseball did its utmost to keep a lid on dissent and maintain the goals of cooperation and consensus.

Another contemporary issue which threatened the baseball consensus of the 1960s was the civil rights movement and a more assertive black population. The response of baseball officialdom to racial unrest in America was self-congratulatory. After all, baseball had shown the way toward peaceful integration with Jackie Robinson years before Brown vs. Board of Education. Thus, the *Sporting News* lauded the fact that Little Rock, Arkansas welcomed the first black player, Richie "Dick" Allen, to ever don a Traveler uniform. Governor Orville Faubus, who had long championed segregation, was given the honor of throwing out the first ball. Obviously, the turmoil brought about by the desegregation of Central High had abated, and baseball would continue the healing process. As for integration, the *Sporting News* stated, "Baseball provided the means for making it work in Little Rock as it has in almost every section of the country since integration became a reality after World War II."[18] It is interesting to note, however, that Dick Allen had a very different perception of the events in Little Rock. Allen maintained that life in Arkansas was a nightmare, and he was often on the verge of quitting baseball. He received threatening phone calls, had the windshield of his car plastered with "nigger go home" signs, and, of course, could not be served in a restaurant unless accompanied by a white player.[19]

While Allen was suffering through these indignities, Baseball Commissioner Frick was testifying before the Senate Commerce Committee extolling the virtues of integration in Little Rock. In response to an inquiry from Senator Warren Magnuson of Washington as to the number of blacks currently involved in major league baseball, Frick replied that he simply did not know as no such records were kept. In a classic example of overstatement, Frick continued, "We keep batting averages, pitching records, fielding and other statistics, birth dates and so forth, but no records on color or religion. We have no figures on whether players are black, white, or yellow because they are selected on the basis of whether they can pitch, hit, play second base...." The *Sporting News* had nothing but praise for Frick's testimony and termed integration in baseball as a "fait accompli."[20] This sense of complacency, of course, was the type of consensus thinking which fueled the civil rights movement and helps explain the violent turn race relations would take in America during the late 1960s. As for baseball, blacks were well represented on the field, but in 1963 there were no black managers and front office personnel; issues which would provide plenty of controversy for a "fait accompli" well into the 1960s.

Condescending attitudes were also evident in baseball's dealings with Latin ballplayers. Shocked that hemispheric solidarity and consensus could be disrupted by a communist government in Cuba, Americans looked to baseball as a diplomatic tool to prevent the spread of Castro and his cancer. Thus, organized baseball was encouraged by the *Sporting News* to provide more baseball equipment for the peace corps in the Dominican Republic, as more balls and bats would "keep a bunch of kids out of the clutches of Castro's agents." Owners such as Boston's Tom Yawkey earned praise for helping Red Sox outfielder Roman Mejias get his family out of Cuba. In exchange, Mejias promised, "I will kill myself for the Red Sox."[21] Other Latin players, however, were less enthusiastic in their attitudes regarding Organized Baseball and its established practices. San Francisco Giants outfielder Felipe Alou observed that while the sport was concerned with combating the spread of Castro, it was doing little to win the hearts and minds of most Latin players. Alou was upset over fines levied by Commissioner Frick against himself and Juan Marichal for playing winter ball in the Dominican Republic. Alou maintained the two Dominicans had to play as "these are our people and we owe it to them to play for them." The Commissioner simply did not understand the problems confronted by Latin players, and Alou demanded that a Latin representative be appointed to the Commissioner's staff.[22]

Thus, major league baseball in 1963 sought to maintain a veneer of consensus and conformity, while restless players and minorities were voicing discontent with the status quo. However, some of the most important blows to the established notion that one should always place the sport above individual gain were dealt by the owners. Following President Kennedy's assassination in November, 1963, the *Sporting News* called Kennedy the "best friend" the sports world ever had in the White House and, although a little vague with specifics, urged all in baseball to band together "to carry out the objectives for which he stood."[23] While Lyndon Johnson was able to fashion a legislative agenda with the memory of the martyred President and, thus, maintain the illusion of consensus for another year, baseball owners were once again shattering the baseball consensus with the panacea of shifting franchises. Kansas City owner Charlie Finley wanted out of his municipal lease and was wooing the cities of Dallas, Louisville, and Oakland. To disconcerted Kansas City fans, Finley simply explained, "You see, this is a business." The eccentric owner and insurance magnate would later encounter considerable difficulty with his players when they exemplified his attitude. Meanwhile, John McHale, President of the Milwaukee Braves, while negotiating with the city of Atlanta and sounding a little like Alabama Governor George Wallace, insisted, "The Braves will be in Milwaukee today, tomorrow, next year, and as long as we are welcome." These rumors of team moves alarmed the *Sporting News* which editorialized that franchise shifts would bring law suits, and baseball might lose its privileged exemption from the antitrust laws. Furthermore, if baseball could not keep its own house in order the specter of federal legislation, baseball's equivalent of the outside agitator, loomed.[24]

The jeremiads of the *Sporting News* notwithstanding, 1964 was a year in which discussion of baseball franchise shifts dominated headlines and further undermined the fragile nature of the baseball consensus. The winds of change were blowing from both within and without baseball's establishment. In January, Finley announced that he had signed an agreement with the city of Louisville which would bring the A's and major league baseball to Kentucky. However, a franchise shift would require the approval of the other owners, and at a January 16, 1964 American League meeting in New York, Finley was the odd man out as permission to move to Louisville was denied. In turn, Finley threatened to sue the Commissioner and Organized Baseball for being in violation of antitrust law.[25] Finley's activities made his fellow owners very uncomfortable as they led to confrontation with influential politicians and presented the threat of federal regulation. Missouri Senator Stuart Symington blasted Finley for his failure to negotiate with Kansas City officials, proclaiming, "Is there anyone who would deny that Mr. Finley has lowered the respect of the American people for professional baseball?" Symington's views were echoed by the junior Senator from Missouri Edward L. Long who labeled Finley as "irresponsible" in his attitude toward the people of Kansas City and fans of the Athletics.[26] While Finley withdrew his law suit in February and signed a new four year Kansas City stadium lease in one of his periodic attempts to rejoin the baseball establishment and consensus, officials of the sport were supporting a new strategy to head off law suits and maintain baseball's privileged position.

Accordingly, Commissioner Ford Frick testified before Michigan Senator Phil Hart's Senate Monopoly Subcommittee in favor of a sports bill which would extend to all professional team sports the exemption from antitrust legislation now enjoyed by baseball and dating back to Supreme Court Justice Oliver Wendell Holmes's 1922 opinion that baseball was not a business.[27] For a "sport" in the process of negotiating a new twelve million dollar television contract, there was always fear that the courts might reverse Holmes. Thus, Commissioner Frick's strategy was to abandon baseball's lone wolf status and establish a consensus with baseball's emerging competitors in basketball, hockey, and football. But while Frick was lobbying for sport legislation that would be sidetracked by the Great Society agenda and Finley was temporarily under control, management decisions in Milwaukee and New York further tarnished the image of baseball and exposed the shortcomings of consensus rhetoric.

Although in April, 1964 Braves management had declared, "We are positively not moving. We're playing in Milwaukee, whether you're talking of 1964, 1965, or 1975," by mid-summer, reports persisted that the Braves were already committed to Atlanta. John Doyne, Milwaukee County Executive, threatened a law suit if the Braves attempted to leave Milwaukee and pointed out that the club still had a year to go on its stadium lease. Doyne criticized Commissioner Frick for not blocking the Braves management, pleading, "How a ball club is permitted to come into a city like this, milk it for a dozen years and then jump elsewhere, I can't understand." Voices of reason and consensus, exemplified by organization men William Bartholomay and John McHale of the Braves, were uncomfortable with Doyne's moralistic rhetoric and calmly replied that while Milwaukee attendance was up, Atlanta offered a mere lucrative radio and television market. They would render their decision at the conclusion of the 1964 season. Sportswriter Dick Young also ridiculed Doyne for elevating the proposed franchise shift to the level of a moral issue. After all, Young reasoned, Milwaukee shed few tears over Boston losing the Braves in 1953. Of course, Young ignored the fact that, unlike previous franchise transfers in Boston, Philadelphia, St. Louis, and New York, Milwaukee would be left with no major league outlet. But regardless of any moral considerations, on October 21, 1964 Braves management voted to ask the National League for permission to shift the franchise to Atlanta. Approval was quickly provided by the other owners, although legal obstacles were able to keep the Braves in Milwaukee for the 1965 season.[28]

Those who criticized the actions of Finley and Braves management as proof that baseball was no longer a sport, but simply a business with little room for sentiment or ethical considerations, were given further ammunition in August, 1964, when CBS announced that it had purchased the New York Yankees from Dan Topping and Del Webb for $11,200,000. With the CBS acquisition, the Yankees emerged as the perfect corporate symbol. They represented big business, mass media, New York City, and monopolistic success (from 1949 to 1964, the Yankees won fourteen American League pennants and nine world championships); while their most successful manager Casey Stengel emphasized a strategy of platooning in which the men in pin-stripes appeared to function as interchangeable parts.[29] Just as many Americans in the 1960s rebelled against bureaucracy and the organizational society which seemed intent on circumventing individualism, so others concerned with maintaining competition in the baseball world assailed the CBS acquisition of the Yankees; not realizing that the world would be turned upside down during the 1960s in both Vietnam and the baseball standings.

Chet Huntly, of rival NBC, simply stated that the CBS action was "just one more reason to hate the Yankees." A more serious note of dissent was sounded by Congressman Emmanuel Celler of New York, a long time critic of baseball's monopolistic practices. Celler observed that the deal confirmed his view that baseball was big business and should be investigated by the Justice Department. He also feared the impact corporate control might have on competition. Thus, the Congressman argued, "If the corporations which own these clubs are given an antitrust exemption permitting them to equalize the competitive strength of teams there is a possibility that players may be traded around to provide closer races, and therefore more entertaining fare." Celler was joined by Representative Henry Reuss of Wisconsin, already angry with Braves ownership, who proclaimed that baseball should forfeit its antitrust exemption. Letters to the *Sporting News* echoed the sentiments of Celler and Reuss. Representative is the comment from P. V. Ball of Avon, Connecticut who argued that baseball was "deteriorating into a monopolistic organization."[30]

To quiet the storm CBS issued assurances that the network would continue to air the game of the week and would not dabble in baseball business at the clubhouse level. Also, as the initial owner approval for the transaction was gained through a telephone poll, public outrage seemed to call for a more judicious discussion of the Yankee sale. Accordingly, on September 9, 1964, an American League owners meeting was held in Boston. The gathering was basically for appearance's sake, as after a five hour debate the CBS purchase was approved by a vote of ten to two, with Finley and Arthur Allyn of the White Sox expressing their dissent. The quotable Finley maintained that other owners were intimidated by the Yankees, and that he was "disappointed, disgusted, disillusioned, disenchanted, discouraged, and depressed."[31] It is interesting to note that Finley, who also championed baseball as a business, was here at odds with the large twentieth-century corporation, while the A's owner was somewhat of an anachronism; a nineteenth-century self-made man, a captain of industry, or perhaps a robber baron.

But as Finley and the Yankees feuded, and while the Braves packed their tepees, what message were the owners sending to their hired hands? If an excess of materialism was threatening the ownership consensus from within, then what could one expect from the players in a society increasingly emphasizing the rights of the individual? One player who took great pride in his independence and rebel image was Yankee shortstop Tony Kubek, who refused to accept the docile and cooperative player concept fashioned by Judge Cannon. If the owners were looking for more lucrative markets, so was the combative Kubek, who asserted that players should be awarded a share of profits from the proposed pay-television market. To support his claim, Kubek uttered the phrase that sent shivers up the collective spine of the baseball establishment. The Yankee infielder insisted that the players had been discussing collective bargaining and were "closer now to a ball players' union than we've ever been before." Kubek's comments immediately brought forth rebuke from Cannon, who termed them "unfortunate and ill-advised." National League Player Representative Bob Friend of the Pirates and his American League counterpart Bob Allison of the Twins were also prompt to maintain their status as organization men and brand Kubek as a malcontent out of the baseball mainstream. Friend agreed that the players had discussed pay-television, but Kubek was off base in regard to a union, as the players had not progressed by using threats. Allison concurred, stating that relations between the players and owners "have never been better." Thus, the player representatives advocated the consensus view of cooperation and conciliation, not confrontation. The *Sporting News* also used an editorial to censure Kubek for stepping out of line. If pay-television were to produce dividends, then the players could certainly depend upon the owners to look out for their interest and award them accordingly. Also, Kubek was criticized for expressing his comments directly to the press rather than working through proper baseball channels.[32] The baseball establishment came together to condemn the radicalism of Kubek, but they were piecing together a fabric that was increasingly becoming unwoven, as Kubek was the voice of the 1960s and baseball's future; demanding and assertive with a labor orientation.

But Kubek's protest was not the only voice of player dissent heard in 1964, as the publishing career of Jim Brosnan once again provoked controversy. In February, General Manager Ed Short of the White Sox warned Brosnan to limit his off season publishing or find other employment. The relief pitcher was violating the privacy of the clubhouse. This was another way of saying Brosnan was ruffling the feathers of management.[33] The *Sporting News* initially supported Brosnan's case, editorializing that the pitcher, while sometimes irreverent, was, nevertheless, entitled to his right of free speech. In a letter to the editor, Brosnan thanked the publication for its stance, stating that arguments on behalf of free speech "should please anyone but the stiffnecked martinets who would control the very breathing of the men who play the game. Overanxious organization men reflect their own insecurities when they suspect that ball players might degrade the game with vocal antics." In March, the unrepentant Brosnan was released by the White Sox as Short maintained that he was unable to swing a trade for a pitcher whose won-lost record in 1963 was three and eight. Of course, Short omitted the fact that Brosnan had compiled an excellent earned run average of 2.84, indicating that he could still pitch. When no teams rushed forth to sign the relief pitcher, some observers saw evidence of a blacklist.[34]

Representative of the baseball establishment was the *Sporting News*, which had originally been supportive of Brosnan exercising his constitutional rights. However, the publication censured the former White Sox player when he asked the A.C.L.U. to present his case. Outside agitators were again intruding into the consensus world of baseball. Squabbles should be settled within the national pastime through proper channels and not question the fundamental principles of the game. Thus, John E. Coons, Chairman of the Illinois A.C.L.U. Freedom of Information Committee, accused White Sox owner Arthur Allyn of engaging in censorship. In an emotional letter utilizing baseball metaphors, Coons argued, "The club's management has driven its well-honed spikes deep into Mr. Brosnan's career. In so doing, they have cut just as deeply into the sporting souls of all Americans who despise the censor's work, whether he strikes at pulpit, *Playboy,* or pitcher's mound." Coons concluded that baseball was in a position to engage in censorship because the sport enjoyed a privileged monopoly through its exemption from the antitrust laws. White Sox owner Allyn exhibited his contempt for both Brosnan and the A.C.L.U. by labeling Coons' charges as "balderdash," while discarding his letter into the waste basket. Allyn's rather pompous reply was applauded by a *Sporting News* editorial which complacently asserted, "The baseball position on civil rights is unassailable and has been since Jackie Robinson's entrance into the major leagues." [35]

Brosnan had written himself out of the baseball consensus, stating that if he could not pitch he would at least have time to finish his novel. But Brosnan and Kubek were not the only restive players in 1964. Management comments and *Sporting News* editorials frequently chided players for their lack of loyalty to the sport and owners who paid their salaries. Bo Belinsky was told to bear down and develop a work ethic, and the pitcher with a reputation as a playboy was returned to the minors by the Angels. Red Sox first baseman Dick Stuart, who gained the infamous nickname Dr. Strangeglove for his fielding prowess, publicly chastised Manager Johnny Pesky for humiliating the slugger by placing him on the B squad for exhibition games. The White Sox benched fleet center fielder Jim Landis when he refused to make television appearances for the club without guaranteed compensation. Landis was dissatisfied with the players' contract which required athletes to make local appearances and endorsements as the club deemed necessary. Pitcher Joey Jay of the Reds also made headlines, demanding that he be traded or else he might quit the game. And last, but by no means least , crusty Cleveland Indian manager Birdie Tebbetts, who was a frequent critic of the modern day player, fined four members of the Tribe for their failure to hustle. The *Sporting News* endorsed the actions taken by Tebbetts and expressed exasperation with the attitude demonstrated by many young players. Sounding very much like a parent who did not understand how their ungrateful children could complain in the midst of affluence, the paper editorialized, "Players today are paid more handsomely than ever, demand and receive more concessions from owners than ever before and live in the lap of luxury. For all of this, all they are asked to do is bear down hard for a couple of hours a day. It is a sad commentary when such dedication can be obtained only by hitting the players where it hurts in the pocketbook."[36] In short, in the eyes of the baseball establishment young players were behaving like permissive children of the Dr. Spock generation. However, some critics of management such as Professor Ralph Andreano, Professor of Economics at Earlham College, maintained that baseball owners were being shortsighted in their endeavor to create bland organization men who would not challenge established rules and policies. Andreano argued that baseball's image problem in the 1960s was due to the fact that the players were becoming faceless corporation figures rather than individuals and characters like the old St. Louis Cardinals Gas House Gang.[37]

While in 1964 baseball officials complacently sought to maintain organizational values, with an increasingly restive player clientele, they also continued to ignore the black revolution in American society by insisting that race relations in baseball were utopian. Thus, the *Sporting News* observed that baseball had been exempt from the civil rights demonstrations sweeping America, for the national pastime had proved that "Negroes and whites could work together in perfect harmony and understanding." Baseball officials loved to laud such black players as Mr. Cub Ernie Banks, who was honored at Wrigley Field on August 15, 1964. Stepping up to the microphone, Banks proudly announced, "First, I want to thank God for making me an American."[38] Success stories like Banks, who had played in the segregated Negro Leagues, were emphasized to demonstrate that baseball, having solved its integration problems and welcomed blacks into the consensus, was immune to the social conflict and debate engulfing the nation.

But baseball was hardly sheltered from the winds of racial change. Critics of the baseball establishment were quick to point out that while equality might exist on the playing field, segregation had not disappeared in the broadcasting booths, front offices, and coaching and managing ranks. Accordingly, in the letters to the editor section of the *Sporting News*, reader H. M. Lasky of Chicago admonished the baseball establishment, requesting "a little less complacency in the future please."[39] While individuals such as Jackie Robinson were taking up the crusade for black inclusion in the higher echelons of the baseball world, the 1964 season also offered an example that racism was hardly dead on the playing field. In the midst of an intense July pennant race Giants manager Alvin Dark was interviewed by reporter Stan Issacs for *Newsday*, a large circulation daily on New York's Long Island. Dark, a native Southerner, was quoted as saying, "We have trouble because we have so many Negro and Spanish-speaking players on this team. They are just not able to perform up to the white players when it comes to mental alertness. One of the biggest things is that you can't make them subordinate themselves to the best interest of the team. You don't find pride in them that you get in the white player."[40] Dark denied the remarks, but Issacs, a respected reporter, stood by his story, and a threatened player revolt by nonwhite players on the Giants roster developed. Reportedly, a player strike was averted, and Dark's job saved, through the actions of team captain Willie Mays. According to clubhouse accounts, Mays asserted that he had nothing but contempt for Dark's racial attitudes; however, the Giants were in a tight pennant race, and Dark did not let his prejudice interfere with his decisions on the playing field (In fact, when Juan Marichal pitched, seven out of nine starters were either black or Latin.) To show his support for Dark after the *Newsday* story broke, an ill Mays came off the bench to hit two home runs in a Giants victory over the Mets. Despite the efforts of Mays, the Giants pennant bid fell short, and owner Horace Stoneham relieved Dark of his managerial duties following the conclusion of the 1964 campaign. But the illusion of complacency and consensus was once again shattered. Baseball was not immune to the conflicts and changes sweeping America.

By 1964 it was apparent that many players were growing uncomfortable with the restraints imposed by the baseball establishment. Players were demanding free speech, increased compensation, and questioning the practices and motives of management. While the consensus was beginning to unravel, an even greater effort was placed by Organized Baseball on appearances of conciliation and compromise. This was nowhere more evident then in the activities of the Players Counsel, Judge Cannon. In the spring of 1964, Cannon was once again touring training camps, disseminating information on what he and baseball management considered to be the major issues of interest to the players; tax saving tips and opportunities for employment during the off season and after an athlete's playing days. Cannon also advised players regarding what the Judge considered to be an outstanding pension program, gained through a "spirit of cooperation among the players and owners, general managers, and administrators of baseball."[41] In other words, Cannon believed players would receive a larger slice of the baseball economic pie and be included in the sport's consensus, if only they would maintain a proper attitude of respect and conciliation rather than confrontation. Thus, the Judge had little patience for a rebel such as Kubek, who would criticize management and raise the red flag of player unionization with the confrontational tactics of American labor.

Cannon's dedication to the values espoused by baseball management was evident by the fact that the Judge's name was brandished about as a possible successor to Commissioner Frick who announced he would not be a candidate for reelection when his term expired in September, 1965.[42] Commentators such as Dick Young insisted that the owners did not want a strong commissioner who would interfere with their actions, and Cannon certainly made it clear that he was not one to rock the consensus boat. Thus, in a speech before the Wisconsin Academy of General Sciences, he again reminded players and fans of the debts they owed to baseball owners, who might lose money but had established "the greatest pension program in the history of this country."[43]

In line with Cannon's conciliatory approach, Pirate hurler Bob Friend, in his tenth year as a player representative, presented the players' "demands" to the owners at the 1964 annual baseball winter meeting. Among the major issues introduced by Friend were increasing player meal money from ten to twelve dollars per day, increasing the number of complimentary tickets available for players, rewarding players monetarily if pay television proved successful, and improving the toilet facilities for players in the Kansas City stadium. In exchange for these considerations, Cannon made it clear that the players would have to reciprocate by demonstrating their loyalty to the baseball consensus and management. Players would be available upon management request to appear without compensation at any noncommercial function to promote baseball, and this duty would be shared by all players, not just a few stars. Cannon, allegedly speaking on behalf of the players, pledged cooperation, promising, "We are going to let the club owners know that we will cooperate with them in any way we can and that we would like their suggestions. This is an honest, concerted, sincere effort to show that we are interested in creating a better image for baseball."[44] Accordingly, the players counsel had little use for those who would criticize the baseball establishment. The proper image for a player was not that of the rebel, as Cannon sought to forge a baseball consensus in which players would benefit from the expanding baseball marketplace. Conciliation, not conflict, would bring progress. In the words of Lyndon Johnson, "Come let us reason together."

But the baseball consensus Cannon sought to fashion was destined to crumble, just as the new consensus supposedly formed by Lyndon Johnson in November, 1964 was based on images and illusions, not substance. Judge Cannon was not elevated to the status of Commissioner, as the owners found an even more pliant candidate in General William Eckert, who knew virtually nothing about the sport. Following the examples of ownership and a society in which established authority was coming increasingly under challenge, players grew restive under the reins of Judge Cannon and management. With the emergence of black power and pride, black players shattered the complacency of the baseball establishment. Athletes were willing to publicly discuss racial slights and slurs, while confronting management with charges of discrimination, especially with regard to the lack of black managers and front office personnel. The seeds of player discontent planted in 1963 and 1964 would continue to sprout throughout the 1960s and 1970s, as players no longer content with a company union selected an experienced labor leader Marvin Miller to head the Major League Baseball Players Association. Under the leadership of Miller the players would strike a more assertive pose, demanding an expanded pension plan, increases in the player minimum salary, and an assault upon the reserve clause, which eventually resulted in strikes, free agency, and arbitration, changing forever the structure of major league baseball.[45] Bob Dylan was right, there was a battle outside raging, which would shake the windows and rattle the walls of American institutions such as Organized Baseball.

However, like many politicians of the early 1960s, baseball officials in 1963 and 1964 did not really recognize that, indeed, "the times were a-changin'." At their 1964 winter meeting owners were in a self-congratulatory mood, having instituted a new free agent draft, approved what sportswriter Red Smith called the "rape" of Milwaukee in supporting the transfer of the Braves to Atlanta, and continued their satisfactory paternalistic relationship with the players. But Ford Frick, the lame duck Commissioner, admonished owners not to ignore the changes and problems on the horizon. While Frick was not really a man to challenge the owners, he had a sincere love for baseball and hated to see Organized Baseball stick its head in the sand. Thus, in a Cassandra-like warning Frick attempted to shatter the walls of baseball complacency, prophesizing, "So long as baseball people refuse to look beyond the day and the hour; so long as the clubs and individuals persist in gaining personal headlines through public criticism of associates; so long as they are unwilling to sacrifice the welfare of the individual for the benefit of the whole; and so long as expediency is permitted to replace sound judgment, there can be no satisfactory solution."[46]

While Frick certainly had a gift for hyperbole and appeared to hanker back to some baseball Garden of Eden which never existed; it was, nevertheless, true that, whether management in 1964 realized it or not, American society and sports such as baseball, which reflected that society, were in a period of transition. The post World War II consensus was being challenged and the times were changing.

Endnotes

A version of this essay was originally published by the Society for American Baseball Research in *Baseball Research Journal* 17 (1988), 54-60.

1. While Bob Dylan would hardly qualify as an expert on baseball, his work does offer some insights into the 1960s. For Dylan see Bob Dylan, *Lyrics, 1962-1985* (New York: Alfred A. Knopf, 1985) ; Dylan , *Tarantula* (New York: MacMillan , 1971); and Robert Shelton, *No Direction Home: The Life and Music of Bob Dylan* (New York: Beech Tree Books, 1986).

2. For a comprehensive attempt to place DiMaggio in historical and cultural perspective see Jack E. Moore, *Joe DiMaggio : A Bio-Bibliography* (Westport, Conn.: Greenwood Press, 1986). DiMaggio has also been the subject of such recent works as Christopher Lehmann-Haupt , *Me and DiMaggio: A Baseball Fan Goes in Search of His Gods* (New York: Simon and Schuster, 1986) ; and Roger Kahn, *Joe & Marilyn: A Memory of Love* (New York: William Morrow, 1986).

3. For an excellent discussion regarding Reagan, baseball, and journalism see Garry Wills, *Reagan' s America : Innocents at Home* (Garden City, New York: Doubleday, 1987), 115–131.

4. For a fine history of baseball in the 1960s see David Quentin Voigt, *American Baseball. Vol. III: From Postwar Expansion to the Electronic Age* (University Park, Pennsylvania: Penn State University Press, 1983).

5. For the role of sport in shaping American society see Robert Boyle, *Sport — Mirror of American Life* (Boston: Little, Brown and Co., 1963); Foster Rhea Dulles, *America Learns to Play* (New York: Appleton Century Co., 1940); Roland Garrett, "The Metaphysics of Baseball," *Philosophy Today*, 20 (Fall, 1976), 209–226; James Michener, *Sport in America* (New York: Random House, 1976); Frederic Logan Paxson, "The Rise of Sport," as cited in Frederic Logan Paxson, *The Great Demobilization and Other Essays* (Madison: University of Wisconsin Press, 1941); Benjamin G. Rader, *American Sports: From the Age of Folk Games to the Age of Spectators* (Englewood Cliffs, New Jersey: Prentice Hall, 1983); and Leverett T. Smith, Jr., *The American Dream and the National Game* (Bowling Green, Ohio: Bowling Green University Popular Press, 1975).

6. U .S. Congress, *Organized Baseball; Report of the Subcommittee on Study of Monopoly Power of the Committee on the Judiciary, House Report*, No. 2002, 82 Cong., 2 Sess. (1952), 12.

7. For works which evoke the spirit of baseball see Roger Angell, *The Summer Game* (New York: Viking Press, 1972); Donald Hall, *Fathers Playing Catch with Sons: Essays on Sport (Mostly Baseball)* (San Francisco: North Point Press, 1985) ; and

Thomas Boswell, *Why Time Begins on Opening Day* (New York: Doubleday and Co., 1984).

   8. George Grella, "Baseball and the American Dream," *Massachusetts Review,* 16 (Summer, 1975), 550; and Jacques Barzun, "America at Play," *Atlantic,* 193 (February, 1954), 40–41.

   9. Peter Levine, *A. G. Spalding and the Rise of Baseball: The Promise of American Sport* (New York: Oxford University Press, 1985); Steven A. Riess, *Touching Base: Professional Baseball and American Culture in the Progressive Era* (Westport, Conn.: Greenwood Press, 1980), 5; Richard C. Crepeau, *Baseball: America's Diamond Mind, 1919-1941* (Orlando: University Presses of Florida, 1960), 25; and Jules Tygiel, *Baseball's Great Experiment: Jackie Robinson and his Legacy* (New York: Oxford University Press, 1983).

   10. The relationship of William Bendix, baseball, and World War II is discussed in Roger Kahn, *The Boys of Summer* (New York: Random House, 1971), xiv. Representative Bendix films of the World War II era include *Wake Island* (1942), *Guadalcanal Diary* (1943), and *Lifeboat* (1944). For general accounts of baseball during the Second World War see Ron Briley, "Where Have You Gone William Bendix?: Baseball as a Symbol of American Values in World War II," *Studies in Popular Culture,* 8 (1985), 18–32; William B. Mead, *Even the Browns: The Zany True Story of Baseball in the Early Forties* (Chicago: Contemporary Books, 1978); David Voigt, *American Baseball. Vol. II: From the Commissioners to Continental Expansion* (University Park: Pennsylvania State University Press, 1970); and Richard Goldstein, *Spartan Seasons: How Baseball Survived the Second World War* (New York: MacMillan, 1980).

   11. For the development of the liberal consensus and its break up see Geoffrey Hodgson, *America in Our Time* (New York: Doubleday, 1976); Allen J. Matusow, *The Unraveling of America: A History of Liberalism in the 1960s* (New York: Quadrangle, 1971); and Charles Maland, "Dr. *Strangelove* (1964): Nightmare Comedy and the Ideology of Liberal Consensus," as cited in Peter C. Rollins, ed., *Hollywood as Historian: American Film in a Cultural Context* (Lexington: The University Press of Kentucky, 1983).

   12. *Sporting News,* January 5, 1963. For the crucial role played by the *Sporting News* in baseball see *Sporting News, First Hundred Years, 1886-1986* (St. Louis: *Sporting News.* 1986). The Bible of Baseball constitutes a primary source for this investigation into the sport during the 1960s.

   13. *Sporting News,* January 26 and March 16, 1963.

   14. *Ibid.,* March 23, 1963. For additional information on Woodling see Dick Darcey, "Woodling Will Be There Opening Day," *Baseball Monthly,* 1 (March, 1962), 22–27.

   15. *Sporting News,* January 5, 1963. For the career of Belinsky see Maury Allen, *Bo: Pitching and Wooing* (New York: Dial Press, 1973); Arnold Hano, "The Wacky World of Bo Belinsky," *Sport,* 34 (September, 1962), 42–45; and T. Thompson, "Brash Bo Comes on with a Big Pitch," *Life,* 52 (June 8, 1962), 13–14. Of course, Belinsky never had much success in the major leagues, compiling a won-lost record of 28 and 51 over eight seasons.

   16. *Sporting News,* April 20, 1963. In hind sight, Pepitone would never fit in as an organization man. For Pepitone's career see Joseph A. Pepitone and Berry Stainback, *Joe, You Coulda Made Us Proud* (Chicago: Playboy Press, 1975).

   17. *Sporting News,* April 13 and May 18, 1963; and Jim Brosnan, *Pennant Race* (New York: Harper and Row, 1962). Of course, Brosnan's account would appear tame following the appearance of Jim Bouton, *Ball Four: My Life and Hard Times Throwing the Knuckle-ball in the Big Leagues* (Cleveland: World Publishing Co., 1970).

18. *Sporting News*, April 27 and May 4, 1963. For an overview of blacks in organized baseball during the 1950s and 1960s see Tygiel, *Baseball's Great Experiment: Jackie Robinson and His Legacy*, 211–344.

19. Dave Nightingale, "The Human Side of Richie Allen," *Baseball Digest*, 31 (July, 1972), 16–24.

20. *Sporting News*, July 27 and August 3, 1963. A more accurate description of some of the difficulties continuing to confront blacks in baseball during the early 1960s may be found in Richard Bardolph, *The Negro Vanguard* (New York: Vintage Books, 1961); Robert H. Boyle, "The Negro in Baseball, "*Sports Illustrated*, 12 (March 21, 1960), 16–21; William B. Furlong, "A Negro Ballplayer's Life Today," *Sport*, 33 (May, 1962), 38–39; Alex Haley, "Baseball in a Segregated Town," *Sport*, 32 (July, 1961), 20–21; and "Negroes in the Major Leagues," *Ebony*, 15 (June, 1960), 99–106.

21. *Sporting News*, February 2 and April 6, 1963.

22. For the views of Alou see Felipe Alou, "Latin American Ballplayers Need a Bill of Rights," *Sport*, 36 (November, 1963), 20–21. Also for a very interesting, but somewhat bizarre observation on Castro, baseball, and the Cold War see Howard Senezel, *Baseball and the Cold War : Being a Soliloquy on the Necessity of Baseball* (New York: Harcourt Brace Jovanovich, 1977).

23. *Sporting News*, December 7, 1963.

24. *Ibid.*, July 27, October 5, and November 30, 1963.

25. For profiles of the controversial Finley see William B. Furlong, "What Charley Finley Is Doing to Baseball, "*Sport*, 34 (September, 1962), 28–30; Bill Libby, *Charlie O. and the Angry A's* (New York: Doubleday, 1975); and Herbert Mitchelson, *Charlie O.: Charles Finley vs. the Baseball Establishment* (New York: Bobbs-Merrill, 1975).

26. *Sporting News*, February 15 and 29, 1964.

27. For Frick's testimony see *Ibid.*, February 15, 1964. For more technical discussions of baseball's position under the antitrust laws see Peter S. Craig, *Monopoly in Manpower: Organized Baseball Meets the Antitrust Laws* (New Haven, Conn.: Yale University Press, 1953); C. P. Rogers, "Judicial Re-interpretation of Statutes: The Example of Baseball and the Antitrust Laws," *Houston Law Review*, 14 (Fall, 1977), 611–634; Arthur T. Johnson, "Congress and Professional Sports, 1951–1978," *Annals of the Academy of Political and Social Science*, 445 (September, 1979), 102–115; and Keith Maxwell, "Developments in the Application of Antitrust Laws to Professional Team Sports," *Hastings Law Journal*, 10 (November, 1958), 119–138.

28. *Sporting News*, July 18, July 23, November 7, 1964. For additional background information on the franchise shift from Milwaukee to Atlanta see Howard Cosell, "Great Moments in Sport: Milwaukee Makes the Majors," *Sport* 31 (April, 1961), 73–99; Charles Dexter, "Milwaukee's Fight for Baseball," *Baseball Digest*, 23 (December, 1964), 6–7; W. C. Heinz, "Baseball Players' Dream Town: Milwaukee and Her Braves," *Cosmopolitan*, 136 (May, 1954), 88–93; and Lyall Smith, "What the Braves Owe to Milwaukee," *Baseball Digest*, 23 (September, 1964), 15–17.

29. For the Yankees in the 1960s and the role of CBS see Jon Bizzelle, *I Hate the Yankees* (New York: Vantage Press, 1971); Melvin Durslag, "C.B.S. and the New York Yankees," *TV Guide*, 13 (July 2, 1966), 26–27; Peter Golenbock, *Dynasty: The New York Yankees, 1949-1964* (Englewood Cliffs, N.J.: Prentice-Hall, 1975); "Keeping C.B.S. in the Big Leagues: Trying to Rebuild the New York Yankees into a Winner," *Business Week* (April 15, 1967), 80–82; and Jack Mann, *The Decline and Fall of the New York Yankees* (New York: Simon and Schuster, 1967).

30. *Sporting News*, August 29 and September 5, 1964.

31. *Ibid.*, September 19 and October 10, 1964.

32. On Kubek see Til Ferdenzi, "Kubek Gets the Job Done," *Baseball Digest*, 22 (July, 1963), 87–90; and Leonard Shecter, "Rational Rebel in Pinstripes," *Sports Illustrated*, 18 (May 13, 1963), 76–78; and *Sporting News*, April 25 and May 2, 1964.

33. For an example of the type of Brosnan literature which infuriated management see Jim Brosnan, "Businessmen are Wrecking Baseball," *Saturday Evening Post*, 238 (May 30, 1964), 8.

34. *Sporting News*, February 15 and March 7, 1964. For Brosnan's employment problems see C. Cilo, "Truth Strikes Out," *Nation*, 199 (October 26, 1964), 281–282; and Jim Brosnan, "This Pitcher May Need Relief," *Sports Illustrated*, 20 (March 16, 1964), 24–26.

35. *Sporting News*, March 21, 1964.

36. *Ibid.*, March 7, April 4, May 30, and August 15, 1964. For the opposing approaches to baseball of individuals like Stuart and Tebbetts see Myron Cope, "An Irrepressible Egotist," *Saturday Evening Post*, 235 (April 28, 1962), 65–66; Arnold Hano, "Dick Stuart: Man and Showman," *Sport*, 37 (June, 1964), 56–67; John P. Carmichael, "Birdie with a Velvet Fist," *Baseball Digest*, 13 (January, 1954), 89–92; and Ed Linn, "The Man in the Dugout," *Sport*, 17 (September, 1964), 50–61.

37. Ralph Andreano, *No Joy in Mudville: The Dilemma of Major League Baseball* (Cambridge, Massachusetts: Schenkman Publishing Co., 1965).

38. *Sporting News*, May 9, May 30, and August 29, 1964. On the irrepressible Banks see Ernie Banks with Jim Enright, *Mr. Cub* (Chicago: Follett Publishing Co., 1971); William B. Furlong, "Ernie Banks' Life with a Loser," *Sport*, 35 (April, 1963), 64–95 and Bill Libby, *Ernie Banks, Mr. Cub* (New York: G. P. Putnam, 1971).

39. *Sporting News*, May 30, 1964. For a more critical account of blacks in baseball see Art Rust, Jr., *Get That Nigger Off the Field* (New York: Delacorte, 1978).

40. For accounts of the Dark interview and player reaction see *Sporting News*, August 15 and 22, 1964; Charles Einstein, *Willie's Time: A Memoir* (New York: J. B. Lippincott, 1979); Orlando Cepeda, *My Ups and Downs in Baseball* (New York: G. P. Putnam, 1968); and Al Dark, *When in Doubt, Fire the Manager: My Life in Baseball* (New York: E. P. Dutton, 1980).

41. *Sporting News*, April 4 and 11, 1964.

42. On Frick as Commissioner see Robert H. Boyle, "The Perfect Man for the Job," *Sports Illustrated*, 16 (April 9, 1962), 36–38; Daniel M. Daniel, "Ford Frick Speaks Out," *Baseball Magazine*, 32 (April, 1949), 373–375; and Ford Frick, *Games, Asterisks, and People: Memoirs of a Lucky Fan* (New York: Crown Publishers, 1973).

43. *Sporting News*, September 5 and October 3, 1964.

44. *Ibid.*, November 21 and December 12, 1964. For background information on Bob Friend and the baseball player as businessman see Myron Cope, "Bob Friend, Symbol of the New Ballplayer," *Sport*, 32 (September, 1961), 72–107.

45. On Marvin Miller see Robert Boyle, "This Miller Admits He's a Grind," *Sports Illustrated*, 40 (March 11, 1974), 22; Robin Roberts, "The Game Deserves the Best: Marvin Miller as Executive Director of the Baseball Players' Association," *Sports Illustrated*, 30 (February 24, 1969), 46–47; and David Q. Voigt, "They Shaped the Game: Nine Innovators of Major League Baseball," *Baseball History*, 1 (Spring, 1986), 5–21.

46. *Sporting News*, November 21, 1964.

12

It Was Twenty Years Ago Today: Baseball Responds to the Unrest of 1968

On February 17, 1968 columnist Dick Young observed that Baltimore Orioles outfielder and future Hall-of-Famer Frank Robinson was complaining that Boston Red Sox star Carl Yastrzemski received more acclaim for his 1967 American League triple crown than Robinson had gained for accomplishing the same feat in 1966. Robinson believed the difference in public reaction was due simply to the fact that he was black and Yastrzemski white. Young concurred with Robinson's analysis as the columnist observed that blacks had done so well in baseball of late and that there had been few white heroes. For some fans Yastrzemski's achievements were really something about which to crow. But Young downplayed this apparent racism in baseball, commenting, "It's nothing to get excited about. We'll outgrow this stuff in another 20 years or so."[1]

Twenty years have passed and allegations of racism continue to plague American society, as well as the baseball establishment. Before the breakdown of the liberal consensus in the mid-to-late 1960s, the so-called national pastime apparently mirrored American faith in the nation's values and institutions. The two cornerstones of the post World War II liberal consensus were anticommunism and a belief that social and racial inequities in American life could be surmounted by an expanding economy and gross national product.[2] Accordingly, there was no need to resort to violence to bring about change. Problems would be solved through the application of reason and orderly expansion. Baseball in the 1950s and early 1960s apparently well exemplified these consensus values. Through barnstorming tours by major league clubs and generous outlays of baseball equipment the State Department often used the sport as a diplomatic tool to indoctrinate wayward Asians and Latins with the benefits of American civilization and values. On the domestic front, baseball's experience with integration following the appearance of Jackie Robinson in a Dodgers uniform was often touted as fulfilling the American dream of social mobility in which an individual is judged by talent rather than skin color or social origins.

But the liberal consensus was shattered in the late 1960s with racial violence, campus unrest, assassinations, and the war in Vietnam. The baseball consensus, which often viewed itself as America in microcosm, was, in turn, disrupted by player unionization, accusations of racial prejudice, and questions of free expression. The sport's status as the national pastime was also challenged by professional football, supposedly more in touch with the values of the 1960s.[3] Perhaps no single year presented a greater challenge to American beliefs in reason and progress than 1968 in which Americans witnessed an escalating Vietnam War with the Tet offensive; student uprisings on major college campuses such as Columbia University; assassinations of Dr. Martin Luther King, Jr. and Robert Kennedy; racial violence in many of America's major cities; street protest and a violent police reaction at the Democratic National Convention in Chicago; and a growing counterculture movement which questioned the moral and economic values comprising the American consensus. An examination of baseball's response to this most troubled and turbulent year should provide some insight into how Americans and American institutions persevered in a time when everything was falling apart and nothing seemed to work.

The new year of 1968 found baseball in somewhat of a defensive posture. In 1967, the American League had enjoyed one of the best pennant races in major league baseball history with four teams in contention during the final weekend of the season. Yet, a league record attendance figure of 11,336,936 was only some 130,000 above the 1948 record. While drawing 12,971,430 fans, the National League gate was off 13 percent from the 1966 pace. The *Sporting News* cited racial fears as a key factor in disappointing attendance figures. The paper observed that too many major league parks were located in ghetto areas, and "the problem had grown acute in recent years with stories of racial violence all over the country making people exceedingly wary of venturing into slum areas, especially at night."[4] This editorial comment sounds almost like a statement Presidential candidate Richard Nixon might have made about the crime problem in America, but it does reflect the increasing economic and racial polarization in 1968 as fear and misunderstanding guided the assumptions of many Americans. The exodus of the middle class and businesses from the inner city had left a crumbling infrastructure and ball parks which symbolized the optimism of a different time.

If assumptions about racial violence were undermining the liberal consensus in baseball and American society, certainly one of the other disruptive questions of the 1960s was the Vietnam War. On this issue baseball sought to maintain its posture as a cornerstone of the anticommunist consensus. As with World Wars I and II, as well as the Korean War, baseball would continue during the conflict, seeking to provide an important morale factor for soldiers at the front and civilians at home. The *Sporting News* offered a program in which patriotic baseball fans could purchase subscriptions for servicemen stationed in Vietnam. In return, the paper relished printing the gratitude of soldiers such as Private J. B. Yanulavich who stated, "Mainly what I want to say is that it's nice to know that most of the people in the U. S. are really proud of us, like I am proud to be an American myself." The Official Baseball Guide was also offered, compliments of the major leagues, to servicemen. Colonel E. Parmly, IV, Commanding Officer, Company C, 5th Special Forces Group, asserted that only a small percentage of the 500 Green Berets under his command could use the book at any one time, but it always remained by the radio for Sunday games. Baseball Commissioner William Eckert received a Pentagon citation for contributing to morale in Vietnam, and, just as in previous military engagements, baseball sponsored visits by athletes to military hospitals to lift the spirits of wounded servicemen.[5]

Los Angeles Angels shortstop Jim Fregosi, visiting hospitals in Guam, Okinawa, Japan, and the Philippines, noted that strains of American dissent intruded upon his mission. Some servicemen were upset that newspaper coverage of demonstrations against the war was crowding out sports stories, and one burly Marine commented, "Just give me two more good Marines and we'll stop all that nonsense." But not all the personnel in the hospital were ready to go back to America and crack some heads. The Vietnam experience had raised doubts in the minds of many young men, such as an eighteen-year-old veteran who had both of his legs blown off. He asked Fregosi how it was possible that he could return to America and still not be able to buy a drink or cast a vote. Fregosi, an athlete rather than a diplomat, simply had no reply, insisting, "What could I say? It really hit me. You just can't answer it."[6]

In previous conflicts the morale-boosting hospital visit had solidified baseball's contribution to the formation of a wartime consensus, but in 1968 for athletes, such as Fregosi, it could be a reminder of the divisions in American society. Of course, the Vietnam War, which was shredding the fabric of the American consensus, was not an issue which baseball usually confronted directly. Morale and the draft status of players were baseball's main contacts with the war, but no major institution in America could completely escape the forces of dissent and division unleashed by this conflict which contributed so much to the breakdown of consensus values in America. In 1968, baseball's version of the American dream in which a young man, regardless of skin color or social background, could achieve success through talent and be appreciative of this opportunity was shattered by more militant players willing to question the assumptions of management. Certainly, baseball has a long history of players disputing the reserve clause and ownership, but the difference in 1968 was that players, operating in a milieu which was more supportive of challenges to authority, enjoyed greater success than their discontented brethren in previous player-management confrontations.

The Baseball Players Association under the aggressive leadership of former steelworker representative Marvin Miller demanded that baseball owners raise the minimum salary of players. Rumors of a strike swirled through the baseball world prior to the 1968 season. A settlement was reached and a strike averted as the minimum salary was raised from $7,000 to $10,000, effective for a two-year period. But the controversial reserve clause, under which a player was bound to the team which originally signed him until traded or released, was left on the negotiating table for further study. Disgruntled players, such as Oakland A's pitcher Jack Aker, made evident their distaste for management and the reserve clause. Aker, who served as player representative for the A's, had several difficult encounters with owner Charles Finley during the 1967 season and was rewarded with a pay cut. Aker complained that the reserve clause left him with no choice but to accept a reduction in salary for the 1968 campaign. He needed a job and still required a couple of years to qualify for baseball's pension plan. Aker reluctantly concluded, "I'm going to play in spite of Mr. Finley and do the best job I can."[7]

As players openly questioned baseball ownership on issues of salary, benefits, and the reserve clause, the baseball establishment also had to consider allegations of racism in its hiring practices. With the civil rights movement challenging the consensus claim of equal opportunity, baseball could point to the increasing presence of blacks on the playing field. But on the executive level in 1968 there were no black managers, only two black coaches (Jim Gilliam of the Dodgers and Ernie Banks of the Cubs), and only one black individual in baseball's front offices (Bill Lucas of the Braves who was related to slugger Hank Aaron). The *Sporting News* called upon baseball management to address the situation, editorializing, "A policy statement would seem very much in order to emphasize that a color line does not exist to bar Negroes from coaching and front office jobs in sports."[8]

But many in the sports world were impatient with liberal promises and demanded action. Harry Edwards, a sociology professor at San Jose State, attracted headlines in 1968 when he organized the Olympic Project for Human Rights to boycott the Mexico City Olympic Games. The articulate Edwards argued that sports such as baseball were not realistic avenues of social mobility for minorities in America. Black youth who spent their time playing games in order to become superstars were missing out on important educational opportunities which would qualify them for jobs in a modern technological society. Edwards concluded, "Big-name athletes who tell Black kids to 'practice and work hard and one day you can be just like me are playing games with the future of Black society." Jack Scott, director of the Institute for the Study of Sport and Society, concurred with Edwards's assessment regarding sports and social mobility. Scott labeled the assertion that sports could serve as an excellent means of social advancement for blacks as myth. He insisted, "For every white youth lifted out of a coal-mining town and every black person taken from the ghetto by an athletic scholarship, there are hundreds of other lower-class youths who have wasted their lives futilely preparing to be a sports star."[9] While critics like Edwards and Scott were leveling most of their criticism at collegiate athletics, it was, indeed, difficult for professional sports such as baseball to ignore the questions being raised regarding the consensus view of athletics as a path to the American dream.

Although criticism of sports was on the increase and the defensive baseball establishment issued nondiscriminatory statements, few management positions for minorities were forthcoming. Reflecting divisions in the civil rights movement between militants and those advocating less confrontational tactics, blacks in baseball disagreed as to how vocal they should be in pushing for racial advances within the game. Jackie Robinson, who had to silently endure racial indignities in his early playing days, was a very proud man. After his status as a player was assured, he wasted few opportunities to confront racism in baseball. Recognizing that he was an important symbol for black Americans, Robinson continued to speak out following his playing days. Robinson criticized black superstar Willie Mays for not living up to his responsibilities in the black community. Using the rhetoric of more militant blacks who sometimes labeled black liberals as "Uncle Toms," Robinson referred to Mays as a "do nothing Negro." The San Francisco Giants center fielder, who was a favorite of many whites, resented Robinson's allegations. Mays observed that he had worked for the Jobs Corps and addressed many black youth organizations, while he maintained faith in the American consensus and that room for blacks could be made in the American dream. Militancy was not required, as Mays asserted, "There has been progress made and we've all been a part of making it so, and it will continue to get better. But even when I get out of baseball, I'm not going to stand on a soap box or preach or picket or carry banners. I have my own way of getting our message across."[10] This exchange between such important symbols to the black community as Robinson and Mays was indicative of the increasing division among blacks regarding the pace of racial progress under such liberal leaders as Lyndon Johnson.

Faced with questions regarding its racial practices, and with voices of dissent challenging such traditional practices as the reserve clause, baseball management sought to reiterate the views of consensus America and the 1950s organization man. Baseball Commissioner William Eckert, a former general known more for his organizing rather than his fighting talents, sought to placate malcontents such as Aker and Robinson with refrains similar to President Johnson's, "Come, let us reason together." Thus, in response to baseball critics Eckert proclaimed, "I believe in cooperation and the creation of good will on all levels. I believe in the most effective organization possible, with progressive working committees, proper delegation of authority and responsibility and extensive, meaningful discussion."[11] Eckert advocated the values of the American consensus in which discussion, organization, and reason would bring orderly change and expansion.

But America in 1968 was becoming an increasingly violent society in which Eckert's values appeared out of place. On April 4, Martin Luther King, Jr. was gunned down by a sniper in Memphis. Rioting erupted in over a hundred cities, and 21,000 federal troops and 34,000 state guardsmen were dispatched to restore order. Given the chaos in America's major cities, there was little that big league baseball clubs could do but postpone home openers. The postponement also gave major league baseball the opportunity to honor Dr. King and appear as a champion of racial harmony, perhaps getting some of its critics off its back. Announcing the altered schedule, Commissioner Eckert dispatched a telegram to Mrs. King conveying baseball's condolences, as well as pledging that the sport would continue to "carry out the goals of Dr. King." The *Sporting News* lauded Eckert's decision to alter the schedule, as it "put baseball on the side of social justice." The publication went on to insist that baseball's unprecedented action was in "keeping with baseball's position as a pioneer in granting the Negro the opportunities which his skills demand."[12]

The *Sporting News* was making an effort to maintain baseball's position within the crumbling consensus of values. According to the paper, protest was not necessary when the opportunity to achieve on the athletic field could lead to acceptance and financial success. In pursuit of this editorial policy, the paper presented interviews with several black players in the wake of the assassination of Dr. King. The black players selected by the paper extolled the virtues of racial progress in baseball. Willie Mays insisted that it was pointless to discuss racism in the sport's past. Baseball had been great to him, and he believed that he owed the sport everything.

If Mays, the star, was reluctant to criticize the hand that fed him so well, what about black players who were not so well known and paid? Tommy Harper of the Cleveland Indians asserted that there was no racial antagonism between the players. The lack of interracial roommates was not evidence of prejudice. Blacks just naturally liked to hang out with blacks, and whites preferred to be with whites. Harper was hardly advocating black separatism when he concluded, "But why make two guys uncomfortable? I think the relationship is great all the way."

Other players picked for the interview did express some reservations. Leon "Daddy Wags" Wagner of the Indians commented upon the fact that many blacks believed teams maintained racial quotas limiting the number of black athletes. He confessed that he had no proof, "just a feeling." Lee Maye of the Senators complained that white players were able to obtain more commercial endorsements than blacks. Maye alleged that Roger Maris had received over a million dollars in endorsements for hitting 61 home runs, and he argued, "No Negro boy could have done that well on the side." Despite these disclaimers from Wagner and Maye, the basic portrait which the *Sporting News* sought to paint was that of the liberal consensus in which cooperation and compromise brought progress.[13]

But the reality of racial relations in America was perhaps more evident when the baseball season did open in Washington, D.C., on April 10, 1968. The Senators had sold over 45,000 tickets for the game, but only slightly over 32,000 fans showed up to watch the Twins defeat the Senators 2-0. D.C. Stadium was only a few blocks from the scene of some of the worst rioting in American history, and the crowd constituted the smallest opening day figure since the Senators moved into their new stadium for the 1961 season. Fearing further violence, President Johnson was not available to throw out the first ball, and that somewhat dubious honor, under the circumstances, was bestowed upon Vice-President Hubert Humphrey. National guardsmen who had been bivouacked in the stadium were given free tickets to the game. But their presence provided an eerie reminder of the turbulence through which the nation had just passed. The guardsmen watched the game in uniform as they were told that if they were needed to quell any further disorder they would be notified over the public address system. Fortunately, the guardsmen were not called upon, and for a change conflict was confined to the playing field.[14]

Despite problems of curfews and crowd control in many cities, the 1968 baseball season did get under way. But the decision to postpone opening day out of respect for Dr. King was not without its critics. A vigorous debate occurred in the pages of the *Sporting News* as many irate readers voiced their displeasure over baseball's honoring of Dr. King. Representative of this view was the comment by a man from Vienna, West Virginia, who observed, "I feel that if they needed a reason to postpone the opening of the baseball season, they could have done it for two Memphis police who, in trying to uphold the law, were killed by rioters." Other readers supported the decision reached by Commissioner Eckert and baseball management. Bernard Winkler of Washington, D.C., argued that the baseball establishment was following the recommendations of the police and military authorities. Besides, "The players wanted to honor Dr. King and not the rioters." Although the King assassination and its aftermath had been divisive, Robert Lipsyte in the *New York Times* hoped that the birth of a new baseball season would help the healing process. Lipsyte suggested that the sport offered a "comfort zone" for Americans as, "Its petty detail and endless speculation holds no import nor danger, and so is balm. And in a world of sharp edges and cruel aftereffects, baseball is slow and soft and sleepy as a fat old dog in the sun."[15]

Lipsyte's desire for a comfort zone was only a dream, for baseball and American society were barely able to deal with some of the scars left by the King assassination before the nation was traumatized by the assassination of Presidential candidate Robert Kennedy in June following his victory in the California Democratic Primary. Failure by Commissioner Eckert to take a decisive position on baseball's response to the assassination resulted in considerable controversy and antagonism which seemed to exacerbate growing player criticisms of management and decline of the baseball consensus. Instead of postponing all games on Saturday, June 8, the day of Kennedy's funeral, Eckert announced that games in New York and Washington, the site of funeral observances for the slain Senator, would be cancelled, while all other games would not start until after the funeral. As for June 9, which had been declared by President Johnson as the official day of mourning for Kennedy, Eckert stated that playing would be up to the individual clubs. Only the Red Sox and Orioles cancelled their home games. However, the huge crowds which turned out to view the funeral train making its way from California delayed the funeral ceremonies and played havoc with baseball's schedule. Why was there no outright cancellation of games as with the King assassination? Although denied by Eckert, reports persisted that the Commissioner had contacted the owners before announcing his decision, and since there was no rioting in the streets which would discourage fans from attending games the owners advised against any mass cancellation.

Regardless of its source, Eckert's ambiguous ruling created considerable confusion and hard feelings, especially in Cincinnati and Houston. The June 8 contest between the St. Louis Cardinals and Cincinnati Reds had been changed from a day to evening game, but the Kennedy rites were running considerably behind schedule. After waiting 45 minutes past the rescheduled starting time, Reds management decided to begin the game. General Manager Bob Howsam defended this action, maintaining, "Our position was that we had scheduled this game in good faith about an hour and a half after the burial was scheduled. We would have waited if the delay had been a short one." To deflect criticism, Howsam also engaged in a little buck passing, asserting that he called the Commissioner to inform him of the situation, and Eckert "felt the only thing to do was go ahead and play." Management's decision to play the contest did not sit well with many players who viewed the decision as placing profit over moral concerns. Consensus values of cooperation were not apparent as Reds pitcher and player representative Milt Pappas led the struggle to cancel the game. Cardinal players did not want to play but insisted that the final determination belonged to the home team. With Reds manager Dave Bristol lobbying in favor of conducting the contest, the Reds took two votes on playing. The first poll was a 12 to 12 stalemate with one abstention. On a second vote the total was 13 to 12 in favor of going on with the game. Pappas believed his teammates had caved in to management pressure, and he shouted to them as they filed onto the field, "You guys are wrong. I'm telling you you're all wrong. If you guys play you'll have to find another player rep." Pappas did not have to worry about resigning as Reds management had no desire to deal with a malcontent, dispatching the pitcher to Atlanta shortly after the incident in a six-man deal.[16]

Meanwhile, a player revolt was brewing in Houston. Astro players voted unanimously not to play the June 9 contest with the visiting Pittsburgh Pirates. Houston General Manager Spec Richardson was intent upon maintaining management control over the players. The game would be played as scheduled and any players refusing to participate would face heavy fines. Astro pitcher and player representative Dave Giusti announced that the players would reluctantly play the game, stating, "We changed our position after the strongest economic pressures had been brought to bear against us by the general manager." However, Houston stars Rusty Staub and Bob Aspromonte decided to sit the game out and, reportedly, were fined by Richardson. Maury Wills of the Pirates also refused to play, explaining, "I was out of uniform when Dr. King died and if I didn't respect Senator Kennedy's memory, too, I felt I would be hypocritical." Initially, star Pittsburgh outfielder Roberto Clemente was going to join Wills, but after a meeting with manager Larry Shepard he agreed to play. In a statement following his discussion with Shepard, Clemente made it clear that he preferred not to participate and blasted teammates who were indifferent to events such as the Kennedy assassination. The aftermath of the aborted player revolt in Houston was that Richardson sought to prevent any dissent among the Astros, imposing a gag rule on players repeating to reporters anything said in the clubhouse. Breaking the gag rule would result in a $500 fine and suspension or both.[17] While Richardson may have won a temporary battle in quelling player discontent, management would tend to lose the war as players would become more assertive later in the year with the pension plan and throughout the late 1960s and 1970s with their challenge to the reserve system.

Baseball's experience with racial tensions and the impact of the King and Kennedy assassinations certainly indicated that the sport could not escape the forces undermining the American consensus. Baseball's place among the chaos and confusion engulfing American society in 1968 was carefully analyzed in a July *Sporting News* editorial which still viewed the sport as a positive symbol of American values, even in the worst of times. The editorial argued that the nation was beset by assassinations, rebellious youth, racial violence, and a challenge to traditional values—all of which were lowering moral standards. And baseball was not mere escapism during this crisis of values, as the sport's continued popularity was evidence that consensus values of "fair play, sportsmanship, and teamwork" were still alive in the country. In a bit of a rhetorical excess, the paper proclaimed, "If you believe that working in harmony with your fellow man is dull stuff, if your kicks are psychedelic, if Bonnie and Clyde are your heroes, then baseball and Willie Mays and Mickey Mantle will be dull." The editorial concluded that baseball might be dull for a radical with a gun, but it would take a man with a bat to provide Americans with "confidence that our country can and will pull together like a championship team." Thus, despite controversies such as the sport's response to the Kennedy assassination, some believed baseball could shun radical change and maintain its position as a bastion of traditional values.[18]

This stance was apparent in baseball's somewhat cosmetic approach to the issue of black hiring. The American League employed former Olympic star Jesse Owens as a troubleshooter to improve racial relations.

Essentially, his job was to keep the channels of communication open with black players. As Owens described it, "I'm going to sit down and talk to them. Then, I'll take it from there. If necessary, I'll go to the managers or owners." The hiring of the conservative Owens, who had been very active in attempting to head off black protests and boycotts in track and field, seemed to be just an effort to prevent further criticism of baseball's racial policies. This apparent policy of co-option was further displayed when Commissioner Eckert appointed the respected former black player Monte Irvin to a position in the Commissioner's office. Despite these efforts at conciliation and window dressing, few other blacks were able to find employment in baseball's executive ranks.[19] And twenty years later this issue still continues to plague the sport.

If the baseball consensus was to some degree successful in muting black protest in 1968, the same certainly cannot be said for a more union-oriented approach by white, black, and Latin players to the economic status of the major league athlete. Baseball management had always taken great pride in the alleged consensus of values between management and players who worked together to achieve financial success and make the sport the great democratic game in which through talent, not protest, one could enhance his status. Accordingly, in 1963, Judge Robert Cannon, legal counsel to the Major League Players Association, gave credit to the owners for their "cooperative and generous dealings with the players." In exchange for these favors Cannon insisted that the players owed loyalty to the owners as well as the great game. It was the duty of players "to get out and preach the baseball gospel, spread good will and improve public relations toward the game."[20]

However, by 1968, Cannon's paternalistic approach was no longer appropriate to baseball or American society. Professional athletes were hardly immune to the protests dealing with freedom of speech, individual liberties, and equal economic opportunity sweeping the nation. In 1966, Marvin Miller replaced Cannon, and a new era in player-management relations was ushered in for the sport. The extent of this change from the cooperation of the 1950s to the confrontational 1960s became apparent in the second half of the 1968 season as Miller and the players demanded that a larger portion of the increasing television revenues be allocated to the players' pension fund. The issue was one of power as well as money. It was evident that television would play a prominent role in the future of the game, and players were determined to establish the principle that they were guaranteed a slice of this lucrative pie. To ensure good faith bargaining on the part of management, Miller urged players not to sign their 1969 contracts until the pension issue was resolved.[21]

Management protested that Miller was introducing the confrontational tactics of labor into the consensus world of baseball. Owners perceived the strategy of not signing a contract as a strike threat, and they attempted to portray Miller as an outside agitator who was misleading players and diverting their attention from the game itself. Thus, like the Old South before the introduction of such so-called agitators as the freedom riders, baseball was tranquil before the arrival of union man Miller. Of course, this was not actually the case as management had often provoked criticism and player challenges to the reserve clause. This provision of the player contract was protected under a 1922 Supreme Court decision written by Oliver Wendell Holmes in which baseball was exempted from the antitrust laws. A challenge to the reserve clause during the 1940s resulted in an out-of-court cash settlement between owners and New York Giants outfielder Danny Gardella. A 1953 Supreme Court decision reaffirmed, by a seven to two vote, the Holmes's ruling of thirty years earlier. However, the climate of opinion in America during the late 1960s seemed to provide an opportune time in which players might again assault the privileges of baseball ownership. With authority and tradition being openly confronted on the streets and campuses of America in 1968, the time seemed right for players to assert their position under a more aggressive leader such as Miller.

Nevertheless, the *Sporting News*, supporting management, sought to ridicule Miller and appeal to the players' pride by insisting that the players' representative had not adjusted to the fact that, "He now represents a group of professionals who take pride in their work (as most do). All too often, Miller acts as if he still is employed by the clock-punching members of the Steelworkers." Players were professionals with high standards and, thus, above blue-collar unionization. But athletes who were bound to service contracts with one club believed that they were not always treated as professionals by team owners. And player representatives such as pitcher Steve Hamilton of the Yankees rushed to the defense of Miller, exclaiming, "The Players Association is fortunate indeed to have a man of Marvin Miller's caliber who is 100 percent behind the players, and I assure you the players are 100 percent behind him." Hamilton also rejected the consensus values of cooperation, arguing that players had only been able to gain a decent pension system because they had fought for their rights. Miller also struck back at what he perceived to be the paternalistic nature of owners who believed players could not negotiate and concentrate on their play at the same time. The players' representative asserted, "The players wonder if they think they should shut their eyes to the war in Vietnam, the demonstrations in Chicago and other current events and think

only about the game. They are insulted by the owners' entire line of reasoning."[22] Miller's comments document the fact that baseball management
and players were not immune to the forces of dissent sweeping through
America. Players could not escape the influence of the "real" world and
changes taking place in American society.

A players' strike was not the only threat hanging over baseball in the
latter months of 1968. Umpires were also on the warpath regarding the
decision by American League President Joe Cronin to fire umpires Al
Salerno and Bill Valentine shortly before the conclusion of the season.
Cronin accused both arbiters of "incompetence." However, Salerno and
Valentine insisted they were let go because of their efforts to organize
American League umpires, whose pay and benefits were below those of the
already unionized National League umpires. Arbiters maintained solidarity and threatened a strike as veteran National League umpire Augie
Donatelli stated, "We'll stand by the American Leaguers if Salerno and
Valentine aren't reinstated."[23] Intransigent owners such as Finley of Oakland asserted that the umpires and players were out of line, and should
they strike, the sport should simply shut down.[24] After all, players and
umpires were dependent upon the owners. Sounding somewhat like a college president who believed the school could exist without students, Finley did not seem to notice that power relations in America were in a state
of flux and that players might be on the verge of enhancing their position
within the game.

As the World Series approached, baseball's establishment was beset
with questions of unionization and individual rights when the repercussions of the Vietnam War again placed the sport in a controversial position.
Before the October 7, 1968 Series contest between the St. Louis Cardinals
and Detroit Tigers, folksinger Jose Feliciano was asked to sing the national
anthem. Feliciano responded with a blues rendition of the anthem which
let loose a storm of protest. The Tiger Stadium switchboard received over
2,000 complaints in less than an hour. To many, Feliciano's experimentation was representative of a society in which tradition was under attack and
patriotism was no longer viewed as a virtue. Reflecting this perspective was
Murphy L. Tamkersley who was recovering from Vietnam wounds in a
Houston veterans' hospital. Tamkersley lamented, "Some of us have seen
people die in Vietnam, soldiers singing part of the National Anthem as they
gave their lives for our country. Then to be in a hospital with injuries and
illnesses we got in the service and to hear that Anthem sung in such a dis-
honorable fashion." Feliciano expressed surprise that anyone was so insecure as to feel threatened by his singing, but reaffirmed that he meant no
disrespect, explaining, "I owe everything I have to this country. "[25]

Organized baseball was also urged to do more to boost morale in Vietnam, and Commissioner Eckert responded by planning more trips by baseball celebrities. A delegation led by Ernie Banks, "Mr. Cub," was dispatched to Vietnam in December, 1968. Banks, a gifted black athlete, was not one to criticize the baseball establishment or American society. Banks believed that he had achieved the American dream through hard work and perseverance, and he had little use for those who were not willing to labor diligently within the system. Banks told reporters that in the U. S. "you see a lot of young people complaining, people who hang out in the streets, and who don't want to work." But in Vietnam young men only nineteen and twenty years of age were piloting helicopters, and young twenty-one-year-old lieutenants were leading men into combat. Banks concluded, "It really proved to me that young people, when they're called upon, can do the job. It was a pleasure meeting them."[26] With players like Banks, baseball was still able to provide its morale boost and support of the consensus even amidst the agitation unleashed by the conflict in Vietnam. Yet, trotting out Ernie Banks to utter support for traditional values was not going to stem the tide of racial, legal, and union issues confronting the sport.

At organized baseball's annual winter meeting, held in December, 1968 in San Francisco, baseball owners moved to dump Eckert as Commissioner. Eckert had been selected for the post in 1965, even though he professed to have little knowledge of the game. Owners extolled his experience as an able administrator and organizer within the military, representing the 1950s values of the organization man. Also Eckert was viewed as an individual over whom the owners might be able to exert considerable influence due to his lack of experience with the game. But if this was the primary motivation, it certainly backfired as after only three years in the job owners were screaming for the scalp of baseball's unknown soldier and calling for strong leadership in the sport. Yankee President Mike Burke, who feared that baseball was losing its hold on young people, argued, "We recognize our problem. It's the attitude of the public at large that baseball is not with it, that it's not as contemporary as football, hockey and basketball, the contact sports. It's an attitude that exists and we've got to decide what to do about it. We need strong, courageous, intelligent leadership." The *Sporting News* believed that the sport's difficulties could be traced back to Ford Frick's long tenure as Commissioner from 1951 to 1965. The paper argued that Frick had not been assertive enough as "problems piled up on the surface, baseball lost ground to the rapid growth of professional football and the game's entire structure began to weaken."[27] Interestingly enough, this line of reasoning seems to parallel the thinking that many of the social problems in America which came to the surface during the 1960s had been quietly simmering throughout the 1950s, but under the unassuming leadership of President Eisenhower these problems were not dealt with in their early stages.

But if baseball owners really believed they needed new dynamic leadership to find a fresh position for the sport in the late 1960s, they did not demonstrate this perspective when a new Commissioner was selected. Stodgy Bowie Kuhn, attorney for the National League, was chosen by the owners to represent baseball.[28] This selection was viewed as an effort to use the commissionership to support the owners in negotiations with Miller and the players. However, in 1968 the tide had turned in baseball, as well as in American society. Bowie Kuhn and Richard Nixon might become chief executives, but they could not always have their way. Black players would continue to be more assertive about race relations, and Marvin Miller would obtain an increased pension compensation plan, while players would persist in their assault upon the reserve system throughout the 1970s. Umpires would also develop a strong union, and Salerno and Valentine would finally gain reinstatement. For better or worse, individual rights would be emphasized over the corporate image of the game.

The changing nature of baseball was also noted in the fall of 1968 by a somewhat nostalgic Senator Eugene McCarthy, whose bid to gain the Democratic Presidential nomination on an antiwar platform had been defeated at the violent Chicago convention. Instead of campaigning for his fellow Democrat Hubert Humphrey against Richard Nixon, a bitter McCarthy agreed to cover the World Series for *Life* magazine. McCarthy's comments on the nature of baseball reveal a great deal of ambivalence about the sport and American society. The Senator lamented the fact that baseball (which he had played on a semi-pro basis), like America, had lost some of its pastoral innocence. Issues of unionization, monopoly, and racism in the sport led the disillusioned Senator to despair for the future of baseball. McCarthy mused about the sport, "It really isn't the national pastime any more. We start kids out in the Little Leagues, and right away the whole thing is very serious. They get too much too soon. The whole thing is overengineered and the only place people want to go is to the top. There's no room in the middle for fun. Perhaps we should abolish organized baseball — the Little Leagues as well as the majors. Then we could just leave a few balls and bats lying around and see if people picked them up."[29]

But McCarthy was wrong in assuming that all the fun had departed from Organized Baseball. Despite allegations of racism, labor confrontations, and the controversy surrounding its response to the King and

Kennedy assassinations, major league baseball was still an exciting spectator sport as pitching dominated during the 1968 season. In the American League, Detroit right-hander Denny McClain became the first pitcher in over thirty years to win 30 games, while in the National League, St. Louis Cardinals ace Bob Gibson set a record by establishing a 1.12 ERA. The World Series was also suspenseful, with the Tigers triumphing over the Cards in seven games with chunky Tiger left-hander Mickey Lolich emerging as the Series hero. In responding to the turmoil of 1968, the liberal consensus in baseball and American society had been altered. The faith of players, both black and white, that the expanding corporate economy and baseball management would look out for their interest was undermined. Players who were coerced into performing during the Kennedy funeral sought a more labor-oriented association under the strong leadership of Marvin Miller which would assert their economic position and individual liberties.

American society in 1968 appeared to be almost coming apart under the strains of racism, violence, assassination, protest, and war, but the nation persevered. The "play" world of professional baseball was also affected by these forces of change, and the 1968 season helped further a shift in the balance of power from the owners to the players. Racial conflicts in American society encouraged debate on the role of blacks in baseball, and a climate of opinion in which dissent was tolerated certainly contributed to player assertiveness on issues of pay and expression. But baseball persevered because in the midst of the chaos of 1968 it retained certain traditional values of fair play and teamwork which had meaning to Americans on both sides of the barricades in the 1960s. In his collection of essays, *Baseball the Beautiful*, Marvin Cohen well captured the place baseball holds in the hearts of many Americans. Cohen wrote, "Fashions come and go, and wars, and social problems, economic crises, political climates. Baseball outlives them all — in our midst. A steady constant that retains its own slow unfolding patterns, while convulsions grip the land outside and tear out the old to plant the new. Baseball serenely glides by — permanent, beautiful, ever itself: insular, yet mildly reflecting, in a peaceful way, in its own terms, the changes going on outside."[30]

The nation and the sport of baseball, which has often so well reflected America, were stronger in 1968 than many observers thought. Yet, baseball which was able to accommodate, under coercion of course, many of the demands made by players has yet to satisfactorily deal with the issue of black hiring in the higher echelons of the game. Commissioner Peter Ueberroth has brought 1960s militant Harry Edwards into the Commissioner's office to help with minority recruitment. According to Ueberroth's figures, the percentage of minorities in front office jobs has increased from 2 percent in 1986 to 10 percent in 1987, but as we approach the 1988 baseball season there are still no black managers in the major leagues.[31] Although many of the events of 1968 may seem recent in our collective memories, it was twenty years ago, and it is high past time to deal with the issue of racial hiring and employment. We do not need to again disprove Dick Young's prophecy that "we'll outgrow this stuff in another 20 years or so."

Endnotes

This essay was originally published in Peter Levine, ed., *Baseball History: An Annual of Original Baseball Research* (Meckler Publishing, 1989), 81-94.

1. *Sporting News*, February 17, 1968. For the key role played by the *Sporting News* in baseball see *Sporting News*, First Hundred Years, 1886-1986 (St. Louis: Sporting News, 1986). The "Bible of Baseball" will constitute a primary source for this investigation into the sport during 1968.

2. For the development of the liberal consensus and its breakdown see Geoffrey Hodgson, *America in Our Time* (New York: Doubleday, 1976); Allen J. Matusow, *The Unraveling of America: A History of Liberalism in the 1960s* (New York: Harper and Row, 1984); and William L. O'Neil, *Coming Apart: An Informal History of America in the 1960s* (New York: Quadrangle, 1971).

3. Studies which have used baseball to investigate American values include Richard Crepeau, *Baseball: America's Diamond Mind, 1919-1941* (Orlando, FL: University Presses of Florida, 1980); Peter Levine, *A.G. Spalding and the Rise of Baseball: The Promise of American Sport* (New York: Oxford University Press, 1985); Steven A. Riess, *Touching Base: Professional Baseball and American Culture in the Progressive Era* (Westport, CT: Greenwood Press, 1980); Leverett T. Smith, Jr., *The American Dream and the National Game* (Bowling Green, Ohio: Bowling Green University Popular Press, 1975); and Jules Tygiel, *Baseball's Great Experiment: Jackie Robinson and His Legacy* (New York: Oxford University Press, 1983).

4. *Sporting News*, January 6, 1968. For a background history of baseball during the 1960s see David Quentin Voigt, *American Baseball. Vol. III: From Postwar Expansion to the Electronic Age* (University Park, PA: Penn State University Press, 1983).

5. *Sporting News*, May 13 and November 18, 1967. For a comparison with baseball activities during World War II see William B. Mead, *Even the Browns: The Zany, True Story of Baseball in the Early Forties* (Chicago: Contemporary Books, 1978); and Richard Goldstein, *Spartan Seasons: How Baseball Survived the Second World War* (New York: MacMillan, 1980).

6. *Sporting News*, January 6, 1968. For an interesting discussion of the connection between American culture and the Vietnam War see Loren Baritz, *Backfire: A History of How American Culture Led Us into Vietnam and Made Us Fight the Way We Did* (New York: William Morrow and Co., 1985).

7. *Sporting News*, February 10, 1968. For background information on Marvin Miller see Robert Boyle, "This Miller Admits He's a Grind," *Sports Illustrated*, 40 (March 11, 1974), 22; Robin Roberts, "The Game Deserves the Best: Marvin Miller as Executive Director of the Baseball Players Association," *Sports Illustrated*, 30 (February 24, 1969), 46–47; and David Q. Voigt, "They Shaped the Game: Nine Innovators of Major League Baseball," *Baseball History*, 1 (Spring 1986), 5–21.

8. Sporting News, April 13, 1968. For background information on racism in baseball and sport during the 1950s and 1960s see Richard Bardalph, *The Negro Vanguard* (New York: Vintage Books, 1961); Robert Boyle, "The Negro in Baseball," *Sports Illustrated*, 12 (March 21, 1960), 16–21; Myron Cope, "The Frustration of the Negro Athlete," *Sport*, 41 (January 1966), 24–25; William B. Furlong, "A Negro Ballplayer's Life Today," *Sport*, 38 (May 1962), 38–39; Jack Olsen, *The Black Athlete: A Shameful Story, the Myth of Integration in American Sport* (New York: Time-Life Books, 1968); Art Rust, Jr., *Get That Nigger Off the Field* (New York: Delacorte, 1976); and Jules Tygiel, "Beyond the Point of No Return: Those Who Came After," *Sports Illustrated*, 58 (June 27, 1983), 40–42.

9. Harry Edwards, *The Revolt of the Black Athlete* (New York: Free Press, 1970); Edwards, *The Struggle That Must Be: An Autobiography* (New York: MacMillan, 1980), 242; and Jack Scott, *The Athletic Revolution* (New York: Free Press, 1971), 181.

10. *Sporting News*, March 30 and April 6, 1968. For Mays and racial issues see Charles Einstein, *Willie's Time: A Memoir* (New York: J. B. Lippincott, 1979); and Ed Linn, "Trials of a Negro Idol," *Saturday Evening Post*, 236 (June 22, 1963), 70–72. For background on Robinson see Tygiel, *Baseball's Great Experiment*; and Jackie Robinson, *I Never Had It Made: An Autobiography* (New York: G.P. Putnam's Sons, 1972).

11. *Sporting News*, April 13, 1968. On Eckert see Barry Kremenko, "The General Takes Command," *Baseball Digest*, 25 (February 1966), 23–25; and John Underwood, "Progress Report on the Unknown Soldier," *Sports Illustrated*, 24 (April 4, 1966), 40–42.

12. *Sporting News*, April 20, 1968. For the King assassination and the ensuing violence see David L. Lewis, *King: A Biography* (Urbana, IL: University of Illinois Press, 1978); and Stephen B. Oates, *Let the Trumpet Sound: The Life of Martin Luther King, Jr.* (New York: New American Library, 1982).

13. *Sporting News*, April 20, 1968. None of the players in this interview were noted for being outspoken on racial issues, with the possible exception of Leon Wagner. For additional information on Wagner see Robert Creamer, "A Free-Swinging Angel Who Never Fears to Tread," *Sports Illustrated*, 19 (August 12, 1963), 46.

14. *Sporting News*, April 27, 1968; and *New York Times*, April 11, 1968.

15. *Sporting News*, April 27 and May 11, 1968: and *New York Times*, April 11, 1968.

16. For detailed coverage of baseball's response to the Kennedy assassination see *Sporting News*, June 22, 1968. For the national response to the assassination and the details of the Kennedy funeral see Arthur Schlesinger, Jr., *Robert Kennedy and His Times* (New York: Ballantine Books, 1978).

17. *Sporting News*, June 29, 1968.

18. *Ibid.*, July 20, 1968. For a discussion of the 1960s counterculture which threatened the baseball and American consensus see Charles Reich, *The Greening of America* (New York: Random House, 1970).

19. *Sporting News*, August 3 and September 7, 1968. For a fine biography which explains Jesse Owens's conservative politics see William J. Baker, *Jesse Owens: An American Life* (New York: The Free Press, 1986). For Monte Irvin see Jackie Robinson, *Baseball Has Done It* (Philadelphia: Lippincott, 1964), 87–96; and Rust, *Get That Nigger Off the Field*, 112–119.

20. *Sporting News*, January 26, 1963.

21. For information on the pension question see Bob Broeg, "$12,000 Pensions Near, Pre-'46 Stars Get Nothing," *Baseball Digest*, 25 (November 1966), 79–81; and Richard Dozer, "After the Cheers Have Faded," *Baseball Digest*, 25 (November 1966), 35–39.

22. For *Sporting News* coverage of the pension issue see August 17, August 31, and September 21, 1968.

23. *Ibid.*, December 21, 1968. For information on umpires in the mid–1960s see John Hall, "The New Breed of Umpire," *Baseball Digest*, 26 (June 1967), 20–23.

24. *Sporting News*, December 28, 1968. For the intransigent Finley see Bill Libby, *Charlie O. and the Angry A's* (New York: Doubleday, 1975); and Herbert Mitchelson, *Charlie O.: Charlie Finley vs. the Baseball Establishment* (New York: Bobbs-Merrill, 1975).

25. *Sporting News*, October 19 and 26, 1968. For the 1968 Series see Roger Angell, "World Series: Detroit Tigers vs. St. Louis Cardinals," *New Yorker*, 44 (October 26, 1968), 171–174.

26. *Sporting News*, December 7, 1968. On the irrepressible Banks see Ernie Banks with Jim Enright, *Mr. Cub* (Chicago: Follett Publishing Co., 1971); William Furlong, "Ernie Banks' Life with a Loser," *Sport*, 35 (April 1963), 64–95; and Bill Libby, *Ernie Banks, Mr. Cub* (New York: G. P. Putnam, 1971).

27. On the firing of Eckert see *Sporting News*, December 21 and 28, 1968; Mickey Herskowitz, "A Farewell to General Eckert," *Baseball Digest*, 27 (April 1969), 12–15; and William Leggett, "Court Martial for a General," *Sports Illustrated*, 29 (December 16, 1968), 24–25.

28. On Bowie Kuhn see Kuhn, *Hardball: The Education of a Baseball Commissioner* (New York: Times Books, 1987); and John J. Smith, "Why the Owners Chose Bowie Kuhn," *Baseball Digest*, 27 (April 1969), 5–12.

29. Eugene McCarthy, "Confessions of a Fair Country Ballplayer," *Life*, 65 (October 18, 1968), 67–72.

30. Marvin Cohen, *Baseball the Beautiful: Decoding the Diamond* (New York: Links Books, 1974), 120.

31. *Sporting News*, December 21, 1987.

13

Baseball and America in 1969: A Traditional Institution Responds to Changing Times

The week of July 19-26, 1969 was a time of celebration for President Richard Nixon and many Americans. On July 20, the Apollo XI mission to the moon culminated in Astronaut Neil Armstrong's one giant leap for mankind. President Nixon, seeking to bask in the adulation for the astronauts, and aware that his major political rival Ted Kennedy's career was in serious jeopardy due to a car crash at Chappaquiddick, Massachusetts only hours before the lunar landing, flew on July 23 to the South Pacific for the splashdown of Apollo XI. On the flight deck of the aircraft carrier *Hornet*, Nixon attempted to make small talk with the astronauts through the window of their quarantine chamber, asking them if they had been able to keep up with the results of the baseball All-Star game while in space. (The National League won the contest over the American League by a margin of 9 to 3.) Although Astronauts Armstrong and Edwin "Buzz" Aldrin seemed a little ill at ease with the baseball chatter, the euphoria of Nixon was not dampened, as the President proclaimed, "This is the greatest week in the history of the world since the creation, because as a result of what happened in this week, the world is bigger, infinitely...." To take maximum advantage of the Apollo publicity, Nixon immediately launched a world tour code-named Moonglow which would take the Presidential party to Guam, the Philippines, Indonesia, Thailand, South Vietnam, India, Pakistan, Romania, and Britain. Relishing state dinners and formal meetings with leaders, Nixon continued to use his love for baseball to establish a connection with the common man, constantly asking servicemen in

Vietnam which baseball team was their favorite, and, while bandishing a baseball cap, telling American embassy employees in Bangkok that "while you can take American boys out of the United States, you can never take baseball out of an American boy."[1]

Having taken full advantage of the Apollo flight's political possibilities, and as usual taking comfort from sport clichés, Nixon returned to the United States with an approval rating of over 60 percent in public opinion polls. But the President's upbeat mood proved to be short-lived. Faced with opposition to his nomination of Clement Haynsworth to the Supreme Court, growing criticism of his policy of Vietnamization as demonstrated by the October Moratorium against the war, and the breaking of news stories regarding American atrocities at the Vietnamese village of My Lai, Nixon moved toward a policy of confrontation with apparent enemies, both foreign and domestic, which would lead to the invasion of Cambodia and an obsession with security leaks, culminating in the Watergate crisis and the unraveling of the Nixon Presidency. Thus, the euphoria over Apollo XI failed to obscure the fact that issues of war and peace, race, poverty, and generational conflict in 1969 were seriously eroding confidence in traditional institutions. While outwardly maintaining a facade of self-assurance, Richard Nixon was beset by insecurities which resulted in his resignation, yet the institution of the Presidency survived the Watergate crisis and remains a bully pulpit for leaders as ideologically diverse as Ronald Reagan and Bill Clinton.

Similarly, the traditional institution of baseball was beset by considerable doubt during the late 1960s. Racked by the storms of racial unrest, confrontations between labor and management, the popularity of football which seemed to reflect the violence of the era, and management which found cultural change in America threatening, baseball maintained, albeit in somewhat of an altered framework, its position with millions of Americans. The turnstiles on summer evenings in the early 1990s indicate record number of spectators for major league baseball in many American cities, and as baseball scholar Richard Skolnik observed in *Baseball and the Pursuit of Innocence,* the remedy for the challenges confronting the sport lie in the game itself, "...in the multiplicity of skills it requires, in its leisurely pace that encourages involvement, conversation and analysis, in the exquisite drama it orchestrates so expertly. The answer will be found in a marvelously executed double play, in a magnetic game-winning home run, in a pitcher extricating himself from a bases-loaded-no-out situation, in a pick off, a suicide squeeze, in a no-hitter in the eighth inning."[2] Thus baseball, like American government, was altered but not crushed by the forces of change afoot in 1969. But how did the increasingly insecure traditional institution of baseball respond to the challenges of a new age symbolized by the Apollo moon landing?

In 1969, the establishment of Organized Baseball sought to find a middle ground between innovation and tradition. Seeking to prop up decreasing revenues, the sport expanded to the cities of Montreal and San Diego in the National League, while adding Seattle and Washington to the American League. To accommodate the additional teams, the leagues would be divided into two divisions, creating a revenue-enhancing new round of play-offs, the League Championship Series. On the traditional side of the equation, Organized Baseball, ever historically conscious, was celebrating its Centennial which was commemorated at the All-Star Game and reception at the White House hosted by Nixon on July 22, the day before flying off to greet the Apollo astronauts.

While the President was unable to attend the All-Star Game at RFK Stadium due to heavy rain which postponed the game for one day, Baseball Commissioner Bowie Kuhn was impressed that Nixon took time out of his busy Apollo week to receive over four hundred baseball dignitaries, including those named by fan vote as the "greatest living players." Full of praise for the President, Kuhn observed, "He gave a bravura performance, with an appropriate comment for almost everyone. He had memories to share with the old-timers, topical comments and advice for those now in the game and pertinent observations for many of the sportswriters and broadcasters." Nixon was awarded a gold lifetime National League pass in addition to a plaque like those given to the greatest team members. Warming to the occasion, Nixon, who was not known for good relations with the press, commented, "If I had it to do over again, I think I'd be a sports writer." Not intending to damn with faint praise, the *Sporting News* thanked the President for taking time out of his busy schedule for baseball and referred to Nixon as "the most knowledgeable and eager baseball fan in the White House since Warren Harding." [3]

Despite all of the glowing tributes, the Baseball Centennial celebration underscored that the sport was finding it exceedingly difficult adjusting to changing times. Prior to attending the White House reception, Hall of Fame players Bob Feller and Jackie Robinson squared off at a press conference in the Sheraton Park Hotel. Irritated by African-American charges of racism in baseball and American society, the conservative Feller lashed out at Jackie Robinson for his criticisms of baseball hiring practices. The former Cleveland pitcher asserted, "Robinson has always been bush. He's always been a professional agitator more than anything else. He's just ticked off because baseball never rolled out the red carpet when he quit playing and offered him a soft front office job." Aligning with baseball management, Feller argued that there had been no discrimination in the sport since Robinson integrated the game and, furthermore, that baseball had contributed more to minority groups than almost any other institution in the country. Feller ended his diatribe by concluding, "Ability alone is what should count in the front office, too. I think there will be a Negro with that ability." Obviously, Feller did not believe that African-Americans in 1969 were yet ready for the responsibilities of management.

An angry Robinson retorted that Feller had grown little since 1947, Robinson's rookie season, continuing to keep "his head in the sand."[4] Expressing some resentment that he was employed as a frozen food executive rather than in baseball management, Robinson proclaimed, "My big thing is I don't believe that the black players are getting an equal opportunity with the whites after their playing days are through. I think the public is much more ready for a black manager than the owners."[5] Despite Robinson's lament, major league baseball did not get around to hiring an African-American manager until Cleveland tapped Frank Robinson to lead the Indians in 1975. The angry exchange between Robinson and Feller reflected that behind the facade of Centennial celebration rhetoric lurked serious questions as to how well the traditional institution of baseball was responding to changes in American life.

1968 had not been an easy year for baseball and the United States.[6] It appeared as if America was coming apart, with the Tet offensive in Vietnam providing further fuel for the anti-war movement; the assassinations of Robert Kennedy and Martin Luther King, Jr. leading to violent explosions in major American cities; campus unrest at such institutions as Columbia University; and the protests at the Democratic National Convention accompanied by what a Presidential commission would term a police riot. Baseball certainly was unable to escape the repercussions of these tumultuous events as games were canceled in the wake of the Kennedy and King assassinations, leading Jackie Robinson, in a nationally syndicated column appearing predominantly in African-American newspapers, to assert, "The American society, whose white rulers spend so much time cautioning black people to be nonviolent, is one of the most violent 'civilizations' on the map, and the rest of the world knows it."[7] While African-American allegations of racism in baseball hiring practices produced little positive response by the baseball establishment, the labors of Marvin Miller as representative of the Major League Baseball Players Association resulted in the baseball owners engaging in collective bargaining and the signing of a "Basic Agreement" to cover the 1968 and 1969 seasons. Lauding this achievement as revolutionizing the game, Miller observed, "The basic agreement incorporated the Uniform Player's Contract, which meant that the form of the player's individual contract could no longer be changed unilaterally by the owners and their lawyers.... In other words, clubs could no longer play sheriff, judge, and jury with ballplayers."[8]

Baseball ownership evidently agreed with Miller that the Basic Agreement constituted a threatening change to the traditional prerogatives of the sport's moguls. Accordingly, at their annual winter meeting in December, 1968, the owners decided to terminate the contract of Baseball Commissioner William Eckert. The former general, who quickly became known as baseball's unknown soldier, claimed to have little knowledge of the game, but was lauded by owners as an experienced administrator. On the other hand, more cynical commentators viewed the appointment of Eckert as an effort by the owners to select an inexperienced baseball person whom they could dominate. However, Eckert proved to be no match for Marvin Miller and the changing climate of opinion in America which encouraged challenges to traditional authority.[9]

The general consensus among baseball executives was that a strong hand was needed to administer the rudder of the game and to place Miller and the players in their place, restoring traditional power relationships within organized baseball. And the baseball establishment was prepared to elect one of its own; however, none of the leading candidates (Mike Burke, President of the New York Yankess; Charles Feeney, Vice-President of the San Francisco Giants; Lee MacPhail, General Manager of the Yankees; and John McHale, President of the expansion Montreal Expos) were able to garner the required three-fourths of all votes in each league. Faced with a united Players Association under the leadership of Miller demanding an increase in pension benefits, the owners could little afford to spend too much time searching for consensus. Accordingly, on February 4, the owners unanimously named National League attorney Bowie Kuhn to a temporary one year appointment as Commissioner of Baseball.[10]

Kuhn's first order of business was to ease fears of a strike over the pension issue which surfaced at a January 20 meeting in New York between Kuhn and John Gaherin, Director of the Player Relations Committee, representing the owners, and Miller. Following this meeting, Miller denounced Gaherin and Kuhn for delivering "a declaration of war with its sole purpose the dissolution of the Players Association." By a vote of 461 to 6, the players rejected a one million dollar increase to the owners' pension share contribution, seeking, instead, a percentage of rising television and radio revenues. To increase pressure on management, Miller produced a list of 315 players, including some of the top stars of the day, who would not sign their 1969 contracts until the pension issue was resolved.[11]

Owner reaction to the gauntlet tossed by Miller and the players was predictable. Sounding like a university administrator chiding recalcitrant students, Braves Vice President Paul Richards stated that he would welcome a strike as it would "get the guys who don't want to play out of the game and let the fellows who appreciate the major leagues play." Meanwhile, General Manager Bob Howsam of the Cincinnati Reds used the familiar outside agitator explanation for player unrest, citing Miller's trade union background and insisting that a majority of the ball players were being swayed by "the thinking of a minority." Howsam went on to express his disappointment that the fraternal relationship between owners and players no longer existed, but "when a player puts his dealings on a purely business basis, management has no alternative but to do the same."[12]

In response to these paternalistic pronouncements and apparent owner solidarity, American League Player Representative and Yankee pitcher Steve Hamilton accused the barons of baseball of seeking to destroy the players' organization and called upon the players to maintain solidarity. Hamilton told his associates, "They're going to test us and we have to be strong or we'll be ruined. All we are seeking is security in the future for our families." Hamilton's appeal for solidarity was supported by 125 players who met in Baltimore and pledged that they were prepared to sit the season out if the pension issue could not be settled.[13]

As the position of both sides hardened, baseball owners planned to open the season with minor league players. However, NBC television made it clear that the network would not be paying major league prices for minor league talent. Faced with losing the lucrative television market, Commissioner Kuhn moved quickly to bring both sides together, fashioning a compromise in which the owners' contribution to the pension fund was increased from 4.1 million dollars a year to an annual figure of 6.5 million, but as a concession to management, the settlement was not tied to television revenues. Although he would later describe Kuhn as an incompetent fool whose "moves consistently backfired" and "attempts at leadership created divisions," Miller praised Kuhn for his handling of the 1969 pension strike as the great exception to the Commissioner's record of mismanagement.[14]

While there were crucial economic incentives to preventing a player strike, a number of owners were most angry that the players had successfully challenged traditional authority. The baseball establishment sought to make it clear that the pension settlement in no way meant that the sport had entered a stage of labor relations and abandoned the consensus values of the 1950s. Visiting the training camp of the Philadelphia Phillies the day after the pension issue was resolved, Kuhn stated that the players did not want a union, as a "normal union relationship is not appropriate for baseball." Meanwhile, President Calvin Griffith of the Minnesota Twins warned his players to report to training camp in good shape or face suspensions, explaining, "If they want to be union men, we'll treat them as union men instead of socialites." Owner Arthur Allyn of the Chicago White Sox tried a less heavy hand with his players, pleading poverty for his inability to pay higher salaries and reminding players of their obligations to the fans. Warning the players that the fans would be scrutinizing them very carefully after a near strike and appealing to a sense of guilt, Allyn said, "If we don't have the right attitudes, if we don't give everything we've got to those who pay their own way into the park, then you can be sure they'll know it, and we'll know it."[15]

The most vitriolic and vindictive assault on the players was reserved for a club house speech which Cardinal President August A. Busch delivered on March 22. Stating up front that he neither liked to lose nor cared for labor ultimatums, Busch angrily accused "baseball's union representatives" of making "derogatory statements" about the owners and contributing to the decline of baseball as America's number one sport. The Cardinal President concluded his remarks with a reminder that the baseball fans pay for the salaries of the players, admonishing the Cardinals "not to kill the enthusiasm of the fans and kids for whom you have become such idols." Busch finished to polite applause, asked for questions, and receiving none, departed from the club house. While Cardinal shortstop Dal Maxvil, who would later be promoted to a management position within the Cardinal organization, termed the speech "classy" and "beautiful," it was obvious that the Busch sermon did not set well with other Cardinal players such as Bob Gibson and Curt Flood. And in Chicago, White Sox pitching ace Gary Peters exclaimed that he simply did not believe the poverty claims of owners such as Allyn. Even if there was some truth to the poor mouthing, Peters, who served as White Sox Player Representative, insisted, "If I have a good year, I'd expect to be paid what I'm worth. How much he makes or loses on the ball club is his problem."[16] Thus in the wake of the 1969 pension agreement, and a social climate encouraging challenges to authority, it was clear that a new era was dawning in player-management relations. The traditional patronizing view of baseball management that they owned and controlled players would be a casualty of the changing consciousness of the 1960s; however, labor relations were not the only problem in 1969 threatening the status of Organized Baseball.

For example, in publications from the *Readers' Digest* to the *Wall Street Journal*, the fate of modern baseball was debated, with many critics providing obituaries for the sport. Bottom line major league attendance figures were of the most obvious concern, from a peak figure of 25.2 million fans in 1966, turnstile counts had slowed to 24.3 million in 1967 and 23.1 million for 1968. (Attendance figures for 1969 when divisional play and expansion were to boost attendance did not prove very encouraging with a total figure of 27.2 million, but without expansion American League numbers would have once again declined.) Seeking to account for this declining popularity, Rosalind Cartwright, professor of psychology at the University of Illinois, perceived baseball's problems as a reflection of changing values in American society, observing, "Baseball is very much 'establishment'—'as American as baseball' has always been a popular cliché—and as youth becomes more anti-establishment, they become more anti-baseball." Lending support to the thesis of Professor Cartwright were the opinions of people such as young Chicago attorney Bob Nichols who described himself as a former baseball fan. Echoing sentiments which seemed to be growing in American society, Nichols criticized baseball, suggesting, "Watching baseball is like watching chess, it's too cerebral. Pro football has a lot of blood and guts action, but baseball grips me about as much as a flower show."[17]

Statistical evidence was not lacking to document these impressions. In early May, 1969, a Louis Harris poll of over twelve hundred Americans who follow sports found 31 percent named football as their number one sport, while baseball finished second with 28 percent, well ahead of basketball which was a distant third with 12 percent. The poll found that baseball enjoyed its greatest support among older and lower income fans. In essence, the Harris report indicated that baseball was "caught in the middle between a large group of fans who want things to stay as they were in grandfather's day and a new breed of sports followers who want more action."[18]

Thus, baseball made concessions to meet apparent declining fan interest with expansion and divisional play-offs, but many traditionalists in the sport saw no reason for tampering with an institution that had reflected America so well for a hundred years. This perspective was well voiced in the *Sporting News* by columnist Wells Twombly, who described baseball as a proud relic of the nineteenth century and capable of resisting "all efforts from radicals who would alter it in the slightest way." Certainly, Twombly continued, the sport was not for everyone, as it puzzled "new generations of females who find its intricacies pretty nearly unfathomable," and baseball held little interest for a new generation of college students "where rioting has replaced beer-drinking as an undergraduate pursuit."[19] The opinions of Twombly, notwithstanding, could the sport really afford to cut itself off from women and the younger generation?

However, many in baseball were less than comfortable with developing female consciousness and the youth culture of the late 1960s. For example, the New York State Human Rights Commission conducted hearings into the complaint of Mrs. Ben Gera that she was barred from the National Association of Baseball Leagues because of her gender. League administrator B. C. Deary testified that female umpires would be accepted if they could meet age, height, and weight standards— standards, which, of course, had been designed for men.[20] In addition, the editorials, columns, and letters from a traditional baseball publication such as the *Sporting News* reflected a preoccupation with issues of youthful protest and counterculture symbols such as long hair. Thus, in a January, 1969 Voice of the Fan letter, Jay D. Conner from Lopez, Washington quoted from recent polls indicating that three out of every four college youths "reject long hair, beards and satorical extremes of dress that go along with such freaks." The editors of the *Sporting News* agreed with reader Conner, arguing, "If you think the hippies and yippies represent young America, you're wrong. For every rabble-rouser on a college campus, there are hundreds of other students finding a wholesome outlet for their energies in sports." The editors could not seem to envision athletes with nontraditional views and styles, asserting that with established institutions all over the country under attack it was incumbent upon baseball to maintain its high standards. The *Sporting News* painted a dark portrait of America in 1969, "We have dissension over the War in Vietnam, racial discord, college rioting, profiteering, religious irreverence, flagrant pornography, and rampant crime."[21]

While the *Sporting News* made no secret of its underlying contempt for cultural change in America, a closer reading of the response by the paper and the baseball establishment to the protests of players Donn Clendenon, Ken Harrelson, and Dick Allen, not to mention the youthful 1969 world champion New York Mets, indicates that traditionalists in baseball were not above seeing that youth was served if it meant more games in the victory column and dollars in the sport's coffers.

After being drafted by the expansion Montreal Expos, former Pittsburgh Pirate first baseman Donn Clendenon, whose departure from the Pirates may have been hastened by his leadership of a team protest against playing games following the King assassination, was traded, along with Jesus Alou, to the Houston Astros for Rusty Staub. Unhappy with his assignment to Houston, on February 28, 1969, Clendenon announced his retirement from the game, leading Houston owner Judge Roy Hofheinz to demand that Commissioner Kuhn invalidate the deal. When Kuhn refused to act, an outraged Hofheinz released a statement blasting Kuhn as a

"Johnny-come-lately," who had done "more to destroy baseball in the last six weeks than all of its enemies in the past one hundred years." Refusing to be bullied, Kuhn demanded and received an apology from the Houston owner. Meanwhile, the trade was restructured with the Expos providing compensation for Clendenon, and Staub still going to Montreal. In his memoirs, Kuhn made it clear that the Staub trade was important for baseball's expansion plans. In Montreal, "the orange-haired Staub was seen as a player of heroic proportions who could win the hearts of French-Canadians and give the Expos a major star in their first season." As for Clendenon, he changed his mind about retirement, playing thirty-eight games for the Expos before being traded to the New York Mets where he enjoyed a successful season (twelve home runs with thirty-seven runs batted in), culminating in his selection as the outstanding player in the 1969 World Series. While one might have expected the *Sporting News* to chastise Clendenon for challenging management's traditional prerogatives under the reserve clause, the baseball publication was more concerned that Roy Hofheinz drop his threatened law suit against Kuhn, for "if baseball cannot govern itself, it may find itself saddled with legislative restrictions much more distasteful than a Commissioner's decision."[22] The Clendenon case indicated an individual could successfully confront the baseball establishment if the challenge did not seriously undermine baseball's expansion or attendance plans.

This perspective was even more obvious in the "retirement" of Boston Red Sox slugger Ken Harrelson. After a 1968 campaign in which the outfielder hit .275 with thirty-five home runs and a league-leading 109 runs batted in, a shocked Harrelson was dealt to the Cleveland Indians ten games into the 1969 season. Not wanting to give up business interests in Boston, the modish "Hawk" Harrelson, who wore a Beatles haircut, lavender suits, and appeared in public sockless, announced his retirement rather than make the move to Cleveland. In another era, the extravagant Harrelson might have been sent packing by traditional baseball barons; however, Cleveland Indian President Gabe Paul told Commissioner Kuhn that he was anxious to complete the deal as "Cleveland needed a colorful character like the Hawk." Accordingly, Kuhn intervened in the Harrelson affair, bringing the slugger and his agent Bob Woolf to meet with Gabe Paul at the Commissioner's New York office. After private negotiations under the auspices of Kuhn, Harrelson emerged to say that he had signed a two year contract, calling for $100,000 a season to play for the Indians. Demonstrating an increasing business-consciousness on the part of players, Harrelson announced Paul had convinced him of the fine business opportunities available in Cleveland and the market potential of the Midwest.

The "Hawk" then flew to Cleveland where he was met at the airport by a crowd of upward to one thousand young fans, including a rock band and several young women who presented him with flowers. An enthusiastic Harrelson pronounced everything "groovy."[23] However, the Hawk's career in Cleveland would prove to be something other than groovy. After a solid 1969 season with twenty-seven home runs and eighty-four runs batted in for Cleveland, Harrelson was injured during the 1970 campaign and retired after the 1971 season, contributing only six home runs and fifteen runs battled in for the last two years of his career.

Despite his embrace of counterculture fashion, Harrelson was a modern young ballplayer who viewed the sport as both a game and a business, and, while there was some grumbling, the baseball establishment could make room for him if he could bolster attendance and baseball's appeal with the youth market. Nor could the powers that be in baseball afford to write off the talents of Richard "Dick" Allen.

On June 24, 1969, Manager Bob Skinner of the Philadelphia Phiilies suspended the power-hitting first baseman for being late to a double header with the Mets. An enraged Allen maintained that Skinner had not even waited to hear Allen's side of the story, and the proud African-American athlete vowed to never play again for Skinner, pointing out that the "suspension was costing me $450 a day — and with three young kids, the loss of money hurt. But I had made up my mind that no fine — no matter how stiff— would ever dictate my behavior again." However, after a month on the suspended list, Allen was urged by his mother to open up negotiations with the Phillies owner Bob Carpenter. Following a meeting with Carpenter at a suburban Philadelphia restaurant, Allen was reinstated with the understanding that he was to be traded after the 1969 season. On his first at bat after a twenty-six day suspension, Allen doubled to left center, driving in a run against Houston. Standing at second base, the Phillies slugger recalled, "They could do a lot to this ol' country boy. They could take my money, take my freedom, take my self-esteem, but they couldn't take my stroke."

However, the 1969 season did not end on an optimistic note for Allen and the Phillies. On August 7, Manager Skinner resigned when Allen, with the support of Bob Carpenter, decided not to accompany the team to an exhibition game with the Phillies farm team in Reading, Pennsylvania. While Allen labeled Skinner an old-school baseball man and a quitter who did not understand the racial taunts which Allen had suffered during both his minor and major league careers, the *Sporting News* in an editorial supported Skinner, suggesting that Allen needed some professional guidance and counseling. Carpenter, who personally seemed to like Allen, was caught between the forces of the old and new in baseball, but he certainly realized that Allen was a valuable property. Keeping his word to the slugger, on October 8, 1969, Carpenter traded Allen, Cookie Rojas, and Jerry Johnson to the St. Louis Cardinals for Tim McCarver, Joe Hoerner, Bryon Browne, and Curt Flood in a transaction which would have severe ramifications for the established structure of major league baseball.[24]

However, before the implications of Curt Flood's challenge to this trade began to rock the baseball establishment at the end of the year, baseball fans were treated to an exciting division race in the National League East between the Chicago Cubs and New York Mets, two teams usually noted for their losing ways. The Amazing Mets of 1969 were not expected to contend, as in 1968, under the traditional National League alignment before divisional play, the Mets had finished in ninth place, twenty-four games behind the pennant-winning St. Louis Cardinals. However, under new manager Gil Hodges, and behind the pitching of Tom Seaver, Jerry Koosman, Gary Gentry, and a young Nolan Ryan, accompanied by some timely hitting from Cleon Jones, Donn Clendenon, and Art Shamsky, the Mets proved to be a respectable team. Nevertheless, going into the month of September, they still trailed the Cubs by four games. But a Cub collapse and Mets surge resulted in the New York team winning an even one hundred games, while finishing eight games ahead of the Cubs

The dream continued for the Mets who swept the Atlanta Braves in three games to win the first National League Championship Series and achieve the first pennant in Mets history. Nevertheless, it appeared it would at last be the stroke of midnight for the Cinderella season of the Mets when they faced the powerful Baltimore Orioles in the 1969 World Series. Featuring three twenty game-winning pitchers (Mike Cuellar, Dave McNally, and Jim Palmer), the Orioles won the American League Eastern Division with 109 victories, finishing nineteen games ahead of second place Detroit. The Orioles easily deposed of the Western Division Champion Minnesota Twins in three games and appeared destined to dominate the Mets. Yet, in one of the greatest World Series upsets in history, the Miracle Mets defeated the Orioles in five games, setting off massive demonstrations of joy throughout New York. New York City's adulation for the Mets culminated on October 20 with a ticker tape parade up lower Broadway which drew more people that a parade earlier in the summer for Apollo XI astronauts Armstrong and Aldrin.

Interest in the Mets contributed to an increase in National League attendance of over three and one-half million fans from 1968 to 1969, providing a much needed shot in the arm for baseball's sagging self-esteem. Many traditionalists, including the *Sporting News*, had to eat their words regarding the proper servile attitude for youth. The paper editorialized that young teams such as the Mets were perhaps "catching the spirit of a youth rebellion sweeping the world. If so, the sports version seems highly preferable to the forms of revolt available elsewhere, including college campuses. The Mets not only epitomized the revolution occurring on the field, they are pacesetters in wardrobe and hair styles as well. No wonder they are the darlings of the mod set." Thus, long hair and youthful questioning of authority, which looked so threatening on college campuses, could be contained within the baseball consensus, especially if the rebellious players excited the popular imagination and filled the empty seats in the baseball parks.[25]

However, the challenge of Curt Flood could not be so easily assimilated by the baseball establishment. A sensitive proud man, Flood enjoyed portrait painting, and at age thirty-one had established himself as one of the best center fielders in baseball. He had no desire to leave the Cardinal organization with whom he had been associated since 1958, having made his home in St. Louis. However, in October, 1969, an early morning phone call from a reporter, informing Flood that he had been traded to Philadelphia, shattered the young outfielder's life. Determined not to accept quietly his fate at the hands of baseball management, Flood was advised by legal counsel that he might question baseball's reserve clause as a violation of antitrust law. Next, Flood asked Marvin Miller for the support of the Players Association as such a legal contest would be expensive. Miller had Flood appear before the Players Association Executive Board Meeting at San Juan, Puerto Rico in late December, 1969. After a grueling interrogation by the players, in which Flood admitted that while he was influenced by changes in African-American consciousness, he was doing the suit as a major league baseball player who found the reserve clause intolerable, the Executive Board voted to support the law suit. Appearing before the same board to discuss baseball's Basic Agreement, Kuhn was unaware of the decision to back Flood and felt betrayed that the issue was not brought forward during his visit to San Juan.

With player solidarity established, on Christmas Eve, Flood dispatched a letter to Commissioner Kuhn, informing him of Flood's desire to be declared a free agent as the reserve clause was invalid. In reply, Kuhn upheld the sanctity of the reserve system, explaining to Flood, "You have entered into a current playing contract with the St. Louis Club, which has the same management provisions as those in your annual major league contract since 1956. Your present contract has been assigned in accordance with its provisions by the St. Louis Club to the Philadelphia Club."[26]

Dissatisfied with this legalistic approach which failed to reflect Flood's own sense of personal freedom, changing power relationships between management and players within the sport of baseball, and a climate of opinion in American society in favor of questioning the status quo, Flood filed suit against Kuhn and the baseball establishment, seeking to have the reserve clause declared in violation of antitrust law. While Flood's case shortened his playing career and was eventually turned down by the Supreme Court, this landmark case helped usher in a new era of arbitration and free agency which would forever alter the structure of player-management relations within the sport.

Thus, 1969 was a watershed year for both baseball and the United States. An apparently self-confident Richard Nixon was growing increasingly uncomfortable with dissent in American society and moving toward the establishment of a White House security network which, in the final analysis, would lead to his own political demise. Yet, while the Watergate crisis altered the way politics would be played in America, the basic Constitutional framework of the American system proved sound. And so it was for baseball. Beset with allegations of racial and gender discrimination and confronted with challenges to the traditional prerogatives of baseball ownership, along with the growing popularity of professional football, the baseball establishment sought to enlarge the sport's consensus by expansionism, division play, and making room for cultural rebels such as Ken Harrelson and the "modish" New York Mets. However, Curt Flood's challenge to the reserve clause and the inevitable rise of free agency fundamentally altered power relations within the game. And Bowie Kuhn, who was awarded by the owners with a full seven year term as Commissioner in late August, 1969, was unable, just as was his friend Richard Nixon, to hold back the forces of change in baseball and American society.

Despite the tremendous changes in the structure of major league baseball in the late 1960s and early 1970s, the game continues to prosper and grow, reflecting both the incredible appeal of this simple but most complex game, as well as the strength of the dominant culture and baseball to absorb change while maintaining continuity. Perhaps we did not get off the track in the 1960s with questioning of the traditional wisdom and establishment, but rather we may have gotten back on the track of emphasizing individual rights whether in the realm of politics, economics, or baseball.

Endnotes

This essay was originally published in *Nine: A Journal of Baseball History and Social Policy Perspectives*, 4:2 (1996), 263-281.

1. For Nixon's reaction to the Apollo landing see Stephen Ambrose, *Nixon: The Triumph of a Politician. 1962-1972*, (New York: Simon and Schuster, 1989), 283–285.

2. Richard Skolnik, *Baseball and the Pursuit of Innocence: A Fresh Look at the Old Ball Game* (College Station, Texas: Texas A & M University Press, 1994), 204.

3. For accounts of the 1969 White House Baseball Centennial reception see Bowie Kuhn, *Hardball: The Education of a Baseball Commissioner* (New York: Times Books, 1987), 58–59; *New York Times*, July 23, 1969; and *Sporting News*, August 9, 1969.

4. In 1946, Feller said of Robinson, "If he were a white man, I doubt if they would even consider him big league material." See Geoffrey C. Ward & Ken Burns, *Baseball: An Illustrated History* (New York: Alfred A. Knopf, 1994), 289.

5. For the Feller and Robinson confrontation see *Sporting News*, August 9, 1969. For additional background information, as well as elaboration on the perceptions of Feller and Robinson regarding race, see Bob Feller with Bill Gilbert, *Now Pitching: Bob Feller* (New York: Harper Perennial, 1991); Jules Tygiel, *Baseball's Great Experiment: Jackie Robinson and His Legacy* (New York: Oxford University Press, 1983); and Jackie Robinson, *I Never Had It Made: An Autobiography* (New York: Fawcett Crest, 1972).

6. For baseball in 1968 see Ron Briley, "It Was 20 Years Ago Today: Baseball Responds to the Unrest of 1968," in Peter Levine, ed., *Baseball History* (Westport, Connecticut: Meckler, 1989), 81–94.

7. Jackie Robinson, "Violent Society: The American Way," *Pittsburgh-Courier*, June 22, 1969.

8. Marvin Miller, *A Whole Different Ball Game: The Inside Story of Baseball's New Deal* (New York: Simon and Schuster, 1991), 97.

9. On the firing of Eckert see *Sporting News*, December 21 and 28, 1968; Mickey Herskowitz, " A Farewell to General Eckert," *Baseball Digest*, 27 (April, 1969), 12–15; and William Leggett, "Court Martial for a General," *Sports Illustrated*, 29 (December, 1968), 24–25.

10. *Sporting News*, January 4 and February 15, 1969; and *New York Times*, February 6, 1969. For background information on Bowie Kuhn see Kuhn, *Hardball: The Education of a Baseball Commissioner*; and John J. Smith, "Why the Owners Chose Bowie Kuhn," *Baseball Digest*, 27 (April, 1969), 5–12.

11. For the pension issue see Andrew Zimbalist, *Baseball and Billions: A Probing Look Inside the Big Business of Our National Pastime* (New York: Basic Books, 1992), 17–24; Bob Broeg, "$12,000 Pensions Near, Pre-'46 Stars Get Nothing," *Baseball Digest*, 25 (November, 1966), 79–81; Richard Dozer, "After the Cheers Have Faded," *Baseball Digest*, 25 (November, 1966), 35–39; *Sporting News*, February 1, 1969; and Miller, *A Whole Different Ball Game*, 99–106.

12. *Sporting News*, January 25, 1969.

13. *Ibid.*, February 8 and 15, 1969.

14. For the pension settlement see *Sporting News*, March 8, 1969; *New York Times*, February 26, 1969; Miller, *A Whole Different Ball Game*, 91, 105–106; Kuhn, *Hardball: The Education of a Baseball Commissioner*, 74–76; and Benjamin G. Rader, *Baseball: A History of America's Game* (Urbana: University of Illinois Press, 1994), 189–192.

15. *Sporting News*, March 8 and 15, and April 5 and 12, 1969.

16. For a text of the Busch remarks see Curt Flood with Richard Carter, *The Way It Is* (New York: Trident Press, 1971), 228–236. For views of Gary Peters see *Sporting News*, April 5, 1994; Joe Falls, "Gary Peters: Boomerangs and Baseballs," *Sport*, 37 (January, 1964), 40–42; and Jerome Holtzman, "Gary Peters, Seven Years on the Way," *Baseball Digest*, 27 (December, 1963), 67–71.

17. Red Barber, "Can Baseball Be Saved?, "*Readers' Digest*, 94 (April, 1969), 155–158; Todd Fandell, "A Crucial Year — Baseball and Its Critics," *Wall Street Journal*, April 19, 1969; and *Sporting News*, November 29, 1969.

18. *Sporting News*, May 3, 1969.

19. *Ibid.*, May 31, 1969.

20. *New York Times*, October 25, 1969.

21. *Sporting News*, January 4 and 25, and July 25, 1969.

22. For the Donn Clendenon story see *Pittsburgh Press*, April 5–8, 1968; Kuhn, *Hardball: The Education of a Baseball Commissioner*, 44–49; *New York Times*, October 22, 1969; and *Sporting News*, April 12, 1969. For the Staub story in Montreal see John Devaney, "Rusty Staub and Montreal: Une Affaire D'Amour," *Sport*, 49 (May, 1970), 38–39; and Mark Mulvoy, "In Montreal, They Love Le Grand Orange," *Sports Illustrated*, 33 (July 6, 1970), 38–39.

23. For information on Harrelson see *Sporting News*, May 10, 1969; Kuhn, *Hardball: The Education of a Baseball Commissioner*, 49–50; John Devaney, "The Hawk Flies High," *Sport*, 46 (October, 1968), 20–23; Phil Elderkin, "New Look Harrelson Eyes 100 RBI'S," *Baseball Digest*, 37 (September, 1968), 51–53; Ken Harrelson with Al Hirshberg, *Hawk* (New York: Viking Press, 1969); and Al Hirshberg, "Why the Hawk Really Quit," *Sport*, 52 (September, 1971), 76–77.

24. On Dick Allen see *Sporting News*, August 2 and 23, and September 6 and 14, 1969; Dick Allen with Tim Whitaker, *Crash: The Life and Times of Dick Allen* (New York: Ticknor & Fields, 1989), 53–81; L. J. Banks, "Richie Allen: I'm My Own Man," *Ebony*, 25 (July, 1970), 80–90; Bill Gutman, *New Breed Heroes in Pro Baseball* (New York: Julian Messner, 1974), 101–115; and Dave Wolf, "Let's Everybody Boo Richie Allen," *Life*, 67 (August 22, 1969), 50–52.

25. On the New York Mets and 1969 baseball season see Rick Talley, *The Cubs of '69: Recollections of the Team That Should Have Been* (Chicago: Contemporary Books, 1989); "Just Call Them Plain Folks: New York Mets," *Sports Illustrated*, 31 (October 20, 1969), 40–44; Leonard Koppett, *The New York Mets: The Whole Story* (New York: MacMillan, 1970); William Leggett, "Maybe It's Time to Break Up the Mets: Pursuit of the Pennant," *Sports Illustrated*, 31 (September 22, 1969), 28–29; Paul O'Neil, "Who Woulda Thunk It?: The Mets Lunge for the Pennant," *Life*, 67 (September 26, 1969), 34–41; Tom Seaver, "Why the Mets are the New Team," *Sport*, 48 (December, 1969), 22–25; Leonard Shecter, "Bring Back the Real Mets: New York Mets in the Pennant Race," *New York Times Magazine* (September 7, 1969), 66–67; Paul D. Zimmerman and Dick Schoop, *The Year the Mets Lost Last Place* (Cleveland: World Publishing Company, 1969); *New York Times*, October 21, 1969; and *Sporting News*, September 20, 1969.

26. For differing perspectives on the origins of the Flood case see Kuhn, *Hardball: The Education of a Baseball Commissioner*, 80–85; Miller, *A Whole Different Ball Game*, 170–193; and Flood, *The Way It Is*, 187–206.

14

The Oakland A's of 1972–1975 and the Counterculture in Baseball: Undermining the Hegemony of the Baseball Establishment

The late 1960s and early 1970s were a time of upheaval and confusion in American society and the sport of baseball. Traditional values were under assault as "pop" philosophers such as Harvard's Charles Reich proclaimed *The Greening of America* and the emergence of a counterculture based upon a new "consciousness." The post World War II consensus values of sustained economic growth, moderation, and anticommunism were openly challenged in the streets, universities, and homes of America.[1] The suburban tranquility portrayed in such popular television shows of the late 1950s and early 1960s as *Father Knows Best* and *Leave It to Beaver* was shattered by racial tensions, a war in Southeast Asia, protest in the streets, and dramatic changes in lifestyle and appearance. The children of the Andersons and Cleavers were returning home from college braless, shoeless, and covered with unkempt hair.

But almost as quickly as this countercultural phenomenon appeared, it receded into the traditional mainstream, a victim of its own excesses and a dominant culture capable of co-opting symbolic, but nevertheless more superficial, aspects of the counterculture. The hegemony of the prevailing culture made countercultural language, fashion, and music "hip" or acceptable, even for the business executive.[2] In other words, co-option by business and government encouraged the process whereby hippies became yuppies. However, this return to apparent routine daily life does not negate the fact that the upheavals of the 1960s did produce change in society, if not an entirely new consciousness. Yuppies may have replaced hippies, but the America of the 1990s is not the America of the 1950s, as questions regarding freedom of expression, the environment, the status of women, and the role of ethnicity within a diverse culture will not retreat into the background and have assumed a place within the hegemony of the main-stream culture.

But these broad strokes are difficult to paint with the brush of a sub-ject as diverse as the counterculture. An examination of an American insti-tution in microcosm may shed more light on this complex phenomenon. In recent years, scholars have found the institution of baseball to provide insights into the American response to industrialization, progressivism, the depression era, World War II, and racial relations.[3] A study of the Oak-land A's from 1972 to 1975 offers an opportunity to examine the cultural impact of changing values and priorities upon a traditional institution. With their bright kelly-green uniforms, mustaches, and long hair, the youthful Oakland A's seemed to embody the values of the counterculture. However, these modern fashions had been encouraged by A's owner Charles Finley, a businessman whose background from the steel mills in Birmingham, Alabama and Peoria, Illinois to a multi-million dollar Chicago insurance executive personified the Horatio Alger saga of from rags to riches.[4] Finley, seeking to boost sagging ticket sales, paid Oakland players $300 each to adorn the facial hair[5] The A's owner sought to co-opt the fashion of the counterculture, but he did not count on having to deal with the questioning of authority inherent in the movement. Albeit, the Oak-land players were not examples of a new consciousness seeking to over-throw established values, they represented a vanguard of baseball players who were willing to protest in order to get their fair share of the baseball economic pie. And the hegemony of the baseball establishment was altered by the A's who mirrored the controversy and unrest sweeping America as they feuded with their owner, managers, and teammates; raising issues of free speech, race, and economic power.

In addition, they were successful on the playing field, winning the American League Western Division in 1971, followed by world champi-onships in 1972, 1973, and 1974, with a final division title in 1975, before Finley disassembled the player components which had contributed to a dynasty.[6] Following the break up of the A's, baseball produced more tra-ditionally-groomed champions in the Big Red Machine of Cincinnati and the pinstripes of the New York Yankees. Yet, Finley's A's, just as the coun-terculture, left an important legacy. Players like Jim "Catfish" Hunter, Reg-gie Jackson, and Rollie Fingers continued to excel after leaving Oakland,

and contract disputes, such as the one between Hunter and Finley, did much to revolutionize the status of players as free agents. Although the impact of the counterculture seemed to reach its Thermidor with the trading and selling of key A's players, the sport was never the same following the tumultuous reign of Finley and the A's as world champions.

Following a Western Division championship in 1971, the youthful Oakland A's seemed poised to enjoy their run as one of baseball's dominant teams. But, just as American society and values were undergoing considerable scrutiny by the counterculture, baseball and the A's found the dawning of 1972 to be a troubling time. The sport could not escape the vicissitudes of America in the 1970s. Russell Means of the American Indian Movement was questioning the Chief Wahoo symbol of the Cleveland Indians. The sport was awaiting the decision of the Supreme Court on Curt Flood's challenge to the reserve clause which the black outfielder claimed unfairly bound players to the services of one team and constituted a form of twentieth-century involuntary servitude. Former pitcher Jim Bouton's muckraking *Ball Four* rocked baseball with allegations of racism and drug use. And rumors of a strike were swirling as the Players Association and their executive director Marvin Miller were unable to reach a settlement with the owners regarding an extension of the sport's pension plan.[7]

Of course, labor problems and negotiations were nothing new in the history of player-owner relations. Interpreted by management as providing stability through binding players to the exclusive service of the club holding their contract, while perceived by players as artificially holding down salaries, the reserve clause was tested before the Supreme Court in the 1922 Federal Baseball decision. Justice Oliver Wendell Holmes rejected assertions that the reserve clause was a violation of antitrust law, maintaining that the sport was not a business subject to the interstate commerce clause of the Constitution. Fearing that the reserve system would not survive another legal test, in the late 1940s owners settled out of court the suit brought by former Giants outfielder Danny Gardella, who had jumped to the Mexican League. Nevertheless, the reasoning of Justice Holmes was reaffirmed in the 1953 Toolson case which continued the recognition of baseball's exemption from the antitrust laws. The desire to follow precedent led the Supreme Court to again decide against the players in the Flood case, but the protests and free speech atmosphere of the 1960s and 1970s appeared to offer a context in which players refused to take no for an answer and were more willing to openly confront the authority of management. Under the leadership of Marvin Miller, who insisted the reserve clause allowed a club to renew an unsigned player for only one year after which a player could become a free agent (an interpretation upheld in 1975 by arbitrator Peter Seitz in the Andy Messersmith case), the players did get an extended pension plan when the opening of the 1972 season was delayed by a walk out on April 1, 1972.

In the midst of this labor turmoil, Finley was engaged in very public negotiations with his star pitcher Vida Blue, who had won 24 games in 1971, while gaining the Most Valuable Player and Cy Young awards in his first full major league season.[8] The twenty-four year old Blue was also a crowd favorite and had pitched to sold-out stadiums throughout the American League. He expected a considerable increase over his 1971 salary of $14,750. Represented by attorney Bob Gerst, Blue reportedly opened the negotiations by asking for $115,000, while Finley countered with an offer of $50,000. The owner labeled Blue's demands as "ridiculous," proclaiming, "My offices are on the 27th floor. He has as much chance of getting $115,000 as I do of jumping out of my office window." Finley was also angered that Blue had chosen an agent to represent him in the talks. The tradition of the owner and his attorney sitting down with the player and arriving at a fair salary would soon be a thing of the past. The idea that the owner was a father figure seeking only what was best for the players would also be a casualty of the confrontational 1970s.

As spring training and the exhibition season opened, Blue and Gerst allegedly lowered their demands to $70,000, while Finley adamantly stuck to his guns at $50,000. Seeking to break the stalemate, on March 16, Blue announced his retirement from baseball, stating that he was going to become a vice-president in public relations for the Dura Steel Products Company. Finley's critics pointed out that nearly one-twelfth of all American League tickets sold in 1971 were for games in which Blue pitched. One good crowd would make up the $20,000 difference between Finley and Blue. But other owners were reportedly concerned about what impact a settlement favorable to Blue would have on the salary structure of major league baseball. Reports out of the A's training camp in Mesa, Arizona maintained that teammates such as Reggie Jackson and Joe Rudi wanted Blue to settle for Finley's figure, asserting that the pitcher could easily make another $50,000 in endorsements. Recognizing that it would be difficult to win the Western Division again without Blue, catchers Gene Tenace and Curt Blefary were willing to take Finley's suggestion that they try some personal diplomacy and bring Blue back into camp. But Blue refused to sign for Finley's figure despite the urging of his catchers and teammates.[9]

It would take more skilled negotiators than Tenace and Blefary to break the Blue-Finley deadlock. Even President Richard Nixon got into the act, although he did not offer the services of Henry Kissinger who was having enough difficulty getting Vietnamese factions to the table. Nixon called upon Finley to compromise, observing, "Vida has so much talent. Maybe Finley ought to pay. It would be a great tragedy if a young player with all that talent stayed out too long." Taking his cue from Nixon, Baseball Commissioner Bowie Kuhn interceded in the talks, developing a compromise package for $63,000, which was essentially a victory for Finley, although it contained a face saving $13,000 for Blue.

While Kuhn's intervention was welcomed by many baseball fans, who would once again have the opportunity to watch Blue perform, it did little to relieve the personal animosity between Blue and Finley. The owner resented Kuhn's meddling. Sounding like a nineteenth-century advocate of laissez-faire economics, Finley complained, "The Commissioner arbitrarily involved himself and forced himself into contract negotiations with Blue, and I don't believe he had the authority to do so. I don't like it one damn bit." Blue also emerged from the confrontation as a bitter individual. He argued that much of the fun had been removed from baseball for him. The sport was a business and not a game, with the owners attempting to acquire players as cheaply as possible. Blue angrily concluded, "Charles Finley has soured my stomach for baseball. He treated me like a damn colored boy."[10]

Although Blue was certainly influenced by the increasing racial awareness of African-Americans stemming from the civil rights movement and black power (Oakland was the home of the Black Panther Party), it is interesting to note that in an interview for *Ebony*, he toned down his anger, placing his holdout in traditional labor vs. management terms. Rather than perceiving the issue in racial terms, Blue criticized Finley for being an unethical businessman who manipulated players and cultural symbols. Defending his quest for a larger piece of the baseball pie, Blue maintained, "Owners seem to be a different breed of people from players. First of all, owners are rich — real rich — or else they couldn't be owners. Major league baseball and other major sports are big business, dealing in millions of dollars every year. Yet, in a way, they are different from other big businesses. Lots of time, the owners use a team like a toy; they just seem to be playing with it. And they use the players like pieces of their toy set, dressing them up in outlandish uniforms, getting them to raise mustaches, and giving them special bonuses...."[11]

Set against the background of the pension strike and the Flood case, the Blue holdout seemed to mirror the discontent in baseball. The *Sporting News*, serving as a spokesman for the baseball establishment, chastised the modern players, editorializing, "They're a bunch of spoiled babies.

Many of them are overpaid, too many have been pampered and most of them have been misled." In other words, ballplayers were behaving like the spoiled children who were disrupting American universities and challenging the traditional authority of their elders. But perhaps the real balance of power in baseball was more apparent in the little known story of Angels catcher Joe Azcue who sat out the 1971 season demanding a pay increase from $26,500 to $35,000. After a year of construction work in Kansas City, he returned to the Los Angeles camp, accepting a $5,000 cut in pay.[12]

Meanwhile, on the field the A's continued to win, despite drawing headlines for third baseman Sal Bando growing his hair over his ears and pitcher Chuck Dobson's admission that he used pep pills or "greenies" to get up for games.[13] However, it should be noted that players such as Dobson were not using drugs to enhance consciousness, but in an effort to bolster performance on the playing field.

When Blue faltered in 1972, his place as a left-handed starter was compensated for by the acquisition of Ken Holtzman from the Cubs for former bonus baby Rick Monday. Following the trade, Holtzman criticized Cubs management, while Cubs coach Peanuts Lowry defended Chicago owner Phil Wrigley, asserting that Wrigley was an owner who looked out for his players. The problem with Holtzman, according to Lowry, was that the pitcher was too much an individualist, who if things did not go his way would resort to a "tantrum like some little school kid."[14] Evidently, the Oakland environment was more conducive to Holtzman's sense of individualism as he recorded nineteen victories for the A's. The individualism attributed to Holtzman seemed to characterize the A's. *Sports Illustrated* reporter Ron Fimrite described traveling with the A's as like being on tour with the musical *Hair*. In July, catcher Dave Duncan informed Fimrite that Oakland was an ideal playing situation. Duncan proclaimed, "There is no bed check, no rules on clothes or hair."[15] In other words, the more superficial aspects of freedom were tolerated, but as Blue had learned, and Duncan was to ascertain by the end of the season, ownership placed limitations on dissent when power and economic relationships were threatened.

In 1972, the A's won ninety-three games, finishing six games ahead of the Chicago White Sox in the Western Division, and manager Dick Williams was rehired by Finley for two more seasons. This would make Williams the first manager to last two seasons with the temperamental Finley, who served as his own general manager and publicly second-guessed his managers and players. On being rehired, the diplomatic Williams insisted, "We don't agree on everything, but no two men can all the time.

He lets me run the club the way I want. There are moves he questions me on, and I'd better have the answers."[16] Although not always happy in the situation, Williams did understand the source of power in his relationship with Finley.

The A's met Billy Martin's Detroit Tigers in an exciting American League championship series, won by the A's three games to two and marred by a bat throwing incident in which A's shortstop Bert Campaneris attempted to spear Tiger pitcher Lerrin LaGrow. Ironically, Blue clinched the victory over Detroit with three innings of shut-out relief. Finley rushed to the clubhouse to shake Blue's hand, but the pitcher remained resentful of both Finley and his manager Williams. A disillusioned Blue complained, "They have no respect for me. Now when I take the field, I don't pitch for Williams and I don't pitch for the Oakland A's. I pitch for Vida Blue. I pitch because it's my job, that's all."[17] The cynical Blue was not fooled by countercultural trappings, he realized baseball was a business and no longer a game for him.

The 1972 World Series showcased the controversial and longhaired A's, champions of the counterculture crowd, against Sparky Anderson's well disciplined and groomed Big Red Machine from Cincinnati. In a well pitched series, the A's triumphed in seven games, with light hitting catcher Gene Tenace emerging as the unlikely hero. The *Sporting News* maintained that many fans were surprised that "the Athletics, garbed in Kelly Green, Fort Knox Gold, and Wedding Gown White, and exponents of mustaches and long hair, could play baseball in a manner acceptable to the most demanding devotees."[18]

Indeed, many fans and critics did perceive the 1972 series as symbolic of the cultural clashes taking place in American society. In his history of the Cincinnati Reds, Robert Harris Walker asserts that the Reds viewed themselves as projecting a conservative working class image, reflective of the dominant values in their host city. On the other hand, the A's, with their long hair, provoked associations with the drug culture in the Haight Ashbury district of neighboring San Francisco. Journalist J. Anthony Lukas also commented on the tendency of fans to see the series in terms of cultural polarities, observing, "The Reds, with their neat red-and-white uniforms, their short hair, and clean shaves, are sound, solid, and stable, full of the substantial virtues that the flacks in the commissioner's office love to associate with our national pastime, while the A's, in their flowing hair and bristling mustaches are bizarre and flamboyant." But Lukas wondered if the A's "hip" image was only hair deep.[19]

And the activities of the team off the field attracted headlines, while demonstrating the limitations on the apparent freedom displayed by the

A's. Blue missed the team victory celebration in Oakland, and Finley responded with a fine. Also, an altercation between Williams and first baseman Mike Epstein on the return flight from Cincinnati apparently led to Epstein's trade. Williams said the shouting match was simply the result of too many drinks, but two months later the power-hitting first baseman (27 home runs in 1972) was shipped to the Texas Rangers for reliever Horacio Pina. Williams and Finley explained that the trade was due to the fact that Tenace's shoulder problem necessitated his shift to first base, making Epstein expendable. A disgruntled Epstein, who earlier in the season proclaimed he was having the best year of his life, blamed his fate on his argument with Williams, insisting, "I thought I would be at least going to a contending ball club. It didn't turn out that way. But sometimes there just isn't any justice in life."[20] The A's of 1972 certainly demonstrated that the bad boys of baseball could play the sport, but not everyone lived happily ever after. Success did not require the 1950s values of consensus, but management, whether Finley or the more popular Williams, placed limits on dissent.

Much of the credit for the A's winning ways went to the controversial owner Finley, who enjoyed the attention and playing the role of patriarch. He spent numerous hours and $80,000 procuring World Series rings for the A's, but he made it clear who was the boss. He would bestow lavish gifts, but the players would have to remember their place. The long hair of the counterculture was tolerated, and mustaches encouraged, but not the dissent. In other words, the superficial aspects of the counterculture were acceptable, but not the substance. Accordingly, Finley informed the press that Vida Blue would sign early in 1973. The owner stated, "I think Vida Blue has grown up a lot in a year." He also made it clear that Blue would negotiate from a base of $50,000. The $13,000 added by Kuhn was simply a bonus. Finley clearly hated to lose.

In a similar vein, Finley traded catcher Dave Duncan and outfielder George Hendrick to Cleveland for catcher Ray Fosse. The A's owner said the transaction was simply to obtain a better catcher, but Duncan, who was engaged in a bitter contract dispute with Finley, disagreed. Duncan proclaimed, "I am a human being with an identity of my own, and I think this is something he tries to strip away from everyone around him. I've had a bad relationship with Charlie Finley for the past three years. I think this trade is going to work out well for me." Evidently, Duncan forgot that he had once praised A's management for lax grooming rules; however, when he challenged Finley on bottom line matters of money the catcher found ownership much less accommodating. Duncan's criticism was unwelcome, as Finley wanted his players to appreciate the kind of freedom they were given. For example, posted on the A's clubhouse bulletin board was a newspaper photo showing San Francisco Giants players shaving off sideburns and beards. Below the photograph was an attached note, saying, "How would you like to be a Giant and be told how to dress?" The note was signed Charles O. Finley.[21]

However, many players refused to accept the type of second class citizenship apparently envisioned by owners like Finley, and the threat of a strike clouded the opening of the 1973 season. But a strike was averted as players and management negotiated a three year extension of the basic playing agreement. The degree of respect on both sides necessary to hammer out an agreement was expressed by A's player representative Reggie Jackson who insisted, "I don't want to sit out. The owners don't want to lock out. They want to play and make money. That is only human. They are businessmen and we're businessmen."[22] Jackson recognized that baseball was, indeed, a business, not simply a boy's game, and his call for players to be treated as economic partners presented a far greater challenge to the hegemony of the baseball establishment than long hair.

But Jackson's "come let us reason together" rhetoric would dissipate in the heat of a pennant race and dealing with A's management. The temperamental outfielder maintained that Williams and his coaches were overly critical of the players. A disgruntled Jackson complained, "It's tough to play here with a smile on your face. The authorities here don't speak to you unless you walk pass them in an alley." Owner Finley responded to Jackson by renewing the contract of each coach for a year, while Williams suggested that Jackson be quiet and concentrate on his play in right field. Williams insisted, "Everything we do is constructive criticism. If you can't stand the heat, get out of the kitchen."[23] The heat also remained uncomfortable for Vida Blue. After becoming the third A's pitcher to win twenty games in the 1973 season, following Jim Hunter and Ken Holtzman, Blue told reporters, "I am looking forward to the playoff because it is a money series. I'm not going to lie to the Little Leaguers by saying anything else than it's the money. It's a business, my job."[24]

While this dissent and cynicism might be viewed as reflective of youthful player identification with the forces of unrest in American society, sportswriter Leonard Koppett believed that in light of the Watergate scandal the problem for American athletes, such as the A's, was that they identified too much with the traditional values of winning at any cost. The articulate Koppett castigated the American sports establishment, asserting, "If the Watergate revelations — regardless of who did what when — truly represent the presence of a flaw in the conscience of many of our finest people, the sports establishment should not shirk its responsibility for its role in helping create the climate of muddy morals. Some heavy soul-searching is in order."[25] Koppett was astute enough to observe that while taking advantage of an atmosphere in which freedom of expression was tolerated, ballplayers were not hippies of the counterculture. Their goal was to gain greater compensation and control over careers. While championing traditional values of economic success and security, players, such as the tumultuous A's, were threats to the power and prerogatives of the baseball establishment.

Whether values were influenced by the counterculture or a perversion of the American dream of success, the A's continued to win and fight as America drifted into a Constitutional crisis over Watergate and the Vietnam War began to wind down. After finishing six games ahead of second place Kansas City in the West, the A's edged Baltimore three games to two to gain the American League pennant. But the championship series was marred by more fighting among the A's. Following a narrow defeat in game four, pitchers Rollie Fingers and John "Blue Moon" Odom came to blows because Odom believed Fingers was criticizing Blue. However, after clinching the pennant, the two shook hands, and team spokesman Reggie Jackson said the outburst was just typical of the A's style, observing, "We've got controversial management, controversial players, and everything else. It was a legitimate argument."[26]

As symbols of a more confrontational period in American history and baseball the A's certainly lived up to their reputation in the 1973 World Series. Although the A's won the series four games to three over the New York Mets, the attention of the sports world was focused on the plight of journeyman infielder Mike Andrews who made two costly errors for the A's during the twelfth inning of game two. Following the A's 10-7 defeat, Andrews was called to the trainer's room where he met with Williams, Finley, and the team orthopedic physician Harry Walker. After a ten minute physical examination, Finley asked Andrews to sign a doctor's statement that his shoulder would not allow him to play anymore. Such a move would allow Finley to add reserve infielder Manny Trillo to the World Series roster. After forty minutes of discussion, Andrews relented and signed the statement, leaving the team and returning to his home in Peabody, Massachusetts.

Following the apparent "firing" of Andrews, the baseball world and the Oakland A's were in turmoil. Finley appeared as an authority establishment figure who coerced a confession out of a young man who had simply made a mistake. After the incident, Williams informed his players that he would not be returning as manager of the A's for the 1974 season. He had been considering the move for some time due to Finley's interference, but the owner's handling of the Andrews case was the "last straw." The players were in a mutinous mood, threatening a strike and wearing pieces of tape with Andrews's number seventeen plastered to their uniforms. Reggie Jackson publicly condemned Finley, asserting, "This thing is a real embarrassment and a disappointment. A team is a team. Finley doesn't seem to understand that. I've never heard of firing a player in the middle of the Series. That's what the man did. I don't care what he says." The players had little toleration for the paternalism of Finley.

With the players, press, and public in an uproar, Commissioner Bowie Kuhn ordered Finley to reinstate Andrews. After conferring with teammate Jim Hunter, Andrews rejoined the team for game four of the Series in New York, telling the press, "I'm sorry I signed it. For the first time in my life I quit. I was embarrassed." In the eighth inning of game four, Williams sent Andrews to pinch hit. He was given a standing ovation by the fans in New York, while Finley sat impassively in his box. But the high drama did not result in a base hit, as Andrews grounded out to third baseman Wayne Garrett. Andrews returned to the dugout as his teammates and the New York crowd voiced their support. Joe Rudi of the A's commented, "The fans were just happy to see a guy who got the shaft come back. The working people can relate to him." With the distraction of the Andrews incident and Williams's imminent departure, it is amazing that the A's were able to defeat the Mets. Perhaps one of the best compliments paid them was by Mets shortstop Bud Harrelson, who toasted the A's in the losers' locker room, "I respected them because they won despite all the bull they had to go through."[27]

It was quite apparent after the series that the off-season was going to be a rough one for the troubled A's and that the team might not hold together much longer. Finley's handling of the Andrews case even offended the baseball establishment and resulted in Commissioner Kuhn fining Finley $5,000 and warning that any further such actions might result in a suspension. However, Finley always liked to get the last word. He blocked the Yankees from hiring Dick Williams unless they compensated the A's with quality players. When the Yankees balked at Finley's demands, Williams was left sitting at home. As for Andrews, he was quietly released during the off-season and was not picked up by another team.

Meanwhile, the A's planned on waging war with their owner. Reggie Jackson, who was the league's Most Valuable Player in 1973, announced that he was going to demand $150,000 from Finley, and not $200,000 because "that's going to take money out of the pocket of people like Rudi and Bando and Hunter and the others. I want to see everybody who contributed to these back-to-back championships given what he deserves."

Finley, apparently paying little attention to the public negotiating of Jackson, offered only $5,000 raises to stars Hunter, Holtzman, Blue, and Fingers. The usually quiet country boy Hunter reacted angrily to Finley's offer, retorting, "From what I understand, the whole Oakland team may be going to an arbitrator. I don't know what Finley is thinking. I do know that we made more money in the World Series for him than we made for ourselves." Hunter's prediction was most accurate as the team's war with the owner resulted in several salary deadlocks being settled by arbitration which was not available for Blue in 1972. Arbitrators decided against Finley in cases involving Jackson, Bando, Holtzman, Fingers, and Darold Knowles; while the owner was triumphant in cases involving Rudi, Tenace, and infielder Ted Kubiak.[28] Hunter reached an agreement with Finley for $100,000 without going to arbitration. Symbolic cultural expression was not enough for A's players as they demanded more money and confronted the paternalistic hegemony of Finley.

With these contract matters settled, the intransigent owner concentrated on selecting a new field manager for the A's. The enigmatic Finley shocked the press and his players by naming Al Dark, whom he had fired seven years earlier, as manager of the A's. The Bible-quoting born-again Christian Dark seemed an unlikely candidate to handle the anarchistic A's, but in the press conference called to announce his signing, Dark provided evidence as to why he was selected. He would not attempt to alter superficial countercultural aspects of player appearance, but there would be limits to dissent. Above all, Dark would be a company man. The manager must work with the general manager, and since with the A's the general manager and the owner were one and the same, Dark insisted, "If the general manager tells you to play catcher Ray Fosse at shortstop, then Fosse plays shortstop." Dark also promised his players that there would be few rules, but he was not particularly attuned to the first amendment, observing, "I think respect should be paid to those who pay their salaries. If you don't like it, just quit." Dark concluded that he would handle his players the way Jesus Christ would, but there was no doubt as to the existence of God, as the manager stated, "If Mr. Finley says this will be done, it will be done."[29]

But Finley's will did not set well with young players who did not learn the lesson of turning the other cheek while growing up in the 1960s. Criticism of the owner remained rampant when he failed to personally deliver the 1973 world championship rings which contained no diamonds, just the synthetic emerald in which the 1972 gems had been set. Jackson called the rings "trash," while Hunter complained that Finley was "cheap." In fact, "cheap" was a word many critics were beginning to apply to Finley's entire baseball operation. He discontinued the use of bunting, fireworks, and ball girls along the foul lines. Restrictions were placed on pregame meals and complimentary tickets for the press. Also, players would stamp and pay the postage for fans seeking autographed photos, and little effort was made to obtain a television contract for the 1974 season. And even when Finley did spend money, he seemed to only antagonize the players, as with his signing of track star Herb Washington to a contract as a pinch runner. Washington, who had no experience with the sport, would take the roster spot of a player who could throw and hit, as well as run.[30]

The Christian principles espoused by Dark were certainly tested by both Finley and his players. A's hurlers were distrustful of Dark taking out starting pitchers too quickly. Evidently believing in conspiracy theories, pitchers such as Holtzman maintained that their early exits were due to the fact that Finley did not want to have to pay so many twenty game winners. Holtzman quipped, "I knew Alvin Dark was a religious man, but he's worshipping the wrong god — Charles O. Finley." Following a tough 3-2 loss in Chicago on May 18, Finley publicly chastised Dark in the clubhouse, shouting, "We won the World Series two years without you, and if you don't get your rear in gear, you're gone." The apparently unflappable Dark went out to dinner with Finley after the tirade, again quoting the *Bible*, "Great peace have they which love thy law, and nothing shall offend them." [31]

Yet the mild mannered manager had difficulty imposing order upon the contentious A's. Sal Bando proclaimed that Dark could not "manage a meatmarket," but eventually apologized for his remarks, saying he did recognize Dark's authority. A June 5 clubhouse incident, however, was not as easily resolved. Outfielders Billy North and Jackson got into a fight, apparently caused by off-the-field social differences. In the struggle, Jackson injured his shoulder and was unable to take a full swing for two weeks, while Ray Fosse, attempting to separate the pair, suffered a slipped cervical disc which placed him on the disabled list. An angry Finley lectured the team, attempting to conjure up images of Abraham Lincoln, insisting, "United we stand, divided we fall." Taking his cue from Finley, Dark assumed a more assertive stance with his players, demanding that pitchers hand him the ball instead of flipping it when the manager changed pitchers. Also, the manager angered some players by singling out North for a lack of hustle, and the center fielder was supported by his antagonist Jackson who did not approve of publicly criticizing players. But the limits of dissent and the strength of Dark's position were made clear when Williams's holdover coaches Irv Noren and Vern Hoscheit were fired by Finley. A disgruntled Hoscheit blasted A's management, asserting, "Charlie Finley is no good. He promised the coaches last year that if we did good, we'd get a raise. He doesn't keep his word. The manager is no good too. He's just a horsemeat manager." [32]

Despite a very open contempt for manager and owner by many of the players, the A's again won the West, finishing six games ahead of Texas and defeating the Orioles in the league championship series. While conquering the Los Angeles Dodgers in the 1974 Series four games to one, the A's continued to make considerable noise off the field. In the clubhouse at Dodger Stadium pitchers Rollie Fingers and "Blue Moon" Odom once again engaged in a brawl. Fingers was going through some marital difficulties, and when Odom asked about his wife, Fingers reportedly replied, "What my wife and I do is none of your damn business." Blows were exchanged, and Fingers ended up receiving five stitches. Afterwards, both players downplayed the incident as just the way the A's were, and both players performed well in the Series. Gene Tenace was also upset when he learned that Finley ordered Dark to replace him with Claudell Washington at first base for the fourth game. An outraged Tenace complained, "I have no respect for Dark for not backing me up. I like him, but I can't respect him as a man." But the compliant Dark remained Finley's man and was rewarded following the Series victory with a one year extension of his contract. [33]

However, a much more dangerous threat than clubhouse fights and disagreements with the manager existed for Finley's dynasty. During the Series, Catfish Hunter and his agent Jerry Kapstein let it be known that they were upset that Finley had reneged on a $50,000 salary payment which was to be part of a deferred-payment scheme on which Hunter would pay no immediate taxes. The Major League Players Association filed a grievance on Hunter's behalf, and arbitrator Peter Seitz ordered Finley to pay the $50,000, plus six percent interest, and the pitcher was declared a free agent. Hunter made it clear that he would not consider playing again for Finley. Referring to Finley, Hunter stated, "He just didn't appreciate what I did for the team. He wasn't gentleman enough to come up to me and try to work things out. He was just trying to beat me out of it. He didn't think I'd take it to arbitration." [34] Finley's appeal was not supported by the courts, and free agent Hunter signed a lucrative contract with the New York Yankees.

Finley had opened the Pandora's Box of free agency, and arbitrator Seitz's decision in the cases of pitchers Andy Messersmith and Dave McNally following the 1975 season completed the process of allowing players to play out their options. On July 12, 1976 an agreement was reached between the owners and the Major League Baseball Players Association incorporating the concept of free agency into the basic playing agreement. Thus, Finley had helped pave the way for the dissolution of one of the owners' most privileged positions; the sanctity of the reserve clause. Finley also oversaw the break up of his own dynasty. Without Catfish Hunter, the A's once again won the Western Division in 1975, but they were swept by the Boston Red Sox in the American League Championship Series. Fearing the impact of free agency on his disgruntled players who wished to seek employment elsewhere, Finley attempted to sell Blue to the Yankees and Fingers and Rudi to the Red Sox during the 1976 season. Commissioner Kuhn voided the sales, maintaining that the transactions were "inconsistent with the best interests of baseball."[35] The courts upheld Kuhn and turned down Finley's appeal. But the A's owner was able to trade Holtzman and Jackson to Baltimore for Mike Torrez and Don Baylor in April, 1976. In November, 1976, Rudi, Bando, and Fingers became free agents and signed with California, Milwaukee, and San Diego, respectively. In March, 1978 a disenchanted Vida Blue was traded to the San Francisco Giants. Charles Finley had dismantled a dynasty.

What did the three year reign of the Oakland A's as champions of the baseball world mean? In historical context, the youthful, longhaired, mustached, more racially conscious, dissenting, and volatile players seemed to embody many of the values championed by the American counterculture in the late 1960s and early 1970s. On the other hand, the A's owner Charles Finley, a self-made male product of depression America, admired the talents of his athletes but never seemed to understand their free spirits. Vida Blue complained that Finley "treated his black players like niggers." Ex-A's catcher Dave Duncan told Blue not to despair, "He treats his non-black players like niggers, too."[36] Caught between these two extremes were managers Williams and Dark and consensus figures such as Bowie Kuhn who attempted to maintain the vital center in baseball.

The success of the A's certainly indicated that countercultural symbols such as long hair were not incompatible with winning baseball. But the volatile mixture of conflicting personalities on the A's with intransigent owner Finley could not be indefinitely maintained. Just as the violence of protest on college campuses and the streets would subside by the mid-1970s, the A's players and their owner could not go on with the fight, but the economic issues of free agency and self-determination for players would continue. Finley dismantled his team and retired from the game. Players like Fingers, Hunter, Bando, Blue, Jackson, Holtzman, and Rudi went on to have fine seasons, but the individual parts never quite equaled the original mixture. More traditionally groomed champions in Cincinnati and New York replaced the anarchistic A's. But just as the protests of the 1960s democratized our society, helped end the war in Vietnam, and made us more aware of racism in our society, the reign of the Oakland A's changed baseball, setting the stage for an environment in which players could more openly challenge management and paving the way for free agency and restructuring of the sport. The A's had donned the appearance of the counterculture and sought greater freedom of expression, but not to usher in the age of Aquarius. They challenged the hegemony of the baseball establishment in order to gain emancipation from the reserve clause and a greater share of baseball revenues. The symbols of the counterculture may have disappeared from baseball with the breaking up of the Oakland A's, but the sport would never be quite the same.

Endnotes

This essay was originally published in *Nine: A Journal of Baseball History and Social Policy Perspectives*, 1:2 (1993), 142–162

1. For the development of the liberal consensus and its breakdown see Geoffrey Hodgson, *America in Our Time* (New York: Doubleday, 1976); Allen J. Matusow, *The Unraveling of America: A History of Liberalism in the 1960s* (New York: Harper and Row, 1984); William L. O'Neil, *Coming Apart: An Informal History of America in the 1960s* (New York: Quadrangle, 1971); and Charles A. Reich, *The Greening of America* (New York: Random House, 1970).

2. For theoretical explanation of hegemonic theory see Herbert Marcuse, *One-Dimensional Man* (Boston: Beacon Press, 1984); and Walter Adamson, *Hegemony and Revolution: A Study of Antonio Gramsci's Political and Cultural Theory* (Berkeley: University of California Press, 1980).

3. Studies which have used baseball to investigate American values include Peter Levine, *A. G. Spalding and the Rise of Baseball: The Promise of American Sport* (New York: Oxford University Press, 1985); Steven A. Riess, *Touching Base: Professional Baseball and American Culture in the Progressive Era* (Westport, Conn.: Greenwood Press, 1980); Richard C. Crepeau, *Baseball: America's Diamond Mind, 1919-1941* (Orlando: University Presses of Florida, 1980); Jules Tygiel, *Baseball's Great Experiment: Jackie Robinson and His Legacy* (New York: Oxford University Press, 1983); and Leverett T. Smith, Jr., *The American Dream and the National Game* (Bowling Green, Ohio: Bowling Green University Popular Press, 1975).

4. For background information on Charles Finley see Herbert Michelson, *Charlie O.: Charles Oscar Finley vs. the Baseball Establishment* (New York: Bobbs-Merrill, 1975); Bill Libby, *Charlie O. and the Angry A's* (New York: Doubleday, 1975); Tom Clark, *Champagne and Baloney: The Rise and Fall of Finley's A's* (New York: Harper and Row, 1976); and Wells Twombly, "Charlie O. and the Missouri Mule," *New York Times Magazine* (July 15, 1973), 12–13.

5. The symbolic value of the mustache issue was certainly important to many in baseball as Marvin Miller observed that American League player representative Bob

Allison questioned Miller's hiring as Executive Director of the Players Association due to his mustache. For Miller's account of mustaches and baseball see Marvin Miller, *A Whole Different Ball Game* (New York: Simon and Schuster, 1991), 40–41.

6. All baseball statistics utilized in this study are from Joseph L. Reichler, ed., *The Baseball Encyclopedia: The Complete and Official Record of Major League Baseball* (New York: MacMillan, 1985).

7. For background information on the issues confronting baseball in 1972 see *Sporting News*, February 5 and 26, March 25, and April 1, 8, and 15, 1972. For the key role played by this publication in baseball history see *Sporting News, First Hundred Years, 1886–1986* (St. Louis: Sporting News, 1986). The "Bible of Baseball" will constitute a primary source for this investigation into the sport during the early 1970s.

8. For background information on Blue see Steve Ames, "Vida Blue, Baseball's Most Exciting Young Pitcher," *Baseball Digest*, 30 (August, 1971), 35–41; Roy Blount, Jr., "Humming a Rhapsody in Blue," *Sports Illustrated*, 35 (July 12, 1971), 22–27; and Vida Blue with Bill Libby, *Vida: His Own Story* (Englewood Cliffs, New Jersey: Prentice-Hall, 1971).

9. On the Blue-Finley negotiations see *Sporting News*, February 26, and April 1 and 15, 1972; and Ron Reid, "Vida Blue Stars in the Great Bathroom Farce," *Sports Illustrated*, 36 (March 20, 1972), 19–20.

10. For the 1972 signing of Blue see *Sporting News*, May 13 and 20, 1972; Bowie Kuhn, *Hardball: The Education of a Baseball Commissioner* (New York: Times Books, 1987), 126–144; and George Vass, "Will the Pressure Get to Vida Blue?," *Baseball Digest*, 31 (June, 1972), 28–34. Blue would, indeed, have trouble recovering from his 1972 dealings with Finley, slipping to only six wins and ten losses for the ensuing campaign. He would have other good years, but he would never regain the enthusiasm and form of the 1971 season. His premature departure from the game would be accelerated by a problem with cocaine.

11. Vida Blue, "Next Year is Going to Be Different," *Ebony*, 27 (October, 1972), 133.

12. *Sporting News*, April 1 and March 18, 1972.

13. *Ibid.*, February 5, 1972.

14. *Ibid.*, April 1, 1972. On Holtzman see Glenn Dickey, "Ken Holtzman Has a Problem: He Likes Living in Oakland," *Sport*, 51 (October, 1973), 56–61: and Bob Hayes, "The Education of the A's Ken Holtzman," *Baseball Digest*, 33 (December, 1974), 72–77.

15. Ron Fimrite, "On Tour with Hair," *Sports Illustrated*, 37 (July 31, 1972), 14–17.

16. *Sporting News*, September 2, 1972. For background information on Dick Williams see Donald Honig, *The Man in the Dugout* (Chicago: Follett, 1977), 198–212.

17. *Sporting News*, October 28, 1972. On the A's 1972 campaign see Ron Birgman, *The Mustache Gang: The Swaggering Saga of the Oakland A's* (New York: Dell, 1973); and Fimrite, "On Tour with Hair," 14–17.

18. *Sporting News*, November 4, 1972. For the 1972 Series see Bob Addie, "Key to the 1972 Series: Relief Pitching," *Baseball Digest*, 32 (January, 1973), 46–49; Roger Angell, "The Pennant Races and World Series," *New Yorker*, 48 (November 11, 1972); and Ron Fimrite, "A Big Beginning for the Little League," *Sports Illustrated*, 37 (Oct. 23, 1972), 26–29.

19. For images of the 1972 World Series as a cultural clash between Oakland and Cincinnati see Robert Harris "Hub" Walker, *Cincinnati and the Big Red Machine* (Bloomington: Indiana University Press, 1988), 53–54; J. Anthony Lukas, "Way to Go, Jonathan Seagull," *Saturday Review*, 55 (Nov. 11, 1972), 7–8; and "Superfreaks v. Super-

stars," *Time*, 100 (Oct. 30, 1972), 66. Oakland's radical image was also evident in racial tensions and Black Panther Party member Bobby Seale's campaign for mayor. For background information on the status of African-Americans in Oakland see "Tame Panthers," *Time*, 100 (December 25, 1972), 13–14; Norman Melnick, "Uncommon Cop: Chief Gain," *New Republic*, 166 (Jan. 22, 1972), 15–16; and Amory Bradford, *Oakland's Not for Burning* (New York: David McKay Company, 1968).

20. *Sporting News*, December 23, 1972; and Arnold Hano, "Mike Epstein: Somewhere Between Journeyman and Superstar," *Sport*, 54 (November, 1972), 66–69.

21. *Sporting News*, January 6, and April 7, 1973.

22. *Ibid.*, March 3, 1973. On the issue of collective bargaining see James B. Dworkin, *Owners Versus Players: Baseball and Collective Bargaining* (Boston: Auburn House Publishing, 1981); and Miller, *A Whole Different Ball Game*.

23. *Sporting News*, July 28, 1973. On Jackson see Maury Allen, *Mr. October: The Reggie Jackson Story* (New York: Times Books, 1981); John Kuenster, *The Reggie Jackson Story* (New York: Lothrop, Lee and Shepard, 1979); and Glenn Dickey, "Reggie Jackson, Super Star (Not Yet!)," *Sport*, 56 (July, 1973), 52–57.

24. *Sporting News*, October 13, 1973; and Ron Fimrite, "Vida's Down with the Growing-up Blues," *Sports Illustrated*, 39 (September 10, 1973), 93.

25. *Sporting News*, July 7, 1973.

26. *Ibid.*, October 27, 1973; and William Leggett, "Hares Against Hairs: Athletics vs. Orioles in American League Playoffs," *Sports Illustrated*, 39 (October 8, 1973), 34–35.

27. On the Andrews case and the 1973 World Series see *Sporting News*, October 27, and November 3, 1973; John Kuenster, "A's at Their Best When Fighting," *Baseball Digest*, 33 (January, 1974), 4–8; Roger Angell, "World Series: Oakland A's vs. New York Mets," *New Yorker*, 49 (November 19, 1973), 183–202; Ron Fimrite, "Buffoonery Rampant: New York Mets vs. Oakland Athletics," *Sports Illustrated*, 39 (October 22, 1973), 24–27; Al Hirshberg, "Dick Williams' Second World Series: This Time the Heroes Wore Mustaches," *Sport*, 56 (October, 1973), 96–110; and William Leggett, "Mutiny and a Bounty: Oakland's Victory," *Sports Illustrated*, 39 (October 29, 1973), 22–27.

28. *Sporting News*, December 1, 1973; and February 2 and March 16, 1974.

29. *Ibid.*, March 9 and 16, 1974. For background information on Dark see Alvin Dark with John Underwood, *When in Doubt, Fire the Manager: My Life in Baseball* (New York: E. P. Dutton, 1980); and Dark, "Rhubarbs, Hassles, and Other Hazards," *Sports Illustrated*, 40 (May 13, 1974), 42–44.

30. *Sporting News*, March 23, April 6, and May 4, 1974; and Ken Moore, "Eff Ell Wyeing on the Bases," *Sports Illustrated*, 40 (June 10, 1974), 69–72.

31. *Sporting News*, April 27, and June 8, 1974.

32. *Ibid.*, June 22, July 13, 22, 27, and August 3, 1974; Murray Olderman, "Reggie Jackson: Blood and Guts of the Fighting A's," *Sport*, 58 (October, 1974), 44–55; and Reggie Jackson with Bill Libby, *Reggie: A Season with a Super Star* (Chicago: Playboy Press, 1975).

33. For the 1974 World Series see *Sporting News*, October 26 and November 2, 1974; Roger Angell, "World Series: Los Angeles Dodgers vs. Oakland A's," *New Yorker*, 50 (November 11, 1974), 156–160; Ron Fimrite, "Triple-Crown to the Clowns," *Sports Illustrated*, 41 (October 28, 1974), 24–27; and Reggie Jackson, "The Dodgers Were Too Cocky," *Sport*, 51 (October, 1975), 90–97.

34. *Sporting News*, December 28, 1974. On Hunter see Roy Blount, Jr., "Opening the Catfish Season," *Sports Illustrated*, 42 (March 17, 1978), 56–60; Bill Libby, *Catfish: The Three-Million Dollar Pitcher* (New York: Coward, McCann, Geoghegan, 1976); Irwin Stambler, *Catfish Hunter: The Three-Million Dollar Arm* (New York: G. P. Put-

nam, 1976); and Jim Hunter and Armen Keteyian, *My Life in Baseball* (New York: McGraw Hill, 1986).

35. On the dismantling of the A's dynasty see Kuhn, *Hardball*, 173–187; Ron Fimrite, "Bowie Stops Charlie's Checks: Attempted Sale of Oakland Players," *Sports Illustrated*, 44 (June 28, 1976), 22–25; Fimrite, "They're Just Mad About Charlie: The Deterioration of the Oakland A's Franchise," *Sports Illustrated*, 50 (May 21, 1979), 36–41; Steve Cameron, "The Night the Oakland A's Dynasty Died," *Baseball Digest*, 37 (April, 1978), 60–63; and William B. Furlong, "Charlie Finley: Triumph and Turmoil," *Saturday Evening Post*, 247 (October, 1975), 30–32.

36. *Sporting News*, October 26, 1974.

15

As American as Cherry Pie: Baseball and Reflections of Violence in the 1960s and 1970s

In an introduction to the paperback edition of *Rights in Conflict*, a report on the riots at the 1968 Chicago Democratic national convention, Max Frankel of the *New York Times* commented on the centrality of violence to American life, stating, "We are known for our violence, we Americans. The creative violence with which we haul down the good for what we fancy is better. The cruel violence with which we treated red men, and black. The intoxicating violence of our music and art. The absurd violence of our comics and cartoons. The organized violence of our athletic and corporate games."[1]

Frankel's commentary was the product of a time in American history when it appeared that the nation was on the verge of disintegrating into riot, rebellion, and revolution. Beginning with the murder of President John F. Kennedy in November, 1963, America was haunted by the specter of political assassination, with the shooting of such figures as Medgar Evers and Malcolm X, culminating in the 1968 assassinations of Martin Luther King, Jr., and Robert Kennedy. Evening news programs were dominated by images of violence in Vietnam, while the body bag count proliferated. The war in Vietnam, cultural changes, and a transition in university clientele led to violent confrontations between students and the educational establishment. Frustrations regarding the lack of economic progress made in fulfilling the promise of the civil rights movement helped ignite America's cities; where high unemployment rates, the assassination of Martin Luther King, Jr., or an incident of police violence might produce the spark to set off an urban inferno.

Black activist Rap Brown shocked Americans, but perhaps accurately captured the mood of America in the late 1960s, by proclaiming, "Violence is necessary and it's as American as cherry pie." [2] Brown looked to the country's past for justification that violence was essential in the struggle for black liberation. While not prepared to join Brown in a call for revolution, many historians began to question the consensus historiography of the 1950s, documenting that violence has, indeed, played a significant role in American history. Richard Maxwell Brown maintains that militant individualism in American life is a reflection of the frontier tradition which eroded the English common law concept that a person has the duty to retreat from violence whenever possible. According to Brown, over time a legal revolution occurred in America allowing a threatened individual to "legally stand fast and, without retreat, kill in self-defense."[3] The historical studies and reports of the National Commission on the Causes and Prevention of Violence supported the conclusions reached by activists and scholars, while insisting, as the Kerner Commission report on racial unrest, that the key component to halting further violence in America's cities was the reconstruction of urban life.[4]

While many scholars looked to the American past in order to explain a propensity for violence, the American sporting tradition and institution of baseball, often described as the national pastime and identified with the American traditions of motherhood and pie, appeared to offer an example of assimilation where conflict could be peacefully resolved on the playing fields of the nation. However, during the 1960s and 1970s, many commentators were convinced that baseball was not immune to the violence sweeping the nation.

An examination of newspaper accounts and sports editorials during this era reflects concern that sport was not an island of tranquility amid a sea of conflict washing over the nation. Sportswriters were worried that violence in the general society was spilling over into the playing fields of baseball, and the sport no longer reflected the values of a consensus society. Challenged by the growing popularity of the more violent sport of football, baseball writers and spokespersons were afraid that the self-proclaimed national pastime was both out of step with the culture of the 1960s and indicative of a growing tendency toward resolving differences through violence. Sportswriters expressed misgivings regarding confrontations among athletes off the field as well as between the foul lines. Any fight between black and white players was feared as possibly triggering racial unrest among spectators. And, indeed, there was considerable speculation that the ballpark was no longer a site where families could safely congregate. Baseball writers lamented that the sport's stadiums failed to provide an environment where a family could escape the social issues of violence, drug and alcohol abuse, and racial unrest. Commentators were apprehensive that the behavior of baseball players as well as spectators was mirroring a society in which violence was becoming the norm. Nonsense, replied such conservative columnists as New York's Dick Young, who proclaimed that, at least on the field, the sport had a rich tradition of beanball wars and physical confrontations. However, the amount of time and space devoted to the relationship between violence and baseball during the 1960s and 1970s certainly indicates that the sport was unable to escape the major social issues of the era, providing a microcosm through which to examine American society in a turbulent time.

As a recent article in *Baseball Digest* attests, violence on the baseball field usually evolves around the question of "beanballs," or pitchers throwing at batters. While some veteran players insist that pitching inside and knocking down batters was once an accepted part of the game, although now rejected by modern athletes, the history of baseball brawls does not necessarily support such an assumption. Thus, most of the confrontations between players during the tumultuous 1960s and 1970s fit well into the brushback tradition.[5]

Perhaps the most celebrated 1960s baseball altercation among players took place on August 22, 1965, during a heated pennant race between the Los Angeles Dodgers and San Francisco Giants. Giants pitcher Juan Marichal, whom the Dodgers accused of throwing at batters, took objection to the Dodger catcher John Roseboro zipping the ball near his ear on the return throw to the mound. An agitated Marichal proceeded to take his bat after Roseboro, opening a gash in the catcher's scalp, before both benches erupted. In an action which many criticized for its leniency, National League President Warren Giles suspended Marichal for eight games and fined the pitcher $1,750. Roseboro filed a civil suit, which was adjudicated in 1969.[6]

Deplored as one of the ugliest incidents in baseball history, the Marichal-Roseboro confrontation hardly reduced the sport's beanball wars. In 1967, the promising career of young Boston Red Sox slugger Tony Coniglario was derailed by the fastball of Jack Hamilton. And the opening of the 1976 season was marred by a brawl when St. Louis Cardinals pitcher Lynn McGlothen hit Del Unser of the Philadelphia Phillies, who the night before had beaten the Cards with a home run in the seventeenth inning. Columnist Dick Young protested when McGlothen was assessed a fine and suspension from the National League office. Stating that fighting was simply part of the competitive spirit, Young made adamant his contempt for liberals and the counterculture, insisting, "We are becoming a little too thin-skinned. Our athletes not only are wearing their hair like girls, they are screaming for cops like girls, as if they were being attacked. And the do-gooders, the bleeding hearts, who weep into their typewriter keyboards, are screaming right along with them." On the other hand, Melvin Durslag, writing in the *Sporting News,* maintained that those who, like Dick Young, perceived the beanball as part of baseball were simply ignorant. Durslag argued that baseball owners could put a stop to throwing at batters' heads by informing their managers that the practice would no longer be tolerated. However, the columnist surmised that the baseball establishment was reluctant to take strong action due to the perception that the fans were attracted to violent spectacles on the field. Thus, baseball management, like their counterparts in the National Hockey League, was placing profits above safety concerns.[7]

Durslag was certainly not the first individual to make the connection between an increasingly violent culture and baseball profits. The baseball establishment was apprehensive with declining attendance figures and the growing popularity of full contact sports such as football and hockey. Media scholar Marshall McLuhan insisted that baseball was out of step with American culture, observing, "When cultures change so do games. Baseball, that had become the elegant abstract image of an industrial society living by split second timing, has in the new TV decade lost its psychic and social relevance for our way of life.... Games are extensions of our immediate lives. And we are living in a violent age. Baseball has no violence." Management figures strongly dissented from the McLuhan prognosis. New York Yankees President Michael Burke, a former executive with the Columbia Broadcasting Company, asserted, "Nowadays everyone is banging everyone else over the head. People will begin to gag on the violence in our lives, from the football field to the college campus. And the relative nonviolence of baseball will become attractive." Baseball Commissioner Bowie Kuhn proclaimed that neither baseball nor American society needed violence, pointing out, "You know, the Metropolitan Opera does not portray violence either. But it is a very dramatic performing art set on a very dramatic stage. So is baseball."[8]

In this quote Commissioner Kuhn displayed considerable ignorance regarding the violent themes in many German and Italian operas, while failing to recognize that the New York City's Met and America's baseball diamonds might not necessarily draw upon the same clientele. Both the Commissioner and media analyst overlooked the sport's tradition of brawling. After all, as columnist and writer Don Atyea remarked, violence was an integral part of the sport which glorified the exploits of Ty Cobb. However, violence was not necessarily the panacea for sagging ticket sales.

Hockey and basketball owners were concerned about the repercussions of mayhem on the ice and court. In 1975, the National Hockey League establishment was rocked by the civil case and criminal complaint lodged against Dave Forbes of the Boston Bruins, who attacked the Minnesota North Stars Henry Boucha during a game in Bloomington, Minnesota. As the two players were leaving the penalty box, Forbes knocked Boucha to the ice, while continuing to pummel the prone North Star, who was carried from the rink on a stretcher, suffering from cuts to his eye which required a twenty-five stitch surgery.[9]

While debates were rampant in the sporting community over whether confrontations between players were a reflection of a violent society or simply an extension of the competitive spirit, there was a consensus that a line was crossed during a 1977 spring training assault by the Texas Rangers Lenny Randle upon his manager Frank Lucchesi. Randle was angry that the Rangers second base position was apparently going to heralded rookie Bump Wills, the son of former Dodger star Muary Wills. Alleging that he was not given a fair chance at earning the position, although his 1976 batting averaged had dipped into the .220's, Randle threatened to leave the team, only to be talked out of it by teammates. When informed of Randle's discontent, manager Lucchesi quipped, "I'm sick and tired of punks making $80,000 a year moaning and groaning about their situation." According to Randle, a few days later and before an exhibition game in Orlando, he approached the manger, still dressed in street clothes, who was standing near the third base coaching box. When Lucchesi again called him a punk, Randle struck him, knocking the older man to the ground. Lucchesi, who denied repeating the offensive word punk, was hospitalized, having suffered a concussion and broken jaw. Randle was suspended and eventually dealt to the New York Mets, where he regained his batting eye.

Perhaps fearing for their own safety, baseball columnists were outraged that an athlete in his mid-twenties had assaulted a fifty-year-old man, although the racial implications (Randle was African-American and Lucchesi Italian-American) of the beating were downplayed. Melvin Durslag speculated whether any manger would now dare to discipline a player, while Bob Addie of the *Washington Post* maintained that the attack was a sign of the times. Addie wrote that the assault exemplified "the disrespect for authority that exists among modern athletes," predicting that even owners might become targets of physical aggression by players.[10] However, the Randle-Lucchesi incident did not establish a precedent for assault and battery against baseball management. The baseball establishment had much more to fear from Marvin Miller and the Major League

Baseball Players Association's challenge to the reserve clause and other prerogatives enjoyed by ownership.

Nevertheless, serious issues of violence did plague the owners during the 1960s and 1970s. Rather than suffering from altercations between ball players on the playing field, management was confronted with incidents of violence in the stadium perpetuated by fans and often directed against the players. Ballpark violence was widespread; mirroring the violence of American society, shattering the notion of a sacred public place where the prerogatives of class and privilege could not be challenged, and cutting into the profits of ownership. Many fearful fans refused to venture out to night games in what they perceived as dangerous neighborhoods. Although not always articulated, these fears reflected America's racial divide during the 1960s and 1970s as the ballpark ceased to be a refuge for white privilege.

It would take considerable time and space to chronicle all accounts of violence in the major league stadiums during these troubled decades. However, a sampling of incidents spread over time and from differing locations offers evidence of the dangers confronting the baseball establishment. Of course, violence had entered the ballpark before the unrest of the sixties. For example, in 1929, a disputed call during a game in Cleveland between the Indians and Philadelphia Athletics resulted in a barrage of bottles being tossed on the field. Third base umpire Emmett Ormsby suffered a concussion, while one spectator from Akron later died from head injuries inflicted by a thrown bottle. The seventh game of the 1934 World Series was disrupted when Detroit fans unleashed a deluge of fruits and vegetables aimed at St. Louis Cardinals outfielder Joe Medwick. And on July 4, 1950, a spectator in the Polo Grounds was killed by a bullet supposedly fired from outside the ballpark.[11] Nevertheless, violence in the 1960s was different, demonstrating the generational, class, and racial divisions exposed by the civil rights movement and Vietnam War.

On April 24, 1964, the Pittsburgh Pirates advertised a special youth admission price of fifty cents. According to the *Sporting News,* over thirteen thousand teens made the ballgame miserable for the nearly eight thousand older fans paying full price. Ushers who had worked at Forbes Field for over thirty years reported that they had never witnessed such unruly behavior. The first aid room was full of youths being treated for sprained ankles and cuts, while other young people stole a huge mustard jar and sprayed the stands. On a more serious note, three other young men were arrested after they assaulted and robbed another youth in the bathroom. And, noted the *Sporting News,* such behavior occurred in a ballpark which did not even serve beer.

Similar manifestations of violence were reported at Milwaukee County Stadium in the spring of 1964, and a young college student attending a game at Busch Stadium in St. Louis was stabbed and killed outside of the stadium. The *Sporting News* editorialized upon the need for curbing youth violence, calling for the law and order policies which would later permeate the political platforms of Presidential candidates George Wallace and Richard Nixon. Warning of "packs of juvenile hooligans and punks," the paper of the baseball establishment pleaded for beefed up security forces at the ballpark, insisting, "People will not risk a beating or worse to watch baseball or any other sport."[12]

Not that they needed any new excuses to lose, but similar concerns with youth violence led some in Boston to acknowledge that the city was better off with the Red Sox dropping the 1967 World Series. Deputy Superintendent Eddie Mannix of the Boston Police Department predicted that if the Red Sox had won the seventh and deciding game in Fenway, rioting would have started with the five to eight thousand "vicious" kids hanging around the ballpark. Police on horseback had scuffled with the crowd during the game, and authorities were girded for a full scale confrontation. But as usual the Red Sox came through, and the Cardinals won the game 7 -2. A relieved head usher Amby Anderson asserted, "If the Red Sox had won that seventh game, I'm positive 400 people would have been either killed or injured. That's how bad the crowd was outside the park. As much as I wanted the Red Sox to win, I was almost hoping they wouldn't."[13]

During the 1968 season which culminated in a world championship for the Detroit Tigers, Joe Falls of the *Detroit Free Press* deplored what the reporter labeled as thuggery in the ballpark. Falls was incensed at Tiger fans, who threw five "cherry bombs" at Red Sox outfielder Ken Harrelson, almost costing Detroit a forfeit. Falls also had little use for what Yankee management labeled a poverty day promotion. Displaying his disgust for the cultural changes taking place in the country, the Detroit columnist concluded that the underprivileged kids in the left field bleachers at Yankee Stadium had tossed so much debris on that field that "the outfield looked like Central Park after a love-in." A *Sporting News* editorial voiced similar concerns about the conduct of bleacher bums in Chicago's Wrigley Field, who poured beer and threw tennis balls at Cardinal outfielders Roger Maris and Curt Flood. The self-proclaimed Bible of baseball concluded, "Unruly conduct should not be tolerated by club officials, because there always is the danger that passions on the field might lead to excesses in the stands. The hooligan who throws an ice cube one night might switch hands to a brick in another game."[14]

However, while the War on Poverty was being dismantled and the

Vietnam War dragged on under a President who was elected in 1968 on a promise to end the conflict; the social, cultural, and generational clashes in America, and in ballparks mirroring the apparent deterioration of the country, only intensified. Following an April 12, 1970 doubleheader with the Indians, in which young fans swarmed on the field disrupting play, officials at Yankee Stadium were considering canceling future twin bills. Cleveland players complained of having full beer cans hurled at them, but the New York crowd played no favorites, making life miserable as well for the home town Yankees. The Yankee mystique, which exemplified so well the affluent and conservative 1950s, offered little protection for New York relief pitcher Steve Hamilton who proclaimed, "I was hit by a sharp object, then I put my glove over my face. The situation in the bullpen is impossible. We get spit on, and billiard balls, nails, fruit, empty cans and just about everything is thrown at us." The chaos reduced Red Foley of the *New York Daily News* to a diatribe with implications beyond the "house that Ruth built." An agitated Foley wrote, "Instead of the plaques they dedicated to Joe DiMaggio and Mickey Mantle, the Yankees should have hung some of the kids on the center field wall at the Stadium yesterday. Considering the tumult that accompanied the split with the Indians, a show of muscle by the Establishment could be a deterrent against future outbreaks."[15]

But the political establishment simply never responded to sports rioting in such an authoritarian manner. Over exuberant fans might still be placed within the context of bread and circuses, or as a safety valve through which the discontented and underprivileged might blow off some steam. Accordingly, in downtown Columbus, Ohio, the violent aftermath of an Ohio State victory over Michigan was tolerated, while the National Guard was needed in May, 1970 at Kent State when protesters burned a political symbol such as the university's ROTC building. In a similar vein, the Associated Press's Pittsburgh bureau chief Pat Minarcin termed the actions of forty thousand revelers celebrating the Pirates 1971 World Series victory "a riot." According to Minarcin, "Police called the violence the worst in the city's history." But the National Guard was not dispatched as was the case in April, 1968, when the African-American community took to the streets in protest of Martin Luther King, Jr.'s assassination. Instead, Pittsburgh Police Superintendent Robert E. Colville blasted what he termed the "gross distortion" of the media. Colville insisted that there was no riot, simply an over exuberant celebration which got a little out of hand. According to Colville's account, there were no reported rapes and most arrests were for intoxication. While over a hundred injuries were reported, none were serious, and property damage and looting were minimal; with two cars overturned, damage to about twenty-five stores, and only two small fires.[16]

In 1973, the Mets triumph over the Cincinnati Reds in a bitter National League Championship Series failed to produce rioting in the streets of New York, but the atmosphere at Shea Stadium was extremely tense. Tempers flared during the Mets 9-2 victory in game three, when Pete Rose barreled into Mets shortstop Bud Harrelson, setting off a bench-clearing fight. The crowd of nearly sixty-thousand reacted by booing and pelting Rose with bottles and debris when he returned to his left field position. After a threatened forfeit and a peace-keeping mission to the bleachers by the Mets Yogi Berra, Tom Seaver, Cleon Jones, and Willie Mays, who had recently announced his decision to retire following the season, a semblance of order was restored. Following Pete Rose's game-winning ninth inning home run in game four, which was punctuated by the controversial player's clinched fist raised in either triumph or defiance, the New York crowd was in a frenzy for the deciding game five of the series. As the Mets pulled away in the game and the crowd grew more unruly, Reds family members were taken out of the stands and escorted to safety. With the recording of the last out, New York fans surged on to the field and, in a scenario reminiscent of the 1969 Miracle Mets, inflicted severe damage to the playing surface. A disillusioned Tom Seaver lamented, "The sad part is that these fans would have done this to the field even if we had lost. I think a lot of them didn't care whether we won or not. They just wanted to rip up the field." An indignant *Sporting News* editorial asserted, "Shea Stadium patrons were terrorized and trampled by hordes of vandals who swarmed out of the stands and engulfed the field."[17]

However, self-righteous editorializing and calls for added security did little to quell ballpark violence, which appeared to reach a crescendo in 1974, as the nation reeled from the disillusionment of military defeat in Vietnam and political corruption at the highest levels with the Watergate scandal. Opening day for the White Sox was marred by heavy drinking and fighting fans, as well as several streakers, both male and female, who pranced through the outfield grass clad only in baseball caps. The rowdy crowd caused White Sox pitcher Terry Forster to fear for his family's safety in the stands, while third baseman Ron Santo simply stated, "I never saw a crowd that bad. It took a lot of concentration away from us." White Sox management blamed the disturbance upon opening-day hysteria and the thirty-seven degree temperature, although the cold day would appear to offer less than ideal weather conditions for streaking in the Windy City.[18]

Following the 1973 National League Championship Series with the

Mets, Manager Sparky Anderson of the Reds had quipped that New York was not part of America. However, during the 1974 season Cincinnati proved to be little different from the Big Apple when it came to obnoxious fan behavior. On May 12, 1974, Houston Astros outfielder Bob Watson crashed into the left field wall at Cincinnati's Riverfront Stadium. With his sunglasses shattered and his face bloodied, Watson was afraid that any movement might endanger his eyesight. Meanwhile, some spectators in the bleachers began pouring beer over the prone and bleeding figure of Watson. Teammates such as centerfielder Cesar Cendeno engaged in a shouting match with unruly fans, while Watson was carried from the field. However, other Reds supporters helped identify the culprits, who, after being subdued by police, ended up in the same hospital emergency room as Watson.[19]

While deploring the behavior of those individuals who harassed the injured Watson, the ever-caustic Dick Young reminded his readers that the Astros Cedeno might want to be careful about calling others hoodlums. In December, 1973, while playing winter ball in the Dominican Republic, Cedeno was involved in a hotel room shooting, which took the life of a young Dominican woman and mother. After initially fleeing the scene of the shooting, Cedeno turned himself into the authorities, explaining that his weapon had been accidentally discharged. With the intervention of Houston management, the charges against Cedeno were reduced to involuntary manslaughter, and the ball player was fined $100 for negligence in allowing the young woman to handle the weapon.[20] While barriers were being challenged in the United States, wealth and privilege certainly counted for something in the Dominican Republic.

The responsibility of fans, management, and players for baseball violence was evident in one of the sport's most infamous incidents; the June 4, 1974 forfeit of the Indians to the Texas Rangers on ten cent beer night in Cleveland. As the evening wore on, inebriated spectators began running on the field, and firecrackers were tossed in the direction of Manager Billy Martin and his Texas players. Despite interruptions, the game continued, with the Indians staging a two out rally in the ninth which tied the score at 5-5. Cleveland had the potential winning run at third base when approximately a half-dozen drunken young men left the bleachers, surrounding Rangers outfielder Jeff Burroughs and tugging at his cap and glove. Led by Martin and armed with baseball bats, Texas players charged out of the dugout to protect Burroughs. Chaos ensued as the appearance of the angry Rangers team on the field induced many drunken spectators to throw debris at the visiting club or climb out of the bleachers to do battle. Now the Indians rushed onto the field in defense of the Rangers. In the resulting confusion and near riot conditions, Cleveland pitcher Tom Hilgendorf was injured when hit on the head with a steel chair, umpire Nester Chylak received a scalp wound, and the umpiring crew declared a forfeit, awarding a 9-0 victory to the Rangers. Burroughs maintained that he was afraid for his life, thanking the Cleveland players for coming to his rescue, "like John Wayne coming over the horizon." When the game was called, over five thousand people were on the field, and nine arrests were made for disorderly conduct.

In the game's aftermath, Cleveland management was censured for staging the beer promotion. The club's financial situation was precarious, and rumors were rampant that the troubled franchise would relocate. Popular promotions such as ten cent beer night were finally putting some people in the seats. However, critics suggested that management was placing profits above player and fan safety. The irrepressible Dick Young urged baseball owners to decide whether they were selling beer or baseball. Young maintained, "In this grab for the buck, they have shed all moral responsibility, then they have the gall to point a finger at the fans they encouraged to become stoned out of their minds." Echoing the sentiments of Young, James T. Carney, Safety Director for the City of Cleveland, stated, "Obviously these young guys went down there and for ten cents had a few beers, got stiff, became wild men and didn't know what they were doing. They just went berserk. Its just an act of God that nobody was killed. These kids get so wild and there were knives and everything else down there."

However, many Cleveland fans found the beer indictment a little too sweeping. After all, there were over 25,000 fans in attendance, and the majority of spectators were not involved in the fisticuffs with the Rangers. Some Indian supporters blamed the media for focusing on a brawl between the Rangers and Indians a few weeks earlier in Arlington, urging fans to exact revenge on the Texas club. According to this line of thought, the Cleveland media played a major role in creating a climate of violence. Some in Cleveland, while condemning unruly individuals, found room to blame the combative Billy Martin. The Rangers were on the verge of losing the game when Martin led his team onto the field, agitating the belligerent fans and triggering the final outburst of violence.[21]

While the sport was engaging in considerable finger pointing after the Cleveland fiasco, players throughout the major leagues insisted that the climate at big league stadiums had changed. Sal Bando, third baseman for the Oakland Athletics, a quality team known for fighting in the clubhouse and whose moustaches and long hair appeared to exemplify the counterculture, maintained that violence in the ballpark was a manifestation of deteriorating values in the country. According to Bando, some fans lacked a proper family structure, "for no one with a decent background would abuse a player the way some have been treated this year." Apparently in agreement with Bando's analysis, Yankee management in 1976 moved to insure that their spectators would have a more proper background, canceling a ten-year program in which Consolidated Edison distributed over one-million Yankee tickets to underprivileged youth. Yankee officials cited a lack of supervision and growing violence as motivating their termination of the popular program. The Yankees maintained a number of violent incidents had occurred in the Con Ed section; including the mugging of a fourteen-year-old girl, a series of fires in the men's room, an assault upon a stadium security guard, and the intimidation of a seven-year-old boy whose head was held in a toilet until he surrendered his baseball glove.[22]

Nevertheless, excessive fan behavior continued to be a problem throughout the late 1970s as the nation attempted to cope with the legacy of Vietnam and Watergate, as well as an economic recession fueled by high energy prices. President Jimmy Carter referred to a cultural and political malaise in America, which was exemplified in baseball by sagging attendance figures, death threats against players, and the continuing rain of debris from the bleachers. Baseball executives, seeking to boost ticket sales, often exacerbated the situation. For example, on the evening of July 12, 1979, White Sox owner and promoter Bill Veeck was convinced by his son Mike to stage Anti-Disco Night. Sponsored by a Chicago radio station, the admission price for the doubleheader between the White Sox and Detroit Tigers was reduced to ninety-eight cents. Over fifty thousand fans filled Comisky Park, while thousands of others milled around outside the stadium. Between games of the twin bill, things got out of hand when a disc jockey exploded thousands of disco records, setting off a frenzy in which many of the spectators, apparently high on marijuana, stormed onto the field, inflicting considerable damage and refusing to return to their seats. Veeck, afraid of violence and injuries, turned down the offer of the Chicago police to clear the field, accepting the umpires' decision to declare a forfeit in the second game of the scheduled doubleheader.[23]

Baseball journalists devoted considerable energy and ink to exploring the reasons for violent behavior in the nation's ballyards, offering various solutions to stem what was perceived as an orgy of violence threatening the national pastime. Joe Falls of the *Detroit Free Press* and a columnist for the *Sporting News* was especially concerned with what he termed a lowering of standards in American society and culture. In a May 16, 1970 column entitled "Insults and Obscenities," Falls acknowledged that he was the voice of the establishment, embarrassed by the language and obscene signs at the nation's ballparks. The columnist chided college students and administrators for fostering a sense of permissiveness on university campuses. Falls complained, "I just can't get it through my head what kind of kicks the students get out of holding dirty signs. I guess it's a defiance of authority, or the right to say what you please. I just couldn't see myself feeling very proud of doing this."

Falls believed that violence among baseball spectators was a manifestation of a society in which many citizens, especially the youth of America, had lost sight of such basic values as civility and respect for property. While unable to reform the larger society, Falls called for law and order in the ballpark, applauding Detroit management for closing the bleachers when unruly fans tossed objects on the field. Like a candidate advocating beefed up police forces and more prisons as a cure for crime, the Detroit columnist campaigned for the baseball establishment to increase security forces at the stadium; the price of which could then be passed on to the fans, who in the final analysis would be paying to police themselves. An added bonus to this approach would be that ticket prices might become too steep for some undesirable elements.[24]

In a series of editorials and columns indicating alarm over the economic impact of violent fan behavior, the *Sporting News* expressed solidarity with the ideas espoused by Falls. However, the conservative slant of editorial policy suggested that problems within baseball would not be solved until the larger climate of violence and cultural change was subdued. Advocating a law and order approach, the *Sporting News* urged baseball management to get tough with unruly fans and expel them from the stadiums. Practical measures for curbing violence suggested by the editors included: limitations on alcohol sales, surveillance cameras, heavy wire fences to prevent the throwing of debris, and increased security. However, the baseball paper despaired of any significant improvements in the sport without a change in the larger moral and political climate. In concurrence with the opinion expressed by White Sox correspondent Edgar Munzel that a permissive society encouraged young people to get out of control and develop an "anti-law-and-order syndrome," the *Sporting News* concluded, "The sports world is confronted with its share of bad actors, but things could be worse. The trouble makers have yet to burn down a stadium. Maybe that's because they lack the advantage of a college education."

Larry Whiteside, the paper's Milwaukee correspondent, insisted that baseball parks would have to be taken back from the rowdy young fans causing mischief and terrorizing patrons. In order to restore baseball as a family entertainment, "every vestige of vulgarity, obscenity, and pugnacity must be stamped out in all parks." But why should such draconian measures be limited to the confines of baseball, editorialized the *Sporting News* in the fall of 1976, observing, "Whatever the solution, sports events are vulnerable so long as the streets of America's cities remain unsafe."[25]

Other commentators, such as William Barry Furlong, writing in *TV Guide*, pointed out the role played by the media in creating an atmosphere for the glorification of violence. While deploring altercations on the field and stands, television executives, nevertheless, recognized that physical confrontations were popular with many viewers, and it was impossible to pretend that they did not exist. In addition to portraying fisticuffs, the new sports journalism of the late 1970s and post Watergate period emphasized the private life of athletes. This demystification of the athlete encouraged fans to become more familiar with players, and in some cases ball players, whose high salaries and life style were common knowledge, were the targets of death threats and hate mail. The salary structure of baseball was especially frustrating to many fans as the American economy contracted during the late 1970s and early 1980s. Pirates outfielder Dave Parker noted that his "hate" mail and threatening telephone calls increased after he signed a 1979 contract extension calling for a salary of over one million dollars a season. Parker sadly related the message of a Chicago man who told the African-American player, "Regardless of all the money you make, you still ain't nuthin' but a stinkin' lousy nigger." To which Parker quipped, "You're right. But the money is good."[26]

The story of Dave Parker demonstrates how the *Sporting News* and columnists like Joe Falls often, in reality, ignored the larger culture about which they so profusely complained. They failed to consider the degree to which the Vietnam War and its atrocities, reported in detail every evening for the network news broadcasts, desensitized Americans to violence and perpetuated an outlook in which a high body count was evidence of victory and success. Also, the vulgarity and obscenity of racism, abandonment of the inner city, and high unemployment rates for minority youth were not the topics of journalistic diatribes. In fact, while issues of race were rarely mentioned in the sporting press, it by no means stretches credibility to read such terms as underprivileged youth and inner city kids, and sometimes stronger descriptions such as hooligan or thug, as euphemisms for young African-American or Latino males. According to the baseball establishment, these were the people who needed to be removed form the ballparks to make them once again safe for family values.

However, the broader historical and sociological implications of violence in American baseball and sport were evident to a growing number of scholars, whose opinions were rarely included in the pages of the *Sporting News*. University of Rochester psychologist Robert Nideffer, in an effort to explain the belligerent reaction of Mets fans to Pete Rose, observed that individuals use sporting events as outlets for frustration in their personal lives. For example, Nideffer asserted, "Someone who has had a hard day at the office or somewhere, who feels the country's falling apart, they can't take it out on the President, so they yell at an umpire or something else."[27]

Other scholars maintained that Nideffer's analysis was too narrow. In an op-ed piece for the *New York Times*, Ross T. Runfola, associate professor of social sciences at Mendaille College in Buffalo, argued that sport violence was a mirror of American culture and society. Concurring with the findings of the National Commission on the Causes and Prevention of Violence, Runfola described America as one of the most historically violent societies in the world. While the National Commission failed to incorporate the domain of sport in its study, the Buffalo professor found ample evidence to support his conclusion that the existing sporting structure in America fostered rather than alleviated violent behavior. Rather than advancing enhanced security and punitive measures, Runfola called for a deeper comprehension of the connections between sport and aggressive actions, writing, "Perhaps the first step in eradicating violence in sport is to work toward a full understanding of the roots of forms of violence in American society. It is, after all, the failure to balance basic goals with the humanistic process that lies at the base of many of the problems both of sport and of American society."

Building upon the arguments of Nideffer, Runfola, and the National Commission on Violence, Stanley Cherin, associate professor at the Boston University School of Medicine, testified before the House Judiciary Subcommittee on Crime, arguing for passage of a proposed sports violence bill. Cherin maintained that American sporting events contributed to a cycle of brutalization, "Wherein seeing violence reduces the impact of that level of violence, raises the general social atmosphere of violence and stimulates the need for more extreme violence." In his testimony, the professor was not calling for the eradication of sport, but rather suggesting that the Congress, media, player associations, and league management structures intervene and establish limits on how far increasing levels of violence will be allowed to go.[28]

While such ideas were an anathema for many in the sporting establishment, who feared federal interference and regulation of their businesses/games, the relationship between sport and American violence was increasingly evident to academics. In the fall of 1982, the University of Toronto sponsored a conference entitled, "War and Violence in North

America." For a panel on sport and violence, Arnold Talentino, a professor at the State University of New York at Cortland, presented a paper equating the territorial acquisitions of manifest destiny with the values of competitive violence found in American sport.[29] However, while historians argued for the centrality of sport and violence to the American experience, violence at the ballpark began to subside in the 1980s and 1990s, with notable exceptions such as the riot following Detroit's victory in the 1984 World Series.

Various explanations may be offered for the decline of spectator violence in American baseball. Certainly, the 1980s, exemplified by the Reagan Presidency, witnessed a conservative backlash to the excesses of the 1960s and 1970s. Others argue that crime rates were reduced by building more prisons and taking a tougher stance against criminals. On the other hand, declining rates of violence may simply be a reflection of an aging population lacking the energy for aggressive behavior. Despite lowered statistical evidence of violent crime, in the 1990s there remains considerable apprehension regarding mass slayings in the schools of America, culminating in the murder of thirteen students and a teacher at Columbine High School in Littleton, Colorado. Although in the Colorado shootings, athletes appeared to be the victims, there has been little analysis of how the "jock" culture of high school and American sport may have played a role in provoking the teenage killers into action. And there has not been enough consideration given to why these acts of mass violence are perpetuated by males rather than females. Does the violent world of male athletics play a role in this process?

But of one thing we may be assured. While the beanball wars continue to rage, the major league baseball park of the 1990s is far different from the monolithic stadiums of the 1960s and 1970s. Baseball's new parks, constructed upon the model of Baltimore's Camden Yards, offer luxury boxes for corporate America, economic revitalization of the urban center, plenty of shopping and food alternatives, along with expensive ticket prices. The "yuppification" of the American baseball environment has supposedly made it safe for families to return to the national pastime. Those minority elements in the inner city, which the National Commission on the Causes and Prevention of Violence credited with rebelling against the inequities of American life, have been removed from the sight of American baseball fans. Attendance of African-Americans at baseball games has declined steadily in recent years. Having weathered labor discontent and a canceled World Series, baseball is back due to the heroics of Sammy Sosa and Mark McGwire, along with upscale ballparks which have once again made the sport secure for women and children. But at what price?

Endnotes

This piece was originally published in Peter Rutkoff, ed., *The Coop-
erstown Symposium on Baseball and American Culture, 1999* (Jefferson,
North Carolina: McFarland & Company, 2000), 115-132. Presented at the
Cooperstown Symposium in 1999, the paper was also honored by the 1999
SABR/MacMillan Award presented at the national SABR convention.

1. A Report Submitted by Daniel Walker of the Chicago Study Team, to the
National Commission on the Causes and Prevention of Violence, *Rights in Conflict:
The Violent Confrontation of Demonstrators and Police in the Parks and Streets of Chicago
During the Week of the Democratic National Convention* (New York: Bantam Books,
1968), v.
2. Rap Brown quoted in Richard Hofstadter and Michael Wallace, eds., *American Violence: A Documentary History* (New York: Alfred A. Knopf, 1972), 39.
3. Richard Maxwell Brown, *No Duty to Retreat: Violence and Values in American History and Society* (New York: Oxford University Press, 1991), i. For other studies on violence see Richard E. Rubenstein, *Rebels in Eden: Mass Political Violence in the
United States* (Boston: Little, Brown and Company, 1970); and Richard Slotkin, *Regen-
eration Through Violence: The Mythology of the American Frontier, 1600-1860* (Mid-
dleton, Connecticut: Wesleyan University Press, 1973).
4. Hugh Davis Graham and Ted Robert Gurr, eds., *Violence in America: Historical and Comparative Perspectives*. 2 vols. (Washington, D. C.: Government Printing Office, 1969); and National Commission on the Causes and Prevention of Violence,
To Establish Justice, To Insure Domestic Tranquility (Washington. D. C.: Government
Printing Office, 1969), xxii.
5. For the Marichal-Roseboro confrontation see *Sporting News,* September 4 and
11, 1965; and Dan Gutman, *Baseball Babylon: From the Black Sox to Pete Rose, the Real
Stories Behind the Scandals that Rocked the Game* (New York: Penguin Books, 1992),
285–288.
6. Larry Stone, "Take Me Out to the Brawlgame: Fights on the Field," *Baseball
Digest,* 58 (August, 1999), 60–66. For a veteran pitcher who enjoyed throwing the
brushback pitch see Kirby Higbe with Martin Quigley, *The High Hard One* (Lincoln:
University of Nebraska Press, 1998).
7. Dick Young, "Brawling a Part of Sport," *Sporting News,* April 25, 1976; and
Melvin Durslag, "The Duster: A Sign of Ignorance," *Sporting News,* May 15, 1976,
newspaper clippings, Violence File, National Baseball Hall of Fame and Museum, Cooperstown, New York.
8. Ira Berkow, "Does Baseball Need Violence?," *Utica Press,* April 4, 1969, newspaper clipping, Violence File, National Baseball Hall of Fame and Museum.
9. Don Atyea, "Blood Sports," *Tampa Tribune,* March 20, 1979, newspaper clipping, Violence File, National Baseball Hall of Fame and Museum. For the Forbes-
Boucha controversy see Parton Keese, "Violence in Sports: What It Could Mean," *New
York Times,* January 26, 1975; and Steve Cady, "Violence in Sports is a Growing Concern," *New York Times,* September 25, 1975.
10. For Lenny Randle's assault upon Frank Lucchesi see *Sporting News,* April 16,
1977, and Melvin Durslag, "Next a Player will Hit a Chaplin," *Sporting News,* April 27,

1977. Also see Bob Addie, *Washington Post*, March 30, 1977, newspaper clipping, Violence File, National Baseball Hall of Fame and Museum; and Bruce Markusen, Senior Researcher Baseball Hall of Fame, "Baseball's Precedent to Latrell Sprewell," unpublished paper, January, 1998.

11. "Pop Bottle Victim Dies," May 15, 1929, newspaper clipping, Violence File, National Baseball Hall of Fame and Museum; and Gutman, *Baseball Babylon*, 316.

12. *Sporting News*, May 9, 1964.

13. Tom Horgan, "Some in Hub Happy Bosox Lost Finale," *Boston Herald*, November 4, 1967, newspaper clipping, Violence File, National Baseball Hall of Fame and Museum.

14. Joe Falls, "Thugs in the Ball Park," *Sporting News*, July 6, 1968; and "Get Rid of Bleacher Bums," *Sporting News*, August 31, 1968. For race relations in Detroit see Thomas J. Sugrue, *The Origins of the Urban Crisis: Race and Inequality in Postwar Detroit* (Princeton, New Jersey: Princeton University Press, 1996).

15. Jim Ogle, "Yanks Map Strategy to Deal with Mob Action," *Sporting News*, May 2, 1970.

16. "What Riot?," *Newsweek* (November 1, 1971), 82; and "Pittsburgh Deflates Riot Report," *New York Times*, October 19, 1971, newspaper clippings, Violence File, National Baseball Hall of Fame and Museum. For the 1968 violence in Pittsburgh see *Pittsburgh Courier*, April 13, 1968.

17. For the 1993 National League Championship Series between the Reds and Mets see *New York Times*, October 9, 1973; Bob Broeg, "Broeg on Baseball," *Sporting News*, October 27, 1973; Red Smith, "Feeney's Peace Brigade Calms Fans in Left Field," *New York Times*, October 9, 1973; "Safety Valve or Time Bomb?," *Sporting News*, October 27, 1973; and Jack Lang, "Mets Clincher Marred by Maniac Mob," *Sporting News*, October 27, 1973, newspaper clippings, Violence File, National Baseball Hall of Fame and Museum.

18. *Sporting News*, April 27, 1974.

19. Joe Heiling, "Cincy Thugs Harass Astros' Injured Watson," *Sporting News*, June 1, 1974.

20. On Cesar Cedeno see Dick Young, "Rowdyism Erupts in Ballparks," *Sporting News*, June 1, 1974; and Joe Heiling, "Cedeno Tragedy Tosses a Cloud over Astros," *Sporting News*, December 29, 1973.

21. For beer night in Cleveland see Russell Schneider, "Incident or Riot?: That Depends on Who's Talking," *Sporting News*, June 22, 1974; and Dick Young, "Young Ideas," *Sporting News*, June 22, 1974.

22. "New Problem: Violence at Ball Parks," June 9, 1974; and "Yankees Halt Free Passes for Youth," June 22, 1976, newspaper clippings, Violence File, Baseball Hall of Fame and Museum.

23. For an amusing account of the White Sox's Anti-Disco Night see John Helyar, *Lords of the Realm: The Real History of Baseball* (New York: Villard Books, 1974), 240–241.

24. Joe Falls, "Thugs in the Ball Park," *Sporting News*, July 6, 1968; "Insults and Obscenities," *Sporting News*, May 16, 1970; "Violence in the Ball Park," *Sporting News*, June 24, 1972; and "Rioting Crowd: It Can Happen in any City," *Sporting News*, June 22, 1974, newspaper clippings, Violence File, National Baseball Hall of Fame and Museum.

25. "Trouble in the Grandstand," *Sporting News*, May 16, 1970; "Problems of Crowd Control," *Sporting News*, July 31, 1971; "Fear Stalks the Stadium," *Sporting News*, October 23, 1976; "Sports Violence... A Disease?," *Sporting News*, December 18, 1976;

and "Get Tough with Unruly Fans," *Sporting News*, May 30, 1981, newspaper clippings, Violence File, National Baseball Hall of Fame and Museum.

26. William Barry Furlong, "When a Fight Breaks Out …," *TV Guide* (December 10, 1977), 30–32; Melvin Durslag, "Temper! Temper!: Why Today's Athletes Keep Losing Their Cool," *TV Guide* (November 10, 1979), 45–46; Terry Taylor, "Spectator Violence," *Utica Observer-Dispatch*, May 10, 1981; and "Death Threats Escalating," *New York Daily News*, October 18, 1981, newspaper clippings, Violence File, National Baseball Hall of Fame and Museum.

27. Steve Monroe, "Why Do Crowds Cause Trouble," *Rochester Democrat*, December 2, 1973, newspaper clipping, Violence File, National Baseball Hall of Fame and Museum.

28. Ross T. Runfola, "Violence in Sports: Reflection of the Violence in American Society," *New York Times*, January 11, 1976; and Stanley Cherin, "Spectators and Violence: A Vicious Cycle Grows," *New York Times*, October 26, 1980.

29. Douglas Martin, "Sports Violence Seen as Ritual Amid the Chaos," *New York Times*, October 26, 1982.

16

Roman Mejias: Houston's First Major League Latin Star

During the 1999 baseball season, businessman and owner of the Houston Astros Drayton McLane was involved in a controversy with the Texas Hispanic community. According to Marco Comancho, general manager of KTMD Television and a subsidiary of the Telemundo Group, and Rod Rodriguez, the station's sales manager, McLane made disparaging and belittling comments regarding Mexicans and Mexican-Americans shortly before a dinner honoring the businessman with the Houston Advertising Federation's Trailblazer Award for service to the community. An outraged McLane vehemently denied having uttered any remarks which might be construed as racist.

Following an investigation of the incident, Telemundo's chief executive, Roland Hernandez, apologized to McLane, stating that he found no evidence of racially-biased comments being made by the baseball owner. In a prepared statement, a relieved McLane insisted, "Having spent a lifetime honoring the values of integrity and honesty, this episode has been unsettling. Despite a rush to judgment by some, this action by Telemundo, hopefully, will help to speed the healing process."[1]

But if McLane devoted his life to the values of integrity, honesty, and community service, why were so many in the Hispanic community so quick to question the baseball executive's motives? The answer to this question may lie in the troubling history of race relations in the Lone Star state of Texas, where, in the words of Carey McWilliams, "Anglos have always been 'gringos' to the Hispanos while Hispanos have been 'greasers' to the Anglos." In *Occupied America: A History of Chicanos,* Rodolfo Acuna asserts that racial animosities in Texas are a result of Anglo economic domination of the Mexican community enforced by official state violence, such as that perpetuated by the Texas Rangers, an organization so much admired by the dean of Texas historians, Walter Prescott Webb. Chicano activists, such as Jose' Angel Gutierrez, argue that education in Texas is presented from an Anglo perspective, ignoring the fact that "the land of the West and Southwest, beginning with Texas, was stolen from Mexicans." While less confrontational and more scholarly in its approach, David Montejano's study of Anglos and Mexicans in Texas, which received the 1988 Frederick Jackson Turner Award from the American Historical Association, maintains that the history of Texas has been Anglo economic control perpetuated by cultural, political, and social Jim Crow legislation, whose hegemony has been challenged by the Chicano civil rights movement.[2]

It is within this historical context that the alleged racist remarks of Astros owner McLane must be placed. While the Houston organization has produced talented Latin players such as José Cruz and Joaquin Andujar, it should be noted that Astros management, unlike the Los Angeles Dodgers with the marketing and pitching success of Fernando Valenzuela, has tended to maintain an Anglo identity; building the team around such stars as Nolan Ryan, Jeff Bagwell, and Craig Biggio. While it is impossible to deny the athletic achievement of these ball players, the failure to develop and especially market more Latin star players flies in the face of Southwestern demographics. From a 1980 base of 8.7 million people, the Mexican-origin population of the United States grew by 4.7 million to a 1990 total of 13.4 million; a 54 percent intercensal increase. And the Mexican-origin people constitute approximately two-thirds of Latins, who, in turn, comprise over 8 percent of the United States population. Nearly 75 percent of all Mexican-origin persons live in California and Texas, both of whom have populations in excess of 25 percent Mexican roots.[3] Yet, the major league baseball establishment in Houston has historically failed to capitalize on these demographics by consistently developing and marketing Latin talent. While perhaps operating on an unconscious level, this policy, nevertheless, may be reflective of the city's conservative to reactionary political traditions. According to Don E. Carlton, the Houston establishment's fears of growing diversity in the city produced a right-wing backlash which labeled efforts at city planning and zoning as communist plots. City biographer George Fuermann argues that Houston has been dominated by merchants and businessmen, whose goals have been material, rather than altruistic, humanitarian, or community-oriented. In fact, Houston's greatest claim to fame, embodied in the hyperbole of the Astrodome as the ninth wonder of the world, may be as the most air-conditioned city in the world. According to city historian David G. McComb, "There is nothing closer to hell in modern American than to be caught after a rain in a Houston traffic jam in an unair-conditioned car. It is possible, at that moment, to appreciate the plight of a steamed clam, and the situation does nothing to improve human temperament." The Houston way of coping with this environment has been to build huge structures of steel and concrete, while paying little attention to zoning and creation of open space.[4]

But while progressive in providing air-conditioned structures, Houston tends to maintain a more reactionary political framework. Francisco A. Rosales and Barry J. Kaplan maintain nineteenth-century values have retained a stronghold in Houston, arguing, "Individualism, opportunity, capitalism, and limited government, virtual dogma in American government before the 1929 crash, have remained sacred in Houston."[5]

Thus, when major league baseball came to Houston in 1962, the city's baseball fathers elected to fashion the team's identity and logo with the Colt .45; the gun that tamed the West and, by implication, the Mexican and Native American populations, making way for the progress of Anglo civilization.[6] While the smoking Colt .45 logo embraced the symbolic values of nineteenth-century Texas, the Houston franchise's handling of its first Latin star, Cuban-born Roman Mejias, demonstrated a lack of sensitivity and appreciation for the potential of its Spanish-speaking community. Drafted out of the Pittsburgh Pirates organization, Mejias would lead the fledgling Houston team in home runs and runs batted in, while hitting for a .286 average. Following his banner year in Houston, Mejias was traded to the Boston Red Sox for singles-hitting Pete Runnels, an Anglo who hailed from nearby Pasadena, Texas. The story of Roman Mejias suggests that Houston management failed to market and develop Mejias as a star, establishing a club tradition of extolling Anglo players, while eschewing the potential of its Latin community and falling into the pattern of racial segregation which has characterized the troubled history of race relations in the Lone Star state.[7]

Roman Mejias was born August 9, 1932 (although some accounts give his birth date as 1930, making the outfielder thirty-two rather than thirty when he enjoyed his first major league baseball season with the Houston Colt .45s) in Las Villas, Cuba, where he was working in a sugar cane field in 1953 when signed to a major league contract by Hall of Famer George Sisler, who was serving as a scout for the Pittsburgh Pirates.[8] Mejias continued to play winter ball in Cuba through the 1960 season, establishing himself as a star of Cuban baseball. However, the diplomatic and economic pressures of the evolving Cold War confrontation between the

United States and Fidel Castro led Mejias in 1961 to become separated from his family in Cuba. While unable to bring his family to the United States, Mejias did embody for Americans the best of Cuban baseball, described by Roberto Gonzalez Echevarria as "conservative, highly strategic," relying upon the "inside" baseball game of bunting and "slapping a grounder past a charging infielder."[9]

Mejias attained considerable success in the Pirate minor league chain. In 1954, the Cuban-born outfielder hit in fifty-four straight games, finishing with a batting average of .354 for Waco of the Class B Big State League. These minor league credentials led to Mejias spending portions of the 1955 and 1956-1961 baseball seasons with the Pirates. But he was never able to crack the starting Pittsburgh outfield of Bob Skinner, Bill Virdon, and Roberto Clemente. Although Mejias did club three home runs in one game at San Francisco during the 1958 season. The next day, however, he was back on the Pittsburgh bench. Mejias's big baseball break had seemingly arrived when he was plucked from the Pirates for $75,000 by the Houston Colt .45s in the 1962 expansion player draft.

However, this brief survey of Mejias's career in the Pittsburgh minor league farm chain hardly does justice to the racial and cultural obstacles confronting the gifted young athlete. First, Mejias was classified as a "Cuban Negro," enduring the racial taunts black ball players were continuing to receive in minor league ballparks of the American Southwest and South.[10] As Peter C. Bjarkman notes in his history of Latin American baseball, "Dark-skinned Caribbean ballplayers were noteworthy during the 1950s and only become commonplace in the 1980s and 1990s."[11] In addition to the issue of race, the Spanish-speaking Mejias was confronted with the English language barrier. Southern segregation forced dark-skinned Latin players to live apart from the rest of the team, and Mejias arrived in the United States unable to speak a word of English. He later recalled:

> I never expec' to be so lonely in the U. S. I couldn't eat.... I thought I would have to go back to Cuba for food. Finally, we learn to go into eating place and we go back in kitchen and point with fingers—thees, thees, thees (sic). After while, somebody teach me to say ham and eggs and fried chicken, and I eat that for a long time.[12]

Mejias's fears that he would not be able to eat in the United States corresponds well with Samuel O. Regalado's characterization of Latin major league ball players as having a special hunger. According to Regalado, competition on America's baseball diamonds carried crucial social and economic implications for Latin players:

> Baseball was a path out of poverty; it helped to bring distinction to their
> homelands; it was a means to ease the pain and suffering of kinfolk and
> compatriots; and it provided a sliver of hope to many younger Latins who
> might otherwise have envisioned a dim future. Their determination to
> succeed in the face of an unwelcoming culture reveals the human spirit
> of Latin players. For they, unlike so many other newcomers, faced these
> barriers alone, without the aid of support groups. And it was this will-
> ingness to break through cultural roadblocks that made their hunger
> "special."[13]

When the fledgling Colt .45s drafted Mejias and awarded him the
starting right field position, the native Cuban was determined to cash in
on his opportunity. During spring training, Mejias's slugging carried the
Houston franchise to the championship of the Arizona Cactus League,
Mejias completed the spring with five home runs and seventeen runs batted in. And the Houston power hitter continued his onslaught against big
league pitching by clubbing two three-run home runs in support of former Yankee pitcher and American League Most Valuable Player Bobby
Shantz's 11-2 opening day win against the Chicago Cubs in Colt Stadium.
The *Houston Chronicle* described the Mejias home runs as a "double-barreled salute" to the introduction of major league baseball "in the land of
the Alamo." Any irony that this shot was fired by a Latin ball player was
lost upon *Chronicle* sports editor Dick Peebles, who focused upon Shantz's
contribution to the opening day victory. Nevertheless, Peebles did not
entirely ignore Mejias, commenting that if the outfielder kept up the pace
of opening day, he would hit 324 home runs. The editor, in a rather stereotypical fashion, noted that Mejias's response to the ridiculous prediction
was a "toothy-grin."[14]

Stereotyping aside, Houstonians celebrated their new found hitting
star and a three game sweep of the Cubs to begin their inaugural campaign. However, behind these accolades, there were troubling signs that
Houston management and many of their fans were not prepared to
embrace Latins and racial toleration into the Texas fold. Mejias was the
only Latin player on the team, while Jim Pendleton, also drafted from the
Pirate organization, was the team's sole African-American player, until
shortstop J. C. Hartman was recalled from the minors at mid season.
Unlike Mejias, Pendleton got off to a slow start at the plate in 1962 and
was the object of fan abuse, which included racial slurs. A taciturn Pendleton attempted to minimize the taunts, insisting, "I turn a deaf ear, that's
the best way."[15]

And sensitivity to Mejias's Cuban heritage was certainly lacking in a
featured *Houston Chronicle* article on Colt .45s pitching Coach Cot Deal's

exploits in Cuba as the Batista regime was falling to the revolution led by Fidel Castro. According to Deal's account, a July, 1959 game between the Rochester Red Wings, whom the Houston coach was managing at the time, and Havana Sugar Kings was marred by soldiers firing bullets into the air in support of their "bearded leader." The game was suspended when Rochester's player-coach Frank Verdi and Havana's shortstop Leo Cardenas were wounded by stray bullets. Deal observed that he was lucky, for he had been ejected from the game for disputing an umpire's decision and was in the clubhouse when the shooting commenced. Demonstrating a lack of cultural and historical understanding, Deal attributed the violence to the "emotional Latin temperament." Engaging in cultural stereotypes, which would long plague Latin players in the United States, the Houston coach described the Cuban baseball fan as governed by unchecked emotion: "When his team loses he sulks the long day through. When it wins, he's the happiest fella."[16] It apparently never occurred to Deal and the Houston press that their Cuban-born right fielder might find such racial commentary offensive.

Cuban pitcher Manuel Montejo, who was attempting to win a spot on the Colts staff after being obtained in a trade with the Detroit Tigers organization, was also the object of stereotyping by the Houston management and press. Manager Harry Craft thought the Cuban might help the club if he could control his temper. On the other hand, Zarko Franks of the *Chronicle* emphasized the pitcher's enthusiasm and poked fun at continuing language difficulties, writing, "The Cuban tiger and English harmonize like the calico dog and the gingham cat. Let's just say that Senor Montejo hacks his way through the word jungle after four years in this country." However, when the Colts broke their spring training camp in Apache Junction, Arizona, Montejo was returned to the minor leagues; leaving Mejias as the only Latin on the major league roster.[17]

And this lack of sensitivity to Cubans was also carried over into the Houston management's negligence in cultivating the local Latin market of Mexican-Americans as well as that of neighboring Mexico. Certainly, the Houston franchise was not unaware of the importance of marketing, for the club had hired Mrs. Ginna Pace as a publicist to lure female fans to Colt Stadium. Writing for the *Sporting News,* and reflecting the gender-biased journalism of the time period, Clark Nealon described Pace as an "attractive, imaginative blonde with a journalistic background and rare enthusiasm for baseball," who would organize radio spots, fashion shows, and baseball clinics for female fans. Houston's Executive Vice-President George Kirksey insisted that the club's success was dependent upon attracting families and mothers, observing, "Even our stadium was built to appeal to the women. The colors are turquoise, chartreuse, and Rio Grande orange, hues that would dress up a rainbow."[18]

However, marketing efforts at broadening the team's ethnic appeal seemed beyond the horizon of what Houston management perceived as an aggressive promotional and publicity strategy. For example, Colt Vice-President Kirksey estimated that if the club drew one million spectators, then approximately sixteen million dollars would be generated for the Houston economy. Kirksey predicted that the Colts would draw support from Texas, New Mexico, Oklahoma, Colorado, Arkansas, Mississippi, and Louisiana. Missing from the executive's equation was any consideration of Mexico as an economic base. In fact, officials expressed surprise that a survey of the stadium's parking lot included vehicles from Mexico. And when the Colts did reach out to Mexico with Spanish-language radio broadcasts and press tours to Monterey, the *Houston Chronicle's* Morris Frank resorted to racial caricature when he described the use of Spanish by approximately two-hundred "senors and senoras" from "good ole' Mexico."[19] The Houston baseball establishment seemed more comfortable perpetuating the Western myth of the cowboy conquering the savage frontier, for the Colts were required to don traveling Western style outfits, featuring wide-brimmed Texas hats, bright blue suits, orange accessories, and boots.[20]

However, symbols of Western mythology extolling the Anglo taming of the frontier and lack of appreciation for Latin culture by the Colt establishment had little impact upon Mejias, who continued to wreck havoc upon National League pitchers during the early months of the 1962 season. By May 7, Mejias had homered seven times and was being touted by the press as Houston's answer to such National League sluggers as the San Francisco Giants Willie Mays and Orlando Cepeda. And even these hitting stars were shut down on May 11 by the Colts Dick "Turk" Farrell, who was emerging as the team's pitching leader and a challenger to Mejias's stature as Houston's most outstanding player.[21]

Meanwhile, the Colts right fielder continued to dominate senior circuit pitching, entering June with eleven home runs and leading the team in hits, runs batted in, runs, and batting average (.297). Mejias was achieving these power figures in a home ballpark whose dimensions were less than conducive to the home run. The Colt .45s played in a temporary structure, Colt Stadium, with a seating capacity of 32,000 and located on the same lot as the projected Harris County domed stadium. The playing dimensions of Colt Stadium were cavernous, with 360 feet down the foul lines, 420 feet in center, and 395 feet in the left and right power alleys. In jest, the *Sporting News* reported, "Our scouts tell us that Colt Stadium extends from the Pecos on the west to the Sabine on the east, and from the Red River on the north to the Gulf of Mexico on the south. The Gulf side is the comparatively short fence because even Texas peters out in this southerly direction."[22]

With seven out of his first eleven home runs coming in Colt Stadium, accolades were forthcoming for the Cuban outfielder, although media treatments of Mejias were still framed through the lens of ethnicity. Regalado's perception of the special hunger of Latin players was also evident in press accounts of Mejias's meteoric rise in the 1962 season, although many of these stories developed the metaphor of hunger on a quite literal level. Referring to Mejias's language difficulties in being able to order food during his early days in the United States, reporter Mickey Herskowitz wrote in the *Sporting News* that the outfielder, who had a bit of the "gaucho" in him, had emerged as, "Houston's ham, eggs, bread, butter, milk, and poultry man." But in reality, Mejias was not necessarily in a position to be purchasing too many heavy cholesterol breakfast foods. In a player profile for the *Houston Chronicle*, Zarko Franks reported that the "handsome Cuban" was earning only $12,500 annually, and the team's most valuable player was far from being the highest paid Colt .45. And in the era of the strict reserve clause and weak players' union, Mejias could hardly expect any mid-season correction to his contract. Franks observed that Mejias was succeeding in Houston despite personal problems. His wife and two young children remained in Cuba, and Mejias expressed concern for their well being, exclaiming, "There is not much food there, and I worry if they are eating properly."[23]

Despite salary and family concerns, Mejias remained the model minority, refusing to publicly complain about his problems. A sense of modesty, along with his prolific hitting, made Mejias a fan favorite in Houston. After having only hit seventeen home runs in part of six seasons with the Pirates, Mejias found it difficult to account for his newly discovered power. He told Franks, "I am more surprised than anyone else that I hit the long ball. In spring, I worked hard just to be patient and wait for the ball. I hit with my wrists and arms only. Before I was a line drive hitter. Not a home run hitter. The fences were a thousand miles away. Today, none of the fences are too far away. I think of the home run more because I know I can hit the ball far." In addition to his work ethic, Mejias attributed his success to clean living. Claiming that his only vice was an occasional Cuban cigar, the athlete maintained, "Even if you are strong, sometimes you can not do your work on the baseball field. So how can you hope to do it if you drink too much and don't sleep enough."[24]

While salary issues remained and Mejias was unsuccessful in getting his family out of Cuba, he continued to make the most out of his opportunity to play every day in Houston. By July 3, when National League All-Star rosters were announced, Cincinnati Reds manager Fred Hutchinson failed to select Mejias to the squad despite the fact that the Houston player was third in the National League in home runs with nineteen, while driving in forty-eight runs and hitting for a .311 batting average. The All-Star outfield for the National League, as elected by the players, included Tommy Davis of the Los Angeles Dodgers, Willie Mays of the San Francisco Giants, and Roberto Clemente of the Pittsburgh Pirates. Instead of Mejias, Hutchinson picked Dick Farrell as Houston's representative to the All-Star team. Used both as a starter and reliever, Farrell had a record of five wins and eight losses, while saving five games, striking out ninety batters, and compiling an earned run average of 2.48. Despite his more than respectable marks for an expansion ball club, Farrell expressed dismay that was he was picked over Mejias. On the other hand, Mejias refused to raise issues of racial discrimination in the selection process and, while disappointed by player balloting and Hutchinson's decision to tap the New York Mets Richie Ashburn and Phillies Johnny Callison as reserve outfielders, stated, "How do you like dot (sic)? Well, nothing to do but jus' keep swinging."[25]

But Mejias did not keep swinging as effectively during the second half of the 1962 season. Slowed by nagging injuries and the adjustment of National League pitchers, Mejias's power numbers declined. Meanwhile, Farrell emerged as Houston's featured player. Born in the Boston suburb of Brookline in 1934 and the son of Irish immigrants, Farrell had already established a reputation for being a prankster and heavy drinker as a member of the Philadelphia Phillies notorious Dalton Gang. His good ole' boy persona appeared a perfect match for a team whose identity was forged in the image of a gun taming the Texas frontier. In fact, Farrell may have taken this image too literally. Farrell was rumored to have reported to the Colts spring training camp with a .22 caliber pistol, which he carried with him on the two mile walk from the team's hotel to the training facilities at Geronimo Park. Along the way, he allegedly shot at beer bottles, rabbits, and rattlesnakes. When asked about his favorite targets, Farrell quipped, "Anything shootable that don't shoot back." Yet, to go along with his reputation as a character, Farrell had a good fast ball and a strong competitive streak (which sometimes included use of the illegal spit ball pitch).[26]

During the baseball dog days of July and August, the hard throwing and partying Anglo, Farrell, became the darling of the Colt fans and media, while the slumping Latin, Mejias, received generally respectful but certainly reduced attention. (Moving away from Latin stereotypes, but keeping a Latin focus, the *Houston Chronicle* often referred to Mejias as "the noblest Roman of them all.") This point is well documented by the *Houston Chronicle's* coverage of a July 20 contest in which the Colts defeated the St. Louis Cardinals by a 4-3 margin. Mejias singled in the bottom of the ninth with the bases loaded and two out, propelling Houston from defeat to victory with one swing of the bat. Yet, newspaper coverage focused upon Farrell who struck out twelve Cardinals in the complete game victory. According to Colts manager Harry Craft, Farrell's fast ball was "hopping like bunny cottontail," and the right-hander's curve ball was "exploding." Interviewed after the game, Farrell exclaimed, "This is the biggest charge I ever got out of winning a game. When Mejias hit that single with the bases loaded in the ninth to win the game, I didn't know who to hug. I was so happy." A logical choice for embracing would have been Mejias, yet in the post game comments of Craft, as reported by the *Chronicle,* there was no mention of the Cuban player. The newspaper account of the game also omitted any interview with the game's hitting star.[27]

Talk of the Colts finishing in the first division and Mejias attaining thirty to forty home runs faded in the hot Texas sun of August and September, but the club and its Latin star completed the season with respectable numbers. While many baseball people had predicted a last place finish for the Colts, the team finished in eighth place, completing the season with a record of sixty-four wins and ninety-six defeats. While completing the season thirty-six games out of first and sixteen out of seventh place, the Colts were six games ahead of the ninth-place Chicago Cubs and twenty-four wins in front of their expansion team rivals the New York Mets, who had compiled a record of just forty wins against one-hundred-and-twenty losses. The Colts finished sixth in National League attendance, drawing 924, 456 fans and falling just short of their goal of one million, which had been negated by a team tailspin in July and August along with the humid Houston climate. The Colts had defeated the Mets in the attendance battle as well, out drawing the New York club by 1,926 spectators. Vice-President Kirksey summed up the year, "Most of our objectives were realized. We did not lose 100 games or finish last. We licked our expansion twin, the Mets, and out drew them at the box office. We have a foundation to build on, and by blending upcoming players in with the 1962 team, we should begin the long, hard climb up the National League ladder."[28]

But would the club's first Latin star Roman Mejias be part of management's elusive plan to climb the National League ladder and claim a pennant. Manger Harry Craft announced that any Houston player, including Turk Farrell, was expendable in an off-season deal if the transaction would improve the team's prospects. The Colts planned to build around such prospects as twenty-four year old third-baseman Bob Aspromonte.

And when the *Chronicle's* sports editor Dick Peebles compiled a review of Colt highlights for the inaugural campaign, the contributions of Roman Mejias were conspicuously missing.[29] While Mejias led the Colts in home runs (24), runs batted in (76), and batting average (.286), nagging injuries had contributed to a late season slump, and Mejias hit only six home runs during the months of July, August, and September.

Thus, it was not a total surprise when Mejias was traded after the 1962 season. But the transaction was hardly part of a youth movement by Houston management. Mejias was dealt to the Boston Red Sox, where the right-handed hitter could take advantage of Fenway Park's inviting Green Monster in left field, in exchange for American League batting champion Pete Runnels. While Mejias was either thirty or thirty-two, depending upon which birthday one chose to count, there was no doubt as to Runnels's rather advanced baseball age of thirty-five. Also, Runnels had little to offer in terms of speed and power, hitting only ten home runs and driving in sixty-one runs for the 1962 campaign. So why did Houston make the trade?

Marketing may be part of the answer. While Houston executives apparently saw little potential in exploiting the Mexican-American market in Texas by signing talent from the Mexican League or celebrating a Spanish-speaking star such as Mejias, they were very interested in acquiring Runnels, who was a native of Lufkin, Texas and resided in the Houston suburb of Pasadena. According to Houston sportswriter Clark Nealon, who filed a piece for the *Sporting News* on the trade, "Acquisition of Runnels ended a two year Colt effort to land the batting star who starred in Southeast Texas as a football and basketball standout at Lufkin High, left Rice University to seek a baseball career and now is the top sports resident of suburban Pasadena."[30]

In his history of the Houston Colts, Robert Reed illustrates the role played by racial stereotypes in the controversial trade, arguing that Houston General Manager Paul Richards was convinced that the "affable Cuban" was thirty-nine years of age rather than the official thirty. But the transaction was risky because Mejias had "become somewhat of a fan favorite for his happy-go-lucky nature and occasionally unintentionally humorous turn of a phrase." Writing in 1999, Reed, whose training is in journalism, seemed to have no problem with perpetuating the image of the smiling, but somewhat lackadaisical, Latin ball player.[31]

As for Mejias, he was wished the best of luck by his former manager, Craft, who insisted, "He is a fine competitor. He carried us for the first two months of the season.... There were two reasons for his slump. He had played winter ball and started to run out of gas. Then he got hurt, missed a couple of weeks and when he got back into the lineup he couldn't generate the steam he had before."[32] However, Craft failed to mention Mejias's growing concerns regarding his family in Cuba. Distractions regarding the fourteen month separation from his wife and two children as weighing upon the Cuban's performance appeared to be of little concern to Houston management.

On the other hand, following the acquisition of Mejias, Red Sox owner Tom Yawkey instructed his front office to spare no expense in laboring for the reunion of the ball player with his family. Red Sox management worked with the State Department and Red Cross to, in the overwrought Cold War rhetoric of reporter Hy Hurwitz, "ransom the outfielder's brood from the clutches of Castroism." Accordingly, on the evening of March 16, 1963, Roman Mejias's spring training in Phoenix was interrupted with the arrival of his wife, Nicholosa; their twelve-year-old daughter Rafaela and ten-year-old son José; and the athlete's sisters, Esperosa and Santa. Following this joyous reunion, Mejias expressed his appreciation for the Red Sox organization, exclaiming, "Now, I don't have to worry any more, and I can't thank the Red Sox enough. I want to do everything possible for the Red Sox, and I hope very soon I'll be helping them win the pennant."[33]

However, baseball reality failed to mirror the happiness of the Mejias family reunion. For, like so many before and after him, Mejias was unable to help the Red Sox win a pennant and World Series. By August, 1963, Mejias was hitting an anemic .233, with only nine home runs and thirty-one runs driven in, and sitting on the Boston bench. While Mejias may have placed too much pressure on himself to show his appreciation for the Red Sox, George Vecsey argued that Mejias was another victim of Fenway Park's fabled Green Monster. Only 315 feet from home plate, Fenway's left field wall is thirty-seven feet high and represents a cozy target for powerful right-handed batters. Mejias assured the Red Sox organization that he "could hit it every time." But like many before him, in his eagerness to reach the Green Monster, Mejias was trying to pull every outside pitch to left; hitting pop ups and weak ground balls to shortstop. While pledging to amend his aggressive style and "just try to go with the pitch," Mejias was never able to regain the glory days of his 1962 campaign with the Houston Colts.[34]

After completing the 1963 season with eleven home runs, Mejias's marks declined even more during his second season in Boston, with a batting average of.238, two home runs, and four runs driven in. Although he continued to play minor league ball for several more seasons, Mejias's major league baseball career was over. He had slugged twenty-four of his fifty-four major league home runs during his 1962 season in the sun with the Houston Colts. However, the Cuban outfielder might take solace from the fact that Pete Runnels's return to his native Texas did little for his career. In 1963, Runnels was only able to hit for a .253 average with two home runs. After beginning the 1964 campaign with a .196 batting mark, Runnels retired from the game.[35]

What conclusions may one draw from this examination of Roman Mejias and the Houston Colt .45s during the 1962 season? The way Mejias was handled by the Houston management and media did little to alleviate the long-standing animosity and distrust between Anglo and Mexican in Texas. While Mejias was a Cuban of African ancestry, there was little recognition by the Houston baseball establishment regarding the potential of a Latin market which might have been reached by publicizing the exploits of the club's first Spanish-speaking power hitter. Instead, the Cuban's struggles with the English language were often a topic of amusement for the Houston press. Although in this regard, perhaps Houston was reflective of organized baseball in general. For example, in a November 3, 1962 editorial, the *Sporting News* called for Latin ball players to refrain from playing winter ball in Latin America, and, instead, spend the time learning English. The paper concluded that even though many Hispanic players "have spent several summers in this country, some of them still barely speak the language. As a result, there is a widespread tendency in baseball to blame the so-called language barrier for collisions and other misplays."[36]

But in any language, Mejias carried the Houston ball club for the first half of the 1962 season, but as he was slowed by injuries and worries, while being snubbed by the All-Star selection process, the Houston baseball establishment focused its attention upon such Anglo stars as Dick Farrell and Bob Aspromonte. The long separation from his family appeared to be of little concern to Houston management, for the Red Sox were able to arrange a Mejias family reunion within four months. Mejias's thanks for his stellar contributions to the inaugural campaign of major league baseball in Houston was to be traded for an aging Anglo and native Texan. The story of Roman Mejias's 1962 season in Houston tends to reinforce the legacy of racial exploitation and suspicion in the Lone Star state. And over the years, the Houston baseball establishment has done little to alleviate this sense of mistrust, organizing and marketing the team around such Anglo stars as Ryan, Biggio, and Bagwell, who despite their achievements have never been able to lead the Houston franchise to a National League pennant. It is within this historical context that the rush to judgment by many within the Hispanic community regarding allegations of racism against Astros owner Drayton McLane must be understood.

Endnotes

Initially presented at the 2000 meeting of the North American Society for Sport History, this paper was originally published in *Nine: A Journal of Baseball History & Culture*, 10:1 (2001), 73-92.

1. For an account of the controversy between Drayton McLane and representatives from KTMD-TV see *New York Times*, July 13, 1999.
2. For race relations in Texas between Mexican-Americans and Anglos see Carey McWilliams, updated by Matt S. Meier, *North From Mexico: The Spanish-Speaking People of the United States* (New York: Praeger, 1990), 112; Rudolfo Acuna, *Occupied America: A History of Chicanos* (New York: HarperCollins, 1988), 40–41; José Angel Gutierrez, *The Making of a Chicano Militant: Lessons from Cristal* (Madison: The University of Wisconsin Press, 1998), 16–17; Armando Navarro, *The Cristal Experiment: A Chicano Struggle for Community Control* (Madison: The University of Wisconsin Press, 1998); and David Montejano, *Anglos and Mexicans in the Making of Texas, 1836-1986* (Austin: The University of Texas Press, 1987).
3. Susan Gonzalez Baker, "Demographic Trends in the Chicano/a Population: Policy Implications for the Twenty-First Century," in David R. Maciel and Isidro D. Ortiz, *Chicanos/Chicanas at the Crossroads: Social. Economic, and Political Change* (Tucson: University of Arizona Press, 1996), 6–23.
4. For the history of Houston, see Don E. Carlton, *Red Scare: Right-wing Hysteria, Fifties Fanaticism, and Their Legacy in Texas* (Austin: Texas Monthly Press, 1985); George Fuermann, *Houston: The Once and Future City* (Garden City, N. Y.: Doubleday, 1971); and David G. McComb, *Houston: A History* (Austin: University of Texas Press), 192.
5. Francisco A. Rosales and Barry J. Kaplan, eds., *Houston: A Twentieth Century Urban Frontier* (Port Washington, N. Y.: Associated Faculty Press, 1983), 3.
6. For the efforts to bring major league baseball to Houston see Clark Nealon, Robert Nottebart, Stanley Siegel, and James Tinsley, "The Campaign for Major League Baseball in Houston," *The Houston Review,* 7 (1985), 3–46; Ron Briley, "The Houston Colt .45s: The Other Expansion Team of 1962," *East Texas Historical Journal*, 27 (1994), 59–74; and Robert Reed, *A Six-Gun Salute: An Illustrated History of the Houston Colt .45s* (Houston: Lone Star Books, 1999). For the New Western history see Patricia Nelson Limerick, *The Legacy of Conquest: The Unbroken Past of the American West* (New York: Norton, 1987); and Richard White, *"It's Your Misfortune and None of My Own": A New History of the American West* (Norman: University of Oklahoma Press, 1991).
7. Many thought the Houston Astros (which replaced the Colt .45s logo following the 1964 season) had found their Latin star with Cesar Cedeno. However, after a December, 1973 incident in which a young woman in the Dominican Republic was killed while allegedly playing with Cedeno's gun, the young player never reached his early potential, and in 1981 the Astros traded Cedeno to the Cincinnati Reds.
8. For biographical sketches of Roman Mejias see Larry Moffi and Jonathan Kronstadt, *Crossing the Line: Black Major Leaguers, 1947-1959* (Jefferson, North Carolina: McFarland & Company, Inc., 1994), 138–139; and Roman Mejias File, Baseball Hall of Fame Museum and Library, Cooperstown, New York.
9. Roberto Gonzalez Echevarria, *The Pride of Havana: A History of Cuban Base-*

ball (New York: Oxford University Press, 1999), 7. For Mejias's career in Cuban baseball see Echevarria, *Pride of Havana,* 319, 323, 328, 330, and 342.

10. For issues of segregation in minor league baseball see Bruce Adelson, *Brushing Back Jim Crow: The Integration of Minor-League Baseball in the American South* (Charlottesville: University of Virginia Press, 1999).

11. Peter C. Bjarkman, *Baseball with a Latin Beat: A History of the Latin American Game* (Jefferson, North Carolina: McFarland & Company, Inc., 1994), 6. For other works on Latin American baseball see Alan M. Klein, *Sugarball: The American Game and the Dominican Dream* (New Haven, Connecticut: Yale University Press, 1991); and Rob Ruck, *The Tropic of Baseball: Baseball in the Dominican Republic* (Westport, Connecticut: Meckler, 1991).

12. Mickey Herskowitz, ".45s Charge Puny Attack with Missile Man Mejias," *Sporting News,* June 2, 1962, clipping from Roman Mejias File, Baseball Hall of Fame Museum and Library.

13. Samuel 0. Regalado, *Viva Baseball: Latin Major Leaguers and Their Special Hunger* (Urbana: University of Illinois Press, 1998), xiv.

14. *Sporting News,* April 18, 1962, clipping from Roman Mejias File, Baseball Hall of Fame Museum and Library; and *Houston Chronicle,* April 11, 1962.

15. *Houston Chronicle,* April 15, 1962. For additional background information on Jim Pendleton see Moffi and Kronstadt, *Crossing the Line,* 99–100; and William B. Furlong, "A Negro Ballplayer's Life Today," *Sport,* 33 (May , 1962), 38–39.

16. *Houston Chronicle,* March 21, 1962.

17. Zarko Franks, "Montejo a Happy Man But Doesn't Like to Lose," *Houston Chronicle,* March 21, 1962.

18. Clark Nealon, "Colts Will Lasso Gal Fans— Hire Woman Publicist," *Sporting News,* April 4, 1962.

19. *Houston Chronicle,* April 8, 1962; *Sporting News,* May 23, 1962; and Morris Frank, "200 Fans from Mexico Boiled at Colt Stadium," *Houston Chronicle,* June 11, 1962.

20. For the Colt .45s traveling Western outfits and player complaints regarding the outlandish costumes see *Sporting News,* May 23, 1962; and *Houston Chronicle,* June 1, 2, 3, and 4, 1962.

21. *Houston Chronicle,* May 7 and 12, 1962.

22. For Colt Stadium see *Sporting News,* January 10 and February 21, 1962; and *Houston Chronicle,* January 11 and 25, 1962.

23. Mickey Herskowitz, ".45s Charge Puny Attack with Missile Man Mejias," *Sporting News,* June 2, 1962, clipping from Roman Mejias File, Baseball Hall of Fame Museum and Library; and Zarko Franks, "Mejias's Season of Milk, Honey?," *Houston Chronicle,* May 30, 1962.

24. Franks, "Mejias's Season," *Houston Chronicle,* May 30, 1962.

25. *Houston Chronicle,* June 30, 1962; *Sporting News,* July 14, 1962; and Reed, *Six-Gun Salute,* 112–113.

26. For background information on Dick Farrell see Clark Nealon, "Farrell Rated Double-Barreled Dilly by .45's," *Sporting News,* November 3, 1962; and Reed, *Six-Gun Salute,* 126–136.

27. *Houston Chronicle,* July 21, 1962.

28. *Sporting News,* October 13, 1962; and *Houston Chronicle,* October 1 and 4, 1962.

29. *Houston Chronicle,* August 28 and September 24, 1962.

30. For the Mejias and Runnels trade see *New York Times,* November 26, 1962,

clipping from Roman Mejias File, Baseball Hall of Fame Museum and Library; and *Sporting News*, December 8, 1962.

31. Reed, *Six-Gun Salute*, 140.

32. *Sporting News*, March 3, 1963, clipping from Roman Mejias File, Baseball Hall of Fame Museum and Library.

33. Hy Hurwitz, "Red Sox Worked to Rescue Mejias's Family From Cuba," *Sporting News*, March 30, 1963, clipping from Roman Mejias File, Baseball Hall of Fame Museum and Library.

34. George Vecsey, "Boston's Dream Wall is Really a Nightmare," July 13, 1963, clipping from Roman Mejias File, Baseball Hall of Fame Museum and Library.

35. Baseball statistics from John Thorne and Pete Palmer, eds., *Total Baseball: The Ultimate Encyclopedia of Baseball* (New York: HarperPerennial, 1993).

36. "English Course for Latins," *Sporting News*, November 3, 1962.

17

Houston's Latin Star Cesar Cedeno and Death in the Dominican Republic: The Troubled Legacy of Race Relations in the Lone Star State

When major league baseball came to Houston in 1962, the city's baseball fathers elected to fashion the team's identity and logo with the Colt .45; the gun that tamed the West and, by implication, the Mexican and Native American populations, making way for the progress of Anglo civilization.[1] While the smoking Colt .45 logo embraced the symbolic values of nineteenth-century Texas, the Houston franchise's handling of its first Latin star, Cuban-born Roman Mejias, demonstrated a lack of sensitivity and appreciation for the potential of its Spanish-speaking community. Drafted out of the Pittsburgh Pirates organization, Mejias would lead the fledgling Houston team in home runs and runs batted in, while hitting for a .286 average. Following his banner year in Houston, Mejias was traded to the Boston Red Sox for singles-hitting Pete Runnels, an Anglo who hailed from nearby Pasadena, Texas. The story of Roman Mejias suggests that Houston management failed to market and develop Mejias as a star, establishing a club tradition of extolling Anglo players, while eschewing the potential of its Latin community and falling into the pattern of racial segregation which has characterized the troubled history of race relations in the Lone Star state.[2]

However, at the peak of the Chicano civil rights movement of the

1960s and early 1970s, Houston management, while continuing to ignore Mexican talent, made a concentrated effort to develop Cesar Cedeno, whom baseball scouts lauded as possessing exceptional athletic qualities. Cedeno was born February 25, 1951 in Santo Domingo, Dominican Republic to a family of modest means. Cesar's father Diogene worked in a nail factory, but he aspired to be a small businessman, purchasing a family grocery store. According to biographical portraits of Cedeno placed in sporting publications after the Dominican cracked the major leagues, Diogene perceived of baseball as a meaningless pursuit and wanted his son available to help with family chores and delivering groceries. However, Cesar's passion for baseball was abetted by his mother who purchased him a glove and shoes without the knowledge of the family patriarch. Despite the ambitions of the elder Cedeno, the family continued to struggle economically, and Cesar, one of four children, dropped out of school in grade eight, working as a laborer in the nail factory which employed his father.[3]

Contrary to the wishes of Diogene, Cesar continued playing baseball in Santo Domingo, where the sixteen year old boy was discovered by Houston scouts in the fall of 1967. Astro representatives Pat Gillich and Tony Pacheco were combing the Dominican Republic searching for prospects, and they stumbled upon Cedeno while looking at another young player. According to Gillich, "We saw him throw and then we saw him go up and get a hit and go up and get another hit. We decided we wanted to look at him. After the game, we arranged for him to go with us and some more players to San Pedro, about sixty miles away, for a workout."[4] The reason for moving the try out to San Pedro was to escape the notice of other scouts, as under Organized Baseball's rules the Caribbean was open territory to which the sport's draft laws were inapplicable. In addition, with a growing cadre of major league Latin stars, such as Orlando Cepeda, Roberto Clemente, Rico Carty, Juan Marichal, and the Alou brothers, the Houston organization was finally becoming aware of the talent pool available in Latin America.

Gillich and Pacheco were even more impressed after observing Cedeno in San Pedro, and the Houston agents moved quickly to sign the young Dominican who had also been scouted by the St. Louis Cardinals. However, there was a stumbling block in the person of Diogene Cedeno, whose signature on a contract was necessary for his underage son. The elder Cedeno reportedly wanted his son to either work in Santo Domingo or return to school, but not to pursue something as frivolous as baseball. Gillich initially offered the Cedeno family a contract for $1,200; however, when Gillich learned that a Cardinal representative was on his way to the Cedeno home, the Houston scout, on his own initiative, upped the ante to $3,000. To the economically-strapped Cedeno household, this amount of money was persuasive, and the elder Cedeno, despite misgivings, gave his assent to his son pursuing a baseball career in the United States. Allegedly, as Gillich and Pacheco were departing the Cedeno residence, a Cardinal scout was just getting out of his car. An elated Gillich waved the Cedeno contract, exclaiming, "You're a few minutes too late."[5]

Houston club officials had little reason to question the judgment of their talent agents, for Cedeno quickly established himself as a first-rate prospect. In 1968, at age seventeen, he hit .374 in thirty-six games for Covington, Kentucky of the Appalachian League and .256 for Cocoa of the Florida State League. The following season, Cedeno continued to impress, hitting .274 with a league-leading thirty-two doubles for the Newport News of the Carolina League. The teen prospect was working his way through the Houston organization, while coping with the challenges of learning English and racial relations in the American South.[6] He also maintained an affinity for ham, eggs, and chicken; a literal representation of what Sam Regalado termed the special hunger of Latin American ball players. According to Regalado, competition on America's baseball diamonds carried crucial social and economic implications for Latin players:

> Baseball was a path out of poverty, it helped to bring distinction to their homelands; it was a means to ease the pain and suffering of kinfolk and compatriots; and it provided a sliver of hope to many younger Latins who might otherwise have envisioned a dim future. Their determination to succeed in the face of an unwelcoming culture reveals the human spirit of Latin players. For they, unlike so many other newcomers, faced these barriers alone, without the aid of support groups. And it was this willingness to break through cultural roadblocks that made their hunger special.[7]

Although he possessed a special hunger and was making steady progress with his mastery of the English language and baseball fundamentals, the Houston organization challenged the sport's conventional wisdom by promoting the nineteen-year-old Cedeno to their AAA affiliate in Oklahoma City for the 1970 season. Apparently, one of the reasons for the assignment was the fact that Oklahoma City 89ers' manager Hub Kittle spoke Spanish and possessed an established reputation "for keeping the Latin players loose and happy." The Houston baseball establishment, which had essentially ignored the cultural and racial barriers confronting the organization's first Latin star Roman Mejias, was making an effort to support the assimilation of its Latin players. However, Cedeno's predominantly Anglo teammates insisted upon referring to the Dominican as "Sandy." Nomenclature aside, Cedeno devoured AAA pitching, hitting safely in all but three of Oklahoma City's first thirty-four games. Manager Kittle refused to tinker with Cedeno's aggressive batting style, observing, "I tell him to go up there and take his cuts. Believe me, if anybody gets this kid messed up, I'll shoot the guy."[8] Ironically, Kittle's comment foreshadowed a 1973 Dominican shooting which would cast a cloud over Cedeno's career and life.

However, in 1970 Cedeno was the toast of the baseball world. After terrorizing AAA pitching (in fifty-four games for Oklahoma City, Cedeno hit .373, with 14 home runs and 61 runs driven in), the nineteen-year-old teenager was promoted to the major leagues in July, playing in ninety games for the Astros, while hitting for an average of .310 with 7 home runs, 42 runs batted in, and seventeen stolen bases; coupled with outstanding defensive play in center field. This phenomenal performance by one so young immediately established Cedeno with a "can't miss" reputation. Astro manger Harry Walker, who was an excellent hitter during his National League career, described Cedeno as a natural, insisting, "He's cat-quick in the outfield, he can throw with the best of them and he can hit. Barring injury, he'll be one helluva ball player by the time he's 22 years old." Praise for Cedeno's performance was also forthcoming from the Pittsburgh Pirates Roberto Clemente, who proclaimed, "He's one of the best young players I have ever seen. He has great control of his movements in the outfield." When asked if he expected to live up to such accolades, Cedeno reportedly grinned sheepishly and replied, "I guess so."[9]

Nevertheless, the young Houston player suffered through a sophomore slump during the 1971 baseball campaign, in which Cedeno hit for a .264 average with 10 home runs, 81 runs in, and 20 stolen bases. The over-swinging twenty-year-old continued to excel in the field, and reporter John Wilson, representing the views of the Houston organization and many baseball talent scouts, concluded, "He still is a young player with the seeming natural ability to do it all, and do it big."[10]

Cedeno more than met the expectations of the Houston baseball establishment with banner seasons in 1972 and 1973; hitting for a .320 average in both campaigns, coupled with power and speed figures of 22 and 25 home runs, 82 and 70 runs batted in, and 55 and 56 stolen bases. The center fielder's defensive contributions were recognized with consecutive golden glove awards. The young Dominican was the shining star of the baseball universe, with pundits as well as players suggesting that Cedeno was as talented as the superstars Willie Mays, Hank Aaron, and Roberto Clemente. Baltimore Orioles scouting chief Jim Russo described the Houston athlete as "the best young player in the baseball." Meanwhile,

Harry Walker, who had also managed Clemente in Pittsburgh, favorably compared Cedeno with the Puerto Rican icon, asserting, "Clemente and Cedeno are the two most exciting players in baseball today. Whether they're catching the ball or throwing it or running the bases or batting, they do it all-out and with a flair. When they're involved, you're always on edge expecting something to happen. They make things happen." Of course, the emphasis upon the similarities between Clemente and Cedeno was partially based upon stereotypes of Latin American ball players as emotional and flamboyant individuals who embraced a flashy or "hot dog" style over that of more disciplined and serious Anglo athletes.

On the other hand, Clemente was uncomfortable with both the stereotypes and comparisons. Acknowledging that Cedeno possessed more talent than anyone entering the league during his time, the Pittsburgh outfielder, nevertheless, believed it was unfair to label Cedeno as another Clemente. The Puerto Rican athlete concluded, "I don't think it is fair to him. When I came up, I did not like to be compared with other players." Cedeno concurred, adding, "I don't want to be the second Clemente, I would rather be the first Cedeno."[11]

Yet, Cedeno's reservations did little to silence his boosters. Cincinnati Reds manager Sparky Anderson labeled the Houston center fielder as the best young player in the game; while Atlanta Braves slugger Hank Aaron observed, "He's the youngster with the greatest ability to hit this league since me." However, perhaps the most dramatic pronouncement regarding Cedeno's unlimited potential came from baseball legend Leo Durocher, who replaced Walker as Houston's manager late in the 1972 season. Durocher, who had managed Willie Mays early in his brilliant career and claimed to be a father figure for the Giants center fielder, maintained that Cedeno was a better player than Mays at a similar stage in his career.[12]

Such hoopla obviously placed tremendous pressure upon the Houston star, but during the 1972 and 1973 baseball seasons Cedeno responded superbly at the bat and in the field. But off the playing field, there were signs that Houston management had little prepared their young Latin star for the price of fame. More might be needed than a Spanish-speaking manager at the AAA level. Rumors of heavy drinking followed Cedeno, and his private life was tumultuous. In 1970, Cedeno married a Puerto Rican woman with whom he fathered a child. Following a divorce, he was married again, this time to a twenty-year-old Houston woman. Nevertheless, Cedeno was still perceived by the sporting press as a man who had it all. In a 1973 profile entitled "Rendering Unto Cesar," Arthur Daley of the *New York Times* concluded. "On what meat doth this, our Cesar, feed? Apparently he also feeds on luck. He's got everything else. This has to give him an unbeatable combination."[13]

However, Cedeno's luck was about to desert him. During the winter of 1973, he was playing baseball in his native Dominican Republic. In the early morning hours of December 11, Cedeno, who had apparently been drinking, checked into a Santo Domingo hotel. He was accompanied by nineteen-year-old Altagracia de la Cruz, the mother of a three-year-old daughter and an acquaintance of Cedeno, for found in the hotel room was a photograph of the ball player and de la Cruz in an embrace. After arriving at the hotel, Cedeno ordered beers from room service, and there were reports of an argument and loud noises coming from the hotel room. Shortly thereafter, a shot was heard, and Cedeno phoned a hotel employee to report that de la Cruz was dead. The athlete then fled the scene in his sports car, reportedly finding sanctuary with his wife Cora in their Dominican home. The next day, Cedeno, accompanied by his wife, turned himself into authorities, almost eleven hours after the shooting. Although Cedeno claimed the death of de la Cruz was accidental, the ball player was initially held on charges of voluntary manslaughter, which under Dominican law called for prison sentences ranging from three to ten years upon conviction. The severe charges levied against Cedeno made him ineligible for bail, and he spent the Christmas holidays in jail. However, according to newspaper accounts, Cedeno was being held in "preventive custody" in Santo Domingo's most modern jail with a room of his own. An anonymous prison source was quoted in an Associated Press account as saying, "The Cedeno case is a special one. He is no common prisoner."[14]

Nor was Cedeno a common prisoner for Houston Astros management, who saw the future of their franchise and a valuable investment about to be extinguished by gunfire in a Santo Domingo hotel. The Houston baseball establishment had refused to intervene when their first Latin star Roman Mejias's family was unable to get out of Cuba in the early 1960s. However, within months of his trade to the Red Sox, Boston management was able to arrange a reunion between Mejias and his family.[15] In Cedeno's case, within days of the shooting, a delegation of Houston officials were dispatched to the Caribbean island. The Astro representatives included General Manager Spec Richardson, Assistant General Manager John Mullen, minor league operations chief Pat Gillet, and Dominican scout Epifanio Guerrero. After visiting with the incarcerated Cedeno, the delegation expressed confidence that the shooting was accidental and the Houston star would be acquitted of all chargers, free to assume his position in center field at the Astrodome, which team hype had begun referring to as Cesar's Palace.

In public statements to the press, Mullen and Richardson described de la Cruz's death as a tragedy and demonstrated paternalistic attitudes regarding Cedeno, and, by inference, Latin culture. Mullen stated, "Cesar was very quiet and subdued.... You know Cesar. He's usually so effervescent, so outgoing. Now he has very little to say and is obviously feeling very downcast." General Manager Richardson echoed the sentiments of Mullen, concluding, "I came down here to cheer up Cedeno and give him confidence and find out for myself what state the boy is in. He's very concerned about what happened and a little frightened." Concerned about the future of their franchise player, Houston executives failed to express much concern or sympathy for de la Cruz and her family.[16]

Meanwhile, back in the United States, teammates and baseball officials weighed in with support for Cedeno. Jim Wynn, who had yielded his center field job to Cedeno and was traded to the Los Angeles Dodgers only days before the shooting, said that he was not surprised to learn that Cedeno was carrying a pistol in a Latin American nation. Wynn asserted, "I played one year over there, and I think it is a fairly common thing. I know a lot of people do it. They have so much trouble down there and a lot of it has to do with changes in government." While Wynn's comments revealed common assumptions and misconceptions regarding Latin America, Houston third baseman Doug Rader insisted that Cedeno was innocent until proven guilty. Rader argued, "Just because he's a ball player doesn't mean he is guilty. If he was Joe Blow he'd get the benefit of the doubt. Why shouldn't he (Cedeno) get the same benefit? Sometimes when something sensational happens to someone in the public eye, people automatically feel he's guilty. I say Cesar Cedeno is a human being. More than that, he's a good person. Like anyone else, he should get the benefit of the doubt until proven guilty."[17]

Tal Smith, Executive Vice-President of the New York Yankees, and who as a Houston executive had approved the contract bringing Cedeno to the United States, told the *New York Times* that he was stunned regarding Cedeno's involvement with the death of de la Cruz. Smith observed that in the United States it was all too common to take a young man from another culture and "give him all the adulation and expect him to handle it. I know guys that can't. But Cesar could." Cedeno's character was also vouched for by the Dominican Ambassador to the United States, Federico Antun, who also happened to be president of the team for which Cedeno played before inking his contract with the Astros. Antun characterized Cedeno as "a very nice boy; he never used bad words." However, he acknowledged that exposure to American culture, fame, and money might have changed the Dominican athlete. The Ambassador asserted, "Cesar was the best player my country gave you, better than Rico Carty. He didn't smoke or drink, but I knew he liked the girls. They said he was drunk when he went to the motel with the girl that night. Maybe he was. Maybe he changed. But when I knew him, he didn't drink."[18]

While there is little evidence that the Astros prepared Cedeno to deal with his new found fame and fortune, which the team had hyped in order to sell tickets, the club certainly rushed to his defense after the Dominican shooting and arrest. In late December, Cedeno's attorney Quirico Elpidio Perez, who had been retained by Houston management, was successful in getting the charges against the ball player reduced to involuntary manslaughter, allowing Cedeno to leave jail after posting a ten thousand dollar bond. In mid January, District Attorney Frank Diaz appealed to Judge Porfirio Natera to dismiss all charges against Cedeno, citing a police report which indicated that paraffin tests proved de la Cruz had fired Cedeno's weapon in her right hand. The paraffin test apparently corroborated Cedeno's testimony that the young woman had grabbed the loaded revolver, and he had tried to take it away from her. In the ensuing struggle, a shot was fired and de la Cruz was dead. After taking the prosecutor's motion into account, Natera, nevertheless, found Cedeno guilty of involuntary homicide. However, the judge assessed Cedeno only a one hundred dollar fine and determined that the ball player would receive no period of incarceration. Cedeno and his wife Cora, who appeared at all court proceedings by her husband's side, made immediate plans to return to the United States.[19]

Felicia de la Cruz, an aunt of the young woman killed in Cedeno's hotel room, termed the verdict "an injustice." Family members filed a civil suit on behalf of de la Cruz's three-year-old daughter, whose father was not acknowledged to be Cedeno. Meanwhile, the ball player was free to leave the Dominican Republic. Ostensibly, the law suits initiated by the de la Cruz family were settled out of court, amid accusations, although never documented, that the Houston franchise had arranged a financial settlement with the family as well as Dominican legal officials.[20] While the Houston organization had generally ignored both the athletic talent and marketability of its first Latin athlete Mejias, the ball club certainly invested time, effort, and money in the case of Cedeno. However, management involvement on behalf of the ball player in the death of de la Cruz provides little indication that the Houston baseball establishment was appreciative of Latin American culture and sensibilities. Instead, the action of the Astros in the Cedeno–de la Cruz affair appeared to coincide more with American military interventions in Central America and the Caribbean to protect business investments.

While Houston officials breathed a sigh of relief upon the release of their superstar, other observers were less comfortable with the deliberations of the Dominican justice system. Columnist Dick Young believed the Houston club was overly focused on how the promising career of its center fielder might be impaired by the events of December, 1973 in a Dominican hotel room. Young pointed out, "Maybe Altagracia de la Cruz, 19, did not have a promising career, but whatever it was, it is ended." In another column, Young speculated, "In America, a man would be innocent by reason of accidental death. If guilty, you get a prison sentence; if innocent, you get off, but how does anyone put a $100 price tag on a human life?"[21]

Cedeno recognized that many baseball fans and players shared Young's questions about what had transpired in the Dominican Republic. To those who maintained that the tragedy of de la Cruz had been obscured by concerns over Cedeno's baseball career, the athlete replied, "I feel very sorry because that happened ... that she got herself killed. I will say it this way: God and me know that I didn't do it. She killed herself. I tried to take the gun away from her. I knew it was dangerous. I told her not to get it ... because it was loaded. What else could I do?" As for hecklers, Cedeno insisted, "Some players on other teams will try to take my concentration away, but it's not going to work. I won't pay any attention to those players. I'll just put on my uniform and play my game." The Houston athlete maintained that he had learned from the Dominican tragedy, which would make him a better person. He also expressed his appreciation for his wife who had supported him throughout the ordeal. But the bottom line for Cedeno was apparently neither de la Cruz nor his domestic and personal life. When asked why he had not immediately turned himself into the police, Cedeno explained, "I was scared. I saw my baseball career was in danger."[22]

While the intervention of Houston officials had succeeded in saving the athlete to play another day, Cedeno's 1974 performance failed to match the expectations established by the 1972 and 1973 seasons. Nursing a knee injury, and bothered more by the de la Cruz affair than he was publicly admitting, Cedeno slumped to a .269 batting average, although he still managed 26 home runs, 102 runs batted in, and 57 stolen bases.

And Cedeno was reentering a baseball world in which ball park violence, reflecting the larger culture, reached a crescendo in 1974. As the nation reeled from the disillusionment of military defeat in Vietnam and political corruption at the highest levels with the Watergate scandal, opening day for the Chicago White Sox was marred by heavy drinking and fighting fans, as well as seven streakers, both male and female, who pranced through the outfield grass clad only in baseball caps. A ten cent beer night promotion in Cleveland resulted in a riot and forfeiture by the Indians to the visiting Texas Rangers. And on May 12, 1974, Houston Astros outfielder Bob Watson crashed into the left field wall at Cincinnati's Riverfront Stadium. With his sunglasses shattered and his face bloodied, Watson was afraid any movement might endanger his eyesight. Meanwhile, some spectators in the bleachers began pouring beer over the prone and bleeding figure of Watson. Teammates such as Cedeno engaged in a shouting match with unruly fans, while Watson was carried from the field. While deploring the behavior of those individuals who harassed the injured Watson, the ever-caustic Dick Young reminded his readers that the Astros' Cedeno might want to be careful about calling others hoodlums.[23]

In 1975, Cedeno raised his batting mark to .288, but his power figures declined with only 13 home runs and 63 runs driven in. The center fielder was also gaining a reputation as a malcontent, which Cedeno blamed upon the publication of Leo Durocher's autobiography *Nice Guys Finish Last.* In this book, Durocher maintained that while the Houston player possessed as much talent as anyone in the game, Cedeno often did not give 100 percent. Cedeno objected to such accusations, asserting that he always gave his best, but that he would not play injured for anybody as that would endanger his career. (Interestingly enough, this was almost the same reasoning used by Cedeno to defend his actions in the de la Cruz shooting.) Cedeno also complained about being labeled by the media as immature for emotional outbursts such as throwing a batting helmet. A frustrated Cedeno insisted that he was tired of being compared with such veteran ball players as Mays and Aaron. Cedeno pointed out that he was still only twenty-five years of age, and he assumed that the great Mays must have done his share of equipment tossing during his earlier years.[24]

Frustration on the part of Cedeno led to rumors that the Dominican would be dealt to the New York Yankees. However, Houston management was not prepared to turn its back on Cedeno as it had done with Mejias following the 1962 season. Bill Virdon, who assumed the managerial reins in Houston late in the 1975 season, made it clear that he wanted Cedeno to remain an Astro, calling the Dominican the "number one player in the National League." Houston executives agreed with Virdon's evaluation, and, in an effort to forestall Cedeno from declaring free agency, provided the Houston outfielder with a ten year, three and one-half million dollar contract, making him the highest paid player in the game.[25]

However, the return on Houston's investment was mixed. While Cedeno continued to be a fine player, he never again amassed the .320 batting averages of 1972 and 1973. In fact, only in the 1980 season would

Cedeno ever again cross the .300 batting average plateau, and Houston, although it came close in 1980, would never win a National League pennant during his tenure. Cedeno missed more than half of the 1978 campaign due to a seventeen stitch wound inflicted when he smashed his fist into a Plexiglas dugout roof after failing to drive a run in from second base, followed by a knee ligament injury suffered when he slid into second base in Chicago. Cedeno's increasing vulnerability to injury and failure to attain the elite status predicted by pundits led many baseball people to wonder what had happened to Cesar Cedeno. For example, Joe Morgan, who played with Cedeno in Houston before gaining Hall of Fame credentials as the second baseman for Cincinnati's Big Red Machine, asserted, "I don't think Cedeno's been as good a player as I thought he would be." Such great expectations might be blamed upon Houston officials' use of public relations in likening the Dominican to Mays, Aaron, and Clemente.

Since Cedeno would only hit .300 once in his career after the de la Cruz shooting, the baseball press began to wonder whether that traumatic event might have taken away from him that slight edge that a truly great athlete must have. Teammates and Houston management asserted that they never discussed the shooting and that it had no effect on the Houston star. Cedeno was also in a state of denial. In response to the allegation that he was never the same after that December, 1973 evening in Santo Domingo, Cedeno maintained, "Like I say, I don't want to talk about it. I feel satisfied, and as long as I feel satisfied I can live with myself. The incident means nothing, nothing at all. I'm a better ball player than I was then."[26]

The Houston ball player's batting statistics failed to support such an assertion, and the de la Cruz shooting continued to haunt Cedeno. In 1981, Cedeno suffered through another sub par campaign, batting only .271 and missing over half the season due to a broken ankle sustained during the 1980 play-off series with the Philadelphia Phillies. Late in the season, Cedeno was fined $5,000 by the National League, but not suspended, for climbing a fence and entering the fourth row of box seats in Atlanta Stadium, confronting three hecklers who were taunting Cedeno and his wife. National League President Chub Feeney condemned Cedeno's actions, but he observed that there were mitigating circumstances. According to witnesses, three male spectators were continuously shouting "killer, killer, killer," in the direction of Cedeno and his wife Cora, who accompanied her husband to Atlanta. In explaining his actions, Cedeno proclaimed, "I'm not going to say what he called me, but it has to do with something that happened a long time ago, something I will have to live with the rest of my life. I don't like people calling me something I'm not.... If I had been here alone, I probably would not have reacted that way. But my wife has been subjected to the same language and treatment. She was near tears. I don't think any man would want to have his wife hear people call him that."[27]

Houston management defended Cedeno for his actions in Atlanta, refusing to impose any additional fines upon the player. However, Houston's patience had worn thin with its increasingly temperamental and oft-injured Latin star. Before the 1982 season Cedeno was traded to the Cincinnati Reds for Ray Knight. Cedeno was unhappy during his tenure with the Reds. After starting in center field during 1982, Cedeno became a platoon player his last years in Cincinnati, while gaining a reputation as a malcontent. For example, after a 1983 game in Chicago, Cedeno was incensed when he was denied a first class seat on the team's return flight to Cincinnati. There were only nine seats available in first class, and they were all assigned to players in the starting line-up. Cedeno demanded a seat in first class, tore up his coach ticket, and stormed out of the terminal, refusing to accompany the team on the flight. The Reds responded with an undisclosed fine, and manager Russ Nixon, alluding to Cedeno's reputation as a malingerer who would not play in pain, remarked, "There were only nine seats in first class, and if he feels that he has to have priority over people who beat their brains out for nine innings, that's his problem."[28]

Late in the 1985 season, the disgruntled Cedeno was dispatched by the Reds to the Cardinals for the stretch drive. Cedeno, insisting that leaving the Reds was like "getting out of jail" (and apparently Cedeno was not being ironic about his past), played an instrumental role in the Cardinals winning the National League pennant, although St. Louis was defeated by the Kansas City Royals in the World Series.[29]

Cedeno finished out his major league career by playing briefly with the Los Angeles Dodgers during the 1986 season. Leaving the game at the relatively early age of thirty-five, Cedeno amassed impressive major statistics; playing in over two thousand games, with a lifetime batting average of .285, 199 home runs, 976 runs driven in, and 550 stolen bases.[30] The Dominican enjoyed a successful major league career, most of it employed with the Houston franchise, but he failed to achieve the Hall of Fame numbers associated with Mays, Aaron, and Clemente. Injuries and, perhaps of utmost importance, the death of Alagracia de la Cruz had prevented Cedeno from attaining the status of greatness predicted by so many observers of baseball talent.

On the other hand, Houston management, perhaps learning a lesson from how the club had handled Roman Mejias, attempted to break the cycle of troubled race relations in Texas between Anglo and Latin by marketing and building the team around a Latin star in the person of Cedeno. While the Houston baseball establishment lavished money and publicity (Although the club's public relations machine may have been responsible for raising unrealistic expectations for Cedeno.) upon Cedeno, the athlete's involvement in the death of de la Cruz offers scant evidence that the Houston franchise had prepared their young player to deal with the pressures of fame and fortune. Also, in its intervention with the criminal justice system of the Dominican Republic and apparent disregard for a dead Latina woman, Houston officials demonstrated little respect for Latin culture and institutions in their efforts to preserve the team's economic investment in a valuable commodity, Cesar Cedeno.

However, Houston's endeavors to build a pennant-winning franchise around Cedeno failed. Although the Astros have signed popular and successful Latin players, such as José Cruz, Joaquin Andujar, and José Lima, the club has not tied its identity to a Latin player since Cedeno. Instead, the Houston baseball establishment has done little to alleviate the legacy of racial distrust between Anglo and Latin; organizing and marketing the team around such Anglo stars as Nolan Ryan, Craig Biggio, and Jeff Bagwell, who despite their achievements have never been able to lead the Houston franchise to a National League pennant.[31] The Houston Astros, based upon their experience with Cedeno, seem to have, assumingly on an unconscious level, bought into the racial stereotype that Latin ball players, albeit talented, are overly emotional, temperamental, and unreliable, lacking the leadership, work ethic, and marketing characteristics around which one should organize a team.

Endnotes

A version of this paper was presented at the 2000 Cooperstown Symposium on Baseball and American Culture. It was originally published in William M. Simons, ed., *Cooperstown Symposium on Baseball and American Culture, 2000* (Jefferson, North Carolina: McFarland & Company, 2001), 219-236.

1. For the efforts to bring major league baseball to Houston see Clark Nealon, Robert Nottebart, Stanley Siegel, and James Tinsley, "The Campaign for Major League Baseball in Houston," *The Houston Review*, 7 (1985), 3–46; Ron Briley, "The Houston Colt .45s: The Other Expansion Team of 1962," *East Texas Historical Journal*, 27 (1994), 59–74; and Robert Reed, *A Six-Gun Salute: An Illustrated History of the Houston Colt*

.45s (Houston: Lone Star Books, 1999). For the New Western history see Patricia Nelson Limerick, *The Legacy of Conquest: The Unbroken Past of the American West* (New York: Norton, 1987); and Richard White, *"It's Your Misfortune and None of My Own:" A New History of the American West* (Norman: University of Oklahoma Press, 1991).

2. For biographical sketches of Roman Mejias see Larry Moffi and Jonathan Kronstadt, *Crossing the Line: Black Major Leaguers. 1947-1959* (Jefferson, North Carolina: McFarland & Company, 1994), 138–139; and Roman Mejias File, Baseball Hall of Fame Museum and Library, Cooperstown, New York.

3. For background information on Cesar Cedeno see John Wilson, "Cesar Cedeno … The Next Superstar?," *Sporting News*, August 19, 1972; David Pietrusza, Matthew Silverman, and Michael Gershman, *Baseball: The Biographical Encyclopedia* (New York: Total/Sports Illustrated, 2000), 186–187; and Charles Morey, "Cesar Cedeno—The Next Willie Mays," *Pro Sports* (May, 1973), 34–37 and 62–63, clipping from Cesar Cedeno File, Baseball Hall of Fame Museum and Library.

4. Morey, "Cesar Cedeno—The Next Willie Mays," 62–63.

5. *Ibid.* For background information on baseball in the Dominican Republic see Alan M. Klein, *Sugarball: The American Game and the Dominican Dream* (New Haven, Connecticut: Yale University Press, 1991); and Rob Ruck, *The Tropic of Baseball: Baseball in the Dominican Republic* (Westport, Connecticut: Meckler, 1991).

6. Bob Dellinger, "Astros Hail 89ers' Cesar as Minors' Top Prospect," *Sporting News*, June 6, 1970; and Bob Moskowitz, "Teen-Ager Cedeno a Terror at Bat," *Sporting News*, n.d., clipping from Cesar Cedeno File, Baseball Hall of Fame Museum and Library.

7. Samuel O. Regalado, *Viva Baseball: Latin Major Leaguers and Their Special Hunger* (Urbana: University of Illinois Press, 1998), xiv. For issues of segregation in minor league baseball see Bruce Adelson, *Brushing Back Jim Crow: The Integration of Minor-League Baseball in the American South* (Charlottesville: University of Virginia Press, 1999).

8. Dellinger, "Astros Hail 89ers' Cesar as Minors' Top Prospect."

9. "Great Cesar—And Only 19!," Binghamton, New York *Press*, July 27, 1970, clipping from Cesar Cedeno File, Baseball Hall of Fame Museum and Library.

10. John Wilson, "Astros' Super Baby Goes Hungry at Plate," *Sporting News*, May 29, 1971.

11. For the comparisons of Cedeno and Clemente see Wilson, "Cesar Cedeno … The Next Super Star?" For the racial stereotyping of Latin American ball players see Regalado, *Viva Baseball*; and Peter C. Bjarkman, *Baseball with a Latin Beat: A History of the Latin American Game* (Jefferson, North Carolina: McFarland & Company, 1994).

12. Morey, "Cesar Cedeno—The Next Willie Mays," 37; and Leo Durocher and Ed Linn, *Nice Guys Finish Last* (New York: Simon & Schuster, 1975).

13. Arthur Daley, "Rendering Unto Cesar," *New York Times,* July 15, 1973. For a survey of Cedeno's marital history see Gerald Eskenazi, "Astros' Outfielder, 22, Is Called Proud and Dedicated Player," *New York Times*, December 13, 1973.

14. For coverage of Altagracia de la Cruz's death see "Cedeno Questioned, Stays in Jail in Fatal Shooting," *New York Times*, December 13, 1973; and "Cedeno Slated to Stay in Jail During Holidays," *New York Daily News*, December 19, 1973, clipping from Cesar Cedeno File, Baseball Hall of Fame Museum and Library.

15. Hy Hurwitz, "Red Sox Worked to Rescue Mejias's Family From Cuba," *Sporting News*, March 30, 1963, clipping from Roman Mejias File, Baseball Hall of Fame Museum and Library.

16. Joe Heiling, "Cedeno Tragedy Tosses a Cloud over Astros," *Sporting News*, December 29, 1973.

17. *Ibid.*; and Milton Richman, "Cedeno Never Liked Publicity," *New York Times*, December 13, 1973, clipping from Cesar Cedeno File, Baseball Hall of Fame Museum and Library.

18. Eskenazi, "Astros' Outfielder, 22, Is Called Proud and Dedicated Player."

19. "Prosecutor Calls for Cedeno's Full Acquittal," *New York Times*, January 15, 1974; and "Cedeno Guilty," *New York Times*, January 16, 1974, clippings from Cesar Cedeno File, Baseball Hall of Fame Museum and Library.

20. "Cedeno Found Guilty," *New York Daily News*, January 16, 1974, clipping from Cesar Cedeno File, Baseball Hall of Fame Museum and Library. For allegations that Houston management influenced the court settlement in the Dominican Republic see Abby Mendelson, "Whatever Happened to Cesar Cedeno?," *Baseball Quarterly*(Winter, 1978), 47–57, clipping from Cesar Cedeno File, Baseball Hall of Fame Museum and Library,

21. Dick Young, "Cesar Cedeno Goes on Trial," *New York Daily News*, January 14, 1974; and Dick Young, "Cheap Price for Justice," *Sporting News*, February 2, 1974, clippings from Cesar Cedeno File, Baseball Hall of Fame Museum and Library.

22. Joe Heiling, "Cesar Set for Brickbats: 'I May Be Better Player,'" *Sporting News*, February 9, 1974; and "Cedeno Expects Reaction by Fans, Players," *New York Times*, January 23, 1974, clipping from Cesar Cedeno File, Baseball Hall of Fame Museum and Library.

23. For a discussion of baseball violence in 1974 see Ron Briley, "As American as Cherry Pie: Baseball and Reflections of Violence in the 1960s and 1970s," 115–134, Peter M. Rutkoff and Alvin Hall, eds., *The Cooperstown Symposium on Baseball and American Culture. 1999* (Jefferson, North Carolina: McFarland & Company, 2000).

24. Harry Shattuck, "Questions Arise Over That Which Is Cesar's," *Sporting News*, June 21, 1975; and Durocher, *Nice Guvs Finish Last.*

25. Harry Shattuck, "No Swap Sign on Cedeno, Says Skipper Virdon," *Sporting News*, October 18, 1975; and Harry Shattuck, "New Cedeno Sheds His Loner Image," *Sporting News*, May 15, 1976.

26. Mendelson, "Whatever Happened to Cesar Cedeno?," 45–57.

27. "Cedeno Is Fined: Goes After Fan," *Sporting News*, September 26, 1981, clipping from Cesar Cedeno File, Baseball Hall of Fame Museum and Library.

28. "No First-Class Plane Seat, No Cesar Cedeno," *Albany Times Union*, March 24, 1983, clipping from Cesar Cedeno File, Baseball Hall of Fame Museum and Library.

29. Rick Hummel, "Cedeno's Baseball Life Takes on New Meaning," *St. Louis Post-Dispatch*, n. d.; and Jared Hoffman, "What a Move: When the Cardinals Acquired Aging Cesar Cedeno for '85 Stretch Run, They Found the Ultimate Difference Maker," *Sporting News*, n. d., clippings from Cesar Cedeno File, Baseball Hall of Fame Museum and Library.

30. All baseball statistics used in the preparation of this paper are from John Thorn and Pete Palmer, eds., *Total Baseball: The Ultimate Encyclopedia of Baseball* (New York: HarperPerennial, 1993).

31. The Texas Rangers, who relocated to Arlington from Washington following the 1971 baseball season, while failing to win an American League pennant, have been much more successful in marketing and attracting such premiere Latin players as Juan Gonzalez, Ivan "Pudge" Rodriguez, and Rafael Palmeiro. This contrasting approach to Latin ball players by the two major league entries from Texas is a topic which merits additional study and analysis.

18

The Albuquerque Dukes and the Summer of 1981: The Best Baseball in America

The summer of 1981. A cloud hangs over the cities of Los Angeles, New York, Boston, and Chicago as the boys of summer have departed from Dodger Stadium, Shea, Fenway, and Wrigley Field in a bitter strike over the issue of compensation for teams losing free agents. But while the major metropolitan centers of America were deprived of the sights, sounds, and smells of major league baseball, the sport refused to die and even flourished with minor league franchises in cities such as Albuquerque, New Mexico.

It is the evening of June 29, 1981, and while major league parks were silent and President Ronald Reagan pondered whether to support an extension of the Voting Rights Act, the Albuquerque Dukes prepared to play the Phoenix Giants before a crowd of nearly eight thousand fans at the Sports Stadium in Albuquerque. With the desert air cooling due to a gentle breeze and with a majestic view of the surrounding Sandia Mountains provided by the waning rays of the setting sun reflecting brilliant shades of purple, the crowd settled in for another night of baseball in the Duke City. The park was filled with the laughter of children anxious to behold the antics of the San Diego Chicken, but baseball thrills would also abound that evening. Trailing by a margin of 9-3 after five and a half innings, the Dukes began one of their patented 1981 comebacks, rallying for five runs in the bottom of the sixth to cut the Phoenix margin to one run, and setting the stage for a dramatic ninth timing. With two outs in the bottom of the ninth, the Dukes struck for two runs to take a 9-8 victory and send the home throng away happy. The winning run was knocked in by former Dodger center fielder Rudy Law who was still angry over his demotion and

281

the fact that the major league strike had frozen his status. He was taking his revenge on the pitchers of the Pacific Coast League with a batting average of .358.[1]

The game on the evening of June 29, and the experience of Rudy Law, in many ways epitomized the history of the Albuquerque Dukes during the 1981 season. With the major league game absent much of the summer and with the Dukes fielding what Peter Gammons of the *Boston Globe* called "the best team in baseball,"[2] the Dukes achieved a great deal of national attention, attracting sportswriters from around the nation and national television games on the fledgling ESPN network. The attention was certainly warranted, as the Dukes dominated the Pacific Coast League, winning 94 games and dropping only 38, for a winning percentage of .712, the highest in the league since 1934. Although the word is often misused, Duke hitting was simply awesome as the team batted .325, scored 875 runs, for an average of over six runs per game, and was not shut out all season.[3] And while major league baseball was not available to provide some relief for the concerns and issues of 1981, of which there were many, such as the attempted assassinations of President Reagan and the Pope, the Reagan tax cut and defense build up, the air controllers strike, and the Israeli air attack upon supposed nuclear installations in Iraq, diversions were provided by the royal British wedding of Charles and Diana and for the baseball fan by the accomplishments of the Albuquerque Dukes. (It seems the contributions of the Dukes may have the more permanent standing of the two.)

Albuquerque was also in need of the positive psychological strokes provided by a successful sports franchise. Albuquerque historian Marc Simmons noted that by the early 1980s, Albuquerque citizens, confronted by growing congestion, crime, drug traffic, and a 1979 scandal regarding the highly esteemed men's basketball program at the University of New Mexico, were finding it more difficult to maintain their traditional optimism that "Albuquerque, as cities go, was an agreeable and, indeed, a preferable place in which to live."[4] Indeed, the Dukes seemed to provide a rallying point for the city which not even the trial and conviction of former University of New Mexico basketball coach Norm Ellenberger could negate. Albuquerque residents flocked through the turnstiles at the Sports Stadium, resulting in the Dukes leading the PCL in attendance by drawing 244,464 fans during the regular season, an increase of nearly 50,000 over the 1980 season.[5]

In recent decades, historians have found baseball a useful analytical tool through which to investigate the formation of American values and ideology in microcosm.[6] While most of these studies have focused on the development of major league baseball, the role of minor league baseball is beginning to receive more detailed study. However, the examination of the minor league game has oftentimes tended to concentrate on either romantic treatments of baseball in a more pure form than the corrupted billions of the big leagues or explorations of the economic impact of a franchise on local urban growth and development.[7] Sometimes lost in the discussion of baseball as a reflection of American values, nostalgia, and economic development, whether major or minor leagues, are the boys of summer who play the game which has made some of them millionaires and developed into a big business. The Albuquerque Dukes of 1981 provided an important diversion for the baseball-deprived public during the summer of 1981, and certainly the attendance figures offer evidence for the economic impact of the Duke season, but what of the players? The Dukes of 1981 were an excellent team who established some marks which will long continue to grace the pages of PCL record books. Despite these achievements, the individual stories of the Dukes of that year are a mixed lot. Some went on to fame and fortune in the major leagues, while others were disappointed that despite the impressive marks at Albuquerque they were simply viewed as good minor league players, players who were considered as commodities to be traded if found unworthy of further investment. In the final analysis, minor league baseball is a business pursued by young men eager to climb the ladder of success. Nevertheless, there is a game played between the chalk lines, and the story of the athletes who play the game deserves as much attention as the impact of the strike and economic conditions.

Having won the PCL pennant in 1980, many of the Dukes hoped to be promoted to the parent Los Angeles Dodgers, who had narrowly lost the 1980 Western Division of the National League to the Houston Astros. However, as spring training and the exhibition season unfolded, it became apparent that the Dodgers would prefer to stay with their established veteran players. Thus, former Dukes such as pitcher Ted Power, shortstop Gary Weiss, second baseman Jack Perconte, and outfielders Bobby Mitchell and Ron Roenicke were optioned back to Albuquerque. Meanwhile, Duke veterans signed to contracts included infielder Wayne Caughey, outfielder Tack Wilson, pitchers Kevin Keefe and Bill Swiacki, and first baseman Kelly Snider. New faces expected to contribute to the 1981 Dukes were outfielder Candy Maldonado and pitcher Alejandro Pena from class A Lodi, and pitchers Brian Holton and Ricky Wright and first baseman Mike Marshall up from class AA San Antonio.[8]

The arrival of the much heralded twenty-one year old Marshall created problems for the Dukes and parent Dodgers as what to do with the popular incumbent first baseman Snider, who had contributed much to the Albuquerque pennant drive of 1980. A disappointed Snider realized he was an expandable commodity and was not surprised when he was included in a deal for Minnesota Twins center fielder Kenny Landreaux. Of the Dodgers, Snider commented, "They said I have no future with them, so there's no point of sticking around. And it's not just my situation — a lot of players are in the same boat." Snider certainly knew what he was talking about as the Dodgers preference for veteran players, evident in the Landreaux deal, led the Dodgers to return center fielder Rudy Law, who had stolen forty bases and hit .260 in 1980, to Albuquerque. A disgruntled Law was not happy about his return to the Duke City and told reporters, "They (the Dodgers) might think differently, but there's nothing I can get out of being here. I'm just waiting for a trade." Although a starting position had been opened for him with the trade of Snider, Marshall was also wary of his position within the Dodger organization. After all, veteran Steve Garvey remained a fixture at first base for the Dodgers. The young six foot-five inch, two hundred fifteen pound prospect termed playing for the Dodgers frustrating, but concluded that if he hit for both power and average, the Dodgers would eventually find a place for him. Meanwhile, he would probably buy a home in Albuquerque as he reluctantly admitted, "There's no two ways about it — I'm going to be here for a while."[9]

These disgruntled Dukes did not get off to a good start. The home opener set for April 14 was canceled due to gale force winds and a wind chill factor more appropriate for the Canadian Football League. Although a twenty-five cent beer promotion helped attract a crowd of over three thousand fans the next evening, the Dukes lost the opener to the Phoenix Giants, a club which lost ninety-five games during the 1980 PCL season. The Dukes lost again to Phoenix, before taking two out of three from the Tucson Toros, leaving the Dukes with a mark of two wins and three losses for their initial homestand. On the other hand, the parent Dodgers were off to a fast start, winning their first six games. Seemingly, the veteran Dodgers would need little help from many of the unhappy Dukes.

The Dukes then journeyed to Phoenix for a short road trip where they split two more games with the Giants, returning home one game under the five hundred mark to face the Salt Lake City Gulls. Based upon this less than inspiring start, Dukes manager Del Crandall predicted a competitive race for first place in the Southern Division of the PCL. But many Duke fans were disenchanted, and the *Albuquerque Journal* editorialized that Albuquerque sports fans were impatient for a winner because of embarrassment and frustration surrounding the so-called Lobogate scandal at the University of New Mexico. The paper advised, "The jaded cynical Lobo fan might do well to take up a seat in the Sports Stadium one fine and sunny afternoon and sink into a pleasant stupor of beer, hot dogs, and gentle conversation while the game and the warm day wear on. The lesson is the game's the thing."[10]

Nevertheless, the Dukes play improved considerably on the home-stand, making it much easier to relax while watching the Albuquerque nine. The Dukes took three out of four from Salt Lake and then swept a four game series with Tucson. During this homestand a new crowd favorite emerged in Candy Maldonado who homered in four consecutive at bats on April 30 and May 1, tying a PCL record. The Spanish-speaking native of Puerto Rico was much admired by local Hispanics. Proud of his Puerto Rican heritage and an admirer of Roberto Clemente, Maldonado had decided to try his baseball talents as a path for social mobility in Amer-ica. Coming from a poor family, Maldonado said of his baseball career, "This is my future. I left school in junior high so this is my job. I had to make my own life." Making the most of his opportunity, the young outfielder slammed his ninth home run on May 8 and led the Dukes to their first winning streak of the year.[11]

After dropping the first road game to Salt Lake, the Dukes won the last three games of the series to return home for a five game sweep of the Phoenix Giants, which left the Dukes on May 11 with a nineteen win and seven loss record, as well as a six game lead in the Southern Division of the PCL. After a rocky start, the players were beginning to sense that there was something special about the 1981 Albuquerque team. Dukes left-handed relief pitcher Steve Shirley captured the team's confidence, asserting, "We're going on the field every day, knowing we're going to win."[12]

This attitude prevailed as by June 1, and before departing on a four-teen day road trip, the Dukes had improved their won-loss record to a mark of thirty-three and eleven, and led the Southern Division by eleven games. Although paced by the M and M boys, Maldonado and Marshall who had each driven in over forty runs by the end of May, everyone on the team seemed to contribute to the winning ways. Yet, the pressures of minor league status continued to cause stress for the successful Dukes. Ron Roenicke complained about having to share outfield time with Mal-donado, Mitchell, Wilson, and Law, while Wilson voiced his discontent about being delegated to a designated hitter role, insisting, "You just wait around, waiting for the next time you bat. In order for me to know what's going on, I have to play." Sportswriter Dennis Latta of the *Albuquerque Journal* observed that some of the upset Dukes were victims of major league baseball's labor negotiations. Latta concluded, "The big league teams aren't going to be doing much until it's known if there will be a strike. Once that's settled, watch for the Dukes to lose some players."[13]

An optimistic Latta maintained that the labor issues could be negotiated, but as the Dukes departed for a fourteen day road trip to the Pacific Northwest and Hawaii, with a final stop at Tucson, the dark clouds of a baseball strike seemed ready to unleash a major storm for the national pastime. On June 10, the National Labor Relations Board refused to grant an injunction against the owners for unfair labor practices, and the Major League Baseball Players Association issued a call for a strike on June 12 which would prevent the owners from implementing their plan for free agent compensation. Preparing for what many predicted might be a protracted strike, George Foster, player representative of the Cincinnati Reds, echoed player solidarity, asserting, "As the Beatles say, there'll be a revolution. All the players, period, are behind the strike."[14]

But minor league players were not part of the union, and the long road trip for the Dukes continued. The Dukes proved to be mortal on the road swing, dropping seven of thirteen games and complaining of boredom on the road. Of course, the exception to these negative rumblings was the four day set in Hawaii. As Duke shortstop Gary Weiss quipped, "If every place was like Hawaii, I'd rather stay on the road." However, the promise of Hawaii did not mean much to reserve infielder Alex Taveras whose season was cut short with torn knee ligaments suffered while playing in the islands. And veteran pitcher Kevin Keefe did not make the trip to Hawaii, after being advised to rest his arm for three weeks. While members of the Major League Players Association defended rights gained with free agency and young players such as Marshall and Maldonado dreamed of future glory, Keefe, age twenty-seven, represented the reality of many players in the minor leagues. He had been stuck in Albuquerque since 1978, and the Dodgers appeared to have given up on him, yet they had not been willing or able to trade him. Now, with arm trouble, his aspirations for a major league career seemed slim indeed.[15]

The rest of the Dukes maintained their winning ways, taking seven out of ten on the final homestand of the first half. The Dukes won the first half Southern Division flag with a mark of forty-six wins and twenty-two losses, finishing with a ten and one-half game lead over second place Salt Lake. During the homestand, considerable interest was generated by the appearance of the Portland Beavers with former major leaguers Willie Horton and Luis Tiant on the roster. On the evening of June 16, Tiant, who had achieved fame with the Cleveland Indians and Boston Red Sox, faced the Dukes in the first game of a double header. The appearance of Tiant on the mound attracted a crowd of over eight thousand who watched the forty-year-old Cuban hurler pitch five innings, leaving with a 7-4 lead which Portland relievers were unable to hold. The Duke youngsters were in awe of Tiant as Maldonado, who homered off Tiant, gushed, "Just seeing my name in the game with Luis Tiant is exciting."[16]

With the major league strike showing no signs of termination, the minor league comeback of Tiant received considerable national attention as did the success of the Albuquerque Dukes. The new cable all sports station ESPN announced that it would carry nationally from Phoenix the June 22 opening game of the second half of the PCL season between Albuquerque and the Giants. In addition, Los Angeles media focused on the Dodgers top farm team with some television stations doing daily segments on the Dukes. According to Dukes General Manager Pat McKernan, the increased publicity was the main impact of the strike upon the players. They were not members of the Major League Baseball Players Association and many years away from being concerned with their potential free agency, but the strike gave them an opportunity to demonstrate their skills to the baseball public. And if the path to major league advancement was blocked by veterans in Los Angeles, perhaps other teams would notice and be prepared to deal after the strike.[17]

On June 22, the Dukes started right up where they had left off in the first half, defeating Phoenix 7-4 before a national television ESPN audience. Mike Marshall knocked in three runs and was one of five Dukes who had two hits. Tom Lasorda, the Dodger manager, was the color commentator on the game for ESPN, and he observed that he was especially impressed with Marshall, Maldonado, and relief pitcher Alejandro Pena. On the hitting-rich Dukes, Pena had received little publicity, but had quietly amassed some impressive numbers, with nine saves and an earned run average below one run per game. Lasorda lauded the Horatio Alger work ethic of the twenty-two year old Pena who had quit school after the fourth grade to find a job in order to help support his five siblings. Dodger Director of Player Personnel Al Campanis was also in Phoenix to watch the Dukes play, but he was a little less enthusiastic about Duke prospects. He conceded that the Dukes were a fine team, but the parent Dodgers were a veteran team, explaining, "It's sort of a cycle movement. We have players who took over the team in 1972-1973. You just hope that you have the replacements for them when you need them. Some players last longer than others." Campanis, never noted for his sensitivity, viewed the players as interchangeable parts, and concluded that most Duke players would have to wait until the following spring to impress the Dodger brass. If any further evidence was needed that Dodger management interest in some of the Dukes was limited regardless of how many games they won, it was provided in Phoenix when Lasorda approached Duke third baseman Wayne Caughey, who was hitting over .300 and fielding spectacularly, stating, "I don't believe I know you." The Duke third baseman insisted that he was not embarrassed and he understood the Dodgers were looking for a third sacker with more power.[18]

Although Lasorda and Campanis were unable to see any further games in Phoenix due to lighting problems which led to the cancellation of the remainder of the series, Caughey and his teammates did not let these mixed signals deter them from playing winning baseball. The Dukes opened the second half of the season with thirteen consecutive wins. The streak was stopped in Tucson on July 9 when God intervened with rain, and the game was stopped after six innings with the Toros ahead 3-2. The highlight of this streak was a four game sweep of the Salt Lake City Gulls at the Sports Stadium, which was broadcast on Los Angeles radio station KMCP with former Dodger pitching ace Don Drysdale doing the play-by-play. The Fourth of July game was telecast by Los Angeles cable station KTLA which normally carried the games of the Los Angeles Angels. For the fireworks display on the evening of July 3, a record crowd of 19,003 saw the Dukes keep their perfect second half mark with a 2-1 victory over the Gulls. According to the *Albuquerque Journal*, "For the first time in the history of the Sport Stadium, the ballpark was completely sold out. The gates were closed and there wasn't even standing room left. Late in the game, several fights broke out, and extra police were called in."[19]

Excellent baseball, coupled with the continuing absence of the major league game, enhanced the amount of attention being given to the Dukes. Herman Franks, General Manager of the Chicago Cubs, allegedly offered to trade his team for the Dukes who were hitting .325 in early July. Don Drysdale pointed out that with the thin mountain air of Albuquerque averages were inflated and would probably be thirty-five points lower in the majors. However, that would still amount to an impressive figure of .290. As national accolades poured in for the team, older players such as Power, Perconte, Law, Roenicke, and Mitchell remained disenchanted regarding their status. However, Al Campanis remained noncommittal with this rich blessing of talent, insisting, "It's a good position to be in, when you're trying to decide who to play. It means you have another choice."[20]

While hopes were raised and dashed throughout the month of July regarding a settlement for the major league strike, the Dukes had no choice but to continue playing good baseball. And, indeed, they did, compiling a mark of twenty-two wins and eight losses for July, with a nine and one-half game lead in the PCL Southern Division. While the Dodger organi-

zation provided Albuquerque with a collection of fine players, much of
the credit for the 1981 Dukes success belonged to manager Del Crandall,
who never allowed his players to let up or show their frustrations on the
field. Mark Rupert, Administrative Assistant to Pat McKeman, recalled
that 1981 was his rookie year working with the team. He was impressed by
how veteran players such as Power and Law begrudgingly acknowledged
Crandall's leadership in constantly pushing them. The former All-Star
catcher of the Milwaukee Braves and manager of the Milwaukee Brewers
was a disciplinarian who stressed teamwork. Explaining his philosophy,
Crandall told sportswriters, "If they put their statistics first, they don't
know how to win. One of the things I talk about at the beginning of the
season is not worrying about statistics. If you know how to win, the statistics will be there anyway." Crandall also enforced a dress code on Duke
road trips. While some might consider dress codes in the 1980s old fashioned, Crandall as a traditionalist exclaimed, "When we travel, we wear
jackets. We represent one of the finest things in the country. Baseball."[21]

After August 1, the Dukes would have plenty of competition in representing the sport as the owners and players union, with strike insurance
nearly exhausted and the entire season in jeopardy, settled their differences
over compensation (teams would be able to protect twenty-four of twenty-
six players from being selected for compensation, but teams losing a free
agent would receive a proven player rather than a draft choice), and the
season was to resume on August 8 with the All-Star Game in Cleveland.
The Dodgers invited the Dukes to Los Angeles for an exhibition game on
August 6. To honor the Dodger request, the Dukes would have to resched-
ule as a doubleheader a game with the Edmonton Trappers, but as McK-
ernan explained, "They are paying our expenses. They'll give us some
money to make up for the night we're going to be giving up at the gate."
Crandall believed the players had earned the opportunity to display their
abilities in Dodger Stadium, and the players appeared anxious to be near
"the show." As for the Dodgers, they needed the game to help get back into
shape following the lengthy strike, and it might not be bad for business.
Bill Schweppe, Dodger Vice President for Minor League Operations, stated,
"With all the publicity Albuquerque has gotten here during the strike, we
thought it might be a good idea. The Los Angeles press has really done a
job to promote Albuquerque."

Indeed, the game did draw a good crowd of over forty thousand,
although it was evident the Dodgers and their fans were not as serious
about the game as the Dukes. Fans yelled taunts such as, "Do you use metal
bats in the minors?" Dodger second baseman Davey Lopes put the game
in perspective for the established players. "If by some mere coincidence

should win the game, what the hell am I going to do? I'm not going to cut my throat. What are they going to do, ship us all down." Lopes was right. The game was simply an exhibition, and the long lay off left Dodger batters only able to score two hits off of Duke hurlers Holton, Ricky Wright, and Pena. The only run of the game was driven in by Maldonado who was the only player to collect two hits in the game. While the Dodgers may have been going through the motions, the Duke players were elated, as was the city of Albuquerque. While the rest of the nation focused on the confrontation between President Reagan and the air controllers union, the citizens of Albuquerque gathered around their television sets to watch a local broadcast of the game by an independent station. The only sour note for the Dukes in the game was that the Dodgers had brought up second baseman Steve Sax and pitcher Tom Niedenfuer from San Antonio for the game, indicating that the Dodger management might be more interested in these Double A prospects rather than top Duke candidates Jack Perconte and Ted Power.[22]

Even if there was little that the Dukes could do to change the minds of the Dodger brass, Del Crandall would not let his team coast through the month of August, as Albuquerque completed the month with a record of twenty wins and eight losses, easily capturing the second half of the division race with a record of forty-eight and sixteen. This was achieved despite the call up of relief pitcher Pena on August 13, the first roster move of the season with the Dukes by the Dodgers. The summoning of Pena, who had compiled twenty-two saves for the Dukes, was somewhat expected, but the mid-August Dodger call to San Antonio for Sax and Niedenfuer was shocking, although their use in the exhibition of August 6 indicated the thinking of Dodger management on the two prospects. Nevertheless, the Dukes were infuriated by the snubbing of their teammates. Right-handed starting pitcher Power who had compiled a mark of eighteen wins against only three losses made his anger over being bypassed in favor of Niedenfuer apparent by burning a Dodger hat in effigy, hanging it in his locker, and letting anyone within earshot know his opinion of Dodger management. However, the greatest sense of outrage was reserved for the failure to call up Perconte to replace the faltering Lopes. Clearly, Lasorda and Campanis had spent more time in San Antonio than in Albuquerque, and it was apparent that Sax was their favorite. Yet, in the eyes of the Dukes and the city of Albuquerque the popular Perconte, who was probably the most respected player on the Duke roster, deserved his chance after the incredible team and individual accomplishments of the 1981 season. (Perconte hit .346 with fifty-eight runs batted in and forty-five stolen bases.) Pat McKernan stated that the anger in the Duke clubhouse over the decision to bypass Perconte in favor of Sax was the most volatile he has ever witnessed regarding a personnel decision by a parent club in the minor leagues. The sense of betrayal felt by the Dukes was well exhibited in a fiery column by *Albuquerque Journal* sportswriter Dennis Latta who wrote:

> None of the opposition has been able to slow the Dukes this season. Albuquerque has made a mockery of the PCL. There is no match for the Duke's minor league baseball. But the Dodgers have demoralized the team. Attitude hasn't been a problem all season but Los Angeles might make it one. If you work hard and do well and then watch someone below you move above you, you lose your incentive and become bitter. The Dodgers have the best farm system in baseball when it comes to developing talent. But they obviously don't know what to do when the players are ready for the big leagues.[23]

Unable to manhandle Steve Sax and Dodger management, the Dukes took their frustration out on the Tucson Toros on August 19. Following Mike Marshall's second home run of the game in the fifth inning, Tucson pitcher Rick Aponte hit Maldonado for the second time in the season. Maldonado charged the mound, and both benches cleared. An enraged Crandall also went after Aponte, taking a swing at the pitcher who succeeded in blocking the blow. For his efforts, Crandall received a blackened eye from Toros first baseman Danny Keep, not to mention an expulsion from the game and a suspension from the league office. The disgruntled Dukes refused to let up on the field despite the harsh realities of life in the minors exemplified by the Perconte situation.

Nevertheless, the Dukes received some consolation from the Dodgers when Ron Roenicke was recalled by the parent club on August 30 so he would be eligible for the National League playoffs. Dodger management also announced that Power, Maldonado, Mitchell, Marshall, Weiss, and Perconte would be joining the Los Angeles franchise following the PCL playoffs, while Holton and Law would be placed on the major league roster but would not report to Los Angeles. After winning both halves of the Southern Division race, the Dukes had almost a week off waiting for the Tacoma Tigers to defeat the Hawaii Islanders in a preliminary round of playoffs to decide the Northern Division of the PCL. Accordingly, the Dukes opened the best three of five series for the PCL crown on September 4 in Tacoma. Just as Albuquerque dominated the regular PCL season, the Dukes defeated the Tigers twice in Tacoma before returning to Albuquerque on September 6 for what promised to be the last game of a memorable season. The Dukes were up to the occasion before a record Albuquerque playoff crowd of over five thousand fans who greeted their returning heroes with a standing ovation. Ted Power exclaimed, "These

fans are great. I went out on the field before the game, and they were standing. I got goose bumps." Behind the three hitter pitched by Brian Holton
and a three run home run by Weiss, the Dukes defeated Tacoma 9-2, and
the incredible season of 1981 was history.[25]

The year was a rough one for air traffic controllers and baseball fans.
The mid season strike resulted in cancellation of over seven hundred
games, totaling more than one third of the scheduled contests. As major
league baseball players vacationed and negotiated, a nation desperate for
baseball news turned its attention to the city of Albuquerque where
between June 12 and August 14, the Dukes won fifty games while dropping only twelve contests, for an unbelievable winning percentage of .807.
National columnists conceded that during much of the summer of 1981
the best baseball in America was to be found in Albuquerque, New Mexico. The final mark of ninety-four wins and only thirty-eight losses established a record for the most wins by an Albuquerque club. Mike Marshall
won the triple crown in the Coast League, batting .373 with thirty-four
home runs and one hundred thirty-seven runs batted in. Marshall's triple
crown achievement had not been equaled in the PCL since 1956, four years
before Marshall was born. The summer of 1981 was described by Crandall
as "one of those seasons you dream about." In December, the baseball
world officially recognized the fulfillment of this dream campaign when
the *Sporting News* selected Del Crandall as Minor League Manager of the
Year, Mike Marshall as Minor League Player of the Year, and Pat McKernan as Minor League Executive of the Year. The Dukes had filled an important void in the baseball world during the strike of 1981, and as Pat
McKernan remarked, in baseball "timing is everything."[26]

The timing was perfect as the Dukes enjoyed their moment at the
center of the baseball world, but the Dodger success in winning the 1981
World Series encouraged Los Angeles management not to promote the
Albuquerque team en masse as had happened with the successful 1972
Dukes team. Baseball is a business and unsentimental team executives
determined that most of the Duke talent would best benefit the Dodgers
as trade bargaining chips. Split up, the 1981 Albuquerque boys of summer
would never quite achieve individually what they collectively registered
during that special season. Third baseman Wayne Caughey and pitcher
Kevin Keefe never made it to the big leagues, Gary Weiss played in only
twenty-two major league games, Tack Wilson achieved six major league
at bats, and Brian Holton won twenty games in six major league seasons.
Ron Roenicke played seven years as a part time outfielder, hitting a career
total of seventeen home runs. Rudy Law got his wish and was traded from
the Dodgers to the Chicago White Sox where he spent four seasons. The

Dodgers stayed with Sax, and Jack Perconte was also dealt away to the American League, where he enjoyed some success with the Seattle Mariners, hitting .294 in the 1984 campaign. Perconte was reunited with Crandall in Seattle for the 1984 campaign, but the former Duke manager was dismissed late in the year, failing to turn around the disappointing Mariner franchise. Crandall never had the opportunity to manage a major league team with the talent of the 1981 Dukes.

Other members of that dream team went on to more distinguished careers. After a promising start with the Dodgers, including the 1985 season when he slammed twenty-eight home runs and drove in ninety-five runs, Mike Marshall developed a reputation as a malcontent who would not play with an injury or discomfort. In 1990, he was dealt to the Mets, and he last appeared in the majors with the California Angels in 1991. His major league marks include one hundred forty-eight home runs, five hundred thirty runs batted in, and a .270 lifetime batting average. Not bad numbers, but not equal to the promise of 1981's triple crown season. Ted Power continues to pitch in the major leagues, and through the 1992 season he registered sixty-six major league victories and fifty-seven saves. The two Latin American stars from the 1981 Dukes, Alejandro Pena and Candy Maldonado, confronted each other in the 1992 World Series between Atlanta and Toronto. Through the 1992 campaign, Pena achieved fifty big league victories and sixty-seven saves, while Maldonado posted one hundred twenty-four home runs, five hundred forty-one runs batted in, and a .258 lifetime batting average. The players from Albuquerque made their presence felt on the major league level, but residents from the Duke City will always remember them for that magical summer of 1981 when the baseball world was turned upside down, and the Albuquerque Dukes were the best team in baseball.

Endnotes

As an Albuquerque resident it was, indeed, a pleasure to watch the 1981 Dukes. This piece was originally published in *Nine: A Journal of Baseball History and Social Policy Perspectives*, 3:1 (1994), 66-84.

1. *Albuquerque Journal*, June 30, 1981.
2. Peter Gammons, "The Best Team in Baseball: Albuquerque's Duke of Flatlands are Tearing up Triple A," *Boston Globe*, July 25, 1981, copy in Albuquerque Dukes 1981 Scrapbook, Albuquerque Dukes, Sports Stadium, Albuquerque, New Mexico; hereafter cited as Dukes Scrapbook.

3. *Albuquerque Dukes 1982 Program*, 4, copy in Dukes Scrapbook. For additional background on the history of the Pacific Coast League see Neil J. Sullivan, *The Minors: The Struggles and the Triumph of Baseball's Poor Relation from 1876 to the Present* (New York: St. Martin's Press, 1990), 208-229; Richard Beverage, *The Angels: Los Angeles in the Pacific Coast League, 1919-1957* (Placentia, California: Deacon Press, 1981); Beverage, *Hollywood Stars: Baseball in Movieland, 1926-1957* (Placentia, California: Deacon Press, 1984).

4. Marc Simmons, *Albuquerque: A Narrative History* (Albuquerque: University of New Mexico Press, 1982), 377.

5. *Albuquerque Dukes 1982 Program*, 28, Dukes Scrapbook. In assessing these attendance figures, Dukes General Manager Pat McKernan pointed out the strong team fielded by the Dukes and the fact that Duke attendance had been on an increasing curve before the 1981 season and downplayed the impact of the big league strike. Pat McKernan, General Manager, Albuquerque Dukes, interview with author, February 19, 1993.

6. Studies which have used baseball to investigate American values include Richard Crepeau, *Baseball: America's Diamond Mind, 1919-1941* (Orlando: University Presses of Florida, 1980); Peter Levine, *A. G. Spalding and the Rise of Baseball: The Promise of American Sport* (New York: Oxford University Press, 1985); Steven A. Riess, *Touching Base: Professional Baseball in the Progressive Era* (Westport, CT: Greenwood Press, 1980); Ben Rader, *Baseball: A History of America's Game* (Urbana: University of Illinois Press, 1992); and Jules Tygiel, *Baseball's Great Experiment: Jackie Robinson and His Legacy* (New York: Oxford University Press, 1981).

7. Examples of the growing literature on minor league baseball include David Lamb, *Stolen Season: A Journey Through America and Baseball's Minor Leagues* (New York: Random House, 1991); Arthur T. Johnson, *Minor League Baseball and Local Economic Development* (Urbana: University of Illinois Press, 1993); J. A. Bosco, *The Boys Who Would Be Cubs* (Toronto: MacMillan, 1990); Roger Kahn, *Good Enough to Dream* (New York: Doubleday, 1985); and Sullivan, *The Minors*.

8. For early Dukes roster moves in 1981 see *Albuquerque Journal*, March 19, 21, and 26.

9. *Ibid.*, March 27, 31, and April 12, 23, 1981. Rudy Law would get his wish and be dealt to the Chicago White Sox after the 1981 season. The pressures of playing in the minor leagues are well developed in a series of *Sports Illustrated* articles, including: Peter Gammons, "Making the Grade," *Sports Illustrated*, 73 (July 23, 1990), 53-57; and Franz Lidz, "Trying to Get in the Swim," *Sports Illustrated*, 73 (July 23, 1990), 59-63.

10. *Albuquerque Journal*, April 26, 1981.

11. *Ibid.*, April 19, 1981. For an investigation of the difficulties confronting Latin American players see Sam Regalado, "The Minor League Experience of Latin American Baseball Players in Western Communities," *Journal of the West*, 26 (Spring, 1987), 65-70.

12. *Albuquerque Journal*, May 11, 1981. For a daily account of the Dukes in 1981 see "Day by Day with the Dukes: Pitcher of Record," Dukes Scrapbook.

13. *Albuquerque Journal*, May 22, 24, 26, and June 1, 1981.

14. For the baseball strike of 1981 and the economic issues involved see Bowie Kuhn, *Hardball: The Education of a Baseball Commissioner* (New York: McGraw-Hill, 1988); Marvin Miller, *A Whole Different Ball Game: The Sport and Business of Baseball* (New York: Birch Lane Press, 1991); Gerald Scully, *The Business of Baseball* (Chicago: University of Chicago Press, 1989); and Andrew Zimbalist, *Baseball and Billions* (New York: Basic Books, 1992).

15. *Albuquerque Journal*, June 11, 13, and 14, 1981.

16. *Ibid.*, June 17, 1981. For national coverage of the Tiant comeback see J. McCallum, "El Tiante Makes His Peetch," *Sports Illustrated*, 54 (April 27, 1981), 60-64.

17. McKernan, interview with author, February 19, 1983.

18. *Albuquerque Journal*, June 24, 26, and July 3, 1981. On the Dodger organization see Peter Golenbock, *Bums* (New York: Putnam, 1984); Tommy Lasorda, *The Artful Dodger* (New York: Arbor House, 1985); and Neil Sullivan, *The Dodgers Move West* (New York: Oxford University Press, 1987).

19. *Albuquerque Journal*, July 4, 1981.

20. Mark Heisler, "In Albuquerque They'll Put Up Their Dukes Against Anyone," *Los Angeles Times*, n. d., copy in Dukes Scrapbook.

21. Mark Rupert, Administrative Assistant to General Manager Pat McKernan, interview with author, February 19, 1993; and *Albuquerque Journal*, July 3 and 27, 1981.

22. *Albuquerque Journal*, August 1, 6, and 7, 1981; *Los Angeles Times*, August 6 and 7, 1981; and "Dukes Blank Dodgers 1-0 in L.A.," *Albuquerque Dukes 1982 Program*, 10-15, Dukes Scrapbook.

23. *Albuquerque Journal*, August 19, 1981; and Pat McKernan, interview with author, February 19, 1983.

24. *Albuquerque Journal*, August 19, 1981.

25. *Ibid.*, September 5, 6, and 7, 1981.

26. "Mike, Del and Pat Lead Dukes Award Parade," *Albuquerque Dukes 1982 Program*, 28-30, Dukes Scrapbook; and Pat McKernan, interview with author, February 19, 1981.

27. For the Dodgers in 1981 see Pete Axthelm, "Los Angeles Rat Pack," *Newsweek*, 98 (November 9, 1981), 63-64; Ron Fimrite, "Last Hurrah for Los Angeles," *Sports Illustrated*, 55 (November 9, 1981), 28-31; and "Looking for that October Magic," *Time*, 118 (November 2, 1981), 90.

28. All statistics and records are from John Thorn and Pete Palmer, eds., *Total Baseball: The Ultimate Encyclopedia of Baseball* (New York: HarperCollins, 1993).

19

Baseball and the Women's Question: Participation, Gender Stereotypes, and the Consumption Ethic

In 1946, following a global conflict which modern memory equates with the egalitarian gender image of Rosie the Riveter and its baseball equivalent the All-American Girls Professional Baseball League, *Collier's* published an article by Stanley Frank entitled, "Cheesecake at the Ball Park." Myths of gender equality were laid to rest in Frank's piece, which made it quite clear that women in the male domain and proving ground of baseball remained quite disconcerting for men already threatened by the transformation of gender roles in the work place. With photographs and a short text, the article encapsulated the images of baseball and women which have dominated the social construction of gender within the self-proclaimed national pastime.

Despite the fact that women were playing baseball in the 1940s, *Collier's* photographer David Peskin-Pix includes no pictures of women as athletes. Instead, women are depicted in the more passive and traditional role of spectator. These photographic images also reflect the gender stereotypes of female spectators perpetuated by the baseball establishment and patriarchal order of American society. Women as sexual predators and threats to the male order are exemplified by models in swim suits interacting with members of the Brooklyn Dodgers atop the male preserve of the dugout. Male insecurities that the friendly confines of the ball park will cease to provide a refuge from the shrew's violent, scolding, or nagging temperament are characterized through a photograph of the legendary "Howling" Hilda Chester, a fixture at Brooklyn's Ebbets Field in the 1940s noted for her foghorn voice and clanging cowbell. The caption under Chester's picture reads, "She is being taken away on transports of delight — but not far enough, perhaps." Nevertheless, the dominant visual image of the *Collier's* text is the one most embraced by the capitalistic structure of Organized Baseball: the woman as consumer. Thus, female fans attracted to the game by the promise of free nylons are shown hoisting their skirts to reveal shapely legs adorned by consumer goods often unavailable during the war.

In support of these photographic images, Frank's brief printed text complains of female intrusion into the male world of baseball. He laments the "violent crushes" which some women get on players, insisting that female promotions are not profitable for baseball ownership. Frank concludes, "Male patrons will even go to work rather than expose themselves to the yammering and the yattating that make the afternoon hideous. It further is significant that serious women fans prefer to pay full admission and sit where they choose instead of taking full advantage of the cut rates which oblige them to remain in segregated sections with their shrill sister."[1] While an examination of baseball marketing and media representation of women in the twentieth century finds the *Collier's* stereotypes of sexual predator, shrew, and consumer to be the prevailing societal constructs of gender within the sport, Frank was inaccurate in blaming St. Louis Browns President Robert Lee Hedges for introducing Ladies Day to baseball in 1912. According to baseball historians, promotions to attract a female clientele to the ball park have their origins in the nineteenth century.

David Voigt observes that while there was male opposition, by the 1880s a grudging acceptance existed for women at major league parks, complete with Ladies Days' promotions offering free admissions for escorted women. According to Voigt, insisting that women have a male escort constituted an effort to control female sexuality and maintain "prevailing patrist norms." On the other hand, some baseball officials, such as manager Harry Wright of the Philadelphia Phillies, believed a female presence would increase profits by contributing to improved crowd behavior and enticing a more middle-class family clientele to the ball park.[2]

Other scholars credit the increasing accommodations made for female spectators as indicative of the dominant male social order's efforts to place women within their proper realm: that of the more passive baseball spectator rather than participant. Recent scholarship by Horatio Seymour, Barbara Gregorich, and Gai Ingham Berlage well documents the presence of women on the playing fields of collegiate and professional baseball in the late nineteenth and early twentieth centuries.[3] However, this participation presented a crisis for masculinity threatened by female power exhibited through athleticism. Some touring women's professional teams were even branded as prostitutes, while the dominant social order and baseball establishment sought to channel women's interest in sport through the more proper roles of spectatorship and consumption. In *A Brief History of American Sports*, Elliott J. Gorn and Warren Goldstein describe nineteenth-century baseball management's efforts to attract female spectators as both keeping women within circumscribed roles and legitimizing the sport in the eyes of the larger culture. Gorn and Goldstein argue, "Just as women were supposed to preside over the emotionally calm and nurturant domestic hearth in middle-class Victorian homes, they were encouraged to bring their domesticating influence to bear on the occasionally raucous scene on the ball field."[4] Using the feminist theory of Simeone de Beauvoir, Karlene Ferrante asserts that it was essential for males to exclude women from the baseball playing field, so the sport could remain a realm for defining masculinity. Ferrante concludes, "The analogy of women and baseball is common. Baseball is a forum in which young men compete and in which the best men may become heroes. It is clear from this analogy that sex and womanhood are objectified into a sort of forum in which young men compete and in which the hero 'scores.'"[5] In a similar vein, Michael S. Kimmel perceives the promulgation of baseball as an urban spectator sport to be part and parcel of the implementation of a white male middle-class hegemonic order in early twentieth-century America."[6]

This critical perspective of an early twentieth-century male order based upon female exclusion is well established in a 1909 article for *Baseball Magazine* by New York stage actress Lulu Glaser. Representing a profession which was once an exclusive male preserve, Glaser, nevertheless, recognized that baseball performance opportunities for women were contracting rather than expanding. Recalling a childhood in which her baseball skills surpassed those of many male friends, Glaser lamented, "If I were a man I would surely try to get out and make good with one of the big league teams." Yet, Glaser was only too aware that as a mature woman who was relegated to the role of a spectator, she would have to pursue her baseball thrills through contemplating the actions of male athletes. Accordingly, the actress concluded, "In every big city in which I am playing I go out to the ball games every possible chance I get. There's nothing in the world, not even the first night appearance with a new play, that's so exciting as watching a man smash out a long hit with three men on base. Why, it makes one feel glad to be living for days afterwards."[7]

While Glaser's acquiescence to the male order of things in baseball carried plenty of Freudian implications, another *Baseball Magazine* profile

featuring actress Stella Hammerstein, daughter of composer Oscar Hammerstein, sent no such mixed signals. A follower of the New York Giants,
Stella, who was described as quitting rehearsals early to view games at the
Polo Grounds, portrayed baseball as American as pie. The values of genteel womanhood described by Stella Hammerstein were celebrated in a
letter to the editors of *Baseball Magazine*, suggesting that women be admitted to baseball games free of charge, for their presence "would tend to
eliminate foul language and make the game cleaner in every way."[8] Asserting that women could elevate the moral tone of baseball paralleled increasing political and reform activity by women. Thus, baseball promoters in
Newark, New Jersey scheduled a Suffragette Day, complete with bands,
parade, and speakers sponsored by the Women's Political Union.[9] However, the progressive search for order in American life ran afoul of World
War I and the post war reactions of the Red Scare, immigration restric-
tion, and racial strife, while in baseball the Black Sox scandal of a fixed
World Series in 1919 exemplified the limitations of progressive reform for
the national pastime.

In order to restore public confidence in the sport, baseball owners created the office of Baseball Commissioner, appointing Judge Kenesaw Mountain Landis, who promptly suspended for life the eight Chicago White Sox
players alleged to have conspired with gamblers. In addition, baseball management embraced what cultural historians identify as a transition from
the values of production to consumption. In *Culture as History*, Warren
Susman argues that in the early 1920s a conflict emerged in America
between two cultures, "...an older culture, often loosely labeled Puritan-
republican, producer capitalistic culture, and a newly emerging culture of
abundance."[10] The values of production — associated with words such as
competition, rivalry, conquest, and individualism — were replaced by an
emphasis on consumption — reflected by the vocabulary of plenty, play,
leisure, gratification, and personality.

This transformation in baseball was perhaps best illustrated by the
instant gratification of the home run and the cult of personality surrounding Babe Ruth.[11] In *American Sports* Ben Rader suggests that the
emergence of the modern sports hero in the 1920s served a "compensatory
cultural function." According to Rader, athletes, such as Ruth, "...assisted
the public in compensating for the passing of the traditional dream of success, the erosion of Victorian values, and feelings of individual powerlessness."[12] For female baseball fans, the sense of powerlessness was even
more pervasive, because, as usual, they were expected to identify with the
other and seek their gratification through the observation of male achievement. While the baseball establishment welcomed women as paying cus-

tomers and consumers of their product, the image of the female as sexual predator — perhaps associated with such popular images of female independence as bobbed hair and smoking in public —continued to indicate the sport's insecurity regarding the intrusion of females, even as spectators, into the male proving ground of baseball. In a piece originally published in *Collier's*, former player turned sportswriter Al Demaree described baseball as a male idyllic Garden of Eden, which could be destroyed by the intrusion of a female serpent. Demaree argued baseball was "not a woman's sport, and for that reason whenever the ladies intrude they usually cause trouble." While Demaree complained about nagging and gossip among players' wives, he reserved most of his sexist rhetoric for what he termed "baseball Daisies." According to the former major league pitcher, the "Daisies" were sometimes known as a home team's fifth pitcher, because "she takes the hurlers of the visiting club out for a round of the cabarets at night and they are not as effective as usual in the game the next day." And simply the mere presence of female sexuality had the potential to disrupt the game. Demaree chronicled the distractions suffered by male athletes, observing, "In some parks the players cut peepholes in the back of the dugout to spot the 'knockouts,' and then they send notes to them by the ushers. Some players carry field glasses to survey the stands from the bench."[13] While much of the sexual aggression was exhibited by the male athletes, the *Collier's* piece made it clear that women, simply by their physical appearance in a male enclave, were seeking these attentions and distracting men from their competitive endeavors.

However, from 1929 to 1933 the baseball establishment had more pressing concerns than containing female sexuality. In 1930, a tight pennant race in the National League, in which the top four teams finished within six games of each other, was mostly responsible for a major league net income of $1,462,000. Nevertheless, it proved impossible for baseball to escape the impact of the massive economic slump, and in 1931 net income declined to $217,000, while the profit margin of major league teams dwindled to 2.3 percent. Financial prospects for the sport dimmed further in 1932 and 1933 with losses of $1,201,000, a margin of 15 percent in the election year of 1932, and with net losses totaling $1,651,000 in 1933, for a "loss" margin of 23.9 percent.[14]

The conservative baseball owners sought to weather the crisis by reducing player salaries, maintaining ticket prices, and eschewing more radical solutions such as revenue sharing and expanding the number of night games. Female fans as consumers of a product in jeopardy were certainly welcomed. Many minor league operators resorted to such gimmicks as a pajama parade in Dayton, Ohio, where seven hundred women marched and bleacher spectators selected the prize-winning "fannette." In a *Police Gazette* interview, James J. Tierney, club secretary for the New York Giants, extolled the virtues of female fans and ladies day promotions at the Polo Grounds. Tierney insisted that women comprised no threat to the integrity and enjoyment of the game, for their appreciation of the sport could extend beyond rooting for individual heroes and the home team. The club official concluded, "The women are as capable as the men of understanding the technicalities of baseball."[15] Confronted with a financial crisis, baseball images of the woman as consumer rather than sexual predator predominated in the depression decade.

With the advent of World War II and an expanded role for middle-class married women in the work place, the democratic virtues of the game were extolled in an effort to justify the continuation of baseball during the war emergency. In a piece for the *New York Times Magazine*, renowned broadcaster Red Barber argued that baseball was essential to the war effort, for fans wanted and deserved the continuation of the game. Summoning up images of baseball as egalitarian and symbolic of American democracy, Barber wrote, "Fathers and mothers with sons and daughters in the armed forces have sat in the stands and watched and been content." However, in seeking to include women within the democratic umbrella of baseball, Barber perpetuated the shrew stereotype of the female baseball fan. Describing female fans as rabid, Barber told the story of an umbrella-wielding grandmother in Cincinnati who chased umpire Cy Pfirmen out of Crosley Field. Barber also could not resist depicting Brooklyn stalwart Hilda Chester, "clanging a cowbell and shouting advice," as typical of female participation in the game.[16]

With the advent of recent scholarship and the popular 1992 baseball film *A League of Their Own*, the public today is generally aware of the fine baseball played by the All-American Girls Professional Baseball League in World War II through the early 1950s.[17] While women's baseball certainly found a niche in the Midwest during World War II, a more widely-shared perception of women and baseball during that time period may perhaps be found in the popular 1942 film *Woman of the Year*. The film, co-written by Ring Lardner, Jr., demonstrates the distress experienced by men due to changing societal constructions of gender in the work place. The conclusion of *Woman of the Year*, in which Tess Harding (Katherine Hepburn) must sacrifice a career to save her marriage, appears to anticipate the post war *Feminine Mystique* described by Betty Friedan. The basic plot of the film is concerned with the rather unlikely love affair and marriage between internationally-acclaimed political reporter Harding and sportswriter Sam Craig (Spencer Tracy). In one of the film's most memorable scenes, Craig takes Harding to her first baseball game. Initially, Sam's colleagues resent her presence and ignorance of the game, while an irate fan has his view obscured by Harding's oversized sun hat. However, by the game's conclusion, which, of course, goes into extra innings, Harding has removed her hat, is munching peanuts, and with her feminine charms has won over her male cohorts. But the key point here is that Harding's acceptance comes after she sheds her active careerism and becomes a flirtatious feminine spectator.[18]

The post war years were difficult ones for both baseball and women. After a post war attendance boom in the late 1940s, major league baseball would not exceed the figure of twenty-million paying customers, a feat achieved in both 1948 and 1949, until 1962, an expansion season with new National League franchises in New York and Houston. Meanwhile, minor league baseball was in serious financial difficulty. In 1949, minor league attendance peaked at nearly 42,000,000 fans, with 464 teams represented in 59 leagues. But turnstile counts dipped by more than 7,000,000 in 1950, followed by another 7,000,000 the next season. By the end of the decade, minor league fan support tumbled to just a little over 12,000,000 in only 21 leagues.[19] Baseball officials and publications such as the *Sporting News* blamed baseball's attendance woes upon a multiplicity of factors, including: television, air conditioning, growing availability of major league broadcasts, and increased leisure choices in the suburbs.[20] Of these reasons, perhaps suburbanization deserves additional attention, for traditional entertainment industries such as Hollywood were suffering a post war slump even before television ownership became widespread. Leisure in the baby-booming suburbs became focused upon the neighborhood barbecue rather than a long family drive to the ball park, located in the inner cities where parking remained a major problem.[21]

While baseball needed female customers and their growing families as consumers, the sport in the 1950s did little to accommodate or recognize the changing lifestyles of American women. In fact, baseball appeared to support the reactionary position taken by many in industry to the employment of women. Stanley Frank's 1946 piece in *Collier's* reflected the perspective that women did not really belong in male enclaves such as the ball field or assembly line. By 1954, many women were out of the factories and the All-American Girls Professional Baseball League had folded, but women in the work place, June Cleaver and the women of 1950s television situation comedies notwithstanding, retained an important role in the economy and work force. Female employment showed a steep upturn in 1947, and by 1950, female employment once again reached wartime peaks. However, rather than pursuing careers, many of these working women perceived their employment as supplementing disposable family income and sustaining the family's status in the affluent society.[22]

As baseball ticket sales declined in the 1950s, the sport continued perceiving women as consumers, perpetuating stereotypes, and refusing to recognize women, whether pursuing a career or supplementing family income, as active participants in the American economy. Considering how little baseball was willing to do in providing new opportunities or changing perceptions for women, it is amazing, and a testament to the game itself, that young women, such as historian Doris Kearns Goodwin, were able to develop and retain a love and attachment to the sport. In her memoirs, Kearns Goodwin relates how baseball and the historical record keeping of maintaining a score book allowed her to foster a closer relationship with her father.[23]

While many fathers may have inoculated their daughters with an appreciation for baseball, officials of organized baseball continued to belittle women's contributions and perpetuate sexist stereotypes. For example, few in baseball raised an eyebrow when Washington Senators Manager Charlie Dressen complained about communication difficulties on a club which included several Latino players. Of course, Dressen pointed out that things could always be worse. If Latinos and the Spanish language were problems, women were far more troublesome. Evoking the shrewish image of the female fan or player wife, Dressen remarked that if he could keep "wives from talking to each other and starting trouble, in any language, he didn't care what his players said in Arabic, Spanish, or Hindustani (sic)."[24]

Like death and taxes, Dressen was resigned to accept the shrewish wife or fan as something that baseball men would have to endure, but the baseball establishment was more adamant in its condescending treatment of those women who might dare to challenge the male domains of the executive suite or press box. In January, 1956, the *Sporting News* reported that the Hamilton, Ontario franchise in the Class D Pony League was purchased by two young women (although the article insisted on referring to them as "girls" or "gals"), Carroll Hodge and Jean Marini. The article commented upon their appearance and physical attractiveness, something usually missing in a sports page depiction of baseball's male executive oligarchy. Some of the money to purchase the franchise was put up by Marini's uncle, but he maintained, "The girls will be running the show, and I think they can get the job done." In the article's emphasis upon the novelty of female ownership, Hodge's considerable baseball experience was downplayed. At age twenty-two, Hodge was a graduate of the School of Baseball Administration at Florida Southern College, with executive experience at Galveston (Big State League), Ottawa (International League), and Winston-Salem (Carolina League). Nevertheless, the press conference concluded with a condescending question as to whether Hodge was interested in romance. Hodge replied that she was, indeed, looking for a man, "Several men, in fact, all .400 hitters."[25]

In a story reminiscent of the film *Woman of the Year*, female reporter Doris O'Donnell received even more hostile treatment than the condescending tones reserved for Hodge and Marini. O'Donnell, who had written a series of prize-winning articles for the *Cleveland News* on her travels in the Soviet Union, found baseball officials less accommodating than Soviet bureaucrats when she was assigned to cover the Cleveland Indians for an Eastern road swing. Barred from the press box in Boston and New York, O'Donnell penned a blistering exposé of the male sports writing fraternity, asserting, "Personally, I'd rather see a son of mine drive a bus than be a baseball writer." After pointing out that baseball writers lacked journalistic integrity and were little more than hirelings of the local ball clubs, O'Donnell concluded, "I charge baseball writers with discrimination against the fair sex in their own profession. On the job, they are snobbish hermits who don't realize the journalistic world around them has changed."

Responding to O'Donnell's charges, Dan Daniel, President of the Baseball Writers' Association of America (BBWAA), observed that membership in the organization was limited to males, and, thus, O'Donnell was not eligible to enter the press box. However, Daniel promised that he would bring up the issue of female membership at the next annual meeting of the BBWAA. On the other hand, the veteran baseball writer stated that he was adamantly opposed to lifting the ban on women in the press box. Acknowledging that women were making important contributions to the field of journalism, Daniel, nevertheless, maintained, "But women are not wholly qualified to be baseball writers. The way the game is reported today, locker sniffing, player interviews, and talks with managers are ultra-important, especially for an evening newspaper." In conclusion, Daniel returned to sexual stereotyping in the guise of a compliment, asserting, "To have you and some other good-lookers in the press box would be much too distracting."[26]

From Daniel's sexist commentary and the coverage of female ownership of the Class D Ontario franchise, it seems apparent that those reporting baseball were much more comfortable with women as sexual objects than as competitors. These writers were much more at ease with a 1957 *Sporting News* story announcing the marriage of actress Kathy Grant to Bing Crosby, who was then an owner of the Pittsburgh Pirates. Featuring a cheesecake photograph of Grant in a swim suit, the story by reporter Jack Gallagher detailed how Grant got her start in the beauty and entertainment business in 1951 when she was selected Queen of the Buffs (Houston's franchise in the Texas League). Following other baseball beauty pageants in which Grant was chosen as Golden Girl of the Texas League and runner-up for the title of Miss Baseball, Grant landed a modeling contract and headed to Hollywood. According to Houston General Manager Art Routzong, "There were several girls in the contest that year who were better stacked, but she won the judges over with her smile and personality."[27] Thus, in the 1950s, professional baseball was uncomfortable with women as competitors against men, preferring to perpetuate the gender stereotypes of shrew, sexual object, or consumer.

But most of all it seemed that the sport elected to ignore women during the 1950s, but change was afoot in the country and the increasing independence and experience of women in the work force was paving the way for an ideological change with the women's movement of the 1960s and 1970s. While baseball, as well as politicians, would have to pay more attention to women, gender objectification and efforts to control women within the male preserve of baseball would persist. Perhaps in response to feminist critics who questioned masculine hegemony, much of the nation's sports reporting, a male domain, insisted upon depicting female fans as shrews, whose antics of nagging male authority figures such as umpires, obnoxious unladylike behavior, and spinster-like appearance fed into anti-feminist stereotypes.

In a February, 1963 piece for the *Sporting News*, Dan Daniel, who evidently preferred more attractive females like Doris O'Donnell, described the loudest fans he had ever witnessed — Hilda Chester of Brooklyn, Lollie Hopkins of Boston, and Mary Ott of St. Louis. Daniel wrote, "They were loud, they were raucous, they were acutely demonstrative. Mrs. Ott neighed like a herd of horses with incredible lung power. She was the bone of visiting players and the umpires." In a side bar to his feature story, Daniel quoted an anonymous New York psychiatrist who found women like Ott, Hopkins, and Chester as overly enthusiastic, but at least committed to a cause. However, men who constantly ridicule the umpire's authority were venting frustrations from their personal lives. "Joe Blow has a shrew for a wife and is henpecked beyond human endurance. So he comes out to the ball game and hurls vituperation at the players and umpires who are the captive receivers in place of his wife."[28] While Daniel's psychiatric source placed shrewish female fans in the more positive light of boosterism, it never seemed to occur to him that boisterous female spectators might be seeking outlets from male domination.

Regardless of what interpretation one gives to the origins of the shrill, female heckler in the stands, a perusal of newspaper clippings in the National

Baseball Hall of Fame and Museum indicates the shrewish imagery was often used in the 1960s. Housewife Sadie Hirsch of Portsmouth, Virginia was labeled the "queen of the hecklers" in the Carolina League. Hirsch prided herself as an umpire-baiter. When it was pointed out to her that the game could not function without umpires, she quickly replied, "Why Not?" In an obituary, Mary Ott was eulogized for her "shrill voice" and "laughing scorn," which few umpires and visiting players in St. Louis had been able to escape since her 1926 confrontation with umpire Bill Klem. The *Newark Evening* News described the deceased Rita Kennedy as a "baseball nut," who followed the New York and San Francisco Giants religiously, even taking a vacation from her job as a staffer at the Prudential Life Insurance Company and traveling to Japan so she could watch her beloved Giants play an international exhibition game.[29]

While organized baseball always approached the female fan's sexuality and shrewishness with considerable condescension, women as consumers were perceived as the possible salvation for a sport under siege by the emerging popularity of professional basketball and football. In 1969, C. C. Johnson Spink of the *Sporting News* editorialized on baseball's need to better market itself to women. Relying upon the marketing research of Spangler & Company, headquartered in Norwood, Pennsylvania, Spink reported that adult men, eighteen years of age and older, named football over baseball as their favorite sport by a margin of 33.0 to 27.0 percent. On the other hand, the editor observed, "The women — and baseball can say 'God bless 'em' — stick with the diamond. They named baseball their favorite sport by a margin of 22 percent to 16.3." Perhaps to better promote the female consumer, New York Yankees President Michael Burke invited poet Marianne Moore to throw out the symbolic "first pitch" at the Yankees 1969 home opener. In a piece for the *Saturday Review*, Joseph Durso attempted to capture Moore's fascination for the game of baseball. Durso portrayed Moore as, "...an eighty-two-year-old beauty with braided white hair and the wit of Casey Stengel, who was born in Kansas City three years after she was born in St. Louis." Durso's portrait of Moore is a flattering one and does not descend into the gender stereotyping of most reporting on female baseball enthusiasts. Perhaps Moore escaped such a fate because she was depicted as an intellectual; a description usually reserved for males.[30]

A more traditional female consumer perspective was provided by writer Eleanor McMenimen's explanation of why she was a Yankee fan. McMenimen found the ball park to be a place of refuge where she could relax free from domestic concerns and social pressures such as the telephone. In addition to commenting upon the appeal of Yankee baseball,

McMenimen depicted herself as a frequent visitor to the concession stand. Portraying herself as an expensive date, McMenimen wrote, "In the ball park I become a compulsive eater, and I'm the best friend of almost every vendor in sight. Hot dogs were never that good at home. Ice cream I seldom eat, but at the ball game it's something else again. And if I'm not ankle deep in peanut shells by the ninth inning, I always suspect that I'm coming down with a virus."[31]

Similar to McMenimen, Marcy Bachmann, writing for the *Oakland Tribune*, asserted that in the 1970s, female fans were coming out of the closet, and that baseball was just as large a component of women's lives as "beauty parlors, shoe stores, and supermarkets." Placing baseball firmly within the consumer pop culture of the period, Bachman argued that women had to love baseball, for:

> It's as all-American as Mt. Rushmore and the Big Mac. As all-American as Snoopy and the Supremes. Not to love baseball is not to love the Grand Old Opry and political conventions. Not to love baseball is not to love T. V. dinners and permanent press, no-iron pants. It's not to love Neil Armstrong and Ethel Kennedy, and freckled faced kids, and floppy eared mutts, and the DAR and YWCA, and licorice candy, and split level ranch houses, and hometown newspapers and biodegradable soap, and two for one sales, and no run pantyhose....[32]

However, baseball's effort to cater to women spectators in the late 1960s and early 1970s could not deter the sport from its traditional gender stereotyping. Amid the cultural clashes in American society regarding the Vietnam War, race, class, and gender, baseball usually supported the conservative side of the ledger, continuing to view female consumers as sexual objects. For example, 1972 marketing research for the California Angels indicated that forty percent of their fans were women, but one of the major promotional endeavors of the club was a three-inning exhibition softball contest between the Angels and Hugh Hefner All-Stars, a team comprised of Playboy Club Bunnies and labeled by Angel promoters as an "eyeful exhibition." Women were also objectified in a 1971 press release by the Kansas City Royals, announcing that since thousands of women "have selected hot pants for their most comfortable attire while watching a baseball game at Municipal Stadium," the Royals would "honor the women of all ages who wear hot pants with a free night." Royals management selected September 13 as "Beauty in Hot Pants Night," with women dressed in hot pants admitted free to the box seat or reserved grandstand area. Women in hot pants attire would also be eligible for a pregame beauty contest and cash prizes.[33]

These sexual promotions appeared to celebrate the sexual revolution in baseball exemplified by pitcher Jim Bouton's controversial books *Ball Four* and *I'm Glad You Didn't Take it Personally*. Bouton shocked many in the baseball establishment by speaking openly of sexual liaisons between players and baseball groupies or Annies. Similar tales were told regarding Babe Ruth and so-called baseball Daisies in the 1920s, but post World War II baseball endeavored to produce a sanitized version of the game and its heroes. Bouton's exposé blew the lid off of baseball's ostensible allegiance to family and consensus values. In his study of sex and baseball, David Voigt found positive possibilities in baseball's shift from patrist to matrist values, arguing, "It is fair to say that Bouton learned that freedom to talk about sex is directly related to freedom to criticize other institutions. Which is after all the essence of the matrist trend-that matrism is ladened with opportunities for expanded personal freedom provided that enough Americans are willing to exercise the right."[34] However, the freedom celebrated by Bouton offered opportunities for men to sexually exploit women in the gendered tradition of "studs" and "sluts," rather than providing a sexually egalitarian playing field.

The objectifications of women contained in *Ball Four*, hot pants promotions, and Hugh Hefner nights at the ball park were hardly isolated incidents. In 1969, the *New York Times* reported that the unprecedented success of the Mets was drawing huge crowds, of whom at least a quarter were female. The article focused upon the sex appeal of the Mets players, quoting a twenty-year-old blond model as saying, "Women like winners. Successful men, whether they're ball players or businessmen, are sexy. Right now, the Mets are very successful." And if a woman could not woo a ball player, then, "They may still find a doctor or lawyer or salesman at Shea. These days the stadium is one of the best spots in town to find a date." The image of woman as sexual predator was also encouraged by Associated Press reporter Hubert Mizell, who chronicled the story of stewardess Mary Cahill arranging her flight schedule to catch as many games as possible of her favorite team, the Baltimore Orioles. Cahill was portrayed as a "blond, shapely, and leggy" twenty-five year old divorcée, "stacking" her summertime flying schedule for key games. And sometimes the shrewish and sexual images of women overlapped as in a piece on Arkansas Travelers fan Bulah Burton. A visiting radio announcer was describing a Travelers game when Burton emerged from her first base box seat to roar at an umpire. The announcer turned his attention to the box seats and, "being a man with an admiring eye," quipped, "That woman's too good-looking to have a voice like that."[35]

No ambiguity existed in an article by *Chicago Sun-Times* correspondent Randy Harvey, whose description of baseball groupies gave credence to Bouton's claims regarding female predators. According to Harvey, the women who wanted to sleep with star athletes came from all walks of life: stewardesses, middle-aged housewives, secretaries, waitresses, models, actresses, teachers, etc. In this scenario, every woman was a potential predator and the male athlete an innocent victim of female aggression. Harvey concluded his piece by quoting a woman who was married to a baseball player for nineteen years before the marriage ended in divorce. "Baseball played a great part in breaking up our marriage due to the traveling he had to do. You have to be very broad-minded. A man has got to be a man. I don't care who he is. A lot goes on on the road. The players are human. The women are going to go after them."[36]

In addition to facing condemnation for their lustful sexual appetites, traditional baseball writers such as the crusty Dick Young of the *New York Daily News* blamed women's liberation for causing the cancellation in New York of "one of the oldest and sturdiest of promotional gimmicks—Ladies Day." Young failed to understand why some women would find ladies day at the ball park objectionable, unless, of course, they were not ladies at all. Meanwhile, the conservative Young could not resist quipping that with modern hair and fashion styles it was becoming increasingly difficult to differentiate male from female. Joining Young in a litany of complaints regarding changing gender roles in America was Joe Durslag, who wrote a column for the *Sporting News* stating his objections to the intrusion of uninformed female spectators into the male preserve of baseball. But women in the 1970s were not as passive as Young and Durslag might have preferred. In a letter to the *Sporting News*, Lauren Applebaum of Bayside, New York found Durslag to be "unfair, bigoted, patronizing, condescending, and stupendously stupid." Displaying a good grasp of baseball history, Applebaum concluded her letter, stating, "Mr. Durslag's equally degrading, insinuated image of the parasol-twirling, hoop-skirted, banana-curled, eyelash-batting, dumb broad belongs to the same antiquated garbage pail as Cap Anson's venomous racial remarks of 90 years ago."[37]

While the more assertive women of the 1970s made many in baseball uncomfortable, traditionalists could take some heart from stories placing women in more dependent and even child-like roles. Sharon McLaughlin, a twenty-seven year old receptionist who was going blind chose to spend the last flickering hours of her eyesight watching the Cincinnati Reds battle the Pittsburgh Pirates. McLaughlin described herself as a Reds fan since she was five years old. Despite fading sight, she preferred the ball park to baseball on the radio, insisting, "I'd rather be with the crowd. I can tell from the fans if the Reds do something. You can tell from the sound of the bat." Pam Cable, age twenty-two of Newark, Ohio, was also a Reds fan and an admirer of Johnny Bench, with whom she corresponded every week. Cable, who was paralyzed since age fifteen, was reported near death in the fall of 1974, and the Reds catcher rushed to her side. Pam's mother gushed, "Ever since Johnny kissed her, the nurses have called her up to say they're jealous. But she's getting stronger and stronger since Johnny told her to start eating again and get well."[38] This sentimental scene is reminiscent of the William Bendix version of the *Babe Ruth Story* in which the Bambino was a miracle worker for sickly children around the nation, except that in these 1974 versions with the Big Red Machine women have replaced children.

But female baseball fans in the 1970s refused to accept the male-defined roles of child, shrew, female predator, or simply consumer. In the decade, women moved beyond the role of the other, seeking to find a niche on the competitive field of play, filing law suits to open up the baseball training ground of Little League for young girls and lobbying for passage of Title IX which attempted to assure equality of sports competition in the nation's colleges and universities. Tilla Vahanian, a New York psychiatrist, told the *New York Times* that competitive play enhanced the self-esteem of women. According to Vahanian, "The old stereotype was that sport was a purely masculine endeavor, and women did not attend sports events for fear of losing their femininity. But now we find that a greater comradeship exists between men and women when they can share roles." And more self-confident women were unapologetic regarding sexual attraction for athletes. In a piece for *TV Guide*, Grace Lichtenstein stated matter of factly that baseball players were sexy. On the other hand, in the same article another woman was quoted pointing out male ideological inconsistencies dealing with sport and sexuality. "Guys have this obsession that girls who like baseball are groupies. I mean, if a guy likes one of the Pittsburgh Pirates does that mean he is after him sexually." [39] This kind of commentary challenging the male hegemony in baseball is what Voigt had in mind when he suggested that sexual freedom could bring greater equality to the sport of baseball.

With Little League forced to include girls and Title IX firmly in place allowing some women to play competitive baseball, optimists for gender equality saw the 1980s as a proving ground culminating in the 1994 establishment of the Colorado Silver Bullets, an all-women's baseball team sponsored by the Coors Brewing Company and affiliated with the independent Northern League. However, in the midst of this 1980s and 1990s apparent blooming of gender equity, there remained troubling signs that baseball was not yet prepared to surrender its role as a male enclave. For example, much of the attention bestowed upon the Silver Bullets was due to the team's novelty appeal, while others believed the team had arrived after engaging in fisticuffs, another male proving ground, during a 1997 game with the Americus Travelers, the state champions of the male Georgia Recreation and Parks eighteen-and-under league.[40]

And while professional basketball was incorporating female officials into its men's game and promoting a women's league, major league baseball refused to find a place for Pam Postema, who was released from her umpiring contract in 1988 after thirteen seasons in the minor leagues. A bitter Postema concluded, "I'll never understand why it's easier for a female to become an astronaut or a cop or fire fighter or soldier or Supreme Court justice than it is to become a major league umpire. For Christ sake, it's only baseball."[41] But for many males baseball remained one of the few bastions of privilege left relatively unscathed by the women's movement, and they were determined to maintain their hegemony. In a 1991 article in *Ms.*, Kate Rounds lamented baseball's failure to pursue an egalitarian playing field, remarking, "One of the biggest tragedies of baseball's failure to embrace women and girls is that girls who grew up loving baseball often end up disillusioned and embittered."[42]

The ambiguous nature of popular attitudes toward women and baseball in the late 1980s and early 1990s was revealed in two commercially successful baseball films, *Bull Durham* (1988) and *A League of Their Own* (1992). Film critics as well as audiences seemed to fall in love with writer/director Ron Shelton's *Bull Durham*, a tale of minor league baseball and redemption in the Carolina League, featuring big name stars Kevin Costner and Susan Sarandon in the lead roles. Enthusiastic about an adult baseball film, *Commonweal's* Tim O'Brien found *Bull Durham* "colorful, wacky, and brilliantly written," while Steve Wulf of *Sports Illustrated* asserted Shelton's film captured "the reality, the language, and the humor of the game as no baseball film ever has." Yet, Wulf's review also contained the observation that *Bull Durham* was superior to Barry Levinson's film version of *The Natural* because the latter film's sentimentality "was for girls." Wulf's comment is revealing, for few of the glowing accounts of *Bull Durham* in the popular media, and most reviews were penned by men, expressed any reservations regarding Sarandon's character of Anne Savoy; an English teacher and intellectual whose goal was to worship in the church of baseball, while offering herself sexually each season to one fortunate player on the Durham Bulls who would be initiated into both the secrets of baseball and sex. Few critics objected to Savoy as a stereotypical baseball Daisy or Annie, but David Anson of *Newsweek* did point out that

Sarandon's performance was so captivating that many viewers and critics failed to notice that she was a "total male-fantasy figure-muse, sex kitten, and intellectual rolled into one compliant and adoring whole." In other words, while Savoy knew her baseball, her knowledge was transmitted from the bedroom rather than on the playing field. Male prerogatives remained unbreached in *Bull Durham*.[43]

But that seemed to change with the 1992 blockbuster film *A League of Their Own*, a fictionalized account of the All-American Girls Professional Baseball League. Director Penny Marshall and stars Geena Davis, Lori Petty, and Madonna, along with Tom Hanks as the manager of the Rockford Peaches, found audiences interested in a story long ignored by the general public. While long lines formed at the box office, critics were less kind to what they perceived as an overly sentimental film, or perhaps to some it was just another Girls baseball film. John Simon of the *National Review* described *A League of Their Own* as a "piece of sentimental claptrap, derivatively directed by Penny Marshall, and anthologizing every cliché of the run-of-the mill sports picture." Beyond accusations of sentimentality, several reviewers observed that Marshall's film often came up short in confronting the sexism of American baseball and society. Stanley Kauffmann of the *New Republic* found the film to be a sanitized version of what women ball players had to endure in a sexist society. Kauffmann asserted, "No one ever makes a sexist gibe at one of these short-skirted players; no one in the stands ever shouts a salty crack when one of them leaps or twirls. The picture might be more telling as a forgotten feminist enterprise if we heard some of the macho guff those women surely had to endure." And Richard Alleya of *Commonweal* maintained that *A League of Their Own* often embraced rather than challenged traditional gender roles. Alleya makes the rather astute point that when a particularly homely player finally fulfills herself it is not through achievement on the playing field, but rather "by getting drunk and wild enough at a roadhouse to attract the attention of a local boy who will later marry her."[44]

Thus, the film texts of *Bull Durham* and *A League of Their Own* indicate continuing societal confusion regarding the gender construction of baseball. The efforts of women to gain a foothold within the male hegemony of the playing field, umpiring, and executive suite remain a struggle. The role of women in baseball continues to be primarily perceived by Organized Baseball through the lens of consumerism. In a 1997 press release, the management of the Chicago White Sox insisted that aggressive marketing aimed at women could be an avenue out of the sport's malaise resulting from the 1994 strike and canceled World Series. White Sox marketing chief Rob Gallas maintained that women already comprised approximately half the crowds attending games at Comisky Park, and efforts would be made to enhance that percentage by adding Ladies Night every Thursday, when any female could enter the park for one dollar, and advertising in local magazines with strong female readership. Gallas concluded, "Our research shows women make most buying decisions so we want to speak to them directly."[45]

As we approach the twenty-first century, one of America's greatest sporting traditions— major league baseball — stubbornly clings to a gendered definition of the woman as consumer. Perhaps in a more competitive sports marketplace women can use their buying power to force baseball to move beyond the stereotypes of shrew and sexual predator. The deconstruction of such gendered constructs of female spectators may be an important first step in altering the male hegemonic order of baseball, in which the woman has served as the other who witnesses male achievement, and ushering in a more egalitarian relationship on the playing field and in society.

=====

Endnotes

This piece was originally presented at the Baseball Hall of Fame and published in Thomas L. Altherr, ed., *The Cooperstown Symposium on Baseball and American Culture, 1998* (Jefferson, North Carolina: McFarland & Company, 2002), 182-202.

1. Stanley Frank, "Cheesecake at the Ball Park," *Collier's*, 118 (July 27, 1946), 62-63,

2. David Voigt, "Sex in Baseball: Reflections of Changing Taboos," *Journal of Popular Culture*, 21 (3), 395.

3. Harold Seymour, *Baseball: The People's Game* (New York: Oxford University Press, 1990); Barbara Gregorich, *Women at Play: The Story of Women in Baseball* (New York: Harcourt Brace & Company, 1993); and Gai Ingham Berlage, *Women in Baseball: The Forgotten History* (Westport, Connecticut: Greenwood Press, 1994).

4. Elliot J. Gorn and Warren Goldstein, *A Brief History of American Sports* (New York: Hill and Wang, 1993), 206-207.

5. Karlene Ferrante, "Baseball and the Social Construction of Gender," in Pamela J. Creedon, ed., *Media and Sport: Challenging Gender Values* (Thousand Oaks, California: Sage Publications, 1994), 238-256.

6. Michael S. Kimmel, "Baseball and the Reconstitution of American Masculinity, 1880-1920," in Michael A. Messner and Donald F. Sabor, eds., *Sport, Men, and the Gender Order: Critical Feminist Perspectives* (Champaign, Illinois: Human Kinetics Books, 1990), 55-65.

7. Lulu Glaser, "The Lady Fan," *Baseball Magazine* (September, 1909), 19-22.

314   Class at Bat, Gender on Deck and Race in the Hole

8. E. W. Dunn, "Stella, the Stellar Star," *Baseball Magazine* (September, 1908), 58; W. C. C., Minot, North Dakota to Editors of *Baseball Magazine* (August, 1908), 42; "Suffragette Day," June 26, 1915, newspaper clipping, Female Fan File, National Baseball Hall of Fame and Museum, Cooperstown, New York.

9. For baseball and progressive values see Steven Riess, *Touching Base: Professional Baseball and American Culture in the Progressive Era* (Westport, Connecticut: Greenwood Press, 1980); and G. Edward White, *Creating the National Pastime: Baseball Transforms Itself, 1903-1953* (Princeton, New Jersey: Princeton University Press, 1996).

10. Warren I. Susman, *Culture as History: The Transformation of American Society in the Twentieth Century* (New York: Pantheon Books, 1973), xx. For other studies which emphasize the cultural shift from production to consumption see Mark Dyreson, "The Emergence of Consumer Culture and the Transformation of Physical Culture: American Sport in the 1920s," *Journal of Sport History*, 10 (Winter, 1989), 261-281; Stuart Ewen, *Captains of Consciousness: Advertising and the Social Roots of the Consumer Culture* (New York: McGraw-Hill, 1976); Richard Merchand, *Advertising the American Dream: Making Way for Modernity, 1920-1940* (Berkeley, California: Beacon Press, 1985); and Richard Wrightman Fox and T. J. Jackson Lears, eds., *The Culture of Consumption: Critical Essays in American History, 1880-1980* (New York: Pantheon, 1983).

11. For Babe Ruth and American values see Richard C. Crepeau, *Baseball: America's Diamond Mind, 1919-1941* (Orlando: University Presses of Florida, 1980), 70-74; and Tristram Potter Coffin, *The Old Ball Game: Baseball in Folklore and Fiction* (New York: Herder and Herder, 1974), 76-101; F. R. Lloyd, "The Home Run King," in Christopher D. Geist and Jack Nachbar, eds., *The Popular Culture Reader* (Bowling Green, Ohio: Bowling Green University Popular Press, 1983), 217-228; Roderick Nash, *The Nervous Generation: American Thought. 1917-1930* (Chicago: Rand McNally & Company, 1970), 126-137; and David Q. Voigt, *America Through Baseball* (Chicago: Nelson-Hall, 1976), 147-161.

12. Benjamin G. Rader, *American Sport: From the Age of Folk Games to the Age of Spectators* (Englewood Cliffs, New Jersey: Prentice-Hall, Inc., 1983), 176-177.

13. Al Demaree, "Grandstand Girls: Bring a Bit of By-Play Gathered from Behind the Scenes by a Veteran Player," newspaper clipping (originally published in *Collier's*), Female Fan File, National Baseball Hall of Fame and Museum.

14. For the economic conditions of baseball during the depression era see U. S. Congress, *Organized Baseball: Report of the Subcommittee on Study of Monopoly Powers of the Committee on the Judiciary, House Report*, No. 2002, 82 Cong., 2 Sess (1952), 1600-1615; Bill Rabinowitz, "Baseball and the Great Depression," in Peter Levine, ed., *Baseball History* (Westport, Connecticut: Meckler Books, 1989), 49-59; and Ben G. Rader, *Baseball: A History of America's Game* (Urbana: University of Illinois Press, 1994), 126-140.

15. "Hard Times Hit the Minors," *Literary Digest*, 114 (July 30, 1932), 37; and Harry Shelland, "Fair Fans 'Crash' Ball Games, Cheer Plays," *Police Gazette*, July 11, 1931, clipping from Female Fan File, National Baseball Hall of Fame and Museum.

16. Red Barber, "Fans Make Baseball," *New York Times Magazine* (October 3, 1943), 10.

17. Lois Browne, *Girls of Summer: The Real Story of the All American Girls Professional Baseball League* (New York: HarperCollins, 1983); and John Fincher, "The 'Belles of the Ball Game' Were a Hit with their Fans," *Smithsonian*, 20 (July, 1989), 88-94.

18. For *Woman of the Year* see Manny Farber, "More Sound than Fury," *New Republic*, 106 (February 16, 1942), 237; "The New Pictures," *Time*, 39 (February 16, 1942), 82; "Films," *Nation*, 154 (February 21, 1942); and Philip T. Hartung, "Love vs. Careers," *Commonweal*, 35 (February 26, 1942), 437-438.

19. For discussions of major league attendance figures see John Thorn and Pete Palmer, eds., *Total Baseball: The Ultimate Encyclopedia of Baseball* (New York: Harper Perennial, 1993), 143-147; Bill O'Neal, *The Texas League, 1888-1987: A Century of Baseball* (Austin: Eakin Press, 1987), 108; and Neil J. Sullivan, *The Minors: The Struggles and Triumphs of Baseball's Poorer Relation from 1875 to the Present* (New York: St. Martin's Press, 1990).

20. *Sporting News*, September 24, 1952.

21. For the post World War II lifestyle of the suburbs see John Belton, *American Cinema/American Culture* (New York: McGraw-Hill, Inc., 1994), 257-274; and William H. Chafe, *The Unfinished Journey: America Since World War II* (New York: Oxford University Press, 1995), 111-145.

22. Betty Friedan, *The Feminine Mystique* (New York: W. W. Norton & Company, Inc., 1963); and William H. Chafe, "Social Change and the American Woman, 1940-1970," in William H. Chafe and Harvard Sitkoff, *A History of Our Times* (New York: Oxford University Press, 1995), 224-231.

23. Doris Kearns Goodwin, *Wait Until Next Year: A Memoir* (New York: Simon &Schuster, 1997).

24. *Sporting News*, February 8, 1956.

25. *Ibid.*, January 25, 1956.

26. *Ibid.*, May 9, and June 5 and 12, 1957.

27. *Ibid.*, November 6, 1957.

28. *Ibid.*, February 2, 1963. For Hilda Chester see Neil J. Sullivan, *The Dodgers Move West* (New York: Oxford University Press, 1987), 38-39; and Peter Golenbock, *Bums* (New York: Putnam, 1984), 432-433.

29. "Housewife Sadie Hates Umps— Meet the 'Queen of Hecklers;'" "Obituary," *Sporting News*, January 4, 1964; and *Newark Evening News*, April 22, 1970, newspaper clippings, Female Fan File, National Baseball Hall of Fame and Museum.

30. *Sporting News*, September 27, 1969; and Joseph Durso, "Marianne Moore, Baseball Fan," *Saturday Review*, clippings, Female Fan File, National Baseball Hall of Fame and Museum.

31. Eleanor McMenimen, "Yankee Fan," *Newark Sunday News*, March 30, 1969, newspaper clipping, Female Fan File, National Baseball Hall of Fame and Museum.

32. Marcy Bachmann, "Back to the Old Ball Game," *Oakland Tribune*, November 7, 1975, newspaper clipping, Female Fan File, National Baseball Hall of Fame and Museum.

33. Dick Miller, "Angels Find 40 Percent of Their Fans Are Women," January 29, 1972; Kansas City Royals, Press Release, September, 1971, clippings, Female Fan File, National Baseball Hall of Fame and Museum.

34. Jim Bouton with Leonard Shecter, *Ball Four: My Life and Hard Times Throwing the Knuckleball in the Big Leagues* (New York: World Publishing, 1970); Jim Bouton with Leonard Shecter, *I'm Gold You Didn't Take It Personally* (New York: William Morrow & Company, Inc., 1971); and Voigt, "Sex in Baseball," 402.

35. Nancy Moran, "For Women, Home is Where the Plate Is," *New York Times*, September 26, 1969; Hubert Mizell, Associated Press, 1971; and Fred Morrow, "Big Bulah," newspaper clippings, Female Fan File, National Baseball Hall of Fame and Museum.

36. Randy Harvey, "Oakland Annies: It's Not Jocks' Autographs They Crave," *Chicago Sun-Times*, August 14, 1977, newspaper clipping, Female Fan File, National Baseball Hall of Fame and Museum.

37. *Sporting News*, December 3, 1971; February 20, 1971; and March 6, 1971, newspaper clippings, Female Fans File, National Baseball Hall of Fame and Museum.

38. *Sporting News*, May 19, 1974; and September 5, 1974, newspaper clippings, Female Fans File, National Baseball Hall of Fame and Museum.

39. Gerald Eskenazi, "In the Stands, Many Cheers Have a Higher Pitch," *New York Times*, June 6, 1977; and Grace Lichtenstein, "They'd Rather Break a Date Than Miss a Game: Women Sports Fans Are Coming Out of the Closet," *T. V. Guide* (March 6, 1976), 8-11.

40. Katrine Ames, "A Whole New Ball Game," *Newsweek*, 123 (May 9, 1994),58-59. For the Silver Bullets fight with the Americus Travelers see *New York Times*, June 14, 1977.

41. Pam Postema and Gene Wojciechowski, *You've Got to Have Balls to Make It in this League* (New York: Simon & Schuster, 1992), 255.

42. Kate Rounds, "Where Is Our Field of Dreams?," *Ms*, 2 (September/October, 1991), 44-45.

43. On *Bull Durham* see David Anson," A Major League Romp," *Newsweek*, 111 (June 20, 1988), 69-70; Steve Wulf, "Diamond Film With Clout," *Sports Illustrated*, 69 (July 4, 1988), 93; and Tim O'Brien, "On the Screen," *Commonweal*, 115 (August 12, 1988), 441-442.

44. On *A League of Their Own* see Steve Wulf, "Field of Dames," *Sports Illustrated*, 76 (July 6, 1992), 4; Stanley Kauffmann, "Minor League and Major," *New Republic*, 207 (August 3, 1992), 28-29; John Simon, "*A League of Their Own*," *National Review*, 44 (August 3, 1992), 46-47; Richard Alleya, "On the Screen," *Commonweal*, 115 (August 12, 1992), 431-432; and Michael Sragow, "Current Cinema," *New Yorker*, 68 (July 13, 1992), 66-67.

45. Chicago White Sox Press Release, January 23, 1977, Female Fan File, National Baseball Hall of Fame and Museum.

Index

318

Index

McCarthy, Eugene 191
McClain, Denny 192
McGaha, Mel 88
McGlothen, Lynn 233
McHale, John 164
McLane, Drayton 250
McLaughlin, Sharon 309–10
McMenimen, Eleanor 306–7
McNally, Dave 225
Medwick, Joe 236
Mejias, Roman: in 1963 261–62; and the
    Pirates 252–53; and racial barriers
    253–54; his success 125, 131, 136, 254,
    257–58; trade to Boston 163, 260
Messersmith, Andy 225
Miller, Marvin: and Kuhn 201; in
    1972 214–15; and the Players Associa-
    tion 151, 172, 180, 187–89, 191; and
    the Uniform Player's Contract 199–-
    200
Milwaukee Braves: and the American
    League 66; beer ban 144; move to
    Atlanta 140–41, 153, 165; 1962
    changes 143–44; and Robinson 80, 95
Milwaukee Brewers 116
Milwaukee County Stadium 237
minor leagues: decline of 86, 87, 89;
    during the Great Depression 25; and
    the Giants 112–13; and the major
    league 118, 285–86; in the 1940s 302;
    1981 strike 287
Misselwitz, Henry 28
Mitchell, Bobby 291
Montejo, Manuel 255
Montreal Expos 204–5
Moore, Marianne 306
Mullen, John 271

NAACP 79–81, 89, 98–100
New Deal 24, 25–26
New York Giants 26, 109, 112–13, 170
New York Mets 110, 123, 134, 136,
    207–8, 239
New York Yankees: and CBS 165; and
    Consolidated Edison program 242;
    in 1952 64; and racism 65, 95; and
    Ruth 12–16; and women 306–7
Niedenfuer, Tom 290
Nixon, Richard 196–97, 198, 215–16

Noren, Irv 224
North, Billy 224

Oakland A's 213
O'Connor, Hap 43
Odom, John "Blue Moon" 221, 225
O'Donnell, Doris 304
O'Donnell, Maj. Gen. Emmett "Rosey"
    62
O'Malley, Walter 77, 111
Ott, Mary 305
Owen, Mickey 59
Owens, Jesse 186–87

Pace, Mrs. Ginna 255
Pacheco, Tony 267–68
Pacific Coast League 113
Pappas, Milt 185
Parker, Dave 244
Paul, Gabe 205
Pena, Alejandro 287, 290, 293
Pendleton, Jim 126–27, 254
Pepitone, Joe 161
Perconte, Jack 290–91, 293
Perez, Quirico Elpidio 272
Perini, Lou 66, 142
Peters, Bonneau 85, 87–88, 89
Peters, Gary 202
Pfirmen, Cy 301
Philadelphia Athletics 109, 236
Philadelphia Phillies 91, 94
players: and arbitration 223; conduct
    of 65; Cuban 162–63, 253; and Flood
    208–9; and free agency 225–26; and
    free speech 161, 167; and manage-
    ment 160, 167–69, 185–86, 188–89,
    202; 1981 strike 286, 287, 289; orga-
    nization of 146–47, 151, 180; and
    owners 215; pension plan 170–71,
    187–89, 191, 200–201; and the Uni-
    form Player's Contract 199–200
politics: and baseball imagery 24,
    29–31, 196–97; during World War II
    34; and expansion 109–10, 111, 118; in
    Houston 251, 252; in Louisiana 86; in
    Milwaukee 145–46, 148–50; progres-
    sive reformers 11; and sports riots
    238; *see also* communism; liberal
    consensus